THE BRITISH IN EGYPT

Peter Mansfield

VICTORIAN (& MODERN HISTORY)
BOOK CLUB
Newton Abbot 1973

© 1971 Peter Mansfield

First published by Weidenfeld and Nicolson

This edition was produced in 1973 for sale
to its members only by the proprietors,
Readers Union Limited, PO Box 6,
Newton Abbot, Devon, TQ12 2DW.
Full details of membership will
gladly be sent on request

Reproduced and printed in
Great Britain for Readers Union
by Redwood Press Limited,
Trowbridge, Wiltshire

THE BRITISH
IN EGYPT

Also by Peter Mansfield

NASSER'S EGYPT
NASSER

To Luis Cañizares

CONTENTS

146411

CONTENTS

ILLUSTRATIONS

between pages 82 & 83

Arabi Pasha's fortifications in Alexandria after bombardment by the British
Arabi Pasha (Mansell Collection)
Lord Cromer (National Portrait Gallery)
Wilfrid and Anne Blunt (Mansell Collection)
Shepheard's Hotel (Mansell Collection)

Punch cartoon of the 'Egyptian Pet'
Construction of the first Aswan Dam (Popperfoto)
English officers in the Egyptian army (Mary Evans Picture Library)
Victoria College, Alexandria (Popperfoto)

Sir Eldon Gorst
Khedive Abbas II (Mansell Collection)
Lord Kitchener at the opening of a new quay in Cairo (Mansell Collection)
Saad Zaghlul Pasha (Popperfoto)
King Fuad I (Popperfoto)

'A Picnic on the Great Pyramid' (Mary Evans Picture Library)
'Waiting to see the Khedive' (Mansell Collection)
Sir Miles Lampson (Keystone Press Agency)
King Farouk I (Mansell Collection)
Port Said after the British landing in 1956 (Popperfoto)

FOREWORD

In the summer of 1882 British troops occupied Egypt. They remained for a period of seventy-four years during which Egypt was under varying degrees of British political control. The relationship between the two nations was unique. There was little sense of imperial mission behind the original occupation; officially Britain claimed that its sole purpose was to prevent anarchy and restore the authority of the Khedive (the hereditary viceroy of this part of the Ottoman Empire) which was menaced by an army-led revolt. But Britain's real interest lay not in Egypt itself but in Egypt as a stepping-stone on the road to India – the imperial possession which alone gave Britain the right to regard itself as a world power. Among the other powers, France was the principal rival. Russia was a distant menace and the challenge of the growing power of Bismarck's Germany was still confined to Europe. In landing troops on Egyptian soil, Britain was first and foremost ensuring that France did not arrive there first. Britain would have been prepared to share the occupation with France, but because of the fragility of governments of the Third Republic, this was not to be.

Late Victorian statesmen sincerely believed that Britain would shortly be able to leave Egypt and, to the bitter amusement of Egyptian nationalists, they said so on numerous occasions.* But there always seemed to be good reason why Britain should stay: stability had not yet been secured or the Egyptians had not proved capable of governing themselves. Over the years, British control of Egypt came to be regarded as part of the natural order. Egypt's financial prosperity was apparent and there were few at that time to question whether its foundations were sound or whether it benefited the people of Egypt as much as the foreigners who lived there. Invariably it was attributed to the wise government of the

* According to one estimate, seventy-two times between 1882 and 1907.

formidable Sir Evelyn Baring (later Lord Cromer) who dominated Egypt from 1883 to 1907. The paradoxical consequence of this assumption of Britain's responsibility for Egypt was that Cromer became perhaps the most famous of all British imperial proconsuls in spite of the fact that Egypt was never formally incorporated into the British Empire and his title was never more exalted than that of British Agent and Consul General in Cairo. Cabinet ministers bowed to his judgement more than to any Indian Viceroy living in semi-regal splendour in Calcutta or Simla.

Although the immediate reason for the British invasion of Egypt in 1882 was the desire to suppress the national movement led by Colonel Arabi, the Egyptians appeared remarkably passive in their initial attitude towards foreign occupation. It is all the more surprising because, unlike India or the African colonies which were united by British rule, Egypt was most certainly a nation. The reason for this apparent passivity was that the mass of the people lacked political leadership; Arabi was a rarity who in the end proved inadequate. Egypt's traditional leaders – the *ulema* (that is the Islamic religious authorities including teachers, scholars and judges) – had declined in influence with the break-up of traditional society under western influence in the nineteenth century. The village sheikhs, on the other hand, who formed a sort of rural aristocracy, acted as intermediaries between the people and the Ottoman ruling class which they did not think of trying to displace. These Turks and Circassians 'identified themselves with Egypt but not with Egyptians, whom they tended to despise'.[1] They were not the men to lead a national movement which was certain to lead to their own downfall. The mass of Egyptians, the *fellahin* or peasants, although unmistakably the descendants of a Great Imperial Race (to employ one of Cromer's favourite terms) had become accustomed to foreign rule after more than two thousand years. The Persians in the sixth century BC had been followed by Greeks, Romans, Byzantines, Mamlouks and Ottoman Turks. In 1882 Egypt was still nominally part of the now ramshackle Ottoman Empire but for most of the nineteenth century it had acquired a large measure of political independence under the Ottoman Viceroy Mohammed Aly and his descendants. More than nine-tenths of the Egyptians were Muslims whose loyalty to Islamic beliefs and traditions was the fibre of their lives. Most of the rest were Coptic Christians, descendants of

Egyptians who had been converted by St Mark and his followers when they brought Christianity to Egypt in the first century after Christ but who had not, like most of their fellow-countrymen, embraced Islam when it arrived with the Arabs five centuries later.

The Copts were generally better educated and more prosperous than the Muslim majority but were prevented by their religion from attaining the higher ranks of political leadership except through the occasional patronage of the Ottoman Viceroy (or the British under the occupation). The same applied *a fortiori* to other minorities such as Syrians, Jews and Armenians who played an important role in the country's commercial life.

So it was that when a revived Egyptian national movement emerged in the early years of the twentieth century the British were not inclined to take it very seriously. Cromer did his best to ignore it as long as he could; he was certain that it would take several centuries for the Egyptians to acquire 'governing capacity'. He felt a paternalist concern for the fellahin but for the middle-class, western-educated Egyptians who aspired to lead the national movement he had nothing but contempt. His successor Eldon Gorst tried a more liberal approach but his methods were faulty and his experiment was already considered a failure before his premature death. Lord Kitchener reverted to paternalism, but his career in Egypt was cut short by the First World War. Preoccupied by war, Britain ignored the national ferment in Egypt so that the violent explosion of 1919 took it by surprise. These were the days of President Wilson's self-determination; the Egyptians were granted a measure of independence but it was taken for granted that this could not be total. Those Egyptians who passionately demanded more were regarded as irresponsible demagogues. Britain had now been so long in Egypt that it was considered an indispensable link in the British imperial system. The history of the remaining thirty years of British occupation was one of constant friction which occasionally burst into flame. Periodically Britain made concessions to Egyptian nationalist demands but always too late to satisfy them. This had been a common feature of colonial emancipation but there was an added bitterness in Egypt's case because it was never a colony, Britain originally claimed that it had come to strengthen Egypt's independence by restoring its rightful ruler. It was only with the dismantling of their Empire that the British relinquished what they had come to regard as their seigneurial rights over Egypt. That imperial nostalgia had still not finally disappeared was shown by the ludicrous Suez adventure a few months later.

The story of the occupation is in many ways neither a happy one nor one of which Englishmen can be especially proud. Its unmistakable positive achievements have to be set against the British attitude towards the Egyptians which was at best a patronizing affection and at worst a contemptuous dislike. This changed very little over the years. Lord Cromer referred to Abbas II as 'my poor little Khedive'; forty years later the young King Farouk was still 'that boy' to the British Ambassador Sir Miles Lampson while the late Abdul Nasser remarked of the only occasion on which he met Anthony Eden that the latter treated him as if he was 'a junior official who could not be expected to understand international politics'.

In return the Egyptians' initial servility towards their new rulers bred by centuries of foreign domination, developed into a strident and emotional hostility. But fundamentally they are a mild and generous people. They have forgotten or forgiven the slights and injuries and remembered only the more admirable qualities of those who dominated them for three-quarters of a century. Now that the British as well as the Egyptians are members of an ex-imperial race it is possible to look back on the curious nature of their relationship.

THE ROADSIDE INN

It was Napoleon Bonaparte who first drew Britain's attention to the importance of Egypt. In 1798, the 29-year-old general was wildly popular in France, having defeated the Austrian armies in a series of campaigns and brought peace to the continent of Europe after five years of war. Britain was now the arch-enemy and Bonaparte proposed to the Directory which was ruling France that he should strike at the sources of Britain's wealth by occupying Egypt and threatening the route to India. 'I was full of dreams,' he remarked later, 'I saw myself founding a religion, marching into Asia, riding an elephant, a turban on my head and in my hand the new Koran that I would have composed to suit my needs. In my undertaking I would have combined the experiences of the two worlds, exploiting for my own profit the theatre of all history, attacking the power of England and, by means of that conquest, renewing contact with the old Europe.'[1]

In July 1798 Napoleon landed his expeditionary force near Alexandria; three years later his depleted and abandoned army capitulated to Admiral Keith and evacuated Egypt under the eyes of British troops. But the botanists, astronomers, cartographers, artists and archaeologists who took part in the expedition founded a tradition of French cultural concern with Egypt and Egyptology which has survived to this day and was certainly stronger than any comparable British interest throughout the nineteenth century. It was left to a later generation of Britons to redeem the Philistinism of their earlier compatriots.

The incomparable travel-writer Kinglake had no doubts about what would happen when he admired the Sphinx on his visit to Cairo during the Plague of 1835. 'And we,' he wrote, 'we shall die, and Islam will wither away, and the Englishman straining far over to hold his loved India, will plant a firm foot on the banks of the Nile and sit on the seats of the Faithful, and still that sleepless rock will lie watching the works of the new busy race . . .'[2]

Fifteen years later Gustave Flaubert wrote from Egypt to an old family friend, Dr Cloquet: 'For me it seems certain that one day England will become mistress of Egypt. She already holds Aden filled with troops. It would be easy enough to bring the redcoats to Cairo via Suez. France will know about it fifteen days later and will be very surprised!'[3]

However, this was not the view of the leading British statesmen of the time, who had no desire to plant their feet on the banks of the Nile. But they did have an interest in preventing the French from doing so and this was the basis of the prolonged struggle of Palmerston, who presided over British foreign policy throughout the mid-nineteenth century, against the building of the Suez Canal.

In 1805 the people of Cairo, tired of the bloody anarchy in Egypt which followed the departure of Napoleon's troops, united behind their traditional religious leaders, the sheikhs, and chose the commander of the Ottoman Sultan's Albanian mercenaries, Mohammed Aly Pasha, as their governor. Most Egyptians would date the origin of their modern national movement from this event. Mohammed Aly was not an Egyptian and was an illiterate barbarian, but he had qualities of genius.

Mohammed Aly ruthlessly suppressed the Mamlouk Beys, the military aristocracy that had misruled Egypt before Bonaparte's arrival, and easily defeated a British expeditionary force which had unwisely been dispatched to restore their power. During the forty-four years (1805–49) of his rule as Ottoman Viceroy he put an end to anarchy through a highly centralized administrative system and immensely increased the productive capacity of the country.

His methods were ruthless and arbitrary and his motive was primarily personal ambition. Most of the industries he founded to feed his military power did not survive his death. But it was more important that one million new acres of land were brought under the plough and that the living standards of the great majority of the population – the fellahin – steadily improved. With the help of French instructors, Turco-Circassian officers and the whip, he forged a powerful army from the fellahin which came near to overthrowing the Ottoman Sultan himself.

That it failed in this was primarily due to Palmerston, who had watched the growing power of Mohammed Aly with distaste. His first concern was that Ottoman Turkey should remain a bulwark against Russian expansion southward and eastward into the Levant. As Mohammed Aly, still a nominal vassal of the Sultan, spread his empire into Syria and Arabia in the 1830s he gained control over the two main routes to India – the Red Sea and the Euphrates Valley. He also threatened to extend his power to Constantinople and there was an alarming possibility that Russia might step in as the saviour of the Ottoman Empire.

At first Palmerston was inclined to hope that France might act as a reliable ally in containing Mohammed Aly, but the Pasha had been assiduously cultivating France's friendship. The engineers of Louis Philippe had not only built dams across the Nile; they had also constructed military forts to protect Alexandria.

When the Turkish navy, possibly with the connivance of some French officers, defected to Mohammed Aly in 1839 the threat to Constantinople became desperately serious. Palmerston launched a diplomatic offensive which in some ways was the supreme achievement of his career. The Treaty of London, concluded in July 1841 by Austria, England, Russia and Prussia to settle the problem, declared the Egyptian question to have been resolved. Its effect was to put an end to Mohammed Aly's imperial ambitions as well as his threat to the Ottoman Empire. He was forced to return Syria and Crete to the Sultan and to accept a limitation of 18,000 men to his army, which had numbered 90,000 at its peak. Nevertheless, French diplomatic action was able to preserve for him the hereditary rights of his dynasty and his semi-independent power as Viceroy of Egypt.

This result was satisfactory for Palmerston who did not care whether Egypt was independent of Constantinople provided it kept to itself. Nor did he mind that Mohammed Aly should be a French protégé as long as the protection did not go too far. For the next forty years successive British Governments acted on the principle that there was no need for a British occupation of Egypt unless a French occupation appeared to be imminent.

It was for this reason that Palmerston strongly opposed the Suez Canal scheme. In the secret decree of 12 April 1798 one of the aims of Bonaparte's Egyptian expedition was given as arranging to have the isthmus of Suez cut through to ensure 'the free and exclusive possession of the Red Sea for the French Republic'.[4] This did not endear the scheme to the British Government; although a British engineer's report in 1830 said that it was technically possible, Britain favoured a different plan to build first a canal and then a railway from Cairo to Suez. For similar but opposite reasons France resisted these ideas. 'We do not want Egypt,' Palmerston once said to Lord Cowley, 'or wish it for ourselves, any more than any rational man with an estate in the north of England and a residence in the south would have wished to possess the inns on the north road. All he could want would have been that the inns should be well-kept, always accessible, and furnishing him, when he came, with mutton-chops and post-horses.'[5]

Already in the early 1830s the young French Vice-Consul, Ferdinand de Lesseps, had become interested in the canal scheme, which gained the support of Mohammed Aly and most of Europe except England. It received a setback with the death of Mohammed Aly in 1849 and the succession of his grandson Abbas, who was no Francophile and who replaced his French advisers with Englishmen. But Abbas was murdered in 1854 and his uncle, Said Pasha, who became Viceroy, was a boyhood friend of de Lesseps whose father had been French Political Agent in Egypt. On 30 November the Suez Canal agreement defining the terms under which de Lesseps' Canal Company would build and operate the canal was signed.

England had by no means given up the struggle. The Sublime Porte* still had to give its consent and during the following nine months strong pressure was exerted on Constantinople to prevent the work from starting and when it did start, in April 1859, to halt its progress. De Lesseps enjoyed the steadfast support of Napoleon III but Palmerston maintained the most vigorous opposition. Disraeli also described the canal scheme as 'a most futile attempt and totally impossible to be carried out'. But the canal had a growing number of supporters, even in Britain. Mr Gladstone asked: 'What would be more unwise than to present ourselves to the world as the opponents of a scheme on the face of it beneficial to mankind, on no better ground than remote and contingent danger to interests of our own?'

The Sultan was stirred by Britain into remonstrating with the Viceroy for proceeding with the canal without his permission but Said stood firm in the knowledge that the forces with him were at

* A common term for the Ottoman Government referring to the High Gate into the government buildings at Istanbul.

least as strong as those against. Slowly the cutting of the canal progressed. In 1863 Said died and was succeeded by his nephew Ismail, a man of courage, vision and intelligence who is nevertheless regarded as the cause of Egypt's downfall. He quickly saw the significance of the canal for the world and therefore for Egypt; in the early years of his reign the work was pushed ahead to its completion in 1869, when Ismail played the munificent host to the plump but still handsome Empress Eugenie and other European royalty, including the Prince and Princess of Wales. It was a triumph for de Lesseps and Ismail but it also doomed Egypt to foreign occupation. In this the judgement of Palmerston, who died in 1865, was correct. When Ismail succeeded to the viceregal throne, Britain persuaded the Porte to issue an ultimatum to the Suez Canal Company on the ground that its act of concession had never been ratified by the Ottoman government. But de Lesseps, sure of his strength, appealed to Napoleon III who, with the consent of the Porte, headed a Commission of Arbitration. The Emperor's award was intended finally to determine the status of the Suez Canal Company in Egypt. The Company abandoned its right under the concession agreement to the use of free forced labour and also relinquished its lands on the Suez Isthmus, the freshwater and subsidiary canals and navigation rights on these waterways. In return Egypt and Ismail had to pay to the Company 84 million francs as compensation for the labour and 46 million francs for the lands and canals (for which the Company agreed to accept the interest on Ismail's shares until 1895).

The Company gained in security as a year later, following the Arbitration Commission's decision, the Sultan issued his Definitive Firman of Approval; it also acquired substantial funds at a time when it was in serious difficulties. But for Ismail and, in the long term, for Egypt, the settlement was disastrous.

The truth was that in 1869 Ismail was already deeply in debt. His uncle Said had set an example by raising a loan from Frühling and Goschen of London at 8 per cent. Ismail went much further, and within five years of his accession he had indebted himself for over £25 million at rates of interest nominally varying between 7 and 12 per cent but in reality amounting to between 12 and 26 per cent. One of his troubles when he acceded was that as Viceroy appointed by the Sultan, rather than an independent sovereign, he had no legal power to pledge the revenue of the state. The terms on which he could borrow money were therefore proportionately more expensive. In 1867 he obtained from the Sultan the style and title of Khedive together with permission to change the law of succession in favour of his direct descendants. But it was not until 1873 that with the aid of heavy bribes he obtained an Imperial Rescript making him an independent sovereign with the right to raise loans and grant concessions in Egypt's name without reference to the Porte. Thus what had hitherto been the personal liability of the Viceroy became the liability of the Egyptian state.

Another serious limitation to Egypt's sovereignty remained. In the sixteenth century the Ottoman Sultan had made special provision for the protection of non-Muslims who had established themselves within the Empire for trade. These privileges – known as the Capitulations – exempted them from taxes imposed on Muslim Ottoman subjects and gave them the right to be tried in their own consular courts. As Ottoman power declined these privileges had been reinforced, until by Ismail's time in Egypt they were the subject of flagrant abuse. The foreign communities in Egypt were not only privileged and protected; they were virtually above the law.

Ismail was an ugly man of the greatest charm. His physical appearance was almost grotesque – short, with a sort of seaman's roll which developed into a waddle as he grew more stout. His tangled, bushy red eyebrows half hid eyes which apparently worked independently, for while he was talking one would remain near closed as the other turned on whoever he was addressing. His conversation – usually in French – was intelligent, genial and witty. Hautes Sauternes, his favourite wine, was served at his long and elaborate luncheon parties. But it was in the private interview that he excelled, for he had a prodigious memory, and the gift of convincing even the most sceptical that he was supremely interested in their lives and welfare.

But ultimately his charm was unable to save him because 'next to his power of fascination, his capacity for spending money was his salient characteristic'. He acceded to the viceregal throne with the reputation of a prudent and successful manager of his private estates, but as ruler of Egypt his ambitions grew. Like other great men he failed to understand finance and he was too proud to seek expert advice. His hospitality at the opening of the Suez Canal has already been mentioned. In true Oriental tradition everyone was welcome to the feast but it was Egypt that paid. (*'J'ai mangé le patrimoine de trois fellahs'* a Frenchman was overheard to remark, patting his stomach as he came out of a refreshment stand at Ismailia.)

In the obloquy that fell on Ismail's name many of his achievements were forgotten. Apart from the Suez Canal, 112 irrigation canals of a total length of 8,400 miles were dug, railway track was extended from 275 to 1,185 miles; 500 miles of telegraph were erected, 430 bridges, Alexandria harbour and Suez docks were built, 15 lighthouses and 64 sugar mills were erected, one million and a quarter acres were reclaimed from the desert. Between 1862 and 1879 imports rose from £1,991,000 to £5,410,000 and exports from £4,454,000 to £13,810,000. At the same time many administrative and legal reforms were introduced. Customs and postal services were improved and, above all, the judicial system was radically changed by the introduction of Mixed Courts which ended the immunity of Europeans to a major part of civil law. The educational budget was increased and the first government girls' school in the Ottoman Empire was founded. The 185 elementary schools of 1863 had been increased to 4,685 by 1875. 'Egypt,' wrote the Alexandria correspondent of *The Times* in January 1876, 'is a marvellous instance of progress. She has advanced as much in seventy years as many other countries have done in five hundred.'

Egypt had acquired much of the infrastructure of an advanced mid-nineteenth-century state. But its debts had increased alarmingly. In the summer of 1875 Ismail decided to sell his interest in the Suez Canal Company, amounting to 176,602 shares out of a total of 400,000. When this became known to the British Prime Minister he bought them for £4,000,000 with the assistance of the London House of Rothschild. Except for the French, most people were delighted. The future Kaiser Wilhelm II wrote to his English mother Princess Victoria: 'Dear Mama, I must write you a line, because I know you will be delighted that England has bought the Suez Canal. How jolly.'

In fact England had not bought the Suez Canal but only 44 per cent of the Company's shares. Even this had the gravest implications as some of the members of the Cabinet and of Parliament were aware. Gladstone, as Leader of the Opposition, considered it 'an act of folly fraught with personal danger'. Moreover it had been sprung on Parliament as a *fait accompli*. Even Disraeli could see that it might well involve the British Government in Egypt's internal affairs 'but it was not I,' he commented, 'who built the Suez Canal'.

The financial collapse of the Turkish Empire already seemed imminent and the immediate effect on Egypt's credit was disastrous. But Turkey's financial collapse was not the cause of the British occupation of Egypt seven years later. Not only Turkey but Spain and several Latin American countries repudiated their debts during the nineteenth century and the British Government rejected all appeals from British bond-holders to intervene on their behalf. Egypt was different because it lay astride the route to India.

Following the collapse of Egyptian stock, Ismail asked for the services of a British government official 'thoroughly acquainted with the system followed in Her Majesty's Treasury' to assist his Finance Minister in remedying the confusion which he admitted existed in the administration. The British government took this as a request for financial advice and sent a high level mission headed by Stephen Cave, the Paymaster General. The view of the British public (including the bond-holders) was that Cave had gone to negotiate for a form of financial control over Egypt in return for financial assistance. France at once made a counter-offer of aid and when Cave persuaded Ismail to accept a financial adviser in Rivers Wilson, Controller General of the English National Debt Office, the French sent a financial adviser of their own.

Cave prepared a report on Egypt's finances which the British Government announced its intention of publishing. When Ismail objected the public assumed it was highly unfavourable with the result that Egyptian stocks sank even lower. In fact the report was far from hopeless: it concluded that 'the resources of Egypt are sufficient if properly managed, to meet her liabilities. . . . Egypt is well able to bear the whole of her present indebtedness at a reasonable rate of interest, but she cannot go on renewing floating debts at 25 per cent and raising loans at 12 or 13 per cent to meet these additions to her debt.'

Ismail made a determined effort to pull the country round. Following French advice in May 1876 he established a Caisse of Public Debt and converted the entire debt, floating and funded,

8

into a Unified Debt (amounting to £91 million) at 7 per cent with a large part of the state revenues as well as his personal estates as security.

The British Government disliked the new scheme both because it gave no independence to the Debt Commissioners, who could still be dismissed at any time by the Khedive, and because it was more favourable to the French than to the British bond-holders. It therefore sent George (later Lord) Goschen, financier and former Liberal cabinet minister, to Paris to make a new arrangement with M. Joubert, the representative of French financial interests. He reached a compromise agreement in Paris for a new type of consolidation which was much more to the British bond-holders' advantage. Under this new arrangement Egypt's total debt charges would amount to £16,565,000 a year, or about two-thirds of Egypt's revenue.

Goschen proceeded to Cairo with Joubert to persuade Ismail to accept the new arrangement. Here they came up against the stubborn opposition of Ismail's Minister of Finance, Ismail Sadik Pasha, known as the Mufattish (i.e. Inspector). He objected first to the introduction of foreign financial control and secondly to the 7 per cent interest rate. He claimed – correctly as it later turned out – that 5 per cent was the absolute maximum Egypt could pay. The Mufattish was a power in Egypt and quite prepared to use the argument that Ismail was preparing to sell the country to the Christians. The Khedive, who had decided to give way to the joint Anglo-French pressure, dismissed the Mufattish and announced his arrest and exile to Dongola in the Sudan. A steamer with windows nailed up like a coffin sailed up the Nile, but whether the Mufattish was on it or had been murdered on his arrest is uncertain. In either case he was never seen or heard of again.

One week later Ismail announced his acceptance of the Goschen-Joubert proposals, and Anglo-French Dual Control of Egypt began. As part of the agreement two executive Controllers-General were appointed: Mr Romaine, a former Judge-Advocate of the Indian Army, for revenue and Baron de Malavet for expenditure. Captain Evelyn Baring, formerly secretary to the Viceroy of India, was appointed to the post of English Commissioner on the Caisse with a salary of £3,000 a year.*

* The equivalent of at least four times as much today – a generous, tax-free stipend for a 37-year-old army captain.

9

The Dual Control at once set about proving its worth and in eight months succeeded in producing revenues of £6 million. Some of its methods were ingenious, such as the sale of a concession to a British firm for the use of Ancient Egyptian tombs to store phosphates. Customs dues and railway rates were also sharply increased. But the main burden fell on the long-suffering fellahin and it soon became apparent that Egypt was being squeezed dry. In November 1877 Mr Vivian, the British Consul General, reported to the Government: 'The Treasury chest is empty, the troops and government employees are many months in arrears of pay and among the latter class the greatest distress and misery prevails. The whole administration of the country is at a deadlock.'

Mr Romaine agreed with this view and drafted a memorandum pointing out that the fellahin were being taxed beyond their ability to pay. But Major Baring thought otherwise. He wrote a counter-memorandum comparing Egyptian taxes with those imposed on French, Turkish and Indian peasants, concluding that Egyptian rates of assessment were not excessive. At that time he regarded Romaine as simple and naïve and when he heard that the Controller-General had proposed that the rate of interest on the Public Debt should be cut by half he was outraged. 'He is a dangerous lunatic,' he wrote to Mr Goschen 'and ought to be locked up.'

Baring's aim was to persuade Ismail to accept an international commission of inquiry into his revenues and expenditure. Ismail put up a prolonged resistance but finally gave way. He still had one card up his sleeve; he intended to have the prestigious Colonel 'Chinese' Gordon, whom he had appointed Governor of the province of Equatoria in Southern Sudan in 1873, as the English representative and chairman of the Commission. Gordon accepted and hastened to Cairo. As Ismail had hoped, his solution to Egypt's financial difficulties was abrupt, soldierly and sensible: payment of the interest should be suspended until the arrears owing to government officials had been paid. But Gordon, who was more at home chasing slave-traders in the desert than discussing the complexities of Egypt's debts in the Abdin Palace, was no match for the European officials and especially for Captain Baring whom he found 'pretentious, grand and patronizing', adding 'when oil mixes with water, we will mix together'. Ismail realized that the game was up and allowed Gordon to return to the Sudan.

Gordon continued to believe his was the best solution and no doubt he was right.

The Commission's report was a devastating indictment of the corruption and abuses of the Government, which no doubt were deserved. But in fairness it should have been pointed out that some of the sufferings of the Egyptian taxpayer were the responsibility of the Dual Control. While the Commission was deliberating the situation had worsened. A low flood in 1877 had meant a crop failure in 1878. There had also been an outbreak of cotton blight and a depression of the cotton market. In Upper Egypt thousands died in the summer of 1878 from starvation and disease and the May and July debt coups were only just paid in time. The *Omdehs* (or village mayors) made exceptional use of the *kurbaj* (the whip); the peasants, who had no cash, gave up their furniture, seed-corn and clothing. Their only coins were the women's ornaments.

The sympathies of Major Baring (he was promoted in 1878) for the fellahin had been aroused. In February 1878 he wrote: 'My duty is to do those things which the Decree says I ought to do. Nevertheless I consider the *fellah* quite as *interesting*, to use the French phrase, as the creditors – perhaps more so; and if Romaine had set to work to ameliorate the fellah's lot in a reasonable way he would have had my cordial support.' But he had no doubts that Ismail was the villain and the common enemy of the bond-holders and Egyptian tax-payers.

The Commissioners' chief conclusion was that the evils of Egypt's system were due to the unlimited authority of the Khedive. Accordingly they decided he must delegate his power to 'responsible ministers' and establish a civil list to distinguish between the public revenue of the state and the private income of the sovereign. In exchange for the civil list they insisted that he should cede all his personal estates and those of his family – a total of about 916,000 acres (or about 20 per cent of Egypt's cultivated land).

Ismail gracefully accepted these terms in words which were to become famous: 'My country is no longer in Africa; we are now part of Europe. It is therefore natural for us to abandon our former ways and to adopt a new system adapted to our social conditions. . . .' He authorized Nubar Pasha to form a Ministry. Sir Rivers Wilson became Minister of Finance and, after strong protests that Britain would be monopolizing the centres of power,

M. de Blignières was appointed Minister of Public Works with authority over the railways and postal services.

Nubar was later described by Baring as 'by far the most interesting of latter-day Egyptian politicians' who 'intellectually towered above his competitors'. He deserved Egypt's gratitude for his part in reducing the privileges of the Capitulations and later in abolishing the *corvée* or forced labour. But he was devious and unscrupulous and bore no little share of responsibility for Ismail's extravagance. Moreover he was an Armenian Christian who never learned to speak Arabic properly. To the Egyptians he was almost as much a foreigner as Wilson or de Blignières.

It was not difficult for Ismail to set about undermining the authority of his own 'European' government. When it took unpopular measures – as it was bound to do in view of Egypt's financial condition – it was simple for the Khedive to refuse to share responsibility. Declaring his faith in parliamentary democracy, Ismail proposed to convene the moribund Chamber of Notables which he had created in 1866 largely to convince Europe of his liberalism.

Meanwhile the Government was faced with the task of paying Egypt's debts to the bond-holders and, as the situation in the countryside worsened, the village sheikhs insisted that even the present taxation rates could not be maintained. Most government servants and army officers had received no pay for eighteen months or more. The Government decided to pay the fficers part of the arrears and to retire 2,500 of them on half-pay. It then rashly summoned 2,000 of the officers stationed in the provinces to Cairo to explain the new arrangements and when these angry and embittered men presented themselves to Ismail he blandly referred them to his Ministers. A group of them found Nubar and Wilson driving to their offices; they dragged them from their carriages and locked them up in the Finance Ministry pending a decision of the whole officer corps. Ismail at once came down and released them and when the mutinous officers refused to disperse, ordered the guard to open fire. Several of the mutineers and the guard were wounded and the Khedive's Chamberlain standing by his side received a sabre cut. By this show of courage Ismail had proved that the Government of Egypt still depended on his authority. The next day he was able to dismiss Nubar as incapable of maintaining public order.

The British and French Governments expressed the fervent hope through their representatives in Cairo that Nubar's downfall would not 'shake the experiment of reformed government in Egypt'. Ismail was equally determined that it should. With the Khedive's encouragement, a national memorial signed by the Sheikh ul-Islam (the senior Muslim dignitary in Egypt), the Coptic patriarch, the Jewish grand rabbi, seventy ulema and numerous pashas and army officers demanding Wilson's dismissal was presented to Ismail. On 7 April 1879 the Khedive informed the European consuls that he intended to form a native ministry headed by Sherif Pasha, the leading constitutionalist among the Notables.

The Khedive's right to dismiss his own ministers could hardly be disputed publicly but the British and French Governments were not less determined that his *coup d'état*, as they rather curiously termed it, should not succeed. Ismail had hoped to revive the posts of Controllers-General of Finance and to persuade Baring and the French member of the Caisse to occupy them. He met with a point-blank refusal; Baring resigned and left Egypt on 24 May 1879. Ismail was confronted by what amounted to a general strike of European officials in Egypt.

Neither the British nor the French Government was yet willing to contemplate direct intervention in Egypt. The British Government, in particular, was aware that the public was not over-sympathetic to the bond-holders and there was still a possibility that the Khedive and his new government might be able to manage the affairs of Egypt. On 19 May 1879 the Alexandria correspondent of *The Times* was writing: 'The Khedive, though master in his own house, has now to take account of a so-called national party whose influence on their master is reported sometimes on the verge of dictation. The army, the Pashas, the Ulema, are united in the common object of proving that Egypt can govern herself, and the Parliament, recently increased to the number of 100, has shown signs of vitality that promise a parliamentary future.'

But the experiment was never tried. While the British and French Governments were still considering what to do about Ismail, intervention came from an unexpected quarter. On 18 May a strong protest was presented to the Khedive by the German and Austrian Governments against the manner in which the Sherif Government was proposing to deal with the holders of the floating debt (most of whom were or German or Austrian nationality). In an effort to keep his administration running, Sherif had proposed to pay the May coupon at the reduced rate of 5 per cent. In desperation he now informed the Powers that the holders of the floating debt would be paid in full; but it was too late. Britain and France put pressure on the Ottoman Sultan to order Ismail to abdicate in favour of his eldest son Prince Tewfik.

Ismail, after collecting his crown jewels and £3 million in cash, sailed from Alexandria on his yacht the *Mahroussa* on 30 June. He went first to Naples and later to Istanbul, where he died in 1895. He has had few defenders. The British rulers of Egypt had every reason to encourage the belief of the Egyptian people that Ismail was responsible for their miserable condition while Egyptian nationalists and their sympathizers saw him as the man who threw away Egypt's independence. That Ismail had done much to win this independence was generally forgotten.

One of the features of his reign which did more than anything to stir national resentment among the Egyptians was the sharp increase in the number of foreigners employed in senior administrative posts. Between 1871 and 1875, 201 Europeans were appointed to the Egyptian civil service, between 1876 and 1879, 534. The Alexandria correspondent of *The Times* wrote on 25 December 1878: 'Satirical visitors find amusement in counting the number of disestablished European officials, whose salaries count by thousands of pounds, while hundreds of native State servants cannot get their few pounds a month due for the last year or more for good service actually rendered. In addition there were over 100,000 foreign residents in Egypt who, under the protection of the Capitulations, were paying no taxation at a time when the fellahin were being flogged to disgorge their last piastre.'

Ismail's deposition created a power vacuum in Egypt. The Sultan had been persuaded by the Powers to revoke his Imperial Rescript of 1873 and issue a new one limiting the Egyptian armed forces to 18,000 men and prohibiting the Khedive from raising new loans without the consent of his creditors – a provision which the British Government was to find a severe hindrance to its administration of Egypt within a few years. At the same time the Powers dissuaded the Porte from revoking the 1867 Rescript allowing the succession to pass to Ismail's male heirs. In this event, Ismail's uncle, Prince Abdul Halim, the youngest son of

Mohammed Aly and his eldest surviving descendant, would have occupied the Khedivial throne and, unlike Tewfik, Halim had a strong and decisive character.

Even Tewfik was at first reluctant to submit to the full political Dual Control of France and Britain. Sherif Pasha, whom he appointed President of the Council, strongly objected to any suggestion either that there should be European ministers in the Government, or that the Controllers General, whose office was to be revived, should have executive functions. Eventually a compromise was reached whereby the Controllers should have advisory powers only and a consultative role in the Cabinet but could no longer be dismissed without the consent of their respective governments. When the British Government asked Baring to accept the post for Britain, he hesitated because he was planning to stand as a Liberal for East Norfolk at the next General Election. Eventually he accepted and arrived in Egypt again at the end of 1879.*

Sherif's ministry was short-lived. One of his first actions was to submit a draft constitution to the new Khedive but, affirming that liberal institutions were utterly unsuited to Egypt, Tewfik refused to approve the new constitution which he described as a *décor de théâtre*. Sherif resigned and the Khedive, after being dissuaded from taking the Premiership himself, appointed Riaz Pasha in his place.

Riaz was very different from Nubar, the other leading Egyptian politician of the day. In appearance he was unattractive. He had begun his career as a dancing-boy to the homosexual Abbas I but was now a fragile little man of fifty with a wizened face and a harsh, high-pitched voice. His manner was also unappealing; but he possessed solid qualities. For one thing he was honest and courageous enough to have stood up to Ismail who was disconcerted by his failure to enrich himself. In the eyes of most Egyptians his advantage over Nubar was that, though of Jewish extraction, he was a pious Muslim who believed that Egypt should be ruled by Muslims, although by this he meant himself rather than any

---

* Shortly afterwards Gladstone told him that he had been right not to enter Parliament as all the principal questions which interested Liberals had already been solved. The Prime Minister, Lord Beaconsfield, on the other hand, who interviewed him before his departure, merely inquired if there were many pelicans on the banks of the Nile.

form of popular government, for which he agreed with Tewfik the Egyptians were quite unsuited.

The first part of Riaz's two-year Cabinet was moderately successful and Moberly Bell, *The Times* correspondent in Cairo, even declared four years later that 'with all its faults it was the best administration which Egypt has enjoyed before or since'. Much of the credit belongs to the Controllers General who worked harmoniously together and wisely remained self-effacing. They prepared a report on Egypt's finances which was used as a basis for the final arrangement for the settlement of the country's debts which was embodied in the so-called Law of Liquidation of 1880. Although this provided some relief, after payment of the Sultan's tribute and interest on the Suez Canal shares, the Government was left with only 34 per cent of the reduced revenue. Some of the burden of taxation was partially shifted from the fellahin to the wealthy. After six months of the Dual Control, consular reports from the countryside collected in Cairo by the new British Consul General, Sir Edward Malet, painted a glowing picture of usurers' interest rates cut by half, land values doubled and the *kurbaj* and *corvée* virtually eliminated. That this was wildly over-optimistic had to be acknowledged after the British occupation when all these abuses remained to be tackled. The fact remains that in those early months of 1880 the fellahin felt a lightening of their burdens for the first time in many years.

Meanwhile a spring General Election had taken place in Britain sweeping Gladstone into power with a large majority. Lord Lytton resigned as Viceroy of India and Lord Ripon was appointed in his place. Baring, who had spent 1872 to 1876 in India as private secretary to his cousin Lord Northbrook, was now appointed Financial Secretary to the Government of India and left Egypt in June 1880. His successor as Controller was a former Indian Civil Servant, Sir Auckland Colvin, who had replaced him as Debt Commissioner in 1879.

THE ARABI REVOLT

Tewfik's autocratic inclinations were tempered by his lack of ability. He had no desire to become a constitutional monarch but he might have been made one all the same. This did not happen because of the rise of the national movement which Britain and France both came to regard as a threat to their vital interests. The movement consisted of several disparate and ultimately incompatible elements which were temporarily united against the dangers of foreign domination and arbitrary government. The intellectual or ideological strand consisted of the politico-religious reformers who were disciples of Jemal el-Din al-Afghani. Al-Afghani had come to Cairo after being exiled from Constantinople in 1871. His disciples included the well-loved Sheikh Mohammed Abdu and the young Saad Zaghlul, whom Cromer was to regard in his later years as a promising moderate nationalist, but who was also to develop into Britain's arch-enemy and the champion of unfettered Egyptian independence. Al-Afghani taught his disciples law, philosophy and theology. He believed that Islam must be strengthened by a restoration of its principles, but he also preached the need for national and Islamic unity as a defence against European intervention. Through his disciples al-Afghani was the formative influence on the flourishing intellectual life of Cairo under Ismail, who tolerated and even encouraged his activities. Although al-Afghani favoured constitutional government his political philosophy was primarily opposed to the power of the Ottoman Caliphate. But Tewfik ordered his exile shortly after his accession (almost certainly with the encouragement of the Dual Control). Al-Afghani departed to India but by 1884 he had joined Mohammed Abdu (who was himself exiled for three years after the British occupation) in Paris to found a secret society and publish an Arabic journal dedicated to Islamic reform.

The second element in the national movement was the Constitutional Party led by Sherif Pasha, an indolent, jovial,

French-educated Turk who was 'willing to accept any proposition rather than spare a precious half-hour from his billiard table'.[1] On occasions he could show traces of courage and statesmanship but in general he lacked the energy and application to put his lightly-held liberal principles into practice. As we have seen, Ismail gave encouragement to the Constitutionalists in his fight for survival. His attitude was cynical for he never sincerely intended the Chamber of Notables to become a permanent brake on his arbitrary power. But this was what the Chamber was showing signs of becoming when Ismail was deposed. The fatal flaw in the Constitutionalists' position was that in the final analysis their sympathies and interests were bound to lie with the property-owning classes rather than with the mass of the fellahin. Like most bourgeois liberals, they were easily scared by any threat of radical revolt. The consequence was that the British occupiers could claim, with some justification, that to revive Egypt's fledgeling representative institutions would be against the interest of the fellahin.

With the encouragement of the Dual Control, Tewfik rejected Sherif's draft constitution and asked Riaz to head the new government in which the Circassian Osman Rifky, a thoroughly unpopular reactionary, became Minister of War. The general consequence was to create an alliance between the Constitutionalists and the Egyptian elements in the army.

The fellah officers were the third element in the nationalist movement who shortly took over its leadership. By now they were in a state of angry discontent. One of the reasons for the popularity of Ismail's predecessor, Said, was that he had preferred to promote Egyptian officers rather than Turco-Circassians. This policy was reversed by Ismail and in 1880 virtually all the military posts were held by Turco-Circassians. (It was these elements who had rebelled against the proposal of the Nubar–Wilson–de Blignières government to place half the officer corps on retirement.)

Osman Rifky now proposed to go further with a new law which would have made it even more difficult for Egyptians of fellah origin to enter the Military Academy. In January 1881 three fellah colonels presented a petition against the draft law. Their leader was Ahmed Arabi, commander of the 4th Regiment. A solid, handsome man in early middle age, Arabi was the son of a small farmer of Lower Egypt. His education at the village Koranic school and al-Azhar was limited but he was not illiterate, as his enemies later maintained. He possessed many of the essential qualities of leadership – moral courage, dignity and trustworthiness. Above all, he appealed to the Egyptian masses because he remained part of them and could understand and express their grievances in terms they could understand. Unfortunately for Egypt, he lacked decision and both political and military skill.

Arabi was a member, although not the leader, of a secret society in the army dedicated to the abolition of favouritism for the Turco-Circassian officers and the deposition of Ismail. (Arabi was among those who saw no good in Ismail and at one time planned his assassination.) He had once been charged with insubordination and on another occasion, when in charge of transport at Massawa during Ismail's war with the Ethiopians in 1875–6, with corruption, although this was almost certainly a trumped-up accusation by one of his Turkish superiors whom he had crossed.

He was already regarded as dangerous in Turkish circles when he presented his petition with his two friends. At Osman Rifky's suggestion, the Council of Ministers decided to arrest and court-martial them. On 3 February 1881 they were summoned to the Kasr-el-Nil barracks on the pretext of discussing arrangements for the wedding of the Khedive's sister, and arrested by Osman Rifky and his Circassian officers and placed on trial. But the three colonels, who had been warned, had arranged to be rescued by a friendly regiment. This arrived in time to break up the court-martial and release the men. Realizing that none of the Cairo garrison was prepared to help quell the garrison, the Government capitulated and dismissed Rifky, who was replaced by Mustafa Sami, a brilliant nationalist intellectual.

Arabi had become a national hero. In exiling al-Afghani and repudiating the Constitutionalists, Tewfik had ensured that Egypt's national aspirations would be concentrated on the army. As *The Times* pointed out on 12 September 1881: 'The army, we must remember, is the only native institution which Egypt now owns. All else has been invaded and controlled and transformed by the accredited representatives of France and England.'

The army had begun by protecting its own interests but now found itself championing the national interests. In addition to demanding an increase of army strength to the full 18,000 permitted by the Imperial Rescript, it called for a written constitution and a reform programme of abolition of the *corvée*, restrictions on usury and regulation of water rights. The inspiration for these ideas came from Mustafi Sami, who was the brains of the Hizb al-Watani, or National Party, as the groups who gathered around Arabi came to be known. A poet and intellectual, Sami remained a Turk who had espoused the Egyptian cause.[2]

As the National Party's influence and popularity spread, the initial reaction of Malet and Colvin, the two senior British representatives in Egypt on whose judgement the British Government relied, was cautiously optimistic. They both had some appreciation of the grievances of the colonels and felt that the national movement could be guided into the right channels under European supervision. Yet both lacked any real understanding of the Egyptian mind, while Malet's character failed to rise to the exceptionally difficult circumstances of the time. This 'placid, cold moon-like diplomat', as Moberly Bell described him, had a high reputation when he arrived in Cairo in 1879 as a still youthful Etonian bachelor. He was not liked. He caused a sensation when he first made a joke. But it was recognized that he soon acquired an ascendancy over the admittedly indecisive Khedive. His letters to Lord Granville and his mother which are printed in his Apologia (Egypt, 1879–83) reveal an extraordinary lack of inner self-assurance combined with a powerful ambition.* His dispatches show that he was far too concerned to tell the Foreign Office what it wished to hear while his account of Egyptian events was marred by a lack of critical judgement of his sources of information. His reference to Arabi, no doubt in a moment of stress, as 'an illiterate fanatic' was dangerously misleading. Both Salisbury, who appointed him, and Granville urged him to do nothing which might lead to armed intervention. Since this is what happened his service in Egypt might be considered a disastrous failure. Yet in later years he assured himself that he could not have been in the slightest degree to blame because in no time he had been made Ambassador

---

* 'Do you like a KCMG in the hand or a KCB in a very thick bush?' Granville had written to him in August 1880. Malet chose the KCB but regretted it when the honour arrived a year later for by that time the services which earned him the knighthood had been forgotten and the Egyptian situation had deteriorated, so the matter was widely misconstrued.

to Berlin 'which at that time was the most important Embassy in the diplomatic service'.

Malet remarks that he had been reproached for having fallen under the influence of Sir Auckland Colvin. He does not deny the charge but generously praises Colvin's character. In fact there is little doubt that the older and more self-certain man was the dominant personality The charge that he worked from the beginning for Arabi's overthrow and British intervention is patently unfair. But, unlike Malet, he never wavered once he had made up his mind on these two points and as the Cairo correspondent of the *Pall Mall Gazette* he had a powerful influence on English public opinion.

The third prominent British actor in the Egyptian drama of 1881–2 was the aristocratic rebel Wilfrid Scawen Blunt. Born at Petworth in 1840 and a cousin of the Wyndhams, Blunt had graced several British legations with his beauty and conversation in the 1860s. In 1869 he had married Byron's granddaughter Anne and a year later, on inheriting the Blunt estates in Sussex, retired from diplomacy. Despite her ancestry, Lady Anne had the more prosaic and scholarly mind. Blunt was a good, if uneven, minor poet and a romantic with the will and the means to pursue his dreams. His adventures with women, which continued into an advanced age, produced several illegitimate children.

Politically, Blunt described himself as a Tory anti-imperialist – a fast-dwindling breed in the jingoistic, acquisitive atmosphere of late Victorian England. He possessed extraordinary social courage for his views were anathema to nine-tenths of his friends. But though they often quarrelled with him they usually forgave him before long for the sake of his company. In 1874 he had visited Algeria with Lady Anne where an Arab rising was being suppressed by the French. They had found their sympathies 'going out wholly to the Arabs'. This was the beginning of a life-long anti-imperial campaign which extended first to Egypt, then Ireland (where he went to prison for two months in 1887) and India. He first visited Egypt under Ismail in 1875–6 but returned again for much of 1880 to 1882. He befriended Arabi and Mohammed Abdu and acted for a time as unofficial adviser to the Nationalist Party and negotiator between them on the one hand and Malet and Colvin on the other.

Inevitably he aroused the extreme hostility of his numerous

political opponents against whom he never measured his words. His role in Egypt was regarded as increasingly sinister as the crisis there deepened. There were questions about him in the House of Commons and after the occupation he was forbidden to enter Egypt for three years. In Lady Gregory's words, he 'came to be regarded as the *enfant terrible* in politics just as Samuel Butler was in art and literature'. In later years British writers on Egypt tended to minimize his importance. Cromer dismisses him with courteous contempt as 'an enthusiast who dreamt dreams of an Arab Utopia' and 'had no political training of any value'. Milner ignores him entirely in his *England in Egypt*, while P. G. Elgood in the *Dictionary of National Biography* says of his writings: 'His discretion is questionable, his judgement superficial; he records gossip as fact and allows prejudice to colour his narration.' They are 'interesting supplements to the impressions of more sober writers, but little else'.

Undoubtedly Blunt, as a personal friend or acquaintance of most of the English ruling class, greatly exaggerated his political influence and gravely misled the Egyptian nationalists in this respect. Perhaps his biggest mistake was to take the anti-imperialist professions of Gladstone, Harcourt, Morley and other Liberals at their face value. He pinned special faith on an article by Gladstone in the August 1877 issue of the *Nineteenth Century* entitled 'Aggression on Egypt and Freedom in the East' in which the GOM forcefully attacked Edward Dicey's call for a British occupation of Egypt. 'Our first site in Egypt, be it by larceny or be it by emption, will be the almost certain egg of a North African Empire that will grow and grow . . .' Indeed for someone who had the opportunity to observe Victorian imperialism both at its source and its object Blunt surprisingly misjudged its motives. The country squire was so appalled by the vulgar commercialism of the age that he ignored the strategic 'lifeline of empire' considerations which were uppermost in the minds of British statesmen, and attributed imperial expansionism entirely to the machinations of international finance.

Nevertheless, for all his spontaneous and often rash judgements (the very qualities which make his Journals of incomparable value and much more than 'interesting supplements to the impressions more sober writers') Blunt got much closer to the heart of things than men of more ordered intelligence, such as Colvin or Milner.

He understood why Arabi was a hero to the mass of the Egyptians. He knew that his power was not based on intimidation and that Egyptian resentment of European control was not merely a manifestation of 'Muslim fanaticism'. His articles in British journals such as the *Nineteenth Century*, and his letters to *The Times*, together with those of Sir William Gregory (a former liberal Tory MP and Governor of Ceylon who also espoused Arabi's cause) at least ensured that the British public was aware of the case for Egyptian nationalism. Cromer dismissed Blunt as a dreamer and supporter of lost causes but it was not many years after Blunt's death, in 1922, that he proved to be a better prophet than Cromer who assumed that the 'imperial race' would be governing and civilizing Mohammedan people for several centuries.

In the spring of 1881, the situation appeared to be settling down so that when Malet went on leave in May he could report that he had 'reason to believe that confidence was being restored'.

On Malet's departure, Colvin became the mouthpiece of European influence in Egypt. Largely because of the intrigues of the Khedive, the situation rapidly deteriorated. There is little doubt that Tewfik was plotting a counter-attack against the Egyptian colonels. He only lacked the courage and determination to act like his father, although Ismail was the kind of ruler he wished to be.[2]

The colonels, who were constantly watched by palace spies, were convinced that plans were being prepared to murder them. In August, Tewfik suddenly decided to replace Mustafa Sami as Minister of War with his own brother-in-law, Daoud Pasha Yeghen, a bitterly reactionary Circassian. On 9 September, Arabi's regiment, the 3rd infantry, was given orders to move from Cairo to Alexandria. The colonels believed that Tewfik and Daoud had decided to act against them – as no doubt they had – and resolved to make the first move. They sent a message to the Khedive asking him to meet them at the Abdin Palace and marched there at the head of their regiments. They said they did not go to his private residence 'so as not to frighten the ladies'.

In this moment of crisis, Colvin's advice to the Khedive was to put himself at the head of two regiments which Riaz Pasha said were loyal and march to Abdin to arrest Arabi. As Cromer remarked, Colvin was a member of the Indian Civil Service and had 'heard of mutiny'.[3] The example of John Lawrence, who had prevented the Punjab from rising with the mutineers, pointed the way. But the circumstances in Egypt were somewhat different from India in 1857. In the first place Colvin was no more than an unofficial adviser to the Khedive and there were no British troops in Egypt. It was very doubtful whether even two regiments were loyal; Riaz was notoriously ignorant of the true state of feeling in the army. Eventually Tewfik arrived at Abdin with Colvin and only a handful of Egyptian and European officers. Nevertheless Colvin's advice was still for Tewfik to arrest Arabi personally and presumably to shoot him if he disobeyed. In his account of the incident Colvin wrote: 'I said to him, "When Arabi Bey presents himself, tell him to give you his sword, and to give him the order to disperse. Then go the round of the square and address each regiment separately, and give them the order to disperse." Arabi Bey approached on horseback; the Viceroy called out to him to dismount. He did so, and came forward on foot, with several others and a guard with fixed bayonets, and saluted. I said to the Viceroy, "Now is your moment." He replied, "We are between four fires." I said, "Have courage." He took counsel of a native officer on his left, and repeated to me: "What can I do? We are between four fires. We shall be killed." He then told Arabi Bey to sheathe his sword. The order was obeyed; and he then asked Arabi Bey what all this meant. Arabi Bey replied by enumerating three points, adding that the army had come there on the part of the Egyptian people to enforce them, and would not retire until they were conceded.'

Colvin told Tewfik it was 'not fitting for the Viceroy to discuss questions of this kind with colonels'.[4] Tewfik retired into the palace leaving Colvin talking to the colonels for an hour 'explaining to them the gravity of the situation for themselves', until Charles Cookson, who was Acting Consul General in Malet's absence and who spoke Arabic well, arrived to continue the negotiations.*

* A small but not unimportant mystery remains concerning Colvin's command of Arabic. Blunt told Lord Granville that Colvin 'does not understand what is going on in the Council from ignorance of the language used'. Malet, who relied heavily on Colvin's reports of the Egyptian Council of Ministers' meetings replied indignantly that 'Colvin speaks Arabic sufficiently to hold a long conversation, and he understands the substance of what passes in Council, though when the Ministers speak rapidly he may not understand every word! Blunt himself is always obliged to use an interpreter.' The suspicion remains that Colvin's

In Colvin's eyes, Tewfik's nerve had failed him at the supreme moment. But it is at least possible (and much more characteristic) that Tewfik, realizing the strength of the national movement in the army, had decided to come to terms for the time being. In that case he would have had no intention of attempting to arrest Arabi without the support of loyal troops and had only asked Colvin to accompany him to witness his helplessness. In his autobiographical fragment Arabi said: 'If the Khedive had shot me the guns would have fired on him, and there would have been bad work. But he was quite well pleased with what had passed.' The colonels seem to have felt that the Khedive was at least partially on their side because he wanted to get rid of Riaz. After the incident he sent them a message saying 'You three are soldiers, with me you make four.'

Arabi's three demands were (*a*) that all the Ministers should be dismissed, (*b*) that a Parliament should be convened, and (*c*) that the strength of the army should be raised to 18,000 men. Tewfik agreed to the first and Arabi that the other two could remain in suspense while reference was made to the Porte.

The Colonels wanted Sherif Pasha as President of the Council. After suggesting a few names, which the colonels rejected, Tewfik agreed. Sherif at first demurred. As a Turk and big landowner he was reluctant to owe his office to a movement led by fellahin colonels. However, his doubts were overcome by the members of the Chamber of Notables who had been summoned to Cairo by Arabi and went in a body to Sherif headed by Sultan Pasha, the President of the Chamber, with an undertaking that if Sherif accepted office Arabi would obey the Government's orders. Sherif became President of the Council with Mustafa Sami as Secretary for War.

Sheikh Mohammed Abdu, al-Afghani's disciple and editor of the *Official Journal*, was at first suspicious of Arabi's aims, believing that constitutional government could not be achieved through a military *coup d'état*. But after a meeting at Sultan Pasha's house he became convinced that Arabi was sincerely working for civilian government and decided to join the national movement.

It appeared that a bloodless revolution had been achieved with the enthusiastic support of the Egyptian people. Blunt says:

Arabic was very limited. Possibly he would have been wise to follow Blunt's example of using an interpreter.

'The three months which followed this notable event were the happiest time, politically, that Egypt has ever known. . . . Throughout Egypt a cry of jubilation arose such as for hundreds of years had not been heard upon the Nile, and it is literally true that in the streets of Cairo men stopped each other, though strangers, to embrace and rejoice together at the astonishing new reign of liberty which had suddenly begun for them, like the dawn after a long night of fear.'[5]

Blunt was not impartial but there is no reason to doubt his evidence of the public attitude to the September revolution. Even Colvin was impressed. 'The Liberal movement should be in no wise discouraged,' he wrote a few weeks later. 'Though in its origin anti-Turk, it is in itself an Egyptian national movement.' Arabi himself was behaving with admirable restraint. He made his submission to the Khedive and at once showed willingness to accept the orders of the civil branch of the nationalist movement. On 6 October he left Cairo with his regiment after telling a huge crowd at the railway station that the army was 'well united, well commanded, well disciplined and marching towards its only goal – the welfare of the nation'. When he returned to Cairo to see Colvin the latter informed Malet that he 'produced a most favourable impression. . . . He disclaimed all hostility to foreigners, saying that what the Egyptians knew of liberty, and much that they had gained of it, was due to foreigners. . . . The impression left on my mind was that Arabi, who spoke with great moderation, calmness and conciliation, is sincere and resolute, but not a practical man.'

Ten days after the 9 September revolution Colvin had written in a memorandum: 'All is being done in an orderly and even exemplary manner, but the chance of any final settlement depends (1) on the army dispersing to the several quarters assigned to it, (2) on the moderation shown by the Notables in their demands, and (3) on the tact and firmness of the Ministers in dealing with the Army and the Notables. . . . I do not think it is at all my duty to oppose myself to the popular movement, but to try rather to guide and to give it definite shape.'

For the remaining months of 1881 there were many indications that Colvin's conditions for a 'final settlement' could be met. When the Chamber of Notables was due to be convened Sherif wanted it to be on the restricted basis of the law of 1866, while Arabi argued vigorously, with the support of some of the Notables, for the more democratic electoral law which Sherif himself had proposed to Ismail in the last days of his reign. When Sherif dug in his heels – doubtless with encouragement from Colvin – Arabi gave way. Then disagreement arose between Colvin and Arabi over the army estimates for 1882. If the armed forces were to be increased to 18,000, as the Khedive had promised, the extra cost was estimated at £600,000. Colvin declared that the Treasury could not possibly support more than £522,000 which was enough to raise the army to 15,000. After lengthy negotiations through Blunt as intermediary, Arabi again gave way.

Arabi was behaving with moderation and reason. Malet, who returned from leave on 18 September, wrote to Lord Granville: 'On the whole our horizon seems to be brightening, and I am less anxious about it at present than I have been for some time past. I think an onslaught will be made in the Chamber on the official salaries of foreigners, and I confess that they afford reasonable ground for attack. I see that the members of the administrative Council to be established at Constantinople are to have £1,200 a year. Here similar officials receive £3,000. I feel sure that the proper persons could be found to fill the posts at £2,000. The Caisse is especially open to such criticism, four members doing work which could be done by two, each member receiving £3,000 a year.'*

But Malet's optimism was misplaced. Several factors were tending to destroy the slender framework of mutual confidence within Egypt on which Colvin's 'final settlement' had to be based. These were the double-dealing of the Khedive and the Porte and the attitude of the French Government. Tewfik succeeded in giving the impression that he was sympathetic to the national movement and to the Constitutionalists. This was not in fact so, although he lacked the nerve to confront them openly. He contented himself with refusing to accept any permanent constitutional arrangement in the hope that the Sultan would intervene to re-establish the Khedive's authority. Meanwhile the Dual Control felt that they had no alternative to backing the Khedive as the only legitimate power in Egypt.

In November 1881 the Khedive sent an emissary to Constantinople to tell the Sultan that Egypt was in a state of rebellion, that

* This was the amount of Captain Baring's salary when he was appointed to the Caisse.

it was proposed to form an Arabian Empire and that Arabi and the British Government were agreed on this point. When Arabi heard of Tewfik's intrigues with the Porte he wrote to the Sultan's confidante and spiritual adviser, Sheikh Mohammed Zaffer, whom he knew personally, expressing his 'strong attachment to the fundamental principles of our sacred law, which make it a duty to obey the Ameer El Moumeneen' (Commander of the Faithful). The Sultan's reply through Sheikh Zaffer was encouraging. He said he was satisfied with Arabi's loyalty and commended him to defend Egypt at all costs from invasion, lest it should share the fate of Tunis (recently occupied by France), and that he cared neither for Ismail, Halim or Tewfik but for the man who would carry out his instructions.

The Sultan was backing both Tewfik and Arabi at the same time as he waited to see which came out on top. Early in October he sent two envoys to Egypt, Aly Pasha Nizami and Ahmed Pasha Ratib, to demonstrate the Ottoman interest in Egypt. At this stage the British Government was still anxious for Turkey to bear the responsibility for preserving the *status quo* in Egypt. As Gladstone summed up British policy for Granville three days after the September crisis: '(1) Steady concert with France (2) Turkish general to go if need be (3) Turkish troops in preference to any others (4) No British or French force, unless ships be needful for "bona fide" protection of subjects (5) Apart from all this, I long for information on the merits of the quarrel.'[6]

The trouble was that although the Sultan Abdulhamid was open to Great Power persuasion, British influence in Constantinople had sunk very low. Gladstone, who had long opposed Disraeli and Salisbury's policy of shoring up Turkey as a barrier to Russian expansion in the Levant, had violently denounced Ottoman persecution of Christian minorities in his Midlothian campaign for the 1880 elections. Moreover, it was a cardinal aim of Gladstone and Granville's policy to preserve the Anglo-French entente in the face of Bismarck's ambitions in Europe. They felt bound by the 1878 Congress of Berlin agreements which, among other things, allowed the French a free hand in Tunis in return for a free hand for Britain in Cyprus.

The French, who had occupied Tunisia in May 1881, were nervous that the Porte might try to raise a Pan-Islamic resistance movement through Egypt. They were absolutely opposed to any

Turkish intervention in Egypt and strongly disliked the presence of the two envoys of Abdulhamid in Cairo. The French Foreign Minister, Barthélemy St Hilaire had persuaded Granville to agree to the despatch of a British and a French cruiser as a counter-demonstration. His earlier proposal that a British and a French general should be sent to Egypt to restore order in the mutinous army had been wisely rejected by Lord Granville on the advice of Colvin and Sherif Pasha. The British Government hoped that Anglo-French diplomatic action would be sufficient because it held to the traditional British view that France must not be allowed to gain a predominant position in the Eastern Mediterranean. If diplomacy was not enough Britain would have to involve itself militarily as much as France, and it was Granville's view that this would inevitably lead to war between England and France.* This was why he would rather see Turkish troops than Anglo-French in Egypt, but greatly preferred neither.

Granville honestly favoured non-intervention, a policy which happened to suit his own indolent nature. On 4 November he sent a despatch to Malet (which Malet had previously drafted for him) laying down the principles of the British Government's Egyptian policy. Answering the common charge that Britain favoured Riaz Pasha, he wrote: 'It cannot be too clearly understood that England desires no partisan ministry in Egypt.' He added, 'It would seem hardly necessary to enlarge upon our desire to maintain Egypt in the enjoyment of the measure of administrative independence which has been secured to her by the Sultan's Firmans', and concluded: 'The only circumstance which could force us to depart from the course of conduct which I have above indicated would be the occurrence in Egypt of a state of anarchy. We look to the Khedive and to Chérif Pasha, and to the good sense of the Egyptian people to prevent such a catastrophe. . . .'⁷

Sherif Pasha was sufficiently delighted with this statement to have it translated into Arabic and disseminated.

Superficially, the situation in November-December was much improved. By mutual agreement the British and French cruisers had been withdrawn at the same time as the two Turkish Commissioners. The Egyptian public began to feel that perhaps after all they were not going to suffer the same fate as the Tunisians. But on 10 November an event occurred which ultimately ensured

* Bismarck was of the same opinion.

the British occupation of Egypt. The Jules Ferry Government fell and Gambetta, the hero of the French resistance to Prussia in 1871 and one of the architects of the Third Republic, took office as Prime Minister and Foreign Minister. Seething with nervous energy, he at once determined that dynamic action in Egypt was necessary. The lazy patrician Granville disliked dynamic action of any kind but his very inertia prevented him from opposing Gambetta with resolution.

On 15 December Gambetta proposed that the two powers should take joint action to express their support for Tewfik and to show that they would not tolerate his deposition (although this was being proposed by no one at the time). On 24 December Gambetta expressed greater urgency in view of the fact that the Chamber of Notables was about to meet in Cairo, which would 'produce a considerable change in the political situation of Egypt'.

On 2 January Gambetta's draft arrived in the form of an Identic Note to be sent to the French and British Consuls-General in Egypt:

You have already been instructed on several occasions to inform the Khedive and his government of the determination of England and France to afford them support against the difficulties of various kinds which might interfere with the course of public affairs in Egypt. The two Powers are entirely agreed on this subject, and recent circumstances, especially the meeting of the Chamber of Notables convoked by the Khedive, have given them the opportunity for a further exchange of views. I have accordingly to instruct you to declare to the Khedive that the English and French Governments consider the maintenence of His Highness on the throne, on the terms laid down by the Sultan's Firmans, and officially recognized by the two Governments, as alone able to guarantee, for the present and future, the good order and development of prosperity in Egypt, in which France and Great Britain are equally interested. The two Governments being closely associated in the resolve to guard by their united efforts against all cause of complication, internal or external, which might menace the order of things established in Egypt, do not doubt that the assurance publicly given of their formal intentions in this respect will tend to avert the dangers to which the Government and Khedive might be exposed, and which would certainly find England and France united to oppose them. They are convinced that His Highness will draw from this assurance the confidence and strength which he requires to direct the destinies of Egypt and his people.

The Joint Note was delivered on 6 January. The British Government's only reservation was 'that they must not be considered as committing themselves thereby to any particular mode of action, if action should be found necessary'. Gambetta readily agreed to this apparently meaningless qualification.

This 'most mischievous document', as Blunt had called it, caused a sensation when it reached Cairo.* It produced precisely the opposite effect to that Granville wanted, although if Gambetta had been all along determined on an Anglo-French occupation of Egypt, as seems probable, it was at least consistent with his aims. Moreover it was sent soon after the Foreign Office had received despatches from Malet which affirmed both (*a*) that there was a genuine Egyptian national movement, and (*b*) that it should not be discouraged provided vital Anglo-French interests were preserved. Malet had gone so far as to say 'it would be inadvisable that the Khedive should be encouraged to hope that we should support him in maintaining an attitude of reserve toward the Chamber. It has been convoked with the full approval of Chérif Pasha who looks to it for success and support.'[8]

Admittedly, Malet tended to contradict himself from one day to another as to the danger of 'military dictatorship' presented by Arabi. At one point he was writing: 'It is questionable how long Chérif will be able or willing to remain at the head of the Government if Arabi Bey maintains the attitude of arbiter of the destinies of the country'. Yet Sherif himself was confident that he could handle both Arabi and the Chamber of Notables. One of the troubles was that when Arabi made a public speech about the need for reforms he sometimes added something about the excessive employment of Europeans in Egypt. Although Malet in his despatches had shown sympathy with Egyptian feelings in this matter, Arabi's remarks were always described as manifestations of anti-European and anti-Christian fanaticism. The cry was taken up by the Europeans in Egypt and various sections of the British press. In fact it was unusual to employ the word 'Mohammedan' without the adjective 'fanatical'.† Blunt said of Malet that 'though

* For once Cromer and Blunt are agreed although Cromer merely calls it 'a mistake'.

† As an example of the excitement of the civil population by the 'vernacular' press at this time, Cromer quotes one newspaper as saying: 'Some people pretend that fanaticism is ruinous to progress, yet our best

not unsympathetic towards the Nationalists, I found him very ill-informed as to their views and objects. He knew none of their leaders personally except Sherif Pasha, and depended in regard to the general drift of affairs on what Sherif and the Khedive thought fit to tell him. For what was passing in the street he had no one on whom he could rely except his Greek dragoman, Aranghi, who picked up his news at the cafés of the European quarter.'[9]

In his interview with Colvin on 1 November, Arabi concentrated his criticism on the Turco-Circassian domination of Egypt, saying 'the most ignorant Turk was preferred and honoured before the best of the Egyptians'. He disclaimed any desire to get rid of the Europeans, whether as employees or residents, because they were 'the necessary instructors of the people'. No doubt Arabi was capable of saying something different to Egyptians but his movement, as Colvin acknowledged, was primarily aimed at national independence. Arabi wanted Egyptians to control their own lives and any generalized xenophobia was as foreign to his nature as it is to most Egyptians. Blunt was impressed when Arabi remarked at their first meeting that he welcomed Blunt with especial cordiality on account of his family connection with Byron whom, though he knew nothing of his poetry, he held in high esteem for his work for liberty in Greece.[10] Later he wrote a long letter to Gladstone interpreting Arabi's views. 'The ideas he expresses are not merely a repetition of the phrases of modern Europe, but are based on a knowledge of history and on the liberal tradition of Arabian thought, inherited from the days when Mahommedanism was liberal.' On 3 January 1882 he succeeded in having published in *The Times* (whose editor, Cherney, was sympathetic to Egyptian nationalism despite the fact that he was a bond-holder) a 'Programme of the National Party', which Blunt had drafted with Sheikh Mohammed Abdu and which had been approved by Arabi and Mustafa Sami. This expressed the Nationalists' aims in moderate and reasonable terms: 'The general end of the National Party is the intellectual and moral regeneration of the country by a better observance of the law, increased education and by political

---

days were those in which we conquered the Universe by devotion to our faith.' (*Modern Egypt*, Vol. I, p. 211). Almost certainly 'fanaticism' here is a translation of the Arabic word 't'assub', which in this context would be better rendered by 'zealous faith' since the writer is unlikely to have been calling for something which in English has wholly evil implications.

liberty.' This was something that an English Liberal could hardly oppose.

On 4 January Gladstone wrote to Granville: 'I am not by any means pained, but I am much surprised at the rapid development of a national sentiment and party in Egypt. The very ideas of such a sentiment and the Egyptian people seemed quite incompatible . . . most of all is the case strange if the standing army is the nest that has reared it . . . [But] it seems to claim the respect due to it as a fact, and due also to the capabilities that may be latent in it for the future. "Egypt for the Egyptians" is the sentiment to which I would wish to give scope: and could it prevail it would I think be the best, the only good solution of the "Egyptian question".'[11]

In the light of these wise sentiments the Joint Note only seems more deplorable. One of the troubles was that in London the 'Egyptian crisis' was overshadowed by Irish affairs. The Cabinet could only give a small part of its attention to events in Cairo.

A few days before the arrival of the Joint Note, Arabi was appointed Under-Secretary of State for War 'as it was thought better that he should belong to the government than be outside it'. In *Modern Egypt* Cromer gives some examples of the collapse of military discipline in Egypt at this time. The troops at Suez showed sign of insubordination, due to a soldier having been murdered by an Italian, and the band of a regiment quartered at Cairo refused to obey an order to play at the theatre. The situation was grave but hardly enough to assume that 'there was no public force in Egypt on whom reliance could be placed to maintain order'.

Malet, in a despairing effort to cushion the effects of the Note, allowed Blunt to tell Arabi 'that the meaning of the Note as understood by the British Government was that the English Government would not permit any interference of the Sultan with Egypt, and would also not allow the Khedive to go back from his promises or molest the Parliament'. Arabi's reply was: 'Sir Edward Malet must really think us children who do not know the meaning of words. . . . In the first place it is the language of menace.' And he added: 'Let them come, every man and child in Egypt will fight them.'[12]

Malet cabled his doubts to Granville, who seems to have realized too late that he had misunderstood the Joint Note and miscalculated its effect. He suggested sending an 'explanatory telegram' to Malet but Gambetta bluntly refused, saying the Egyptian government 'had only to listen to the advice of the two Powers and be silent'.[13]

The immediate consequence of the Joint Note in Egypt was to stiffen the resolve of the Chamber of Notables. Its arrival coincided with the drafting of the Organic Law which was to define the power of the representative legislature in the Parliament the Khedive had promised. A difficulty had arisen over the budget. The Financial Controllers had insisted that they should continue to draft it as they had for the past two years and that the Chamber should have no power to vote even on the portion of the revenues which were not assigned to the Public Debt, Porte tribute and items arising out of the 1880 Law of Liquidation.

Sherif Pasha and Sultan Pasha, President of the Chamber of Notables, were prepared to make this concession, despite the fact that it meant abandoning the essential part of self-government. As Mohammed Abdu remarked: 'We have waited so many hundred years for our freedom, that we can well afford to wait some months.' A majority of the Notables opposed the concession but there was hope of reaching a compromise. All this was changed by the Joint Note.

The Chamber now unanimously demanded the right to vote on the unassigned revenues. Malet vainly proposed to Granville various forms of compromise, but Granville did not respond, partly because Gambetta was adamantly opposed to allowing the Chamber any authority over the budget at all, but also because Colvin had swung round to an attitude of uncompromising hostility towards the Chamber. On 31 January Colvin told Blunt that he had changed his mind about the Nationalists. 'He had thought them amenable to reason, but he found them quite impracticable, and he would do his best to ruin them if ever they came into office. . . . He said he had changed his mind about intervention too; that he believed it now to be necessary and inevitable, and that he would spare no pains to bring it about.'[14]

At the same time he was writing in his dispatches to England: 'The Egyptians being, in my opinion, incapable of conducting the administration of affairs, I think we are rapidly approaching a state of affairs which differs little, if at all, from anarchy.'[15]

At the end of January matters had come to a head over the Organic Law and the budget. Sherif was still willing to bow to the views of the European Controllers but the Notables were adamant.

On 2 February a deputation went to the Khedive to ask for a change of government. Tewfik reluctantly agreed and unenthusiastically appointed Mustafa Sami as President of the Council and Arabi Minister of War. As neither Sami, Arabi nor any of the fellah ministers knew any European language, Mustafa Pasha Fehmi, a Turk and a mild liberal, became Foreign Minister.

From this moment Sherif Pasha went over to total opposition to Arabi. He co-operated fully with Malet whom he now told that he favoured the dispatch to Egypt of a Turkish force. He opposed Anglo-French intervention as too dangerous for the European population. The situation was at the same time cause for both jubilation and alarm to the Nationalists. For the first time they had a government dominated by native Egyptians; but they had thrown down the gauntlet to Europe. The encouraging news had arrived on 31 January that Gambetta's 'grand Ministère' had fallen to be replaced by one led by the milder and less chauvinistic de Freycinet.

On 7 February the new Organic Law drafted by the Nationalists was promulgated by the hostile but helpless Khedive.

At the end of February, Blunt left for England 'where I could do more for the Egyptian interests than I could at Cairo, by word of mouth and by a personal appeal to Gladstone'. Just before leaving, he received an apparently reassuring letter from Gladstone in answer to his own explaining Arabi's views, which concluded: 'My own opinions about Egypt were set forth in the *Nineteenth Century* a short time before we took office, and I am not aware as yet of having seen any reason to change them.'

Later Blunt was to write with extreme bitterness of Gladstone's 'betrayal of the Egyptian cause'. With hindsight it is easy to see that Anglo-French 'imperial interests', as they were conceived in Whitehall and the Quai d'Orsay, were incompatible with the rise of a truly autonomous power in Egypt. Gladstone, who woefully misunderstood foreign affairs although he discussed them frequently, took longer to see this than most. When he did he satisfied his Liberal conscience by declaring, as he did to the House of Commons on 27 July 1882, 'It has been charitably believed, even in this country, that the military party was the popular party, and was struggling for the liberties of Egypt. There is not the smallest rag or shred of evidence to support that contention.' Even Cromer, who later had cause to regret Gladstone's intervention in foreign affairs, quoted this remarkable statement in order to deny it.[16]

In 1882 the view was commonplace in Europe that oriental 'subject races' were incapable of self-government. Gladstone's peculiar difficulty was that he had not held this view but had frequently attacked it. Even arch-imperialists on the Opposition benches and among the Gambettists in France accused Arabi of being a self-seeking military dictator when the real cause for their dislike was the fear that he would develop into a genuine national leader.*

During the spring of 1882 the Egyptian army dominated the nation, watched by a nervous and resentful Khedive. But the mass of the people gave the army their enthusiastic support. The fellahin believed that the reign of the moneylenders had come to an end together with the *kurbaj* and the *corvée*. Henceforth Egypt would be ruled by Egyptians. Because of the very real fear of Anglo-French or Turkish invasion the army was now looked on as an essential protection. Malet's dispatches, quoting at length the reports of his consular agents, painted an alarming picture of falling land values and repudiated agricultural debts. Yet the situation was still a long way from a Peasants' Revolt. The fellahin's demands were precisely those that Cromer, with some justice, claimed to have satisfied when he became ruler of Egypt.

The British Government, heavily preoccupied with Irish affairs, still hoped to avoid direct intervention. This was now also the view of the French Government, although the difference over the alternative of Turkish intervention remained. Sultan Abdulhamid remained unco-operative. He protested officially against the Joint Note and bided his time in the hope of re-establishing his authority in Egypt. He made Arabi a Pasha and continued to allow him and the Khedive to believe his sympathies lay with each of them.

In April the situation took a dramatic turn with the arrest of fifty Circassian officers, including Osman Rifky, the former unpopular War Minister, on a charge of conspiracy to murder Arabi. Whether the plot, as Malet believed, amounted to no more than

---

* Thus Gambetta's friend Joseph Reinach accused Gladstone and Granville of failing to see that the 'Chamber of Notables was a sham assembly, Arabi an ambitious intriguer, encouraged and suborned by the fanatic Council of Constantinople, and the national party a ludicrous invention of some badly informed or too well paid journalist.' (*Nineteenth Century*, December 1882).

'outspoken threats to murder him on the part of unpromoted Circassian officers' is impossible to say. Certainly the Circassians were furious as Arabi had recently promoted some 500 Egyptian officers. Arabi himself, with a lively memory of Ismail's reign, was convinced that there was a conspiracy. The court-martial dragged on for three weeks until on 2 May, 40 officers, including Rifky, were condemned to exile to the While Nile in the Sudan. The ex-Khedive, Ismail, was named as the original instigator of the plot.

It is difficult not to believe that Malet saw this as a heaven-sent opportunity for a showdown with the Nationalists. Malet advised Tewfik to refuse to countersign the sentences on the ground that the court-martial's proceedings were improper. The French Consul General also advised the less provocative course of confirming the sentences and then commuting them.

The Khedive followed Malet's advice and the breach between him and the Nationalists was complete. The Government convoked the Assembly – illegally, because under the new Constitution only the Khedive had this power – and an informal meeting of Notables at Sultan Pasha's house considered the possibility of deposing Tewfik if he continued to intrigue with the foreign consuls. But Sultan at once began to waver in his alliance with Arabi. For a time he attempted to reconcile the Khedive with the Government, and when this failed he defected entirely from the Nationalists. Although the great majority of Notables remained firm his action gravely weakened the movement.

On 11 May Granville suggested that the Porte should be asked to send a Turkish general 'with full power to restore discipline in the Egyptian army', accompanied by an English and French general and backed by the threat of Turkish intervention. But the French Government – and still more the French Chamber – were violently opposed to Turkish intervention. Against his own in-stincts, de Freycinet agreed to the dispatch of British and French naval squadrons to Alexandria.

On 15 May the Government of Mustafa Sami offered its resignation after failing to persuade the now stubborn Tewfik to change his mind on the court-martial sentences. The Khedive tried to persuade first Mustafa Fehmi then Sherif Pasha to form a new ministry, but both declined on the ground that they would be powerless as long as effective control of Egypt remained in the hands of the army. Malet betrayed his continued lack of comprehension of the nationalist movement by proposing that he should ask Arabi and the three other leading colonels to go into voluntary exile. Granville and de Freycinet agreed to make this a demand backed up by the threat of force (the combined squadron now being in Alexandria) and a second Joint Note to this effect was dispatched on 25 May. The reaction, as should have been expected, was a virtual uprising of the Egyptian people to demand that the Government and Arabi be reinstated. In Cairo Muslim, Christian and Jewish religious dignitaries combined to implore the Khedive to restore the Sami Government. Sultan Pasha, now frightened out of his wits, persuaded the Khedive to yield, and the ministry was reinstated.

The situation was now alarming. Instead of intimidating the National Party, the arrival of the Anglo-French squadron raised a great wave of patriotic feeling throughout Egypt. Relations between Christians and Muslims deteriorated as every European in Egypt came under the suspicion of wanting an Anglo-French occupation. The nationalist orator, Abdullah Nadim, made fiery denunciations of the new Joint Note to mass audiences.

Sultan Abdulhamid then decided to send a Commissioner to Egypt to reassert his rights and reach an arrangement with Tewfik. He chose Dervish Pasha, a tough and unscrupulous old aristocrat with experience in handling rebellious Ottoman minorities. But, with a supreme act of deviousness, he sent with him Sheikh Ahmed Essad, an Arabic-speaking Pan-Islamic nationalist, with orders to negotiate secretly with Arabi.

Dervish Pasha arrived in Alexandria on 7 June and made a show of asserting his authority, after accepting a bribe of £50,000 from Tewfik. The British liberal press of the time makes curious reading today. John Morley, biographer and uncritical disciple of Gladstone the anti-Turk, was writing in the *Pall Mall Gazette* (15 June):

There is something very impressive in the calm immovable dignity of Dervish Pasha, who is emphatically the man for the situation. After all the shiftings and twistings of diplomatists and the pitiful exhibition of weakness on the part of the leading actors in this Egyptian drama, it is an immense relief to find one 'still strong man' who, by the mere force of his personal presence, can make every one bow to his will. . . . Dervish is a man of iron, and Arabi may well quail before his eye. . . .

Egyptians are less warlike than Albanians and Lazis but even in Egypt the Gordian knot may have to be severed with the sword.

Even in the most pacific English liberals there is often a deep-seated admiration for ruthless power.

In fact when Morley was writing these words the situation was already out of Dervish's control. On 11 June there was a serious riot in Alexandria in which several hundred were killed or injured, including at least fifty Europeans. Charles Cookson, the British Consul, was badly wounded in the head and a petty officer of the British warship HMS *Superb* was killed.

The first reaction of Europeans and British officials on the spot was to conclude that the rioting was started by the military. This version spread through Europe and profoundly influenced the Radicals in the British Cabinet against Arabi. 'I found a clear opinion that it was impossible for us not to take active steps in intervention after this,' wrote Dilke in his diary.[17] Gladstone made a note: 'International atrocity. Wholesale massacre to over-rule the people of that country.'

In later years Dilke came to the conclusion that Arabi had not instigated the riots. Malet also changed his mind after his first impression and Cromer accepted his view in *Modern Egypt* although he felt that a 'considerable moral responsibility' rested on Arabi and his colleagues for having 'done their best to arouse the race hatred and fanaticism of the cowardly mob at Alexandria'. Wilfrid Blunt, on the other hand, believed that the real culprits were the Governor of Alexandria, Omar Pasha Lutfy and the Khedive, who had been urged by him not to allow Arabi to appear to be able to guarantee public order. Blunt produced enough evidence to convince Randolph Churchill who made this charge in Parliament a year later. The truth is unlikely to be known, but the probability is that the riots spread spontaneously after a brawl between a drunken Maltese and an Egyptian donkey-boy. Tension between the communities had been rising and the Europeans had armed themselves. There were many bedouin in Alexandria who were ready to join in the fighting. But in apportioning the moral responsibility no one has mentioned the British and French Governments, who ordered their warships to Alexandria. Malet had predicted long before that if this was done the European residents would be in danger.

Whatever the causes of the rioting its immediate consequence was that Arabi and the army took over responsibility for maintaining order. As Europeans evacuated Alexandria in thousands, the French, Austrian and German Consuls urged the Khedive to entrust Arabi with full powers to maintain public security. Arabi issued a proclamation calling upon the people to keep the peace and obey the law, and charged local commanders with responsibility for maintaining order.

In England the Cabinet was more united on Egypt than at any time before. The worsening Irish situation had some influence on the attitude of the British ministers. The Whigs in the Cabinet, who were led by Lord Hartington (later Duke of Devonshire) the Secretary of State for India, were in favour of coercion rather than conciliation of the Irish. The assassination of Hartington's brother, Lord Frederick Cavendish, in the Phoenix Park murders in May had hardened their attitude towards all nationalists. But Hartington's chief reason for supporting intervention was his belief that the rebellious Egyptians were endangering a vital imperial interest. The Whigs were now joined by the Radicals, Chamberlain and Dilke.

At the end of May de Freycinet had proposed a conference on Egypt of the Powers, including Turkey. The French Prime Minister had reluctantly agreed to the principle of Turkish intervention provided: 'Turkish forces were summoned by England and France, and operated there under English and French control'. Bismarck approved the idea of a conference as a very good expedient for covering the change of policy on the part of the French Government. Not surprisingly, Abdulhamid found the suggestion that his imperial troops should act under Anglo-French control difficult to swallow but he was overawed by British and French land and sea power. He therefore chose to sulk and the conference opened in Constantinople on 23 June with no Turkish representative present and in an atmosphere of bizarre unreality.

In his opening speech at the conference, Lord Dufferin, British Ambassador to the Porte, stated: 'It is no exaggeration to say that during the last few months absolute anarchy has reigned in Egypt.' This was an exaggeration of the first order, for there had been nothing approaching 'absolute anarchy' in Egypt. At the time Lord Dufferin was speaking, a compromise government had just been formed under the aged Ragheb Pasha with Arabi as

Minister of War. The Sultan had enjoined Arabi to co-operate with Ragheb and decorated him. The country was in a state of effervescence but not of chaos. The mass of the Egyptian people, including the great majority of *ulema* (Muslim divines) who, though they had lost some of their power, were still looked upon as representatives of public opinion, enthusiastically supported Arabi. From this time until the British occupation two months later the machinery of administration and justice worked smoothly and Treasury accounts were kept accurately and honestly.

Although the British Cabinet – with the exception of the aged radical Chancellor of the Duchy of Lancaster, John Bright – was now determined on intervention to overthrow Arabi, it still hoped it would be done by Turkey on behalf of Britain, France and the other Powers. Hartington was the first to envisage the possibility of singlehanded British action but he still regarded it as a last resort. The Constantinople Conference dragged on with Lord Dufferin urging the danger of conditions in Egypt. He began each session by reading alarming dispatches from Cairo describing the pathetic impotence of the Ministry of Comedy, as he called the Ragheb Cabinet, and the ever-increasing arrogance of the military faction. All the Powers were agreed that somehow Turkey should be encouraged to take action but prevented from taking it on its own initiative. Finally a draft was agreed on 6 July for an appeal to the Ottoman Government to send troops for a limited period of three months – 'the expenses of the occupation to be borne by Egypt'.

3

ULTIMATUM AND INVASION

Meanwhile the British Government was becoming increasingly suspicious that de Freycinet was secretly preparing to come to terms with Arabi and the Khedive together. These suspicions were increased when, on 24 June, de Freycinet refused a British proposal to arrange for Anglo-French protection of the Suez Canal on the ground that the Canal Company's view was that the only potential danger to the canal came from intervention.

In Alexandria tension was rising dangerously. On 3 June the British Admiralty had been informed that batteries were being raised at Alexandria 'with the intention of using them against the British fleet'. Richards, a Radical MP, was later to illustrate the situation to the House of Commons: 'I find a man prowling about my house with obviously felonious purposes. I hasten to get locks and bars, and to barricade my windows. He says that is an insult and threat to him, and he batters down my doors, and declares he does so only as an act of strict self-defence.' However, Lord Granville protested to the Porte who, by now thoroughly alarmed, replied that no new fortifications were being built or armed, that only some repairs were being carried out but that even these had been suspended on his orders. He added the hope that 'the commanders of the Anglo-French fleet will carefully avoid everything calculated to provoke the slightest conflict'.[1]

Work on the batteries was suspended for one month and then begun again on Arabi's orders. The British Admiral, Sir Beauchamp Seymour, now sent an ultimatum on 19 July demanding that unless the forts were surrendered to him for dismantling within twenty-four hours he would bombard them the next morning. Some mystery still surrounds this ultimatum. On 7 July Seymour had first given warning that the work had been resumed but the Khedive had promptly denied it to the Sultan. It seems that some repairs were being carried out on the forts overlooking the eastern harbour, while the British fleet was out of sight in the western harbour. The First Lord of the Admiralty, Lord Northbrook, who was a Whig supporter of Hartington, had earlier reported to Gladstone: 'If we want to bring on a fight we can instruct B. Seymour to require the guns to be dismantled. My advisers do not think they will do much harm where they are.'[2] Gladstone was therefore surprised and angered by the terms of the Admiral's ultimatum. Lord Northbrook must bear a large share of the responsibility for the bombardment of Alexandria.

The question remains as to how far Gladstone and Granville still believed at this stage that British intervention could be avoided. On hearing of the proposed ultimatum, the French Government had refused to be associated with it and ordered the French ships to sail to Port Said to protect the canal. As de Freycinet wrote later: 'without doubting the sincerity of his [Admiral Seymour] fears, I shall say that our own information was not so alarming and therefore in the circumstances a bombardment would have the appearance of an offensive rather than a defensive act.'[3] This response merely confirmed Granville's suspicions that the French were planning to come to terms with Arabi. 'The Sultan and Freycinet,' he wrote to Lord Dufferin on 7 July, 'are very much on a level as to the pleasure of dealing with them'. On the same day the Khedive had hinted strongly to Cartwright, the acting English Consul-General in Malet's absence,* that he was looking forward to an Anglo-French bombardment. On 9 July, Cartwright reported to Granville that Tewfik had asked him 'to urge on Her Majesty's government the necessity, from his point of view, of the earliest possible action, or at least of an intimation as to what may be expected'. It is highly improbable that Granville had already decided to act on the basis of this information when Sir Beauchamp sent his ultimatum the following day. On the other hand, the Admiral's high-handed action saved him from an awkward dilemma by precipitating a *dénouement* that the Khedive wanted.

The Khedive Tewfik, like his royal master the Sultan, was hedging his bets. No military expert, at this stage he was still

* Malet had been taken ill with a sudden and mysterious fever in Alexandria on 17 June and left on a British ship ten days later. Twenty-five years later, on reading Blunt's *Secret History of the English Occupation of Egypt*, which quoted a cable Blunt received from his agent in Egypt on 15 June imploring him to do his best to have Malet removed, Malet came to the conclusion he had been poisoned. He wrote a letter to *The Times* to this effect (12 October 1907).

uncertain which was the stronger – Alexandria's defences or the British fleet. When the Admiral's ultimatum was received on the morning of 10 July a Cabinet Council was held, presided over by the Khedive and with Dervish Pasha attending as well as Arabi as minister of war. After a long discussion it was decided that it would be 'altogether shameful and dishonourable to remove the guns'. According to Arabi: 'The Khedive now shewed apparently great energy and courage, and repeatedly said that should the war take place he would himself carry a rifle and be to the front with the troops.'[4]

The Council drafted a reply to the Admiral pointing out that the forts and their guns . . .

. . . Could not constitute a threat for the vessels which are in the western harbour . . . and the requirements of the Admiral are contrary to the laws of public international right. Nevertheless, in order to preserve the good relations which exist between the Khedive and the great British Empire, and to give a manifest proof of the good intentions of the Egyptian government towards it, the Council decides on dismounting three guns in the forts in which work may have been undertaken. . . . If he [the Admiral] refuses and persists in his intention to bombard the forts, these must not answer till after the fifth shot has been fired; they will then reply to the fire, and God, the best of judges, will decide between them and us.

This reply to the Admiral's ultimatum, which was sent in the name of the Khedive and with Dervish Pasha's approval, effectively answers the charge that Arabi was a rebel. Sir Beauchamp evidently considered it unsatisfactory. In Arabi's words:

Next morning at the appointed hour a shot was fired from the fleet, which was followed by fifteen others. Then we decided to reply, and so the war began.
The bombardment lasted without interruption for ten hours and a half, and until most of the forts were wholly or partially destroyed. A portion of the Ras el-Tin Palace (the official residence; Tewfik was safely at Ramleh) was demolished, besides several other houses in the town, and particularly those near the railway station, which lies in a line with Fort Demas, where my staff and I were.

The great majority of British residents, including Colvin, had boarded a P & O liner or a warship the previous day. The Egyptian troops then evacuated Alexandria, leaving the city in flames. The burning of the city was subsequently the most substantial charge against Arabi at his trial. When Blunt heard the news in England his first reaction was to believe that Arabi had ordered it as a legitimate military measure. 'This is the policy of the Russians at Moscow, and squares with all I know of their intentions.'[5] However, after hearing all the evidence of eyewitnesses he came to believe that some fires were started by Seymour's shells but that these were spread by looters, including many eager bedouin, who were joined by the army rearguard under the command of Soliman Pasha Sami. Sami was later hanged for his role in the destruction of Alexandria. Arabi vehemently denied the charge of having ordered the burning of the city which his accusers failed to substantiate, although, as Blunt noted, Arabi never called Sami to account for what his men had done.[6]

Another charge against Arabi – that he had made use of a white flag of truce to withdraw his troops – was easily dismissed by his defence, who were able to quote numerous authorities (including Sir Garnet Wolseley, Commander of the British expeditionary force, in his *Soldier's Pocket Book*) to show this to be accepted practice in warfare.

On the evening of 13 July a small force of British marines were landed to be followed the next day by a larger force, who took possession of the smouldering and debris-laden city. One of their first acts was to set up a summary court to deal with looters and incendiaries. Anyone caught in the act was charged and tried in a space of about twenty minutes and then taken away and hanged. Order was soon restored.

The Khedive Tewfik now had clear evidence of English military superiority and hastened to place himself under Admiral Seymour's protection. Dervish Pasha returned to Constantinople where he was promptly arrested. But while the Ottoman press denounced the invasion the Sultan havered.

As soon as Granville had news that the bombardment had started he informed Lord Dufferin at Constantinople:

Her Majesty's Government now see no alternative but a recourse to force to put an end to a state of affairs which has become intolerable. In their opinion it would be most convenient and most in accordance with the general principles of international law and usage that the force so employed should be that of the Sovereign Power (i.e. Turkey). If this method of procedure should prove impracticable, in consequence of the unwillingness on the part of the Sultan, it will become necessary to devise other means.

Abdulhamid finally understood that his fragile authority over Egypt was in danger of being destroyed, and on 19 July announced that he accepted the joint appeal of the powers for Turkish intervention (which asked Turkey to send troops for a limited period of three months).

But the situation in Egypt was not developing as the British Cabinet had hoped. Granville had thought gunboats would be enough to destroy Arabi and restore the Khedive's authority. But as soon as he had withdrawn his troops behind Alexandria, Arabi issued a proclamation stating that 'irreconcilable war existed between the Egyptians and the English'. The country rallied to his support and money and supplies for his troops poured into his camp. It is true that the Khedive was finally induced to declare Arabi a rebel on 24 July, but he did so in a curious proclamation which appeared to condemn him not for disobeying orders but for failing to resist the English more effectively at Alexandria.

It was not until 27 August that a new ministry could be formed under Sherif Pasha with Riaz as minister of the interior. But in Cairo a rival government in the form of a General Council of civil and religious leaders was established, while Arabi declared the Khedive to have defected to the enemy.

Clearly it was of the greatest importance for the British Government to have the Porte declare Arabi a rebel. But true to his own style of diplomacy Abdulhamid still prevaricated; he had not abandoned all hope of appearing to the Egyptians as their protection against the infidel. The other European Powers were not unsympathetic towards the bombardment of Alexandria but they were quite unwilling to give Britain an explicit mandate. France was unwilling to co-operate with Britain except in defence of the Suez Canal and French opinion was turning increasingly hostile to intervention of any kind.

At the end of July, Granville made a formal invitation to Italy to join Britain in an invasion force, which was politely declined. Throughout August Lord Dufferin conducted tortuous, frequently hilarious and ultimately futile negotiations with the Porte on the terms for the despatch of 5,000 Ottoman troops. But still no anathema was declared against Arabi.

The British Government was still far from united on Egyptian policy. Only John Bright resigned with a letter to Gladstone: 'I think on reviewing the doctrines connected with our foreign policy which I have preached and defended during forty years of my public life, you will not be surprised at the decision I am now compelled to take. . . .' All the rest of the Cabinet were now agreed on the need for action of some kind but, whereas Gladstone and Harcourt, the home secretary, wanted only a very limited move to protect the Suez Canal with France, Hartington was now joined by Chamberlain and Dilke in seeking a full-scale invasion to put down Arabi, and one by one other members of the government went over to the forward party. Granville, who had always disliked the idea of an Anglo-French occupation of Egypt, became more enthusiastic as the chances of French co-operation receded.* The last recruit to the forward party was Gladstone himself. Public opinion and the press were in jingo mood. The fears of the Radicals, Chamberlain and Dilke, that liberal opinion might be provoked if Britain appeared to be fighting a bond-holders' war were unjustified. But a British invasion of Egypt to restore the Khedive's authority was contrary to everything Gladstone had stood for – and especially his platform at the 1880 election. In the last analysis he could not ignore the vital imperial interest of the Suez Canal but he needed more than this to justify what he had so recently defined as 'Aggression on Egypt and Freedom in the East'. Thus in his speech to the House of Commons on 22 July asking for £2,300,000 to finance an expeditionary force, he declared: 'The insecurity of the canal is a symptom only and the seat of the disease is in the interior of Egypt, in its disturbed and its anarchical condition.' Arabi and his followers were anti-Christian militarists who cared nothing for the liberties of the Egyptian people. 'We feel that we should not fully discharge our duty if we did not endeavour to convert the present state of Egypt from anarchy and conflict to peace and order.' Thus the invasion was a crusade as well as an act of *realpolitik*.

The voting was 275 to 19 in favour. Fifteen thousand men were ordered to Malta and Cyprus and a further five thousand from India. Sir Garnet Wolseley, Adjutant General of the British Army, was placed in command.

* The French Chamber finally refused to sanction even the dispatch of troops to protect the canal and de Freycinet's government fell on this issue on 31 July.

In Egypt the situation was far from total anarchy. Immediately after the bombardment of Alexandria there were serious incidents at three Delta towns – Tanta, Damanhur and Mehella – in which about one hundred Christians (mainly Syrians and Greeks) were killed. Those responsible were enraged refugees from Alexandria encouraged by agents of the Khedive. The disturbances were promptly suppressed by the Arabists and there was no recurrence for the remaining two months of Egyptian independence. Those Europeans who had remained in Cairo were unmolested, while those who wished to leave were escorted to Alexandria.

Arabi had withdrawn his army to strong lines at Kafr Dewar about fifteen miles south-east of Alexandria. Morale was improved when an attempted advance by General Alison, with several thousand British troops, was repulsed. But Arabi remained here for the next five weeks, holding court in a huge viceregal tent and discussing religion with his favourite *ulema*. This was what Blunt called his 'all too supine conduct of the war'. Arabi was not immune to flattery, especially from ladies of the princely houses, and he knew that his name had spread throughout the Muslim world. He seems to have believed that his strong position in Egypt, combined with Gladstone's oft-expressed liberal sympathies, would cause England to come to terms.

On one vital matter, Arabi showed himself too honourable for an effective military leader. In April, Blunt had written to warn him that an invasion would come via the Suez Canal, but by August nothing more had been done than to trace a defensive line at Tel el-Kebir between Zagazig and Ismailia (which lies in the middle of the Suez Canal). When Wolseley landed at Alexandria on 16 August with the advance troops of the expeditionary force, the Egyptians finally woke up to the danger of their exposed flank opposite the canal. An Eastern army, under one of Arabi's more energetic colonels, Ali Fehmi, hastily began to dig trenches at Tel el-Kebir. But it was also strategically essential to block the canal at the northern end to prevent an invading force from reaching Ismailia. The Egyptians had made preparations to block the canal in four places and Arabi's council now urged him to do this. But Arabi hesitated because he had received assurances from Ferdinand de Lesseps that the neutrality of the canal would be respected. The elderly genius of the canal had an exaggerated belief in his power to influence European governments. Leaving

his son Charles to argue with the British Directors of the Suez
Canal Company in Paris, de Lesseps arrived in the Canal Zone at
the end of July and bombarded Arabi with appeals for Egypt to
respect the canal's neutrality. But British warships were already
in the southern end of the canal. On 20 August British troops
landed at Port Said and the canal was closed at both ends. It remained closed for three days. The justification for this action by
the British Government and the British Suez Canal Company
Directors was that the Company was Egyptian and the Canal
Zone was being occupied on the Khedive's behalf.

Arabi had kept his word but his flank was now turned. Wolseley
sailed up the canal to disembark at Ismailia on 21 August. The
result of the war was no longer in doubt; against a British force of
30,000 Arabi had barely 10,000 trained men and a rabble of hastily
recruited fellahin. Moreover, his camp was torn by dissension.
Already some of the civilian leaders, such as Sultan, had gone over
to the Khedive.* Now some of his senior officers went also. Two
were wounded in a skirmish and Mahmoud Fehmi, the engineer,
his ablest lieutenant, was captured by a British patrol. Nevertheless, Arabi's forces gave a fairly good account of themselves at
Kassassin on 28 August, where they nearly succeeded in capturing
the Duke of Connaught.

But the end was now near. At dawn on the morning of 13
September the British force crossed the Egyptian lines and fell
upon Arabi's forces from two sides. The Egyptian army was
asleep in the delusion that bedouin scouts would warn them if the
British approached. The battle lasted barely forty minutes. Many
of the Egyptian recruits threw away their arms or surrendered
but some in the trenches fought back with hopeless courage and
they left some 10,000 dead. The British lost 57 dead and 22 missing.
In his official report on the battle Sir Garnet Wolseley wrote: 'I
do not believe that at any previous period of our military history
has the British Infantry distinguished itself more than upon this
occasion.'[7]

---

* The Khedive's gold (some of which turned out to be false coin)
played a big part in this. But Britain was not above using the same
methods. Lord Northbrook recruited Edward Palmer, an impecunious
Professor of Arabic, to gain the support of the Sinai bedouin with bribes.
After an initial success, he was robbed and shot by men of the Haiwat
tribe just east of Suez.

Arabi was at his headquarters one mile behind the lines. Awakened by firing he first attempted to reach the battle but was swept away by the tide of retreating Egyptians. He took a train to Cairo to prepare for the defence of the capital but on arrival he found that the Grand Council had already decided to make submission to the Khedive. The matter was decided the next morning when Drury Lowe arrived with his Indian cavalry. Arabi submitted his sword as a prisoner-of-war to the English general.

4

LORD DUFFERIN'S
MISSION

Not for the first time in the two thousand years since Egypt lost
its independence, the mass of the people now declared their
support for their new conquerors and the Khedive who had made
himself their client. Wolseley held a full-scale military review in
Cairo at which English decorations were conferred on the Khedive
and his ministers. The immediate problem was what to do with
Arabi and his associates. The Khedive, Sherif and Riaz were in
favour of hanging them at once as rebels, without trial. There were
very few prominent Egyptians now in the Khedive's camp who
would not find the inevitable revelations of a trial embarrassing.
However, while some of the British press and residents, with the
vociferous support of most other European communities in Egypt,
were baying for Arabi's blood there was a discernible reaction
after Tel el-Kebir among some of the British public. That part of
liberal opinion which had not been won over by the glamour of a
successful imperial adventure felt little pride in military victory
over a fellahin army. If Arabi was to be summarily executed the
reaction would be much stronger. So it was that when Wilfrid
Blunt started a move in England to allow Arabi a fair trial with
European counsel he was backed by *The Times* and Gladstone
and Granville were forced to agree. Blunt opened a fund, to which
both Gordon and Randolph Churchill subscribed, although he
ultimately bore most of the cost himself. Blunt retained A. M.
Broadley, an able QC, who had distinguished himself in Tunisia
where he had acted for the Bey at the time of the French
occupation.

Broadley arrived in Egypt on 18 October and at once set about
preparing the case of Arabi, Mohammed Abdu and others with
his assistant, Mark Napier. He encountered many obstacles which
he met with imperturbable humour. Tewfik and his ministers were
understandably angry and resentful that the British Government
was insisting on a proper trial and had even sent Sir Charles

Wilson as its official observer. Abdu in particular had been shattered by his imprisonment and ill-treatment at the hands of the Khedive's eunuchs, but once Broadley had gained the prisoners' confidence their spirits rallied. Arabi impressed everyone who saw him with the dignity of his bearing. As Blunt shrewdly remarked: 'Whatever may have been his lack of physical courage, he had moral courage to a high degree.' It became increasingly urgent for the British Government to find a solution. As the preliminary interrogation proceeded it became abundantly clear that Arabi could not be convicted on any charge except the highly debatable one of rebellion. His private papers gave proof of the Sultan's approval of his actions, while it was the Khedive who had gone over to the enemy after ordering resistance at Alexandria and was therefore more liable to the charge of treason.

Lord Granville's solution to the dilemma was to send Lord Dufferin from Constantinople on a special mission to Cairo. Broadley soon established a rapport with this urbane and highly civilized Irish aristocrat, a former Governor-General of Canada and future Viceroy of India. A solution was worked out by which Arabi and six of his associates would plead guilty of rebellion and receive the death sentence. This would at once be commuted to exile in Ceylon. Arabi at first demurred, saying that he wanted to vindicate himself in court, but Broadley pointed out that he had already thrown himself on England's mercy 'and as England had just spent some millions of money in putting down what she was pleased to call his rebellion, it was improbable her ministers would support any solution which would involve a complete stultifying of their own acts'.[1]

Arabi's trial took place on 3 December, and he left three weeks later, penniless – he had been stripped of his modest possessions – but with luggage provided by female sympathizers of the Khedivial house.

Arabi spent eighteen years in Ceylon in exile where he was visited by tourists and travellers to Australia as one of the curiosities of the island. From time to time Wilfrid Blunt and other sympathizers raised the possibility of his being allowed to return to form a National Party in Egypt. But nothing happened, and it was not until May 1901 that he was pardoned. His return caused little stir; he was white-bearded and broken in spirit though still in good health. He angered the new generation of Nationalists by telling the press that everything the English had done in Egypt was good. Mohammed Abdu, who had been allowed to return in 1888, at first refused to meet him but was reconciled at a meeting arranged by Blunt.

Arabi eventually died of cancer in 1911. *The Times* said of him: 'Probably few characters in themselves so insignificant have ever so largely influenced the history of our times.' Is this common judgement fair to Arabi? There can be no doubt of the significance of his unsuccessful movement. For the first time a subject oriental people had attempted to throw off the domination of a privileged minority and to establish its own form of constitutional represent-ative government in defiance of the European Powers. As Gordon wrote to Blunt from Capetown on 3 August 1882: 'As for Arabi, whatever may become of him, he will live for centuries in the people; they will never be "your obedient servants" again.'[2] During Arabi's brief spell of power and after his failure, many attempts were made to cast doubt on the scope and aims of his movement. It was said that he had merely frightened the Egyptians into following him. But, as Mackenzie Wallace, who accompanied Lord Dufferin to Cairo as *The Times* special correspondent and in 1883 published the most shrewd and thoughtful contemporary book on the subject, *Egypt and the Egyptian Question*, wrote:

Never since the days of Mahomet Ali – or perhaps from a much earlier date – was there a man in Egypt who had such a firm hold of the country as Arabi, for he had not only the army and police at his disposal, and consequently was in a position to terrorize to any extent he chose, but he also enjoyed, as I have shown, the sympathies of nearly every section of the population. The common theory, for which I suspect some of our diplomatic agents are responsible, that he was merely a military adventurer without any kind of popular support, and that the solution of the Egyptian question consisted simply in having him and a few of his accomplices shot or hanged, is now found to be utterly untenable.[3]

The capacity of Arabi's movement to carry out reforms was more questionable. His critics claim that his slogan 'Egypt for the Egyptians' was a fanatical Moslem appeal to massacre Christians, was slanderous. So also was their charge that he was a dangerous radical because he urged the fellahin to repudiate their debts. As Broadley points out, 'No kind of proof of any such proceeding was ever attempted at the trial. If it was true nothing could have been more easily substantiated.'⁴ In the brief memorandum on Egyptian reform which Arabi drafted in prison a week before his trial he merely proposes that 'The unnecessary European employees to be dismissed, and only such of them to be kept as may be really useful and necessary; their salaries to be fixed in accordance with the resources of the country, and a proportion to be observed between their salaries and those allowed to natives, in order to avoid jealousy and discontent by undue partiality.' This seems reasonable enough. His eleventh point was that 'Special attention ought to be paid to the question of usury, and the means of preventing usurers from employing the most unfair means to despoil the nation;' which was precisely what Sir Evelyn Baring did when he succeeded Arabi as ruler of Egypt.

We have seen how Arabi and his colleagues succeeded in maintaining the machinery of government while they were in control. What is doubtful is whether they could have carried through their reforms even if they had been left alone. A successful republican revolt of young colonels was hardly conceivable at that time; seventy years later it still seemed improbable. They needed the co-operation of Tewfik in establishing Egyptian representative institutions but the Khedive, nostalgically recalling his father's autocracy, had no desire to lend his support for reform. When he appeared to co-operate it was out of simple fear; already he was seeking a chance to doublecross the reformers.

Arabi had neither political experience nor instinctive genius; he therefore depended on the help of Egyptian liberal reformers. This was perhaps his greatest weakness, and ultimately his undoing. For although circumstances drew them together their aims were only apparently identical – to establish constitutional representative government. Cromer somewhat contemptuously refers to Wilfrid Blunt's 'inopportune and mischievous' advice to the Chamber of Notables at the height of the crisis, contained in his telegram: 'If you allow yourselves to be separated from the army, Europe will annex you.' According to Cromer, 'Whatever danger of "annexation to Europe" existed lay rather in the direction of the consolidation of the national and military parties than in their separation. A trained politician would have seen this.'⁵ Here Cromer is disingenuous. As he was well aware, it was the threat of annexation contained in the first Joint Note which first brought the civilian and military nationalists together. He is correct only in the sense that the fear that they might stay together and so create a genuine autonomous power in Egypt, caused Europe to intervene. Blunt, even without political training, was right in seeing that a united national movement would have made intervention much more difficult. But even the liberals in the Chamber of Notables were salon reformers, whose liberalism sat very lightly on their shoulders. Many of them, like Sherif Pasha and Mustafa Pasha Fehmi, were men of Turco-Circassian stock who despised the natives and ultimately could not favour Arabi's 'Egypt for the Egyptians'. Others, like Sultan Pasha, though genuine Egyptians, were millionaire landlords whose interests would suffer from any pro-fellah movement.

This is not to say that at one time all of these were not swept along with a wave of enthusiasm for Arabi. It was not only soldiers, peasants and Egyptian *ulema* who echoed the street-boys' cry of *'Allah yansurak ya Arabi'* (God give you victory Oh Arabi). In the summer of 1882, princes and aristocrats bombarded him with presents and telegrams addressed to 'Defender of the country'. Upper-class ladies of Cairo formed an association to make bandages for the wounded. At the time their feelings were genuine, but Arabi's simple character was deceived into thinking his position much stronger than it was. He was neither the first nor the last national leader to believe that, with God and the people on his side, everything would be well.

If Arabi's capabilities of ruling and reforming Egypt may be disputed, there can be no doubt that the British occupation destroyed Egypt's power to govern itself. It liquidated the National Party and restored the Khedive to his throne but in doing so it permanently shattered his authority. Tewfik was no more than a puppet; he was not even permitted to shoot Arabi, and the wave of Turco-Circassian revenge against Arabi's supporters was swiftly halted. Thus the only two internal forces capable of Governing Egypt – the Nationalists and the Khedive – had been emasculated.

None of this was immediately apparent to the British Government or public. On the day of the Battle of Tel el-Kebir, Lord Granville had telegraphed to Lord Dufferin that he presumed 'that the emergency having passed, His Majesty the Sultan would not now consider it necessary to send troops to Egypt'. Within a few more days the Anglo-French Dual Control was formally abolished, as it had already been in fact when de Freycinet ordered the French fleet to leave Alexandria and the Chamber refused even to sanction an expeditionary force to the canal. For twenty years until the Entente Cordiale of 1904, French policy in Egypt remained impotently and resentfully anti-British. British influence in Egypt was now supreme and, although this was not de Freycinet's view, Turkey and France could be forgiven for believing that perfidious Albion had been secretly bent on the occupation of the Lower Nile since the beginning of the crisis in the 1870s. But this widely held impression (which incidentally was not shared by de Freycinet) was not correct; the great majority of the British Cabinet believed that, having ousted Arabi and restored the Khedive, law and order, British troops could soon be withdrawn. A month before Tel el-Kebir, 10 August, Gladstone had replied to a question in the House of Commons: 'I can go so far as to answer the honourable gentleman when he asks me whether we contemplate an indefinite occupation of Egypt. Undoubtedly, of all things in the world, that is a thing which we are not going to do.' Barely a week after Tel el-Kebir the main occupation force was ordered to withdraw, leaving behind a small garrison until a loyal army for Tewfik had been trained. (The Khedive, in a laconic decree, had already declared the Egyptian army disbanded.)

The Cabinet was, however, divided as to how far the Egyptians could now be trusted to behave themselves. The Radicals, Dilke and Chamberlain, favoured the restoration of a Chamber of Representatives with real powers over the budget, believing that the Egyptians' gratitude to England for their liberation from foreign financial control would be enough to ensure continued British influence. Hartington and the Whigs, sharing Colvin's conviction of orientals' incapability for self-government, wanted a strong Khedive with an English Financial Controller. Gladstone and Granville stood somewhere between these two views. The main purpose of Lord Dufferin's mission was to find a compromise solution to these conflicting views.

During the winter of 1882–3 Dufferin prepared his report which he presented to the Cabinet on 6 February. Elegant and persuasive in style, the report covers every aspect of Egyptian government and society. But its apparent clarity and incisiveness only helped to conceal the conflict of irreconcilable principles on which it was based.

The report repeatedly stated the principle of Egyptian independence:

The Valley of the Nile could not be administered from London. An attempt upon our part to engage in such an undertaking would at once render us objects of hatred and suspicion to its inhabitants. Cairo would become a focus of foreign intrigue and conspiracy against us, and we should soon find ourselves forced either to abandon our pretensions under discreditable conditions or embark upon the experiment of a complete acquisition of the country. If, however, we content ourselves with a more moderate role and make the Egyptians comprehend that instead of desiring to impose upon them an indirect but arbitrary rule we are sincerely desirous of enabling them to govern themselves, under the uncompromising aegis of our friendship (*sic*), they will not fail to understand that while on the one hand we are the European nation most vitally interested in their peace and well-being, on the other we are the least inclined to allow the influence which the progress of events has required us to exercise to degenerate into an irritating and exasperating display of authority which would be fatal to those instincts of patriotism and freedom which it has been our boast to foster in every country where we have set our foot.

Direct and indirect British rule were specifically discarded.

Had I been commissioned to place affairs in Egypt on the footing of an Indian subject state the outlook would have been different. The masterful hand of a Resident would quickly beat everything to his will, and in the space of five years we should have greatly added to the national wealth and well-being of the country by the extension of its cultivated area and the consequent expansion of its revenue; by the partial if not the total abolition of the *corvée* and slavery; the establishment of justice and other beneficent reforms. But the Egyptians would have justly considered these advantages as dearly purchased at the expense of their domestic independence. Moreover H M S Government have pronounced against such an alternative.

Nevertheless, the reforms of law and administration were to be on the Indian model and supervised by British officials. Egyptian independence was to be maintained through two representative bodies – a Legislative Council with thirty members, of whom fourteen were to be nominated and the rest elected by Provincial Councils, and a General Assembly consisting of eighty-two members, of whom forty-six were to be elected on a restricted franchise by the population while the rest would be the ministers and members of the Legislative Council.

Lord Dufferin declared bravely: 'The very fact of our having endowed the country with representative institutions is a proof of our disinterestedness.' Unfortunately these representative institutions were still-born; they had no power to initiate legislation or to control ministers. They could only advise and their advice could be rejected. Consequently they aroused no interest or enthusiasm among the Egyptian people. Labouchere described them in the House of Commons as 'a perfect sham of constitutional Government'.

In theory this system could have been used to favour the Whig alternative – a strong Khedive running the country through loyal ministers. But Tewfik could never be strong and although some of his ministers, such as Riaz Pasha, exhibited the power of independent action from time to time the ultimate sanction was in the hands of the British Consul and the English advisers in the government departments. There was no written undertaking by the Khedive and his ministers that they would obey the English representatives in Egypt, but their obedience was expected all the same. 'The masterful hand of a Resident' was there even if it was rarely seen pulling the strings.

This system, which came to be known (in Milner's phrase) as the Veiled Protectorate, was unique to imperial-colonial relations. It survived even after Egypt gained a quasi-independence in 1922, only the Veils were thicker. On the whole it worked well at the purely administrative level; Egypt was much better governed than any other part of the Ottoman Empire. But it is at least arguable that it was responsible for the peculiarly bitter feelings between England and Egyptian nationalism which can be compared only to the tragedy of Anglo-Irish relations. Egyptian patriots who sought their country's freedom found themselves struggling against an enemy who disappeared behind a smokescreen of verbiage. From Gladstone onwards British statesmen constantly asserted that the British occupation, which would shortly be withdrawn, was chiefly intended to strengthen Egypt's independence. Annexation was out of the question because England had 'pledged her honour' against it. Increasingly exasperated, Egyptians felt that open annexation might have been preferable because it would at least have shown where true responsibility for their Government's policies lay. As it was, they were battering against a rubber wall.

BARING IN COMMAND

The Veiled Protectorate originated to reconcile the continuance of British paramountcy in Egypt with the need to avoid provoking a war with the other Powers, especially France. But its evolution depended upon one man – Evelyn Baring. Without him it could hardly have survived; his successors never attempted to alter it radically but only to adjust it, mostly without success, to changing circumstances. It was with more than an inkling of Baring's qualities that Lord Granville decided in the summer of 1883 that he should replace the unpopular and inadequate Malet as British Agent and Consul-General in Egypt.

Baring was by now well qualified for the task. Earlier in his varied career his rapid promotion had often been attributed to his influential family connections. But in 1883 he had already served twice in Egypt, first as the English Commissioner of the Debt in 1877-9 and then briefly as Financial Controller. He had now just completed three highly successful years as Financial Member of the Council for India in Lord Ripon's Viceroyalty when the first tentative steps towards Indian self-government had been taken.

In 1883 he was just 42 years old. He had been born into the famous banking family of German extraction who, by the end of the nineteenth century, had founded four separate peerages.* His father, Henry Baring MP, was a successful banker but an unsuccessful gambler. His mother, Admiral Windham's daughter, was a strong-minded self-educated blue stocking who once astonished Sir William Harcourt by quoting Lucan at a dinner party to disprove his assertion that there is no mention of Druids in Latin literature.[1]

As the ninth son of the extravagant Henry, Evelyn had no easy start in life. From a Dickensian preparatory school in Norfolk he went to Woolwich whence he passed out, at the age of seventeen,

* Northbrook, Ashburton, Revelstoke and Cromer.

as a subaltern in the Royal Artillery. He served first in Corfu where he met and fell in love with his future wife Ethel, the daughter of a fashionable Catholic baronet, Sir Rowland Errington. His total income at that time was £400 a year and he had to wait fourteen years before he felt he could afford marriage. But his ambition had been fired. Already he had begun a vigorous course of self-education to make up for the philistine years at Woolwich. He became a considerable classical scholar, but also acquired modern Greek, Italian and French.

He served briefly in Malta, and accompanied the Governor, Sir Henry Storks, to Jamaica for the Commission of Enquiry into General Eyre's savage suppression of an uprising. On his return he entered the Military Staff College for two years and after passing out at the head of the list, entered the Topographical and Statistical Department at the War Office, the ancestor of the Intelligence Branch. In 1873 the Viceroy of India, Lord Mayo, was assassinated and on succeeding him Lord Northbrook invited his young cousin, Evelyn Baring, to accompany him as his private secretary.

His first three years in India profoundly influenced his life, for he gained his first experience in what he was later to call 'the government of subject races'. In economic matters he remained a Free Trader and Manchester school liberal but he was already showing signs of the authoritarianism which increased with age. In his view, it would have been ridiculous to apply John Stuart Mill's libertarian principles to uncivilized orientals. But his sympathies lay with the lower stratum of peasants who suffered most from harsh and corrupt rulers.

In India he worked intensely hard, from 6 a.m. to 8 p.m. every day, with only two hours off for exercise. Although still only in his middle thirties he acquired a position of considerable power and the unofficial title of 'Vice-Viceroy'. He also saved money which enabled him finally to marry Ethel Errington in June 1876.

He returned briefly to the Topographical Department but in 1877 he was recommended by Goschen for the position of British Commissioner of the Debt in Egypt on the advice of Sir Louis Mallet, Under-Secretary of State at the India Office, who had been impressed by his abilities when on a visit to India. In August 1878 he was promoted to Major but one year later retired from the army. In 1880 he resigned as Financial Controller General in

Egypt to accept the post of Financial Member of the Council of India in succession to Sir John Strachey and under Lord Ripon, who had just been appointed Viceroy by the new Gladstone government. His highly successful three-year term, during which he converted a £6,000,000 deficit into a £657,000 surplus, earned him the KCSI. Shortly after his return to England he accepted the post of Consul-General in Cairo (despite the doubts that Lord Dufferin expressed to Malet that 'he would be willing to come at the low salary').

In 1883 Baring was patently both able and experienced. Where there were doubts they concerned the aspect of his personality which had earned him the nickname 'over-Baring' in addition to the 'Vice-Viceroy'. Already at 43 he was formidable and with age this characteristic increased. Already at Malet's farewell dinner in Cairo in September 1883 an epigram, attributed to Lady Strangford was in circulation:

> The Virtues of Patience are known,
>   But I fear, when it comes to the touch,
> In Egypt they'll find, with a groan
>   There's an evil in Baring too much.

Even Kitchener quailed as he approached his door, so the effect on a junior clerk can be imagined. Yet he attracted love and devotion from many of his colleagues as well as respect, as is abundantly clear from their memoirs. The truth is that Cromer was a much more complex and interesting character than might be imagined from his bust in the Victorian imperial pantheon or his unflattering portrait in the Egyptian nationalist gallery. He had humour and wit which enlivened his genuine, if somewhat pedagogic, classical learning. He was certainly not a bore. He entertained well and often at the Residency where social intercourse was lively; he avoided depressing the conversation with his dominant personality.

An anonymous friend quoted in H. D. Traill's *Lord Cromer* observed:

His attitude towards his men is not unlike that of Dr Arnold, of Rugby, when he said that he *must* have confidence in the Sixth. Lord Cromer's resemblance to the great headmaster is specially shown in his relations with the junior members of his staff. The Agency at Cairo is an excellent diplomatic school. The Chief treats his subordinates with perfect frankness, and the result is that he is served with unswerving devotion. He requires thoroughness and hard work. His conversation – rich in quotations, historical references, and shrewd criticisms of men and things – is full of instruction and stimulating suggestion. Dull indeed must that Secretary be who does not learn something from the daily talk Lord Cromer pours out over the luncheon table.[2]

He resembled Dr Arnold in other ways.

His knowledge of the English poets is remarkable. Dryden's masculine verse attracts him, but his voluminous note-books contain extracts from writers of every century. He loves a good novel, and enjoys healthy stories, like those of the new romantic school of novelists; but he never fails to express his loathing of the nauseous fiction of the day, and has been known to put chance-found volumes of it into the first fire he could find alight.[3]

In conducting his affairs he was normally courteous even when he was at his most commanding. His old enemy, Wilfrid Blunt, wrote after meeting him in 1890 on his return to Egypt: 'In business matters I found Sir Evelyn a pleasant man to deal with. He was quick to understand a case, and straightforward in his replies, willing always to listen to arguments, however opposed to his opinions, and with nothing of the conventional insincerities of diplomacy. . . . People say that he is stiff and ill-mannered. I did not find him so. On the contrary he was courteous and kindly.'*

But Blunt was a self-assured and independent aristocrat who had no reason to be scared of Cromer. Others were not so fortunate; some found his masterfulness indistinguishable from bullying. One of these was the outstanding irrigation engineer Sir William Willcocks, who had several brushes with Cromer during his service in Egypt: 'I used to imagine that Lord Cromer was never so happy ordering officials to march to the right or the left as he was when ordering them to think to the right or the left.'[4] When Cromer discovered that Willcocks was writing 'a kind of comic history of Egypt under the English' which he regarded as subversive, he blatantly threatened to have him dismissed from Egypt unless he signed a pledge not to write anything more, in

---

* *My Diaries* I, pp. 30–31. Perhaps one of the things that endeared him to his staff was that he often reserved his brusqueness for those in the highest positions. When the Prince of Wales (Edward VII) asked for a third helping of prawn curry at one of the excellent Residency luncheons, Cromer remarked: 'You had much better not. It is rich enough as it is, and you have already had two ample helpings.'

the knowledge that with four children to support Willcocks could hardly refuse. However, even Willcocks agreed that 'though he was a brute, he was a just brute'.

Cromer was unaware of the alarming impression he made on many people. He often complained of Kitchener's brutal manner, and when someone suggested that the Sirdar would like to succeed him, Cromer said 'I do not think that that would do at all. K. has not got enough of the *suaviter in modo* which is so necessary in dealing with Egyptians.'[5] To a supreme degree he possessed the Victorian quality of 'character' but his mind was neither sensitive nor subtle, and 'though it had a humanistic side, was disposed to pass by the things of the soul'.[6]

Lytton Strachey wrote: 'His life's work had in it an element of paradox. It was passed entirely in the East; and the East meant very little to him; he took no interest in it. It was something to be looked after. It was also a convenient field for the talents of Sir Evelyn Baring.'[7] Rennell Rodd, who was Cromer's second-in-command from 1894 to 1902, indignantly rejects the charge of small-minded ambition but adds: 'I readily admit that the Oriental mind did not appeal to him, and that in so far as he understood it he regarded it as an obstacle to be overcome rather than a factor to be studied with sympathetic attention.'[8]

This is abundantly clear from the five chapters in Cromer's *Modern Egypt* on the 'Dwellers in Egypt', which understandably distress and anger present-day Muslims and Egyptians. He saw nothing worth preserving in their traditions or morality. He condescendingly admitted that 'a primitive society benefits greatly by the adoption of the faith of Islam', but this is now largely irrelevant, for 'Islam as a social system has been a complete failure'. Thus wherever there are signs of improvement they are wholly due to Western influence. He variously describes Muslim society as intolerant, oppressive, hypocritical, inartistic and illogical, without apparently pausing to wonder whether any of these characteristics occurred in early twentieth-century Western civilization.

At the same time he implicitly acknowledged the strength of Islam and its hold on the Egyptians in his refusal to consider any campaign to transform their society, still less to convert them to Christianity. He believed that over a very long period they might benefit from Western influence but he was sceptical about the possibilities of fundamental change. In his view they were doomed to be Orientals with all that this implied.

Cromer knew excellent French and some Turkish, the languages of the Khedivial and Pasha classes, but he never attempted to learn Arabic which is spoken by the Egyptian masses. His interpreter and close companion for most of his years in Egypt was Harry Boyle, a brilliant linguist who had never been to school. Boyle arrived in Cairo in July 1885 when he was barely 22 years old, to be characteristically greeted by Cromer with 'I suppose you can speak Arabic perfectly?' 'No, Sir, hardly at all.' 'What the devil does White (Ambassador in Constantinople) mean by sending that boy here? He'll be worse than useless.'[9]

However, Cromer gave Boyle six weeks to learn Arabic. He disappeared into the back streets of Cairo and emerged after five weeks with an amazing knowledge of the vernacular. Very soon he was invaluable to Cromer; he was nicknamed 'Enoch' because he 'walked with the Lord'. An eccentric and exceedingly ill-dressed animal-loving bachelor (he married late after leaving Egypt) Boyle, with his great drooping moustache, became a familiar Cairo landmark. Well-loved by his colleagues, Egyptian nationalists regarded him as more than slightly sinister for Cromer used him unashamedly to report on the activities of anyone he regarded as subversive. Boyle himself revelled in his *eminence grise* role. ('Even if I am there, I always omit my own name from lists,' he wrote to his mother, 'as I inherit the fine old gentlemanly plan from my father of not putting myself forward, and the Lord's school has gone still further in the same direction. Blow semblance of power! I like reality, and you don't often get the two together.') But because he shared Cromer's contempt for Egyptian nationalism he provided no antidote for 'the Lord's' view that all opposition to his policies was trivial and irresponsible. As Oriental Secretary, his task was to keep Cromer in touch with Egyptian public opinion. But his contacts were almost exclusively with pro-British elements. His brilliant gifts as a linguist were not supported by political judgement.

6

SUDANESE DISASTER

When Sir Evelyn Baring arrived in Cairo in September 1883, he discovered an alarming situation. The nationalist movement was crushed and dispirited, and was to remain so for a decade, but the Khedive's authority had also been destroyed. Sherif's government, which lacked either prestige or popularity, was attempting to deal with a bankrupt Treasury.

The principal cause for alarm lay one thousand miles to the south in the Sudan, where the rising power of the Mahdi, Mohammed Ahmed, was already threatening Southern Egypt.

Egypt's quasi-empire in the Sudan dated back to 1820 when two of Mohammed Aly's armies had invaded Central and Western Sudan, bloodily suppressed the resistance of the Sudanese tribes, and established the seat of government of an Egyptian dependency under the nominal suzerainty of the Ottoman Empire at the village of Khartoum near the junction of the Blue and White Niles. In 1840 Egyptian rule was extended to include the future Kassala province in Eastern Sudan, and in 1865 the Red Sea ports of Suakin and Massawa, which had been leased to Egypt in 1846, were ceded by the Porte to the Khedive Ismail. Ismail attempted to develop and extend his Sudanese possessions with only limited success. Darfur, the far western province of modern Sudan, was annexed in 1874 but the efforts of Sir Samuel Baker and his successor Colonel Charles Gordon to assimilate and pacify Equatoria must be counted a failure, despite their extraordinary achievements as soldiers and explorers. In 1875 and 1876 Egyptian armies advancing from Massawa were twice defeated by the Ethiopians.

The sixty years of Egyptian rule in the Sudan were far from being as unredeemedly vicious and corrupt as it has often been described. 'To judge Turco-Egyptian administration by the standards of twentieth-century colonial rule, instead of seeing it as part of the pattern of late Ottoman provincial government, is unwarranted and unhistorical.'[1] The Egyptians created an admittedly fragile administrative system to cover the whole country for the first time in Sudanese history. Egyptian cultural influence was greatest in the garrison towns where primary schools were established under Ismail and Egyptian officials inter-married freely with the Sudanese. But there was no influx of Egyptian settlers and as time went on Sudanese were introduced increasingly into the higher ranks of the civil and military administration and the judiciary.

Rebellion, when it came in 1881, began on a small scale and spread through the inspired politico-religious leadership of one man, Mohammed Ahmed ibn Abdullah, who in July of that year announced that he was the Expected Mahdi of Islam.* He came from the Dongola area in Northern Sudan but he declared himself from Aba Island on the White Nile and achieved his first success among the tribes of Kordofan in the West. In 1882 and 1883 he won a series of striking victories over the Egyptian garrison forces.

His support depended on two factors – first the puritanical Islamic zeal of the Sudanese nomadic people who disapproved of the Turco-Egyptian ruling class of the towns and their Sudanese collaborators less for their corruption and misgovernment than for their apparent religious backsliding. The other factor was the profound resentment of some Sudanese Arabs, particularly the Northern tribes who had penetrated the south-west as merchants and soldiers of fortune when this was opened up by the Egyptians, with Ismail and Gordon's efforts to suppress the lucrative slave trade. The second factor was almost certainly the more important of the two. The purity of Ismail's motives may be questioned but not the reality of his effort to suppress slavery, and in Gordon he had a representative of furious energy.

By 1881 Ismail had abdicated and Gordon resigned. His successor as Governor General of the Sudan was an amiable and indecisive Egyptian, Mohammed Rauf Pasha, who was quite

---

* There is no mention of a Mahdi (literally 'the (divinely) guided one') in either the *Koran* or the *Hadith*, the sayings attributed to the Prophet, but very early in Islamic history the Muslim masses came to believe that one would appear 'to fill the world with justice and equity even as it is now filled with injustice and iniquity'. There were several Mahdi claimants before and after Mohammed Ahmed but he was the most important.

incapable of dealing with the Mahdi and his warlike supporters. He was recalled by the Arabists in December 1881 and replaced by a much more capable officer, Abdul Kader Hilmi Pasha. Despite continued Mahdist successes, Abdul Kader was organizing an effective counter-offensive when he too was recalled in February 1883 by the Sherif Government which had succeeded Arabi.

But the Khedive and Sherif could not afford to abandon the Sudan without a fight. They needed to prove that they were not simply puppets of the British occupiers. In the spring of 1883 they appointed several British officers to the Sudan army of whom the most senior was General William Hicks, formerly of the Indian army. At the head of 10,000 raw and undisciplined troops Hicks marched to reconquer Kordofan on 8 September. On 5 November, in a huge thorn and scrub forest south of El-Obeid, this entire force was annihilated by 40,000 Mahdists.

When news of the disaster reached Cairo and London on 22 November, its effect was shattering. Gladstone's Cabinet began to be aware for the first time of the nature of their involvement in Egypt. The Khedive and his Egyptian collaborators who were to have been left to govern after an early British withdrawal had lost all hope of recovering their prestige; if Khartoum fell Egypt itself would be threatened and defenceless except for the British occupation forces. Northbrook protested to Granville: 'We have now been forced into the position of being the protectors of Egypt.'

In Cairo, Baring, who had been barely two months at his post, was plunged into gloom. He realized that either Sudan must be abandoned or an army of non-Egyptian troops sent to hold it. He sounded out the Cabinet on the possibility of dispatching an Anglo-Indian force or of asking the Sultan to send Turkish troops. Both ideas were flatly rejected. Senior British officers in Cairo agreed that in these circumstances even Khartoum could not be held.

Sherif Pasha and the Egyptian ministers were determined that they would not be responsible for the loss of the Egyptian Empire. Sherif continued to insist that Turkish aid should be sought – doubtless in the hope that this would induce the British Government to send Indian troops after all. Granville finally agreed that the Porte could be asked to send 10,000 men to hold the Eastern Sudan, in the certainty that Abdulhamid would never take such decisive action, but he continued to insist on the abandonment of Khartoum. In a private note to Baring he wrote: 'It is essential that in important questions affecting the administration and safety of Egypt, the advice of Her Majesty's government should be followed, as long as the provisional occupation continues. Ministers and Governors must carry out this advice or forfeit their offices.' In the last resort, English ministers might have to be appointed 'but it will no doubt be possible to find Egyptians who will execute the Khedive's orders under English advice.'

Sherif preferred to forfeit his office and resigned on 7 January 1884. Only Nubar, the wily Armenian, agreed to form a government, adding that he 'accepted cordially the policy of abandoning the whole of the Sudan, which, on mature reflection, he believed to be the best in the interests of the country'.

But it was one thing for Nubar to accept the evacuation policy cordially and another to carry it out. Apart from Khartoum, there were garrisons all over the Sudan – in Darfur under the Austrian Slatin Pasha, in Equatoria under Emin Bey as well as throughout the Eastern Sudan. These could not simply be abandoned to their fate but after the victory in Kordofan, triumphant Mahdism swept across the country to the East where Osman Digna, a former slave-dealer who had been appointed the Mahdi's Emir, had won some decisive victories against the Egyptian troops.

Meanwhile something was happening in England which ultimately insured that the evacuation policy would not begin before it was too late. 'Chinese' Gordon, Ismail's former Governor General of the Sudan, had spent the past two years out of the public eye. After a frustrating year commanding the Royal Engineers in Mauritius, he had been summoned by the Cape of Good Hope Government to help with a war against the Basutos only to resign within a few months after a violent quarrel. In 1883 he had left for Palestine where, with the aid of a bible, he had established for his own satisfaction the sites of Calvary, Christ's sepulchre and other holy places. In October he received a summons from King Leopold of the Belgians to administer his personal estate, the Congo, on his behalf. Owing to Foreign Office opposition he offered his resignation from the British Army.

But Lord Granville had other ideas. A few days after the Hicks disaster, Granville was writing to Gladstone: 'Do you see any objection to using Gordon in some way? He had an immense name in Egypt – he is popular at home. He is a strong but very sensible opponent of slavery. He has a small bee in his bonnet. . . .'

But the Sherif Government objected on the ground that, as a Christian, Gordon was unsuitable to deal with a Muslim religious movement. Baring supported Sherif on this ground, although his real objections 'were in some degree based on General Gordon's personal unfitness to undertake the work in hand'.[2]

Baring's doubts are easy to understand. Charles Gordon was an intensely vivid character who in China, Equatoria and elsewhere had given abundant proof of his courage, endurance, military skill and electrifying personality. At the same time he was so alarmingly eccentric as to border on dottiness. Years earlier he had abandoned all belief in free will. In 1876 he wrote to his sister: 'If my actions are right they are His actions; if evil they are the inevitable produce of the corrupt body in which I am placed by Him. . . .' Now he had persuaded himself that he was God's instrument for some still unspecified purposes. While Colonel Chaille-Long's charge that he was an intermittent drunkard can be dismissed as the malicious retaliation of a man he had sacked, a post-Freudian age can hardly doubt that some violent sexual repression lay behind his daemonic energy and mysticism. Baring rightly divined that such a man was unlikely to obey instructions from London and still less from the Consul-General in Cairo.

But the forces in favour of sending Gordon were too strong. 'Chauvinists and humanitarians', in Cromer's words, united to demand a more forward Sudanese policy. The former wanted to expand the British occupation of Egypt while the latter denounced the revival of slavery that would follow the abandonment of the Sudan to the Mahdi. But their accents were much the same.* On 1 January 1884 *The Times* published a letter from Sir Samuel Baker demanding that British and Indian troops should be sent

* Blunt has some fun at the expense of the Anti-Slavery Society who, he says, deeply resented the idea that slavery might be suppressed by Mohammedan reformers such as Arabi or Mohammed Abdu. They maintained that since slavery was permitted by the Prophet it was illegal for a Moslem to suppress it. 'Our professional humanitarians,' says Blunt, 'were no more anxious to abolish slavery altogether than masters of foxhounds are anxious to abolish foxes.' (Blunt, *Gordon at Khartoum*, p. 98.)

to hold the Sudan. But it was the Liberal *Pall Mall Gazette* and its chauvinistic editor, William Stead (who had succeeded John Morley a few months earlier) which led the campaign. After interviewing Gordon at Southampton, Stead demanded: 'Why not send Chinese Gordon with full powers to Khartoum to assume absolute control of the territory, to relieve the garrisons, and do what can be done to save what can be saved from the wreck in the Sudan?'

The doubts of Gladstone and Baring were overcome and on 15 January the Cabinet offered Gordon the job, which he accepted without demur. No doubt he infinitely preferred Khartoum to the Congo.

Gordon was the obvious choice to go to the Sudan. It was equally obvious that he was the wrong man to carry out a policy of withdrawal. His original instructions were to proceed to the Sudan to report to Her Majesty's government on the military situation and advise on the measures needed to ensure the security of the Egyptian garrisons and the European population of Khartoum. Already when he reached Cairo he was talking of the 'restoration of the country to the different petty Sultans who existed at the time of Mehmet Ali's conquests and whose families still exist'. At his own suggestion he was appointed Governor General of the Sudan by Tewfik, who was fully aware of Gordon's contemptuous feelings towards him. At the same time, on Baring's initiative, Gordon was given 'the widest discretionary powers . . . as regards the manner of carrying out the policy [of evacuation].' Clearly it was not going to be a question of simply reporting back to London. Already his fertile mind was considering such possibilities as going to see the Mahdi personally or sailing up the White Nile to take possession of the Bahr el-Ghazal and Equatorial Provinces for the King of the Belgians. Before he even reached Khartoum he had convinced himself that the Mahdi's popularity was declining and that Egypt's prestige was still high enough to maintain its position as a Suzerain Power. A few days after his arrival he was telegraphing to Baring: 'If Egypt is to be quiet Mahdi must be smashed up.'

It is easy to understand Baring's exasperation with Gordon. Each morning he received a batch of telegrams with a variety of often contradictory proposals. Wisely he waited to deal with them in the evening when another batch would have arrived taking an entirely different line. Somehow he had to fashion a coherent report to refer to Lord Granville. Yet when Gordon's journals came to be published, Baring found them studded with highly derogatory references to his character and behaviour, frequently illustrated with cartoons, and summing him up as a pompous, humourless, time-server.

In his *Modern Egypt*, Baring rightly castigates the Gladstone Government for the costly blunders of its Sudanese policy which did so much permanent damage to Gladstone's reputation. But, he is a little too hasty in denying any responsibility of his own. While he is correct in claiming that he was opposed to sending Gordon from the outset, he also says that 'No Englishman should have been sent to Khartoum.'[3] On this point the watchful Wilfrid Blunt caught him out, for in his dispatch to Lord Granville of 22 December 1883 Baring says clearly: 'It would also be necessary to send an English officer of high authority to Khartoum with full power to withdraw the garrison and to make the best arrangements possible for the future government of that country.' Yet when he came to publish *Modern Egypt* some twenty-four years later he omitted the word 'English' from the letter, thereby giving the impression that he proposed sending an Egyptian officer.

While the Gladstone Government, supported by the British public, was chiefly responsible for Gordon's fatal mission to Khartoum, it refused to send the one man who might have helped him effectively and ultimately succeeded him. This was Zobeir Pasha, an aristocratic Sudanese of energy and ability. The only trouble was that he had mainly employed his talents in slave trading, and his son Soliman had been defeated and killed by Gordon's Italian lieutenant Gessi in 1878. Zobeir himself was detained in Cairo. However, while Gordon was in Cairo on his way to the Sudan he conceived the idea that provided Zobeir had forgiven him for the death of his son, it was absolutely essential that he should accompany him to Khartoum. He was convinced that Zobeir could easily have dealt with the Mahdi and ensured that at least a form of order followed the evacuation.

Baring, who always tended to take a pragmatic view,* was

---

* 'Every Englishman is justly proud of the part which his country has borne in the suppression of Slavery and the Slave Trade. . . . The [Anti-Slavery] Society, however, is not without its defects. Concentration of thought and action on one subject, together with a certain want of

inclined to agree with him but because he felt that Gordon had made this decision on an impulse which he might reverse at any moment, and also because he was certain the British Government would never agree, he refused to allow Zobeir to accompany Gordon to Khartoum. But Gordon did not change his mind, and when he continued to press for Zobeir to be sent, with the support of Colonel Stewart who had accompanied Gordon, Baring strongly urged this course on the British Government. He could point out that if the Sudan was to be evacuated the slave trade was certain to revive anyway. At least Zobeir might ensure there was not anarchy as well. Gordon had already announced to the delighted Notables of Berber in Northern Sudan that anti-slavery was no longer part of his programme. But the British Government was adamant that Zobeir could not be trusted.

Gordon was received with enthusiasm when he arrived in Khartoum on 18 February. He made several popular moves such as remitting taxes and releasing prisoners, but he wholly under-rated the Mahdi and overestimated the strength of his own position. From Berber he had written to the Mahdi offering to recognize him as Sultan of Kordofan in return for ending his rebellion. The Mahdi's reply, which he received in Khartoum on 22 March, rejected the offer with contempt and suggested instead that Gordon should surrender and embrace Islam.

The Mahdi had good reason for his confidence. In the Eastern Sudan Osman Digna's dervishes had inflicted a series of bloody defeats on the Egyptian garrisons, led by General Valentine Baker, Sir Samuel Baker's brother. A British force under Sir Gerald Graham landed at Trinkitat on the Red Sea and twice defeated the dervishes at el-Teb (20 February) and Tamai (13 March), where they destroyed and burned Digna's camp. But the Gladstone Government was not contemplating any more ambitious operations. The British troops withdrew to Suakin and stayed there. The dervishes soon recovered their morale when they discovered that the Eastern Sudan had been left in their possession.

Gordon's position in Khartoum was now desperate. He contin-ued to press for Zobeir to be sent, and also for an expeditionary

---

imagination which occasionally characterizes the conduct of Englishmen in dealing with foreign affairs and which is perhaps in some degree due to their insular habits of thought, produce their natural effect.' (*Modern Egypt*, Vol. I, p. 403.)

force of British and Indian troops to open up the route between Berber and the coast of Suakin. But while Baring supported him over Zobeir he was opposed, on the advice of senior British officers in Cairo, to committing any British troops to the interior of the Sudan. In any case the Gladstone Cabinet flatly rejected both requests on 11 March, ignoring Queen Victoria's expressed wish that Indian troops should be sent to relieve Khartoum. Gordon did not learn of the Government's final decision until a month later because on 12 March the telegraph wire linking Khartoum with the outside world was cut. His reaction was defiant and wholly characteristic: 'I shall hold out here as long as I can, and if I can suppress the rebellion I shall do so. If I cannot, I shall retire to the Equator, and leave you the indelible disgrace of abandoning the garrisons of Sennar, Kassala, Berber and Dongola, with the certainty that you will eventually be forced to smash up the Mahdi under great difficulties if you would retain peace in Egypt.'

He was still determinedly underestimating the Mahdi. A week earlier he had cabled: 'I wish I could convey to you the trumpery nature of this revolt, which 500 determined men could put down. Be assured that for the present, and for two months, we are as safe here as in Cairo.'

In Cairo Baring understood his danger better and now began to press the Government for a small relief expedition to reopen the Berber-Suakin road. Understandably in view of Gordon's continued optimism, the Government refused. On 26 May the Mahdi's forces took Berber and Gordon's escape route to the north was cut.

If Gordon and Colonel Stewart were to be saved a relief expedition was urgently necessary. At home the Cabinet was divided along familiar lines. The Whigs were in favour and the Radicals, suspecting a Whig plot to recover the Sudan and establish a permanent evacuation of Egypt, were opposed. Chamberlain and Dilke soon changed their minds when they were persuaded of Gordon's danger but Gladstone remained adamant. He had reluctantly agreed to the despatch of Gordon to Khartoum in the first place. When he saw the danger of a deep involvement of British forces in the interior it was he who had insisted on their withdrawal from the Eastern Sudan. In a rash moment he had blurted out in the House of Commons the words that were so long to be held against him: 'Yes, those people are struggling to be free, and they are rightly struggling to be free.' That he should allow the Sudanese Mahdists but not the Egyptian Arabists to be a legitimate national movement was the quintessence of self-deception. But he remained adamant, and the crescendo of protest from the jingoes and humanitarians merely increased his obstinacy.

The familiar story of the few remaining months of Gordon's life is hardly relevant to this account. Throughout the summer of 1884 Gladstone held out against Hartington and the Whigs' demands for a relief expedition. Baring continued patiently to point out that the Cabinet's attitude was illogical; that by continuing to reject all responsibility for the Sudan it was storing up endless troubles for the future and the certainty of intervention. Finally, he was slapped down by his cousin, Lord Northbrook: 'We are much better able than you to balance the general interests of the country against the obvious considerations of the Sudan difficulty.'

In April, Baring left for London to attend a financial conference on Egypt and remained there until early September. On 8 August, after Hartington had threatened to bring the Government down by resigning, the House of Commons voted a credit and finally, on 8 October, Baring was authorized to instruct Lord Wolseley to mount an expedition up the valley of the Nile 'to bring away General Gordon and Colonel Stewart from Khartoum'. But the expedition was beset by misfortune. Already in September, Colonel Stewart, who had been sent up the Nile with messages by Gordon, was treacherously murdered. As the expedition moved painfully southwards several senior officers were killed in encounters with the Mahdists. Wolseley lost his initiative and delayed. As his steamers finally approached Khartoum on 28 January it could be seen that the Egyptian flag was no longer flying from Government House which had been wrecked.

Gordon had been besieged in Khartoum by the Mahdi and his forces for five months. He had organized its defences with his usual ferocious energy – maintaining morale in the capital with highly optimistic accounts of the progress of the relief expedition as he vainly scanned the horizon for the sight of steamers' smoke. Finally it was the correct report of the British defeat of a Mahdist force at Abu Klea that convinced the Mahdi to make his final assault. The exhausted and half-starved garrison could offer little resistance. Gordon was speared to death on the staircase of

Government House against the orders of the Mahdi who wanted him taken alive.

The British public, led by Queen Victoria, blamed Gladstone and his Cabinet for Gordon's death. Certainly Gladstone does not come well out of the affair but admiration for Gordon's attractive and remarkable character cannot disguise the fact that he was chiefly responsible for his own fate. He never seriously attempted to carry out his orders to evacuate as he could have done easily before the fall of Berber in May and quite possibly even afterwards. It is hard not to agree with Anthony Nutting's verdict: 'That he ended by sacrificing several thousands of men whom he could have saved, as well as condemning their women and children to years of slavery in the service of the Mahdi's successor, the Khalifa Abdullahi, places on him a terrible responsibility before history, which all the undoubted heroism and endurance of his final stand at Khartoum cannot expunge.'[4]

The fall of Khartoum meant that most of the modern Sudan remained under the control of Mahdism for thirteen years. Of the total Egyptian garrisons in the Sudan about 12,000 were killed, 11,000 returned home and the remaining 30,000 were absorbed into the Mahdists state.

In the first reaction to Gordon's death Wolseley was ordered to 'smash the Mahdi' as Gordon had wished. But it was soon apparent that Wolseley could do no such thing; he failed to advance on Berber while Sir Gerald Graham's forces were severely mauled by Osman Digna near Suakin. When a war scare with Russia arose over Afghanistan, the Government took the opportunity to revert to its former policy of complete evacuation of the Sudan, ignoring Wolseley's protests that at least the Dongola province should be held. At first Baring was apprehensive of the effect on Egypt if the Mahdists reached as far north as Wadi Halfa and favoured at least the establishment of a semi-independent Egyptian Governor of Dongola, with his own British-trained Sudanese troops, to act as a buffer. Later he realized this was impracticable and that the dangers of the spread of Mahdism into Egypt had been exaggerated. He was relieved that when the Tories under Salisbury came briefly to power in June 1885, they dashed Wolseley's hopes that they would reverse Gladstone's decision to evacuate the Sudan entirely. Egypt was in no position to pay and the House of Commons refused to vote any more credits.

On 22 June the Mahdi died and was succeeded by the Khalifa Abdullahi who attempted to carry out the Mahdi's intention of invading Egypt in December 1885. But he was defeated by an Anglo-Egyptian force at Ginnis and the frontier was thereafter held without much difficulty by an Egyptian frontier force at Wadi Halfa backed by British troops at Aswan. Four years later he sent a stronger force headed by the outstanding Mahdist general, Nejumi, which was decisively defeated in a big battle at Toski. Two years later Osman Digna was also defeated in the Eastern Sudan.

Egypt had been made safe from a Mahdist invasion but by 1889 Baring had begun to change his mind about the need for the reconquest of the Sudan. He had always known that one day it would be necessary but the situation altered as the scramble for Africa began in earnest. Egypt's former African empire had been liquidated. England, France and Italy had divided the Somali territories and the fertile province of Harar, which had been annexed by Ismail, was abandoned by a reluctant Egyptian Government and absorbed by Ethiopia in 1887.

Then in 1889 the Italian Government made a Treaty with Ethiopia and laid claim to the key town of Kassala on the River Atbara. Baring, who had always maintained, no doubt correctly, that the Mahdists' control of the Upper Nile did not threaten Egypt, was now seriously alarmed. In December 1889 he wrote to Salisbury saying that if the Italians took Kassala they would soon reach Khartoum and whereas 'the savage tribes' who now ruled the Sudan lacked the means to harm Egypt the situation would be very different if they were replaced by a 'civilized power' which could so reduce the water supply as to ruin Egypt. 'Whatever Powers hold the Upper Nile Valley must, by the mere force of its geographical situation, dominate Egypt.'

Salisbury, who controlled England's foreign policy for most of the period 1885–92, was inclined to agree with Baring but the military reconquest was still postponed for several years. 'Before any thought of reconquest could be entertained, two conditions had to be fulfilled,' wrote Cromer in *Modern Egypt*, 'In the first place the Egyptian army had to be rendered efficient. In the second place, not only had the solvency of the Egyptian Treasury to be assured but funds had to be provided for the extraordinary expenditure which the assumption of an offensive policy would certainly involve.'

In 1890 Egypt's army and finances had improved but not sufficiently in Cromer's eyes. Five years later, however, when Salisbury returned to power again after a Liberal interlude under Gladstone and Rosebury, he had to assume that the reconquest would not be long delayed although he himself would have preferred a delay of several more years. Ironically, it was precipitated by the Italians – not because they threatened the Nile but because they asked for help to relieve the pressure on their forces by the Ethiopians whose country they were unsuccessfully attempting to conquer. The Italian dilemma provided the occasion but Salisbury's real concern was not to help the Crispi Government. Over the years he had reached the conclusion that control of the whole Nile Valley was a vital interest of the British Empire.

In March 1895 a sudden decision was taken to recover the province of Dongola. A force was assembled of Egyptian troops with some British officers on secondment. The commander was the young Sirdar of the Egyptian army, Sir Herbert Kitchener. Slowly and painstakingly he advanced up the Nile laying a railway as he went. He occupied Dongola in September 1895. Casualties were kept to a minimum and so were expenses because, as Cromer dryly remarks, Kitchener possessed a quality rare among soldiers. 'He did not think that extravagance was the necessary handmaid of efficiency.' This was all the more welcome because when application was made to the Commissioners of the debt for a £500,000 grant to cover the expenses of the Dongola expedition, although a majority of the Commissioners approved, the French and the Russians voted against and then sued the Egyptian Government in the Cairo Mixed Courts. A few days after the successful completion of the Dongola expedition the court found in their favour and ordered the Egyptian Government to repay the money to the Caisse.

The Salisbury Government knew that it could not stop at Dongola; Khartoum would have to be recovered eventually. But despite Kitchener's economies it still balked at the cost. Ultimately Egypt would be made to pay for everything but meanwhile, in view of the Mixed Courts' decision, the British Treasury would have to lend the money. In November 1896, the House of

Commons approved an £800,000 loan to Egypt at 2¾ per cent interest.

There was an even more serious matter to be considered. The Cabinet felt that some British troops would be needed to ensure overwhelming superiority for the final assault on Khartoum but it was uncertain how this would be received by the British public. It was not until February 1897 that Hicks-Beach, the chancellor of the exchequer, made the matter public when he said in the House of Commons: 'Egypt could never be held to be permanently secure so long as a hostile Power was in occupation of the Nile Valley up to Khartoum' and that it was England's duty to give the final blow to the 'baleful power of the Khalifa'. Still another year passed before Kitchener, convinced that the Khalifa was about to mount a counter-offensive, made a formal request for British troops. Four battalions were sent immediately and later another infantry brigade, a regiment of cavalry and a field artillery battery for the final advance on Khartoum. On Good Friday (18 April) the Emir Mahmoud's army of 12,000 was defeated on the River Atbara with heavy casualties on both sides. On 2 September 1898 the Anglo-Egyptian force of 22,000 routed the Khalifa's army of 50,000 a few miles north of Omdurman. Sudanese casualties exceeded 27,000, the Anglo-Egyptians lost some 400 dead and wounded. As some of Kitchener's troops continued to shoot the dervish wounded, the ever-economical Kitchener was heard to exclaim: 'Cease fire! Cease fire! Oh, what a dreadful waste of ammunition.'[5]

Cromer speaks of the 'rapid growth of the Imperialist spirit, which about this time took place in England'. Wilfrid Blunt refers as characteristically to the jingoism of the British public in the 1890s. Of the reaction to Omdurman he wrote in his Journal: 'The whole country, if one may judge by the press, has gone mad with the lust of fighting glory, and there is no moral sense left in England to which to appeal.' Salisbury was not the man to be carried away or even influenced by these feelings but they happened to support his strategy. While Kitchener's force was moving slowly southwards he had hoped to forestall the French from gaining a foothold on the Upper Nile, first with a diplomatic mission to King Menelek of Ethiopia and then, when this failed, by a military expedition from Uganda to the east bank of the Nile. But this never got started until much too late and when Kitchener defeated the Khalifa at Omdurman Captain Marchand's gallant little band had already struggled through to plant the tricolour on the Nile at Fashoda. After Omdurman Kitchener sailed on up the Nile to meet Marchand. They treated each other politely and the Egyptian flag was raised beside the French but Britain and France remained on the brink of war for over a month until the French climbed down and ordered Marchand to evacuate Fashoda – which he had already done.

Britain now held a strong position along the length of the Nile Valley; but the problem remained of the future status of the Sudan. The reconquest had been carried out in the name of the Khedive and mainly with Egyptian troops and money; the £800,000 was a loan and not a grant. For these reasons outright annexation by Britain was not feasible. On the other hand, the expedition had been planned and managed by Kitchener (the 'excellent man of business' as Cromer calls him). Salisbury had every intention that Her Majesty's government should have 'a predominant voice in all matters connected with the Sudan, and that they expect any advice which they may think fit to tender to the Egyptian Government, in respect to Sudan affairs, will be followed,' as he wrote to Cromer one month before Khartoum was occupied. He gave orders for the Egyptian and British flags to be hoisted side by side at Khartoum. From this action evolved the juristic innovation of the 'condominium' which, according to the Anglo-Egyptian agreement of January 1899, was intended: 'To give effect to the claims which have accrued to Her Britannic Majesty's government by right of conquest, to share in the present settlement and in the future working and development of the Sudan.'

For a time this was hailed as a masterpiece of British pragmatism. In many ways it worked well and it had the immense advantage of preventing all Egypt's international complications of the financial control and the Capitulations from spreading automatically to the Sudan. Through prudent administration, the country slowly recovered from the devastation of the Mahdia. But as time passed it became clear that the Sudan was the major obstacle to a settlement of outstanding problems between Britain and Egypt. This had mattered little while Egypt was in a state of total subjection to England but not with the resurgence of Egyptian nationalism in the twentieth century. Despite the theoretical equality of the condominium the administration of the Sudan was almost exclusively in British hands. The Governor-General, who was appointed by the Khedive on British advice, was always an Englishman. Egypt was accorded only the doubtful privilege of providing troops and money. 'Once Egypt had passed from under British control, the artificiality of the Condominium could no longer be concealed, and from the end of the First World War onwards, Cromer's clever device was increasingly an embarrassment, both to successive British Cabinets and to the administration in the Sudan, which came to be called the Sudan government.'5*

* Sir Rennell Rodd records an astonishing interview between Cromer and Sir Michael Hicks-Beach the chancellor of the exchequer in 1900 in which the chancellor stonewalled all Cromer's urgent requests for some modest British financial support for the Sudan, on the ground that it was as much a British as an Egyptian interest, with the bleak utterance: 'I have no money'; and 'If you cannot afford to remain there, you had better give it up and come away.' (Rodd, *Social and Diplomatic Memories*, p. 281.)

1883–92

Looking back from retirement, Cromer remarked that although he had experience of hard work in his official career of nearly fifty years he was never in a position of such difficulty 'or in one involving such a continuous strain on the mind, the nerves, and, I may add, the temper, as during the first three months of the year 1884. I was rarely able to leave my house. I had a very small staff to help me. I was generally hard at work from daybreak till late at night.'[1]

It is not difficult to see why. While the flow of contradictory telegrams from Gordon required most of his attention, he had to devise means of staving off Egyptian bankruptcy. At that stage there was no question of financial progress – only of preventing disaster. At the same time he was under the orders of a Cabinet, in general woefully ignorant of foreign affairs, which expected him to achieve the impossible: that is the establishment of a secure and viable Khedivial regime which would enable the occupation to be withdrawn in a matter of months.

Although nominally a Liberal, Baring was so far out on the imperialist wing of the party that he soon established a much closer rapport with the Tory Salisbury than he ever had with Gladstone or Granville, the quintessential Whig grandee. He agreed with Queen Victoria that Rosebery was the only tolerable Liberal foreign minister. But during those first two vital years he had to deal with Gladstone and Granville, who clung to the policy laid down by Palmerston thirty years earlier – to secure Britain's vital interests without direct intervention. They had not appreciated, says Cromer, that 'all history was there to prove that when once a civilized Power lays its hand on a weak State in a barbarous or semi-civilized condition, it rarely relaxed its grasp'.[2]

Initially, according to Cromer's own testimony, he was in favour of evacuation. Within a few weeks of his arrival in Cairo he was recommending the withdrawal of the British garrison from Cairo to Alexandria and the reduction of the total force in Egypt to about 3,000 men. He claimed that some progress in reforming the internal administration had been achieved 'but there is one obstacle which stands in the way of almost every move forward, and that is the necessity of consulting every Power in Europe before any important steps can be taken.' The Dual Control had been abolished unilaterally by Britain soon after Tel el-Kebir but the Caisse de la Dette and the foreign Capitulations still existed. In an urgent plea to Granville to get rid of these international rights of interference in Egypt, he said: 'Give me 2,000 men and power to settle matters between the English and Egyptian Governments, and I will guarantee that in twelve months there shall not be a British soldier in Egypt, and that the country is put in such a position as to render it very improbable that any Egyptian question will be raised again for many years to come at all events.' He later acknowledged that this estimate 'was unquestionably much too sanguine'. No doubt he realized at the time that he could give no such guarantee but he wanted to persuade the Government to take a strong line with the powers to abstain from interference in return for a promise of early withdrawal.

This Gladstone and Granville were not prepared to do. However the question soon became academic as the Hicks disaster and the consequent Mahdist threat to Egypt made it impossible to withdraw and leave the country virtually defenceless. From then on the arguments for evacuation (that is, placating the Powers), though strong, were always outweighed by those for prolonging the occupation – the impossibility of ensuring that a secure and sympathetic Khedivial regime could be left behind. In the 1880s several attempts were made to win the co-operation of the Powers. An international conference on Egyptian finances in London in the summer of 1884 ended in failure but a stopgap agreement granting Egypt a £E9 million loan guaranteed by all the powers involved in Egyptian finances was reached the following year. In June 1885 Gladstone was replaced by his political antithesis, the cool and dispassionate Salisbury, who began conducting his country's diplomacy like a brilliant chess-player. Having appeased Bismarck with Tanganyika he sent Sir Henry Drummond Wolff, a member of Randolph Churchill's Fourth Party, to Constantinople to seek a settlement with the sultan which would also satisfy France. At

July, 1882. After ten and a half hours' continuous bombardment by the British fleet, Arabi Pasha's fortifications in Alexandria were reduced to rubble.

Arabi Pasha during his eighteen years' exile in Ceylon.

Lord Cromer, who was the real ruler of Egypt during the first twenty-four years of the British occupation.

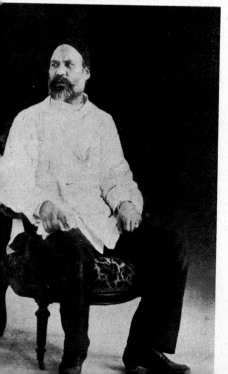

Mr. Wilfrid Blunt, the poet, Arabist and lifelong nationalist sympathizer, with his wife Lady Anne Blunt in 1888. He was a trenchant critic of Cromer's rule in Egypt.

The terrace of the old Shepheard's Hotel c. 1890 known to all tourist visitors as the social centre of Cairo.

THE 'EGYPTIAN PET' Professor of the noble Art of Self-Defence: 'Not up to it yet, young 'un.'

'We desire that Egypt should be strong enough of herself to repel all external attacks, and to put down all internal disturbance' – Lord Salisbury. Cartoon in *Punch*, November 21, 1891.

Construction of the first Aswan Dam, c. 1900. Although now overshadowed by the much larger High Dam it remains the most solid achievement of the British occupation.

'English Officers in the Egyptian Service – Trying on a Fez in Cairo'
c. 1900.

Victoria College, Alexandria, which was run on the lines of an
English public school.

Sir Eldon Gorst, Financial Adviser
and Cromer's successor. His early
death cut short his liberal
experiment.

Khedive Abbas II (1874–1944)
whose attempts to assert himself
against Cromer ultimately failed.
He was finally deposed as pro-Turk
in 1914.

Lord Kitchener, British Consul-General in Egypt 1911–1914, at the
opening of a new quay in Cairo. His status and manner were
semi-regal.

Saad Zaghlul Pasha
(1860–1927) who dominated
Egypt's political life after
World War I. Great orator
and parliamentarian, he
lacked some of the essential
qualities of statesmanship.

King Fuad I (1868–1936)
would have wished to be a
royal autocrat but was
restrained by the British and
by Egypt's parliamentary
constitution.

'A Picnic on the Great Pyramid', 1874. Eight years before the Occupation the British had little doubt who was destined to control Egypt.

'Waiting to see the Khedive.' In an earlier age many British tourists had money and leisure to spend all the winter months in Egypt.

Sir Miles Lampson, Britain's dominating Ambassador, visiting the Palace.

Egypt's last monarch, King Farouk (1920–65) rapidly destroyed his early popularity through his cynical abuse of his position.

Full circle. Egyptian children search among the rubble of their homes after the British landing in Port Said, November 13th, 1956.

first Salisbury was inclined to underestimate the difficulties. As he explained to Drummond Wolff, what he wanted was to be able to evacuate at some date in the not too distant future, but to ensure permanent British supremacy in Egypt by persuading the sultan to acknowledge Britain's right to return whenever it pleased. The Sultan Abdulhamid, who was resigned to a lengthy British occupation of Egypt, was prepared to agree to Salisbury's terms but, not unnaturally, the French were bitterly opposed to an automatic British right of re-entry. They were joined by Russia, Turkey's traditional rival in the eastern Mediterranean.

Drummond Wolff swiftly reached a preliminary agreement with the Turkish Government whereby British and Turkish special commissioners would go to Egypt to study 'the best means of tranquillizing the Sudan by pacific means' and, in concert with the Khedive, to reorganize the Egyptian army. They were also to examine all branches of the Egyptian administration, and introduce into them the modifications which they considered necessary. All this was to lead to 'the conclusion of a convention regulating the withdrawal of the British troops from Egypt in a convenient period'.

The commissioners were Drummond Wolff himself and Ghazi Moukhtar Pasha. Negotiations dragged on for eighteen months. During this time there was a brief Liberal interregnum (February–June 1886). When Salisbury returned to power in June 1886 his attitude on the Egyptian question had hardened. While he continued to give priority to the maintenance of a European balance of power, he foresaw the coming scramble for Africa and Egypt's vital importance as a link in the lifeline to India. While he had not abandoned the belief he had inherited from Disraeli that the survival of the Ottoman Empire was the best protection against Russian encroachment on the eastern Mediterranean, he was beginning to look on the Empire as suffering from a mortal disease and to consider Egypt as a substitute.

The convention that was finally signed by Drummond Wolff and two Turkish plenipotentiaries on 22 May 1887 provided for the evacuation of the British garrison within three years and the British officers in the Egyptian army two years after, leaving Egypt a neutralized territory. However, Article 5 stipulated that British troops would not withdraw 'if there were any appearance of danger in the interior or without'.

The sultan was faced with a dilemma. If he ratified the convention it would set a precedent for other powers to occupy parts of his Empire and then claim the right of re-entry before evacuating. If he refused to ratify he would in effect be abandoning even his nominal suzerainty over Egypt. In the event he chose the second alternative.

No one was more relieved at this result than Baring who by now had gained immeasurably in confidence. The immediate threat from the Sudan had been averted. He felt that Egypt was turning a corner financially and could see his way forward to the achievement of new reforms. Above all he had succeeded in evolving a method of governing Egypt from behind the scenes (the Veiled Protectorate) which, while unconventional and in some ways unsatisfactory, appeared to be working. It is also reasonable to suppose that he was sufficiently ambitious not to want to see a promising proconsular career cut short.

The establishment of the Veiled Protectorate had to await the arrival of Baring – a year after the battle of Tel el-Kebir. But, under Lord Dufferin's supervision, a start had been made on recruiting a small corps of British advisers. The distinguished Anglo-Indian irrigation engineer, Colin Scott-Moncrieff, was invited to Cairo by Dufferin when he landed at Suez on his way home from Bombay, and offered the post of director-general of irrigation. Sir Evelyn Wood, with the title of Sirdar, was put in charge of a new Egyptian army. Some English officers were appointed to form a police force under Colonel Valentine Baker. A British doctor, Dr Fleming Sandwith, had hardly been appointed to form a sanitary department when a severe outbreak of cholera caused panic among the Levantine population of Cairo and Alexandria and the virtual collapse of the Sherif Government. Only emergency measures by the British occupation army prevented a much more serious disaster.

The key post was still that of financial adviser. Colvin remained until June 1883 and when he was appointed to replace Baring as finance minister to the Government of India, Scott-Moncrieff was asked to take his position in Egypt. Although the move from irrigation to finance would have meant a salary increase from £2,000 to £3,000 a year, Scott-Moncrieff's total ignorance of financial matters made him reluctant to accept. He was relieved when Lord Goschen recommended the 26-year-old Edgar Vincent (later Lord D'Abernon). Vincent soon overcame initial doubts about his extreme youth. 'He was a man of great ability,' wrote Sir Colin in his *Reminiscences*, 'and as beautiful as he was able; he looked like a son of the gods.'

Lord Milner, in his able apologia for the first decade of British rule in Egypt, *England in Egypt*, remarked: 'Baring, Vincent, Moncrieff – these were the men who bore the burden and heat of those early days of stress.' But he added that if this trio were the most important they were not at that stage 'the most conspicuous of our countrymen in Egypt'. This was an outspoken and rumbustious ex-magistrate from Ireland, Clifford Lloyd, who in September 1883 was given the newly invented title of 'director-general of reforms'. Nominally this was a position of great power. There was much to be reformed and Lloyd set about his task with explosive energy. Within a year he had quarrelled so violently with Sir Benson Maxwell, an elderly colonial jingo from Singapore ('a great stickler for the letter of the law, and a pedant,' according to Moncrieff) who had been made procureur-général in the newly established native courts, that both were obliged to resign and 'returned to England to fight out their battle in the columns of *The Times*'.

Lloyd's failure was probably inevitable; it is difficult to see how he could have worked in harness with a man of Baring's character. But in his short period in Egypt he succeeded in raising a fundamental question of the nature of the British occupation – this was whether the British 'advisers' were or were not to have executive powers or, in other words, whether the Egyptian ministers were to be treated as mere figureheads. The possibility of establishing direct rule through English ministers was rejected, except as a last resort, by the Gladstone and the Salisbury Governments. But if the English 'advisers' were to deal directly with the subordinate authorities in the provinces to see that their advice was put into effect it would amount to the same thing.

Sherif Pasha resigned over the Sudanese issue and Nubar had been the only Egyptian politician of standing who was prepared to take office on Baring's terms. But although Nubar was anxious for the occupation to continue he was no simple British stooge. As an Armenian he was an honorary member of the Turco-Circassian ruling class but a strong element of Egyptian patriotism mingled with his personal ambition.* As Ismail's minister he had achieved a major step towards Egyptian independence through the establishment of the Mixed Courts.

When Nubar took office in January 1884 he was quite prepared to see full British executive control in certain fields. Scott-Moncrieff records that Nubar sent for him as well as Vincent and Lloyd and told them that, according to British Government policy, all heads of departments must be Egyptian subjects. He then interviewed each of the three Englishmen separately and after repeating to Scott-Moncrieff that the minister of public works would have to be an Egyptian, asked: '*Voulez-vous avoir un homme capable, ou une nullité?*' '*Une nullité s'il vous plaît, Excellence,*' I replied. '*Ah, mon cher, vous avez raison, vous avez raison, je vous chercherai une nullité.*' 'And he was as good as his word, and appointed a very nice old fellow – Rushdi Pasha – to be my nominal chief. . . . I always treated him with respect, for I really liked him, and he, for his part, always backed me up, and agreed with what I wanted.'³

Nubar, a keen agriculturalist himself, was convinced of the overriding importance to Egypt of improvements in irrigation. A favourite saying of his was 'The Egyptian Question is the Irrigation Question'. Having correctly estimated Scott-Moncrieff's abilities, he was prepared to see the department entirely in British hands. His attitude towards Vincent and the finance department was similar. When a dinner party conversation touched on the unveiling of a statue, Nubar remarked to Vincent: '*Ah, vous, vous êtes la statue; moi, je suis la couverture. Mais, mon cher, je vous prie, ne la remuez pas trop vite.*'

The ministry of the interior, however, was quite a different matter in Nubar's eyes. The exuberant Clifford Lloyd produced a plan to place the newly organized police force entirely under the orders of their own officers in all matters of discipline. At the same time the traditional system whereby the police were under the direct control of the local Egyptian officials – Mudirs in the

---

* Scott-Moncrieff shrewdly compared his position with that of Disraeli in England. 'An Armenian Christian who never really learnt Arabic, a Liberal in constant touch with Tory Turks who hated him and yet could not do without him, a man of European reputation, of charming manners, so long as his own personal interests were not injured, he threw himself into the party of civilization.' (Mary Hollings, *Life of Sir Colin A. Scott-Moncrieff*, London 1917, p. 175.)

provinces and Mamurs in the district subdivisions – was radically modified. European inspectors were appointed and made responsible to the inspector general in the ministry of the interior, Colonel Valentine Baker. Inevitably these tended to assume much of the Mudirs' authority.

This new system would clearly do something to remove the manifold corruption and abuses of Egyptian administration of justice, but Nubar, who came to power immediately after Clifford Lloyd's new plan had been announced by Khedivial decree, at once saw that it amounted to a social revolution. It was the first step towards full European control of Egyptian society and was not what Nubar had in mind. He was enthusiastic about the British military occupation because the army did not try to interfere in the civil administration, 'Hence his extreme civility to all British military officers whose praises he was never weary of singing,' says Cromer. 'What, indeed, for all the purposes which he had at heart, could be more perfect than the presence in Egypt of a thoroughly disciplined force, commanded by young men who took no interest in local politics, and who occupied themselves exclusively with polo and cricket.'[4]

Nubar fought Clifford Lloyd's new measure bitterly and, because at that stage he was still regarded as indispensable, he won. He was helped by Clifford Lloyd's temperament because just when their dispute was at its height, Lloyd chose to engage in his quarrel with Sir Benson Maxwell which led to both their resignations. But Lord Granville had already made it clear that he was not prepared to take Lloyd's side against Nubar. Lloyd had written to the foreign secretary: 'The real question is whether Her Majesty's Government will not face the inevitable and appoint an English president of the council, or by withdrawing me deal a death-blow to reformation in this country.' Cromer comments acidly, '. . . if there was one thing in the world which Lord Granville disliked, it was "facing the inevitable".' But the Cabinet had already made up its mind that there was no question of replacing Nubar with an Englishman.

Nubar remained president of the council for four years. During this time he fought a running battle to prevent what he called a British 'administrative occupation'. In this he was fairly successful as long as he was in power but his downfall came because he dazzled himself with his own cleverness. As he ruefully remarked,

'*Les Anglais sont faciles à tromper. Mais lorsqu'on croit qu'on les a trompés, il vous arrive de recevoir un énorme coup de pied au derrière.*'

Baring distrusted Nubar but tolerated him because he considered him indispensable. Nubar could not be certain that the British intended to stay. Until 1885 Gladstone was repeating his intention to withdraw at the earliest opportunity. After this the Drummond Wolff negotiations held out the real possibility of a British evacuation resulting from a settlement with Constantinople. Nubar therefore attempted to insure himself with the National Party. But in doing so he overplayed his hand. On a visit to London in the summer of 1887, he took the opportunity of an interview with Lord Salisbury, at which Baring was present, to launch a violent attack on the British officials in Egypt, especially Vincent, the financial adviser and Baring himself. Salisbury was unmoved but Baring decided that Nubar would have to go. He did not precipitate matters; he waited for a suitable opportunity. This arose early in 1888. Following the death of the chief of police, Valentine Baker Pasha, Nubar proposed to reorganize the police along pre-1882 lines without British officers or a centralized command in Cairo. Baring decided to do battle on the vital principle of the head of the police remaining an Englishman. Nubar still held a few cards. The Khedive Tewfik was nervous about reports that his father, the ex-Khedive Ismail, was intriguing in Constantinople for his restoration and rightly surmised that Nubar had the necessary diplomatic skill to protect him. Moreover, Salisbury was urging Baring to patch up his quarrel with Nubar. In the spring of 1888 France was at the height of the Boulangiste fever and was widely expected to attempt a revival of Napoleonic glory by invading Italy, Germany or England. Salisbury wrote to Baring (17 February 1888) 'If you were to have a row in Egypt, the excited opinion of the French might turn that way. They already, I am told, look upon a war with England as the cheapest of the three alternatives open to them. They are so unreasonable, and have so much incurable hatred of England, that I should dread any very glaring exhibition of our sovereignty in Egypt at this moment.'

Nubar seized the opportunity to send an emissary to London (his son-in-law Tigrane Pasha, under-secretary of state for war) with the Khedive's approval, to make a detailed complaint about Baring to Lord Salisbury. But the response was a stern warning to Tewfik that if he expected Britain's protection he must accept its advice on all matters of internal policy. The Khedive at once realized his mistake and awaited some trivial pretext to dismiss Nubar in June 1888. Baring had already had his way concerning the command of the police.

Because Nubar had accepted office at a time when no one else would, he had consistently overestimated the strength of his position. In the last analysis, he depended on British support and as a Christian Armenian it was impossible for him to pose as a national leader whatever his achievements in resisting the British 'administrative occupation'. Baring's bland denial – 'I did nothing to hasten the downfall of Nubar Pasha' – was literally correct.

The Khedive now turned to the veteran Riaz Pasha to head the Government. Riaz eminently lacked Nubar's charm, wit, presence or subtle intelligence but he was tough and honest and a good administrator. He also had the important advantage of being a Muslim. Although Riaz was a reactionary who did not hide his contempt for the masses he held the respect of Muslim reformers such as Sheikh Mohammed Abdu, who infinitely preferred him to Nubar. Abdu had been allowed to return to Egypt from exile and had been appointed Judge at Benha in the Delta.

Wilfrid Blunt, who had been kept out of Egypt since 1884 by Tewfik and Baring, with Granville's approval, interceded success-fully with Salisbury to be allowed to return in 1888 on condition that he abstained from political activities. He also regarded Riaz as an improvement on Nubar because he felt that, as a zealous Muslim, Riaz was bound to work for the ending of the British occupation.

Certainly Riaz's relations with Baring and other British officials deteriorated steadily after he took office. Unlike Nubar, who usu-ally charmed people, while he was crossing them, Riaz quarrelled with everyone and especially the formidable Alfred Milner who had moved at the start of his career from the sub-editorship of the *Pall Mall Gazette* to be Goschen's private secretary and, on Goschen's recommendation, had been recruited by Baring to the Egyptian ministry of finance, 'nominally for administrative work, but in reality with a mission of organizing a press campaign in favour of the Egyptian occupation'.[5]

Nubar fell over the question of control of the police. Riaz lost a similar dispute over European supervision of the law courts. John Scott, a former judge of the Egyptian mixed courts, who had since had a seat in the Bombay high court, was invited to return to Egypt in 1890 to assist in improving the native tribunals. Scott wrote a report recommending the appointment of European inspectors for the native courts. The minister of justice, acting on Riaz's instructions, rejected his report but was overriden by Baring who insisted that Scott be appointed adviser to the ministry of justice. Riaz tried to counter this by appointing Colonel Kitchener head of police in the hope that he would fall out with Scott just as Clifford Lloyd's dispute with Sir Benson Maxwell led to the resignation of both. But the ruse did not work and in May 1891 Riaz resigned.

Riaz was succeeded by Mustafa Pasha Fehmi, the lukewarm foreign minister in the last Nationalist Government before the occupation, who was now to be prime minister for most of Baring's remaining fifteen years in Egypt. Wilfrid Blunt refers to him as the 'dummy prime minister', and the description is not unfair. He was scrupulous and industrious; he worked well with Baring and the other British officials but at heart they despised him for his weakness. With Fehmi at the head of the Government the protectorate's veil became transparent. Baring was the undisputed ruler of Egypt.

For most of Baring's first decade in Egypt the national movement, which had been scattered and cowed by Tel el-Kebir, remained quiescent. Jacques Berque has shown convincingly (in his *L'Egypte Impérialisme et Révolution*) that the fact that there was no organized political opposition to the occupation during this period does not mean that there was no grass-roots resistance among the fellahin and the urban masses. The alarming growth of brigandage in the countryside was one manifestation of opposition, so also was the increased popularity of local Islamic saints. But it was many years before the Egyptian people found a leader to voice their aspirations.

Although Egyptian nationalism was silent, Baring's assumption that only the Turco-Circassian class was capable of ruling Egypt did not go undisputed. Already in the summer of 1883 Wilfrid Blunt was attempting to press on Gladstone the need for a restoration of the National Party in Egypt. Gladstone's private secretary, Sir Edward Hamilton, gave Blunt the impression that Gladstone was favourable, although 'all depended on the co-operation of our officials'. With Hamilton's blessing, Blunt raised the matter with

Baring in Cairo where he stopped off on his way to India. But he got nowhere. Baring said: 'They could not restore the National Party without another revolution, and another revolution could not be ... as far as he was concerned, he should support the Khedive and the Circassians with all his power.'[6]

Blunt did not give up hope. When Salisbury took office in 1885 he believed he had a chance of persuading him, through his friend Lord Randolph Churchill, secretary of state for India and a powerful figure in the Cabinet, of the need to bring Arabi back from Ceylon. Lord Randolph himself was in favour of deposing Tewfik and formally declaring a British protectorate over Egypt.

But Salisbury had other considerations in mind and in December 1886 Lord Randolph made the fatal resignation which ended his political career. Blunt persisted with a letter to Salisbury in April 1887, setting out the case for including some Egyptian Arabs, Muslim dignitaries or fellahin, in the Government. Salisbury forwarded Blunt's proposals for comment to Baring who replied at length with a letter which reveals much of his attitude to Egypt. 'Egypt is a nondescript country. Take away the Suez Canal, the railways, the telegraph to Europe, the European colonies and trade, the capitulations, the external debt, and the mixed tribunals; make Blunt English consul-general, and a government such as he would have might work. It would be more superstitious, rapacious, ignorant, and corrupt than that of the Turkish aristocracy which he wishes to supplant, and about whom, in spite of many faults, some slight traditional trace of governing capacity still lingers. But it would not be altogether unsuitable to the population which, under these conditions, would alone remain to be governed. Amongst other reforms which would then be affected, the low-class Levantine would no longer continue "the ungodly pursuit" of keeping a public house. He would disappear, as in 1881 "as if by magic", although the magic would not, and in 1881 did not, consist in the hallowing influence of the Ulema, as Blunt fantastically imagines, but rather in a very well-founded belief on the part of the publican that he would get his head broken by some impecunious creditor to whom, in his habitual character of usurer, he had advanced money. Under present conditions, however, I should regard a proposal to make one of Blunt's friends ruler or prime minister of Egypt, as little less absurd than the nomination of some savage Red Indian chief to be governor-general of Canada.'[7]

In the chapter of *Modern Egypt* entitled 'Dwellers in Egypt', Cromer dismisses Blunt's policy of 'Egypt for the true Egyptians' on the ground that a 'true Egyptian' cannot be defined. He points out that the 1897 Census divided the 9,621,000 Ottoman subjects dwelling in Egypt into four categories – Natives (9,008,000); persons born in other parts of the Ottoman Empire – mostly Syrians and Armenians (40,000); semi-sedentary Bedouins (485,000) and Nomad Bedouins (88,000). But this was a semantic quibble. Baring's letter to Salisbury shows that he knew very well what Blunt meant by a 'true Egyptian' as did everyone else who lived in Egypt. He merely considered him incapable of self-government. A more serious criticism of Blunt's proposals, which Baring might have made but did not, was that they showed no sympathy with the Egyptian Christian Copts who certainly had as much right to be regarded as 'true Egyptians' as the Muslims. But Blunt's principal objection – that not a single representative of the overwhelming majority of the Egyptian people was to be found in the Government (in 1887) can hardly be refuted.

Baring's attitude had hardened in the few years since he came from India. His last year as Finance Member of the Indian Government had been marked by the violent controversy over the Viceroy, Lord Ripon's progressive policies, and in particular Sir Courtenay Ilbert's Criminal Jurisdiction Bill by which it was proposed to allow European British subjects throughout India to be tried for criminal offences by native magistrates and judges possessed of certain qualifications. Baring had defended the Bill in Council and in a widely noted article in the *Nineteenth Century* after his return to England. In this he said: 'It is always difficult in politics to decide whether it is wiser to anticipate a difficulty, or to await a solution until the difficulty has become a burning question. Englishmen generally prefer the latter course, because they are accustomed to it. The difficulties of parliamentary government are so great that few ministers will care to take up a difficult question until it is forced upon their attention. The consequence is that reform is often so long delayed as to prevent its producing a full measure of beneficial results when it is ultimately effected. As India is necessarily debarred from the benefit of parliamentary institutions, there can be no reason why it should not reap whatever advantages are incidental to a despotic form of government; and one of these advantages is that it is sometimes possible and desirable to anticipate a difficulty and solve it before it has attained considerable dimensions.'

He believed India was 'necessarily debarred from the benefit of parliamentary institutions' and fated to submit to a 'despotic form of government'. Nevertheless he declared himself to be on the side of those 'who have established a free press, who have promoted education, who have admitted natives more and more largely to the public services in various forms, and who have favoured the extension of local self-government'.

Though he would have regarded the possibility of self-governing independence for India as so remote as to be unworthy of consideration, he had cautiously pronounced in favour of increasing the number of Indians in positions of authority. The consequences of his twenty-four years in Egypt were exactly the contrary; the number of native Egyptians in the higher ranks of the government service declined while Englishmen and other Europeans steadily increased.

His views had not changed fundamentally. His *Nineteenth Century* article shows clearly that he favoured Lord Ripons' progressive 'Indianization' reforms less for any positive good they might achieve than for the trouble that he hoped they would avoid. The ultimate goal was the imposition of European civilization on both Indians and Egyptians and the only important question was the smoothest and most lasting way for this to be achieved. Speed was not essential; he did not expect the goal to be reached for many centuries. Meanwhile he would concentrate on what he regarded as most immediately important: financial reform and, above all, an improvement in the lot of the Indian ryot and the Egyptian fellah through a reduction in taxation and investment in public works.

After his retirement from Egypt, he expounded his paternalist philosophy in an article entitled 'The Government of Subject Races'. In this he said: 'We need not always inquire too closely what these people, who are all, nationally speaking, more or less *in statu pupillari*, themselves think is best in their own interests, although this is a point which deserves serious consideration. But it is essential that each special issue should be decided mainly with reference to what, by the light of Western knowledge and experience tempered by local consideration, we conscientiously think is best for the subject race.'

He saw representative government as an obstacle to progress for 'subject races'. As Edgar Vincent (later Lord d'Abernon) wrote: 'On the vital question of reform in India, Cromer had little sympathy with the Montagu school.* He did not deny the wisdom of associating Indians to a greater extent than heretofore with the executive government of the country, but he thought the policy of effecting legislation through the machinery of representative bodies largely composed of elected members had been pushed to greater lengths than was prudent. He was frankly nervous of these bold experiments, and doubted whether the immediate popularity gained by them would not weaken the force of the executive government and its capacity to deal with emergencies.[8]

In Egypt he saw even more reason to keep political power out of the hands of the people's representatives. In the first place there was no such thing as an Egyptian ruling class; it was only the Turkish minority who retained 'some slight traditional trace of governing capacity'. Also he considered that the European residents in Egypt (Italians, Greeks, Maltese, etc., who in 1897 numbered 113,000 or 1·16 per cent of the total population) 'represent the greater part of the wealth and intelligence, and no small proportion of the rascality and aggressive egotism of the country'. Significantly he refers to them as the 'Brahmins of Egypt'.[9] If wealth, intelligence and governing capacity were largely in non-Egyptian hands, how could the native Egyptians expect to rule themselves?

Wilfrid Blunt still had not given up all hope of bringing Baring round to his point of view. In his letter to Salisbury he had suggested some names for a 'fellah' (i.e. Egyptian and not Turkish) government which included Hassan Pasha Sherei (former governor of Minieh and president of the committee which drafted the 1882 constitution), Saad Zaghlul (later to be prime minister) and Sheikh Mohammed Abdu. The rest were prominent notables, judges, etc. Blunt had been kept out of Egypt since 1883 when he failed to move Baring, who had told him that he intended to support the Khedive and Circassians 'with all his power'.

* Edwin Montagu, the secretary of state for India who introduced the 1919 Government of India Act.

Blunt claims that ultimately Baring was forced to admit his mistake because fifteen years later he made Saad Zaghlul minister of public instruction and declared Mohammed Abdu, who became Grand Mufti of Egypt, 'to be the chief hope of Liberal Islam in Egypt'.

RESTORING EGYPT'S CREDIT

Cromer's admirers had no doubts in their minds that his greatest achievement in Egypt was financial. Contemporary writings by British authors ranging from well-informed studies by Colvin and Milner to the numerous portraits of Egypt by journalists and winter tourists, agree that under his presiding genius the country was raised from a dismal economic stagnation to an unparalleled prosperity.

Cromer himself would not have disputed this judgement; his financial reforms had been an outstanding success. He was equally certain that he had been correct in giving them priority over everything else for he held the Victorian liberal view that the moral regeneration of oriental subject races (as of the English working man) was best achieved through the promotion of the virtues of thrift and self-reliance. As long as the Egyptian masses were at the mercy of a corrupt, extravagant and exorbitant ruling class there was no hope.

In a brilliant essay, Roger Owen[1] has shown the great extent to which Lord Cromer's Indian experience influenced his policy in Egypt. In his two periods of service in India he felt he had seen the full justification of John Stuart Mill's thesis – adopted by Gladstone and absorbed by several generations of Victorian students of economics – that taxation should be as low as possible to allow money to 'fructify' in the pockets of the producing classes. In his *Social and Diplomatic Memories* Sir Rennell Rodd remarks cautiously: 'The objects to be attained during the earlier years of a terminable occupation were purely material. It could not well be otherwise. But it is the exclusively material character of our achievement throughout, to the exclusion of moral development, which might offer ground for criticism. Cromer's positive mind, though it had a humanistic side, was disposed to pass by the things of the soul.' Cromer was unaware of this deficiency since for him the civilizing influence of a thriving *laissez-faire* economic system was the only sound basis for moral development.

The first five of Cromer's twenty-four years in Egypt were marked by almost constant financial crisis. With Cromer's approval, Milner called it 'The Race Against Bankruptcy'. The problem was simple enough to diagnose. The Law of Liquidation of 1880 had placed Egypt in a position where about half the country's revenues were automatically diverted to paying its debts. Debt servicing amounted to about £3·5 million. In addition to the debt charges there was the Ottoman tribute and interest on Suez Canal shares, making a total of £4·5 million at a time when total revenues barely exceeded £9 million in a prosperous year. The consequence was that the salaries of government officials were not paid, government services were cut to the bone and public works were non-existent. By these means the Sherif Government in 1881 had actually succeeded in reducing the debt by £1 million. But it was at a fearful cost and the consequent public discontent had contributed to the Arabi revolt.

This was the situation at the start of the British occupation. Clearly, if British rule was not to be regarded by the Egyptian masses as intolerable or worse than the last years of Ismail, revenues had to be increased without raising taxation. Yet in 1883 there were new burdens on the treasury. The British Government, with the enthusiastic support of British public opinion, had decided that Egypt should pay for the military campaign which led to the occupation (including, as Milner points out, the cost of burying the British dead after Tel el-Kebir). The inhabitants of Alexandria were encouraged to present their claims for compensation for loss of property caused by the bombardment and subsequent burning of the city. In no time the total claims approached £4 million from 210 persons. In 1883 and 1884 a costly military campaign to recover the Sudan from Mahdism was still being pursued. The deficit in 1883 was £600,000, the estimated deficit for 1884 was £1,294,000 and Baring estimated that by the end of the year Egypt's new floating debt would amount to £7,800,000.

Baring and Vincent's reaction to this alarming situation was to attempt to cut expenditure even beyond the ruthless economies of the 1884 estimates. But their necessarily cheeseparing savings were clearly not going to be enough. In the summer of 1884, Lord Granville invited the Powers (France, Austria, Italy, Germany, Russia and Turkey) to attend a financial conference on Egypt in

London. But the other Powers refused to accept the British proposals to lighten Egypt's financial burdens and the conference
broke up in a heated atmosphere.

The Gladstone Cabinet, dispirited and divided over Irish and
Egyptian policy, was expiring slowly. The Whigs still favoured a
prolonged occupation of Egypt and the establishment of exclusive
English control but the dominant Gladstone wing wanted above
all an accommodation with the Powers. When the French made
some fresh financial counter-proposals early in 1885 the British
government at once responded. In return for the permanent
continuation of the Caisse de la Dette and an international loan
guaranteed by all the Powers, instead of Britain alone, France
was prepared to allow the Egyptian government to use any revenue
surplus for administration rather than debt repayment and to tax
the coupon for two years. On this basis a London convention
which regulated Egypt's international financial status for nearly
twenty years, was signed in March 1885. In this the Powers also
took the important step of recognizing the principle that their
nationals resident in Egypt should pay the same taxes as Egyptians
(although it was many years before this principle was put into
practice).

As the French ambassador wrote triumphantly to Jules Ferry,
the premier and foreign minister: 'It implies the eventual supervision of Egyptian finances by Europe. It means the start of
international control for Egypt.' Incorrectly, he also deduced that
it would mean an early British evacuation.

For the same reasons, the convention was highly distasteful to
Baring and the other British officials in Egypt. Baring never
ceased to complain about the perpetuation of international control.
Nevertheless, the convention brought certain immediate advantages
– notably in a £9,000,000 loan for which Egypt was obliged to
set aside the reasonable sum of £315,000 annually to service the
debt – 'something quite unheard of in the history of Egyptian
finance', as Milner remarked. In Ismail's time, not only would
the rate of interest have been much higher but Egypt would
have been fortunate to receive more than two-thirds of the loan in
cash.

Nearly £4,000,000 of the loan was earmarked for payment of the
Alexandria indemnities and a similar sum to cover the budget
deficits of the past two years and the expected deficit of the coming

year. This still left £1,000,000 for irrigation which, as we shall see, was an exceptionally sound investment.*

The loan relieved the Egyptian Government of all its immediate difficulties. The radical amendments to the Law of Liquidation accepted by the Powers also greatly eased the problem of balancing future budgets. Nevertheless, Egypt's financial situation remained extremely delicate; the country still had to recover from the years of turmoil and the effects of the war. The French had insisted on a stipulation in the 1885 convention that if Baring should fail to bring about financial equilibrium within three years an international commission would supersede him and take over the management of the country. Britain's control of Egypt was important but it was not worth a European war.

Baring and Vincent succeeded; the 1886–7 budget actually showed a small surplus of £20,000. But to do this they had to resort to a series of highly unconventional financial measures – which today would be denounced as gimmicks. In one year the payment of salaries of government officials was postponed from 31 December to 1 January in order to include the December salaries in the next year's budget. A much more important device was the institution of payments for exemption from military service. Families were allowed to pay between £40 to £100 to keep their sons at home. By calling up 262,000 men in 1886 about £250,000 was raised in that year. It was mainly the wealthy who paid but some of the small farmers scraped together their £40. The Government in later years was not above increasing the call-up on the bogus excuse of exceptional frontier unrest in order to raise more revenue.

The tax on imported Greek and Turkish tobacco was about three times that on Egyptian tobacco. On the plea that this amounted to heavy protection and contravened the principle of free trade, Baring first had the Egyptian tax sharply increased and then actually limited tobacco cultivation in Egypt to 1,500 acres. Tobacco customs receipts rose to £1,200,000 in 1890 but at the cost of the destruction of Egypt's promising tobacco industry.

Another measure – which had been specifically licensed by the London convention – was to sell off the rich Daira and Domains

---

* Milner went further: 'The history of that million is one of the most marvellous chapters even in the romantic history of Egyptian finance.' *England in Egypt*, p. 228.

lands (formerly Ismail's property, amounting to nearly 1,000,000 acres). This brought in substantial revenues for a time but deprived the Egyptian state of a permanent source of wealth.

All these measures could only be justified by the immediate overriding need for solvency. General economic recovery was painfully slow; between 1884 and 1887 revenue from direct and indirect taxation increased only marginally in spite of the subjection of foreign nationals to certain taxes for the first time. The odium of the economic squeeze, which amounted to a throttle, fell principally on the young Edgar Vincent whose task was to deny funds to every government department except irrigation. He received vital assistance from Gerald Fitzgerald who had come to Egypt to take charge of the accounts department in the last days of Ismail and remained at his post for the first three years of the occupation. As Colvin remarks: 'His task was singularly difficult. He had not only to extract light from the almost visible darkness of Coptic accountancy, but he had to do so under the eyes of a group of very competent French inspectors of finance, who, in one or other capacity, were employed in Egypt, both before and after the occupation. Partly, it may be, from national pique at seeing a department in British hands which they regarded as peculiarly their own; partly, perhaps, from the jealousy of specialists; partly because they honestly believed that the French system of public accounts was the best of all possible systems – these gentlemen were apt to make themselves merry at the cost of Mr Fitzgerald and his reforms.'[2]

With revenue maintained only through a variety of financial expedients and no possible further pruning of expenditure there was no possibility of remission of taxation in the early years of the British occupation. Instead Baring and Vincent concentrated on the aim of substituting paid labour for the *corvée* or forced labour.

In a country such as Egypt there are strong arguments in favour of the principle of the *corvée*. As the British consul in Alexandria in 1871 wrote: 'When it is considered that the maintenance of canals at their proper level is the great desideratum here, without which the country would become a desert, it does not seem to me that there is injustice in making all contribute their share to what is so essential for the welfare of the country.' But like all forms of compulsory national service, if it is not to arouse deep resentment, it has to be equitably applied. In Egypt during the 1880s it most emphatically was not. William Willcocks was horrified by what he saw when he was sent to supervise the clearing of the Rayah Beherah Canal in the winter of 1883. 'It was being silt-cleared by the *corvée*, or the gangs of forced labourers, invariably the poorest and most helpless in the land, who for six months in the year were compelled to clean canals and repair banks. Egypt existed on their work. They received no payment except in blows; they provided their own tools, carrying wet earth on their bare backs when they were too poor to provide baskets; they brought their own sacks full of dry biscuits, on which they existed, they slept out of doors on the bare ground in all weathers, with the bare sky above their heads both night and day. The Government did absolutely nothing for them except punish and imprison them when their stock of food failed and they ran away to beg or steal. In the Delta their lives were made bitter by feeling that all this hard labour benefited them but little; for while they were digging and clearing the canals, their rich neighbours were pumping up the water and irrigating cotton, while their own fields had to wait for the Nile flood. The Turkish pashas never sent a man to the *corvée* off their estates, the European protected subjects were just as bad, except that they made mean excuses which the Turks scorned to do.'[3]

The *corvée* was inhumane and inequitable; as a system it was also already in decline. In a special memorandum on the subject in 1886, Scott-Moncrieff pointed out that owing to the growth of large estates, the drift of the rural population to the towns and other factors, the number available for the *corvée* had declined from 634,000 in 1848 to 376,029 in 1882. Still harsher measures would be needed to obtain the necessary unpaid labour from the diminishing pool at a time, as we shall see, when the Government was aiming to abolish the normal method of coercion – the *kurbaj* or whip.

In the summer of 1886 Nubar, with strong support from his British advisers, proposed that the remaining £250,000 intended for a reduction in the land tax be used to replace part of the *corvée* with hired labour. Scott-Moncrieff at once set about doing this and in 1886 the number called out compulsorily was reduced by more than half.

A majority of the Debt Commissioners had agreed to this measure but the Governments of the Powers, led by France and Russia, protested. They were in a strong position because there was no doubt that the London convention had been contravened. However, Baring hit back by announcing the call-out of the *corvée* in full. 'The result was that public opinion, both in England and Egypt, was moved;'[4] and France, reluctant to bear responsibility for the retention of such an unpopular system, gave way on the principle of eliminating the *corvée* but insisted in return on placing the whole of Public Works expenditure under the control of the Debt Commissioners. This the British Government refused, and the controversy raged for two more years with Scott-Moncrieff at one point handing in his resignation and being persuaded to withdraw it by Baring.

Lord Salisbury, now in power in England, gave Baring his support to the extent of agreeing to the postponement of the payment of interest on the British Government's Suez Canal shares to provide the Egyptian Government with the funds to dispense with *corvée* labour. France had been outmanoeuvred and the principle of abolition of the *corvée* accepted, although it was not until 1892 that enough funds could be found to eliminate the system entirely. Even then the French Government was able to use its powers in the international control to exact conditions for the use of revenues for this purpose.

British contemporary writers on this period have generally agreed with Lady Gwendolen Cecil that 'France's obstruction' was 'inspired, as it was held to be, by pure spite'.[5] There may have been an element of petty jealousy in the attitude of the French Government; it may also be explained by its natural desire to keep the international control alive. As the occupying power, with some responsibility for the welfare of the Egyptians, Britain's view was certain to be different. But it is worth pointing out both that France was not proposing that the £250,000 involved in the dispute should be paid to the bond-holders but used to reduce the land tax, and that the strongest argument used by Nubar and his advisers in favour of eliminating the *corvée* was the practical one that the system was rapidly becoming unworkable anyway.

Gradually Egypt's financial situation improved. When Edgar Vincent retired from Egypt in 1889 he was confident that the country could easily surmount the problems caused by an exceptionally low Nile and the increase in the army. In his comments on the 1889 budget he said, 'I may state my conviction that it would require a succession of bad years to place the present financial situation in any serious peril.'

From 1890 onwards, Cromer was able to pursue the financial policy on which he had set his heart: the reduction of taxation. By the time of his retirement in 1907 direct taxation had been reduced by £2,000,000 and most indirect taxes and customs duties (except on tobacco) had been abolished or reduced. Cromer was able to say: 'There cannot be a doubt that the whole Egyptian population is now very lightly taxed;'[4] although he admitted taxation was unfairly distributed, because 'the urban population do not bear their fair share of the public burdens'.

Despite the cuts in taxation, economic expansion allowed revenue to increase from £8,935,000 in 1883 to £E15,337,000 in 1906. The Gladstonian policy of extreme budgetary prudence was pursued and by 1906 the aggregate surplus of the Egyptian treasury amounted to over £27,500,000. Under Cromer's guidance Egyptian Governments stubbornly held in check the clamorous demands for increased expenditure from the various departments. 'It was clear that, as a wave of European civilization was to sweep over the land, all the paraphernalia of civilization – that is to say, its judges and law-courts, its hospitals, its schools, its reformation for juvenile offenders and so on – would sooner or later have to be introduced; but the main point to be borne in mind was this: that, in introducing all these reforms, Egypt should not be allowed to slip back into the slough of bankruptcy from which it had been so hardly and so recently rescued.'[5] Thus, although public works expenditure was increased after 1890 it was financed almost entirely from revenues rather than borrowing.

Egypt was well out of the red as far as its Government's current account was concerned. But on the general question of public debt Cromer had less reason to congratulate himself. In 1883 the debt in the hands of the public amounted to £96,457,000. In 1906 it had fallen to £87,416,000. Thus in 23 years of steadily increasing prosperity the public debt had been reduced by slightly over £9,000,000. This corresponded almost exactly to the size of the guaranteed loan of 1885 which had been primarily intended to pay off the costs of intervention. In 1887 Drummond Wolff had made a moving appeal for reduction in the interest on Egypt's public debt. 'It would be a blot on any permanent arrangement if some attempts were not made to alleviate the heavy burden entailed on the fellahin by the debt which crushed their industry and often deprived them of their property and means of livelihood.' Drummond Wolff estimated that no less than one half of the revenue 'though drawn from the labour and property of the Egyptian people, was encashed by foreigners and spent abroad. If the debt had been run up by wars, or extravagance sanctioned by the people, it might be right to continue to saddle them with this intolerable load. But they had no voice in the matter, and were passive instruments, almost beasts of burden, in the hands of the rulers, whose vices, ambition and waste had accumulated this mass of debt.'

Very little was done to lighten the 'intolerable load'. It was not that taxation continued to be extortionate; Cromer had some justification by 1907 for his claim that 'the whole Egyptian people is now very lightly taxed'. But twenty years after Ismail's abdication the Egyptians were still bearing the burden of his extravagance and its unscrupulous exploitation by foreign financiers. Half of all the country's revenues could not be used for vital public expenditure for the country's benefit. As Lord Milner remarked: 'The spectacle of Egypt, with her treasury full of money, yet not allowed to realize that money for an object which, on a moderate calculation, should add 20 per cent to the wealth of the country, is as distressing as it is ludicrous.'

The 1880 Law of Liquidation and the 1885 London convention meant the continuation of international financial control and as long as Britain was not prepared to risk a European war over this principle, it would be maintained. It was only when France was ready to bargain its position in Egypt, which had only the negative advantage of limiting British supremacy, in return for the more solid benefit of British recognition of French hegemony in North Africa, that this 'ludicrous' situation could be modified. This was achieved as part of the Anglo-French agreement of 1904 – the original *entente cordiale*.

When the Caisse de la Dette was founded in 1876, its function was limited to receiving certain assigned revenues on behalf of the bond-holders. Since then its powers had grown considerably. On behalf of the Powers its members claimed to control the execution of all the complex international agreements governing the country's finances. No new loan could be issued without their assent and no part of the general reserve fund could be used without their sanction. All assigned revenues were paid directly to them without passing through the ministry of finances. Even the receipts of the railways, telegraphs, and the port of Alexandria were paid to the Caisse after the deduction of expenses.

All this was changed by the Anglo-French agreement of 1904 which re-established the principle that the Caisse should be limited to receiving certain assigned revenues on behalf of the bond-holders and would have no right to interfere in the general administration of the country. Its consent would no longer be required for the issue of new loans and it would have no power to limit the Government's administrative expenditure. As part of the agreement the entire funded debt was to be liquidated by 1912.

The Caisse was allowed to linger on as a vestigial remnant until this date with the six commissioners 'eating the bread of idleness', as Colvin remarks, continuing to receive their handsome salaries from the Egyptian revenues. The consent of the other Powers was theoretically required for this part of the Anglo-French agreement but since France and Britain between them held almost all the Egyptian debt there was little they could do. By the outbreak of the First World War Egypt had finally escaped from the financial bondage of Ismail's debts.

ECONOMIC STRATEGY

Under Cromer's aegis, the Egyptian state acquired a reputation for financial reliability. His influence on the country's general economic development is much more controversial. Egyptians have accused him of maintaining their country in a state of typical colonial independence. According to this view, a truly independent Egypt might have established an industrial base and set out to become the 'Japan of Africa' in the nineteenth century instead of today.

Egypt differed from almost every other country in Africa and Asia in having made a start with industrialization in the early nineteenth century. Mohammed Aly's prime concern in establishing factories as state monopolies was to supply his armed forces with weapons and equipment but, just as Egypt's so-called military factories today turn out a variety of non-military goods, Mohammed Aly's factories produced machine tools, pumps, cloth, paper and glass as well as arms. These industries were heavily protected as they were in every other industrial nation except England at that time but Mohammed Aly, although strong and virtually independent at the height of his power, was not strong enough to maintain the protection against the opposition of the powers. When he accepted defeat and the limitation of his army in 1841, he also accepted the ruin of his industries because the enforcement of the Anglo-Turkish commercial convention of 1838 meant that cheaper and better quality British manufactures could enter Egypt with an eight per cent *ad valorem* duty only.

'Once more it is necessary to repeat that Egypt's economic destiny was shared by a very large part of the globe; it is also necessary to repeat that the colonizing process began not in 1882 but in 1841. Cotton was not an English innovation; nor was irrigation; nor was de-industrialization; nor were the Capitulations and Mixed Courts; nor, above all, was foreign indebtedness. To a much greater extent than he would have cared to admit, Cromer merely carried on Ismail's work, often using the same methods.'[1]

Cromer therefore did not destroy Egyptian heavy industry for it had disappeared many years before he arrived in the country. Mohammed Aly's industries did not survive long enough to take root. The Pasha opened some technical schools and sent Egyptian students for training in Europe. But his policies were not pursued long enough for any native class of skilled artisans, managers or entrepreneurs to be formed. Moreover, under Mohammed Aly and his successors there was a steady influx of foreigners who, under the protection of the Capitulations, came to control the commercial and financial life of the country. The interests of these politically influential foreign communities – many of whom made a living through the importing of European manufactures – were against the growth of Egyptian industry. Thus it was that although, as we have seen, Egypt under Ismail had many of the attributes of a developed nineteenth-century economy, such as railways, telegraphs and insurance companies, it was still more of an appendage than part of Europe, as Ismail chose to believe.

Cromer was a Liberal imperialist and as such his economics were Gladstonian while his politics were closer to Lord Rosebery. Throughout his career he was an ardent, if not a fanatical, free trader. As finance member of Lord Ripon's Cabinet he had supported the imposition of free trade on India. Apart from the classical argument that protection always fosters inefficient industries and raises prices for the consumer (in this case the Indian ryots), Baring maintained that the imposition of protective tariffs on imported British cotton textiles would inevitably cause friction between England and India. He acknowledged that no Indian could be expected to understand this logic: 'There are probably very few natives in India, and there are not many Anglo-Indians, who believe in the advantage of free trade as far as India is concerned,' he wrote in 1883. 'They fail to grasp the conclusive, but occasionally subtle, arguments which prove the fallacy of protection. We were, however, quite justified in imposing free trade upon India, because there could not be a shadow of doubt that the adoption of that measure was in the true interests of the natives of India.' As always, the government of subject races meant giving them what was good for them regardless of their opinions. Moreover, the argument was clinched by the example of Britain which had adopted free trade with such obvious success.

Cromer took precisely the same attitude in Egypt. When in 1895 an Englishman named Wilks secured a concession from the public works department to build a small cotton mill in Egypt, without reference to Cromer, he wrote to the foreign secretary: 'The present enterprise will be on a small scale but should it succeed it is probable both that the works of the company now being formed will be extended and that competitors will spring up. In that case the establishment of factories here will obviously produce serious consequences both in respect of the finances of Egypt and the huge trade in cotton goods now carried on between England and this country.'

In Egyptian eyes this seems damning enough. In his reference to the 'serious consequences' to the finances of Egypt, Cromer had a good point. Imported cotton manufactures paid an eight per cent customs duty and the new mill in Egypt would be enjoying this degree of protection. The larger its output the greater the loss to the Egyptian treasury in revenues; in 1894 customs receipts from imported cottons amounted to about £150,000. It was on these grounds that Cromer was able to persuade successive Egyptian Governments to impose an eight per cent excise duty on home-produced cotton manufactures. But Cromer's alarm at the effect of the new industry on the 'huge trade in cotton goods now carried on between England and this country' looks like a blatant piece of economic imperialism. It seems to bear out the charge made so often by later critics of Cromer's regime, especially Marxists, that 'Egypt as a whole became a vast cotton plantation for the factories of Lancashire'.[2]

Cromer did everything in his power to discourage the establishment of a cotton textile industry in Egypt despite his knowledge, as in India, that public opinion was almost unanimously against him. Apart from persuading the Egyptian Government to impose the countervailing duty there was no direct action he could take against foreign businessmen who wanted to set up textile factories, but in view of his awesome authority in Egypt his moral disapproval had a powerful and discouraging effect. There is good reason to believe, however, that if Cromer had remained strictly neutral in his attitude and no excise duty had been imposed, most of the textile factories that were established would have gone to the wall. This happened to the Anglo-Egyptian Spinning and Weaving Company which never managed to make a profit although the excise duty was waived for five years. The fact is that for Egypt to industrialize itself in the late nineteenth or early twentieth centuries would have required a vigorous and comprehensive policy of protection for native industry and industrial training for Egyptians. To this Cromer and his associates were most emphatically opposed.

Cromer was, above all, a creature of his age. His attitude was based on the assumption that while imperial races were suited to industry their subject races were not. 'Given that Egypt is by nature an agricultural country, it follows that industrial training would only cause the neglect of agriculture while it would divert the Egyptians from the land – both of which would be a disaster for the nation.' It may be said that this attitude survived Cromer by many years and still exists today. It is certainly regrettable that he did nothing to encourage Egyptian industry but it is not surprising.

Today it is generally appreciated that there is no solution to Egypt's economic problems in agriculture alone; in Cromer's time this was only partially understood by very few. Cromer himself had an inkling of it towards the end of his career in Egypt. In his report for 1905 he acknowledges that over the past ten or fifteen years even the remaining light industries in certain quarters of Cairo had given way to little shops selling European bric à brac. In the same report he advocated the need for the expansion of technical education: '... there is a rapidly growing need for skilled labour of various kinds, and scope for the development of various useful industries. The population of the country is rapidly increasing, and though the area under cultivation is being steadily extended, it is probable that a growing proportion of the people must find employment in other occupations.'

Even in the tense years of the 'race against bankruptcy' the underlying assumption of Baring, Milner and their associates was that Egypt was fundamentally prosperous and only required good financial management. In 1884 Scott-Moncrieff wrote after travelling throughout Egypt: 'The Egyptian fellah, in spite of kourbash and conscription, and corvée, cruelly heavy taxation, and a total absence of justice in the land is, I am bound to say, a fatter, jollier, better-to-do individual than the average Indian ryot, for whose benefit earnest, high-minded men have been racking their brains and giving their best years for more than half a century.'

Once the financial problem had been solved there were no

limits to Cromer's optimism about Egypt's future. In 1891 he was writing: 'in the nature of things there is really nothing to prevent Egypt in our grandchildren's time from being one of the most prosperous countries in the world.'

Yet, doubts began to creep in towards the end. Pests and flooding due to over-irrigation with inadequate drainage were causing an alarming drop in cotton yields per acre. In 1882, with 6,800,000 people, Egypt could be said to be underpopulated. But the growth was swift under the British occupation, reaching 9,715,000 in 1897, 11,287,000 in 1907, and 12,751,000 in 1917. Although Cromer wrote, in *Modern Egypt* (Vol. II, p. 453): 'The finance minister had not, as in India, to deal with a congested population, of whom a large percentage were in normal times living on the verge of starvation. He never had to refer to the pages of Malthus or Mill, of Ricardo or Bastiat', it is probable that this passage, like much of the rest of this book, was written some years before Cromer's retirement. By 1907 the dangers of overpopulation in Egypt were apparent to even the most optimistic.

The Cromerian solution to the Egyptian land problem was the multiplication of small-holdings. He agreed with Lord Dufferin that peasant indebtedness to foreign creditors was 'one of the most distressing subjects connected with the present social condition of the country', and he believed that the best way of avoiding this was to have as many small proprietors as possible who would not need to fall into the hands of the Jewish, Syrian and Greek moneylenders. 'The arguments in favour of small-holdings apply with somewhat special force in Egypt. Owing to the fact that there is not generally any serious congestion of the population, competition rents have not as yet resulted in any grave strife between landlords and tenants. Nevertheless, as the population increases, and the area of cultivable but uncultivated land diminishes, there will be, to say the least, a risk that issues will eventually arise between landlords and tenants somewhat similar to those which have caused so much trouble in other countries – notably in India and in Ireland. The best way to postpone this strife, as also to mitigate its intensity should it eventually prove to be inevitable, will be to avoid the adoption of any measures which will tend towards the disappearance of the small proprietors.'[3]

Cromer's hopes were therefore that while he ruled Egypt the amount of rural debt would be reduced and the number of small proprietors – usually defined as those owning less than five feddans – would increase. In *Modern Egypt* – his 'final report' – he says: 'There can be no doubt that these efforts have been crowned with success. On 1 January 1907, only 665,226 acres were held by 6021 foreign landowners, as against 4,765,546 acres held by 1,224,560 Egyptian proprietors. Of the latter, the holdings of 1,081,348 proprietors were of less than 5 acres in extent; the holdings of 132,198 varied from 5 to 50 acres, thus leaving 11,054 proprietors of more than 50 acres.'

This situation was not nearly as satisfactory as at first appears; Cromer was telling the truth but not the whole truth.* In the first place he does not point out that although the number of small proprietors and the total area they owned apparently increased between 1896 and 1906 by about 60 per cent and 30 per cent respectively, they still owned less than 25 per cent of the total cultivated area, whereas the 10,000 proprietors with more than 50 feddans still owned more than 40 per cent. In other words, after 24 years of Cromerism 80 per cent of those who owned land in Egypt possessed less than one-quarter of the whole, while at the other end of the scale one per cent owned more than two-fifths. Secondly, the increase in the number of small landowners was partially deceptive. New survey methods had shown that many small estates which were in fact already divided had hitherto been registered in a single name to avoid payment of registration fees.

The same applies to rural indebtedness – which Cromer does not mention in *Modern Egypt* except in general terms. In his report for 1895 he claimed that a highly satisfactory state of affairs had been achieved in that out of a total of 4,471,000 acres owned by 661,000 Egyptians, only 395,000 acres were mortgaged for a total of £7,323,000 and of this 71 per cent was due by the large proprietors with more than 50 acres. However, in his report of the following year, Cromer admitted that 'in addition to this registered debt, there was, without doubt, a certain amount of unregistered debt, notably due by small proprietors'. This was much more considerable than Cromer implies. In 1913 the total indebtedness of small proprietors was estimated at £E16 million. Moreover anyone who knew the state of rural Egypt intimately was aware

* 'Want of accuracy, which easily degenerates into untruthfulness, is the main characteristic of the oriental mind.' Cromer, *Modern Egypt*, 11, p. 146.

that debts were still the deepest worry of the fellahin. In an interview with the *Egyptian Standard* published on 20 October 1908, Prince Hussein Pasha Kamel, the Khedive's uncle who was later to succeed him, said of the fellah: 'He passes his life burdened with debts, his wages do not exceed the amount of taxes and the interest on his debts. He is continually obliged to run into debt at exorbitant interest, in order to meet his agricultural needs at the proper moment; and as a consequence of this difficult situation, of his lack of money, and of the large number who depend on him, the peasant remains in a sea of trouble from which he can find no means of saving himself.'

The great majority of the fellahin were then, as they still are today, among the most wretched of the earth. Their poverty is very little due to ignorance for as farmers they are skilled and hardworking but only a small minority (that is those who owned more than five acres) have ever had a hope of accumulating enough capital to take advantage of progress in agricultural techniques and until recently there was little attempt to help them. Most of their tools are the same as were used four thousand years ago as can be seen from the paintings on the walls of the Pharaohs' tombs. The typical fellah lives in a two- or three-room hovel of mud brick dried in the sun where the family sleeps for most of the year with its animals. These buffaloes, donkeys and camels are as precious to them as their children and the authorities' attempt to requisition them in the 1914–18 war was a major cause of the violent outbreak which followed. If the fellah does not actually starve in an Asian-type famine he is undernourished on an ill-balanced diet of maize, rice and a few vegetables and he almost certainly suffers from at least one debilitating disease. In these circumstances it is no paradox that he is conservative and suspicious of change and clings to his rural and Islamic religious traditions. Radicalism only comes with new hope which was rarely offered in the past. In his summary of the fellah's character Judge Marshall remarks: 'He is usually devoid of gratitude to man: he reserves that for God' but it is difficult to see what cause he has to be grateful to either.

In economic rather than human terms, however, Egypt was undoubtedly prospering at this time and it remains true that 'real per capita income during the first decade of this century was higher than at any time in modern Egyptian history, with the possible exception of the early nineteen-twenties'.[4] By the modern standard of 'growth rate' the economic consequences of Cromerism were highly successful. Egypt had become more than ever dependent upon a single crop but this must be seen in the light of the country's comparative advantage in cotton growing, which was so great that there would have been a substantial loss in national income if more land had been used to grow wheat and other cereals. Only the deliberate suppression of Egypt's flourishing tobacco industry for the sake of an immediate gain in customs revenues is much more dubious.

The charges against Cromer's economic policies are essentially negative: that he failed to diversify the economy, or to arrest the increasingly uneven distribution of wealth. But it is hardly necessary to point out that little was understood of development economics in Cromer's day. National income statistics, which even today are often misinterpreted and misapplied, were then unknown and maximization of profits was the sole criterion of economic success. Malthus' warnings of the dangers of population explosion had been swept aside by the tide of Victorian optimism which, at least in industrial societies, was broadly justified. Free trade was the accepted dogma among influential Englishmen; heretics were few and Cromer was certainly not one of them. On the face of it the accusation that Cromer's first concern was to run Egypt for the benefit of the Lancashire textile magnates would seem to be justified – especially in view of his family connections with high finance. But it is most improbable that he saw the matter in those terms. With the ineffable self-assurance of the Victorian proconsul, he knew what was right for the people of Egypt. If it happened also to benefit Lancashire then so much the better.

THE WATER ENGINEERS

In present-day Egypt the direct public references to the British occupation have all been removed by the nationalist tide. Only in Zamalek – the spacious residential quarter of Cairo on a Nile island – an unpretentious street is still named Avenue Willcocks.

William Willcocks, the kind-hearted but opinionated eccentric who stood up to Cromer, was one of the small group of Anglo-Indian engineers who in restoring and extending Egypt's hydraulic system created the most enduring monument to the occupation.

From the beginning, Lord Dufferin had been convinced of the primary importance of irrigation and, as we have seen, successfully enticed Colin Scott-Moncrieff from his liner homeward-bound from India to become director of irrigation. In his 1883 report Dufferin noted: 'Egypt is so similar to many of the irrigated districts in India that it is only natural to turn to that country for advice.'* Before the end of 1884 Scott-Moncrieff had been joined by Major Justin Ross RE, Major Hanbury Brown RE, William Willcocks and E. P. Foster, who had all been trained in 'the best of schools' – the public works department of India. They were later joined by William Garstin and 'these six men, together with Col. Western and Mr Reid, who between them restored the barrage, have been the saviours of Egyptian irrigation'.[1]

Herodotus' aphorism that 'Egypt is the gift of the Nile' still bears repetition. The Pharaohs had been enthusiastic hydraulic engineers; some of them showed creative genius. The fleshpots of Egypt were intermittently replenished and preserved by the succession of alien rulers who followed the Persian conquest in the sixth century BC but agriculture fell into stagnation and ruin from the fourteenth century onwards under the Mamlouks and Ottoman

---

* He was thinking of Northern India in particular where 'a system of canals exists far greater than in Egypt, and here, too, irrigation is practised when the heat is the greatest and the canals at their lowest'. (Scott-Moncrieff, 'Irrigation in Egypt', *The Nineteenth Century*, February 1885.)

Turks. The private ownership of land disappeared, the canals were allowed to silt up and the cultivated area rapidly shrank. The Egypt that Napoleon's expedition discovered was half-starved and miserable, with a population that had fallen from six or seven million in Roman times to two and a half million.

Under Mohammed Aly and his successors the situation was considerably restored. Individual land ownership was revived by degrees. With the great expansion of commercial cotton cultivation, river banks were raised and strengthened to protect summer crops from flood water, Delta canals were deepened and small dams built across them to raise the water-level and in 1833 the foundations were laid of the two great barrages over the Rosetta and Damietta branches of the Nile at the point where they divide just north of Cairo. The architect was the French engineer, Mougel Bey, and his object was to regulate the entire hydraulic system of the Delta. Under Said and Ismail, over 8,000 miles of new canals were dug; the cultivated area increased from 3,050,000 feddans* in 1813 to 4,743,000 in 1877, cotton exports increased from 350,000 cantars* in 1850 to 3 million in 1880. The population had reached 6,800,000 by 1882.

Nevertheless there had been a severe setback in the last years of Ismail and under the Dual Control, when the irrigation and drainage systems had been allowed to fall into disrepair.

Mougel Bey's Nile barrages were 'practically useless' when Scott-Moncrieff first examined them. Mougel Bey's great design had never been completed: the Rosetta branch barrage had never been supplied with gates while the one over the Damietta branch had been virtually abandoned after a series of accidents. Whereas the original intention had been to raise an additional head of water of four and a half metres, the most that could be got out of it was half a metre.

As soon as his Anglo-Indian engineers had arrived, Scott-Moncrieff divided the country into five circles of irrigation (three in the Delta and two in Upper Egypt) in which each inspector of irrigation was given wide powers to take action at his own discretion.

They set about unblocking and enlarging old canals, cutting new drainage canals and disentangling the lines of irrigation from

* 1 feddan = 1.038 acres.
  1 cantar = 99 lbs (approx.).

the lines of drainage which had become confused over the years. By altering the system of regulators they were able to reduce the size of the silt deposit on the canal beds and the need for *corvée* labour to clear them.

When Scott-Moncrieff examined the Rosetta barrage shortly after his arrival in Egypt, he was assured by the local French and Egyptian engineers that it was so unsound he had better have nothing to do with it. 'It had been so long neglected that timbers were rotten, iron was rusted. There were no appliances or tools, and attached to it there was a large establishment of superannuated and incompetent men, who for years had done little besides drawing their pay, a duty which they performed with praiseworthy regularity.'[2]

Nevertheless, Sir Colin and his newly-arrived colleagues decided that it was so important to gain control over the Delta irrigation that they would either make an effort to repair the barrage or build a new one. In January 1884 he put Willcocks in charge at the barrage; Nubar Pasha, who was prime minister, found the modest £25,000 which was needed to begin repairs on the Rosetta barrage by cementing over the cracks and replacing the rotten timbers. Gradually the water level was raised to seven feet two inches. Disaster threatened at any moment as the pressure rose with the closing of the gates and the cracks threatened to re-open. Of the three great canals leading northwards from the barrage to irrigate the Delta only the centre one had been properly complete. But in 1884, for the first time in many years, this contained seven feet of water in the low flood months of May and June. As a result the cotton crop increased by 30,000 tons over the previous record. With the price at £35 a ton this meant an extra £1,050,000 'which was not a bad return for the £26,000 we had spent' as Sir Colin drily remarks.

The experiment was repeated with even greater success the following year. Scott-Moncrieff therefore decided to repair the two barrages entirely from their foundations and install gates for the first time in the Damietta branch. He had Baring's support and the money became available from the guaranteed loan which was part of the financial settlement of 1885.

The work proceeded with an army of fellahin workers at a forced pace to beat the flood. In 1887 Scott-Moncrieff conceived the idea of using electric lighting to work at night. He cabled the firm of Frank Albright in Chelmsford and received a satisfactory reply within three hours. The Rosetta branch was completed in 1889 and the Damietta branch in 1891, at a total cost of about £460,000. The increase in the cotton crops was worth about £2,500,000.

Scott-Moncrieff had good grounds for satisfaction, especially as when he started 'there was a host of jealous foreigners delighted to see an English failure'. He sought out the aged Mougel Bey, who was living in poverty-stricken obscurity, brought him to Egypt to see the completion of his great conception and browbeat the Egyptian Government into giving him a pension.

The repair of the barrages was not the only major irrigation scheme carried out in the early years of the British occupation, although it was the most dramatic and the most obvious in its beneficial effects. The great eastern Delta canal was dug and the one on the west repaired. The bed of the Nile above the barrages was actually moved about a quarter of a mile east so that the current would flow more directly on to them. At the same time smaller-scale operations throughout the cultivated areas improved the system of bringing the water to the fields and taking it away. When Scott-Moncrieff left Egypt in 1892 about one thousand miles of drains had been built, while in Upper Egypt, where basin irrigation (i.e. only during the flood period) was still in use,* the river banks were raised and canals widened and deepened to ensure that even in years of low flood the water reached the fields. The Zifta barrage on the Damietta branch of the Nile in the Delta and the Assiut barrage in Upper Egypt were built. Like the Cairo barrages, these did not actually store water but raised the water level to feed the large canals that depended upon them.

Even before the repair of the Cairo barrages and Scott-Moncrieff's departure from Egypt in 1892, it had become apparent that more irrigation water supplies would be needed. Willcocks spent 1890 to 1894 examining the possibilities of building reservoir dams across the Nile in Upper Egypt. In 1894 he presented his final report which proposed building a dam across the granite base of the First Cataract at the Nile, capable of storing 85 billion cubic feet of water.

This proposal aroused a storm of opposition – principally from

* And remained so until the building of the High Dam in the 1960s.

British and French archaeologists who pointed out that it would
drown the great temple of Philae. However, a meeting on the
proposed site of French and English archaeologists and engineers
under the chairmanship of Sir William Garstin, under-secretary
of the ministry of public works, agreed by majority vote that
the dam should be built provided an exhaustive examination of the
ruins were made; that a watertight wall should be built around the
island and the height of the dam be reduced. All these conditions,
except the second, were fulfilled. The height that Willcocks had
planned was lowered so that the reservoir held less than half its
original capacity. However, within a few years it was discovered
that this would not provide enough water to irrigate some desert
land at Kom Ombo north of Aswan that had been purchased by a
company especially formed by the English financier Sir Ernest
Cassel. Despite the Government's promises and against the opposition of all archaeologists (as well as Willcocks*) the dam was
raised between 1907 and 1910 to increase its capacity by over two
billion tons.

Sir Ernest Cassel was in a powerful position because it was he
who had made the building of the dam possible. When the prospect
was first raised seriously in 1894 England and Egypt were about
to embark on the reconquest of the Sudan. Even with the economi-
cal Kitchener in command the difficulties of raising the money for
this were great enough without also building a giant dam. However, Cromer soon shrewdly understood that the increased national
income from the dam was essential if Egypt was to pay for the
administration and development of the Sudan. (England, as we
have seen, was not prepared to pay at this stage.) It was in vain
that Milner pleaded in his *England in Egypt* (p. 321), published in
1892, that 'Indirectly, Great Britain has made a great deal of
money at the expense of Egypt. Sixteen years ago, she bought
for £4,000,000 Egypt's interest in the Suez Canal, which, had
she only clung to it, would soon have become so fertile a source
of income to her. What she bought for £4,000,000 will in another
year or two be worth something nearer £20,000,000. Would it
really be a very enormous sacrifice, or a very extraordinary act of

* Willcocks maintained that it was a 'shocking waste of public funds'
because the supplementary work alone would cost over £1 million,
whereas his original plan for the larger dam would have cost less than
£1 million.

generosity on the part of Great Britain, if we were to devote say one-fourth of the clear profit that we have made out of this fortunate transaction to the benefit of the country at whose expense we have made it . . .?' The canal had been an immense commercial success as the tonnage of shipping using it had increased steadily. When Cassel offered a loan repayable in 30 years, Cromer did not hesitate. The work was begun in 1895 under the direction of Sir Maurice Fitzmaurice and to Willcocks' design and the dam was completed in 1902. As Cromer wrote to Lord Salisbury soon after the work had begun: 'The reservoir business has been a remarkable success here. It is by far the most popular step we have ever taken, all the more so because we have done it ourselves, without French or other co-operation.'

Meanwhile the reconquest of the Sudan, in 1898, had made it possible to examine further possibilities of harnessing the Nile waters. Between 1901 and 1904 Scott-Moncrieff's successor, William Garstin, made a detailed reconnaissance of the White Nile from Lake Victoria to Khartoum, while C. A. Dupuis studied the Atbara and the Blue Nile tributaries. Garstin's report published in 1904 was the basis of Nile development during the next twenty years. Garstin placed the emphasis on the needs of Egypt which would have to pay for the development of the Sudan. He recommended that the waters of the White Nile, which, unlike the Blue Nile, had a fairly even flow throughout the year, should be devoted to Egyptian irrigation and those of the Blue Nile, when it was not in flood, to the Sudan.

In 1905 the Sudan branch of the Egyptian irrigation service was formed and in 1906 Sir Henry Lyons published his *Physiography of the Nile Basin*, in which was collected all the available information from travellers and scientific explorers.

The consequences of all these hydraulic developments could be seen throughout Egypt. While all Lower Egypt and most of Middle Egypt were finally converted to perennial irrigation, the basins of Upper Egypt were assured of a regular supply.* Between 1881 and 1911 the cultivated area increased from 4,764,000

---

* It was unfortunate that the years of the building of the Aswan Dam were years of exceptionally low floods so that the Saidi (i.e. Upper Egyptian) fellahin ascribed the disaster to the building of the Dam. There is little doubt that without the Dam there would have been years of actual famine.

feddans to 5,658,000 feddans, and the crop area (because of the conversion to perennial irrigation which enables more than one crop a year to be grown) to 7,712,000 feddans. In the next fifty years (i.e. until the building of the High Dam) the cultivated area was hardly increased at all although the crop area was raised to 8,474,000 feddans in 1938 and 10,349,000 in 1958 through further conversion to perennial irrigation.

'There is one respect in which the British irrigation officers are more fortunate than most of their countrymen engaged in the service of the Khedive. Their work is not only successful, but it is appreciated', wrote Milner, *England in Egypt* (p. 310). In the earliest days of the occupation, Scott-Moncrieff won his point with his nominal superior, Rushdi Pasha, the minister of public works (the '*nullité*' that, true to his word, Nubar had found for him) that his four Anglo-Indian irrigation inspectors should not, as Rushdi expected, have their headquarters in Cairo and be sent out occasionally to the countryside on mission but 'should live in the native towns and villages, and not come often to Cairo'. Rushdi expostulated: '*C'est une révolution que vouz proposez.*' '*Justement, Excellence, c'est une révolution*,' was Scott-Moncrieff's reply.[3]

The consequence was that the inspectors of the circles, as they were called, became men of immense power and prestige in the Egyptian countryside. The results of their efforts were immediately apparent; in many cases it was a question of restoring an existing system which had fallen into neglect. But when water filled a fellah's basin for the first time in years or a perennial flood was avoided, his response was grateful and warm-hearted. Willcocks was twice the object of thanksgiving prayers in a mosque – on the second occasion he entered the building ('without boots to please them, and without my hat to please myself') and the officiating imam placed his hands on Willcocks' shoulders as he asked God to bless him in all his works.[4]

Very soon the inspectors were being appealed to in matters not directly concerned with their department – such as legal questions of land ownership.

Such a development had its drawbacks. Nubar fought and won a battle at about this time to prevent the undermining of the *Mudirs*' authority by the appointment of European inspectors of police responsible to Cairo. This was not a simple reactionary attempt to preserve the *status quo* and prevent reform. There was much to be said for retaining the traditional fabric of society and patching it up where necessary as long as there was no new and comprehensive system to take its place and this the British, as the 'veiled protectors' limited by the international control, were unable to provide. Certainly the irrigation inspectors alone could not do it, especially when much of their popularity in the countryside depended on the fact that the fellahin did not associate them directly with the British occupation (of which many of them had not even heard at this stage). Also there were not very many of them and they demonstrably worked extremely hard. Unlike other government departments it would be a long time before it could be said of the ministry of public works that there were too many Englishmen occupying too many posts.

On balance the irrigation engineers left behind an immense positive achievement. This is not to say that there are no grounds for criticism of their total domination of Egypt's agricultural policy in the first period of the British occupation. Before Cromer's retirement in 1907, it had become apparent that the immense increases in perennial irrigation were the direct cause of soil exhaustion, spreading pest attacks and, above all, of the rise in the water table through inadequate drainage, which was one of the chief faults that the engineers had set out to remedy. All these combined to cause the alarming fall in yields per acre that we have already noted.

As the *Egyptian Gazette* pointed out in its issue of 29 December 1907: 'However eminent the irrigation engineers may be in their own profession, they are not agriculturalists, and are naturally pursuing their own policy without proper regard to agricultural considerations.'

Cromer's *laissez-faire* principles prevented the creation of a department of agriculture in the Egyptian Government and it was left to the Khedivial Agricultural Society, formed in 1898 by a group of Egyptian landowners, to do what it could with quite inadequate resources to encourage improved farming methods. Significantly, although Milner, Colvin and Cromer himself all write glowingly about advances in irrigation none of them makes any claim in his book that agricultural techniques improved under the British occupation.

The Agricultural Society's most significant achievement was to engage Lawrence Balls as a research botanist in 1904. Balls, who retired only in 1947, laid the foundations of all Egyptian cotton research and he and his associates succeeded in reversing the declining trend in yields after the First World War.

In 1912, when Kitchener – who took a special interest in agriculture – was consul-general, the British finally agreed to the creation of a department of agriculture in the Government. This took over some of the Khedivial Society's experts and in 1914 became a fully-fledged ministry. Serious co-ordinated research on the cotton crop really dates from 1920 when the Cotton Research Board building in Giza was opened and cotton yields began to recover.

LAW AND ORDER

Speaking a few weeks after the bombardment of Alexandria, Gladstone had said that Britain's duty in Egypt was to substitute the rule of law for that of military violence. Atrocities had been committed against European life and property which must not be allowed to occur again. The object of this police action was to be achieved by the restoration of the authority of the Khedive. The trouble was that if this meant the authority of Tewfik it was useless, because he had never had very much; if it meant his father's authority it was impossible. Ismail was an autocrat who ignored the rule of law but achieved a high degree of security within his borders. As Steven Cave, MP, reported to the House of Commons in 1876, Egypt was 'a country in which there is the greatest security for life and property, and the most entire freedom of religious worship, a country in which European ladies unattended except by natives may and do travel from Alexandria to the Second Cataract – and of how many Christian countries can this be said?' Ismail achieved these results by fairly ruthless police methods and summary justice exerted through the provincial *Mudirs*, who combined the roles of local police chiefs and magistrates. The British, who constantly denounced Ismail's blackguardry, could hardly revive his system even if it were possible for an alien power to do so. The consequence was a fairly steady increase in crime throughout the British occupation.

In 1883 General Valentine Baker had been given the task of reorganizing the police. The strength of the Egyptian army – declared officially dissolved by the Khedive Tewfik – had been limited by Lord Dufferin to 6,000 men which, according to Colvin, was 'barely sufficient to guard the southern frontier (there was no apprehension of Dervish invasion at that time), to preserve internal order, and to overawe the Bedouins'.[1] General Baker therefore set about organizing a constabulary on quasi-military lines divided into a city police, a gendarmerie in the provinces, and a reserve.

The infantry gendarmerie were divided into battalions and the cavalry into squadrons; the officers held Turkish military titles.

General Baker's constabulary was intended to supplement rather than replace the existing traditional system which consisted of the *Omdehs* (or headmen) in each village with the *ghafirs* or watchmen and the untrained and unenrolled Turkish *kawasses* attached to the staff of the provincial *Mudir*. The provincial police superintendent (known as the Mamur el-Zabtieh) and his subordinates in the sub-districts were under the control of the *Mudir*.

In September 1883 the energetic Clifford Lloyd, as director-general of reforms, attempted in the absence of General Baker in the Sudan with his gendarmerie, to change this system from the roots by replacing the Mamur el-Zabtieh and his *kawasses* with a properly enrolled police force responsible to the inspector-general in Cairo. Nubar, as prime minister, did battle over this principle; he was able to point to an alarming increase in rural crime due to the hasty abolition of the traditional security system, and the loss of a clearly understood provincial authority in the *Mudir*. Nubar won the battle because he was indispensable as prime minister and Clifford Lloyd aroused opposition through his gross lack of tact. General Baker returned to Egypt from the Sudan strengthened in his conviction of the need for an army-type police force, which he now reinforced with some of the soldiers withdrawn from the Sudanese garrisons. The provincial police were restored to the *Mudirs'* authority but they were no longer a provincial police.

Nubar's victory had not been complete. Formerly the *Mudirs*, as well as being local heads of police, had been magistrates dealing with all but the most serious classes of crime. Clifford Lloyd succeeded in having their magisterial powers taken away from them and given to the recently reconstituted native tribunals. Under the new system, the procureur-général had a number of representatives attached to each tribunal who were described collectively as the Parquet.

The results, as we shall see, were highly unsatisfactory. It was a clear departure from the system instituted by the British in India whereby the 'district magistrate' was also the supreme authority in police matters, responsible for everything except their drill and discipline. The difference was that these district magistrates were normally Englishmen, whereas there could be no question of appointing British *Mudirs* in Egypt unless the country was formally annexed. The problem was partially resolved by a compromise when Nubar returned to office in 1894. The police was left in Egyptian hands but English control of the ministry of the interior was established through an 'adviser' to the minister of the interior and a handful of young English inspectors of police who had been specially trained for the Egyptian service. Over the years the quality of the provincial *Mudirs* steadily improved.

As Nubar and Lloyd struggled and General Baker drilled his gendarmerie, crime continued to increase. In 1884 Baring was obliged to pass on to the British Government the alarming reports from his agents in the countryside of the state of public security. The principal concern was known as 'brigandage', which did not mean attacks by organized bands of outlaws but 'raiding of the bad characters of a village upon outlying houses or hamlets, or, in some cases, upon other villages'. The native tribunals having proved incapable of dealing with the crime wave, special commissions of brigandage were set up by Nubar Pasha in 1884 at first to investigate and then also to try crimes of this description. They were in fact courts-martial sitting under the presidency of the *Mudirs*, who therefore temporarily recovered some of their magisterial powers. The commissions were originally appointed for a few months only but their powers were renewed by successive decrees and for nearly five years they dealt with most criminal offences throughout Egypt. While they had only slight success in diminishing crime, they were guilty of grave abuses. Torture was used to extract evidence and defence witnesses were rarely heard. Anyone arrested and brought before the commission had almost no chance of being acquitted. In 1888 the Belgian, Le Grelle, who had been appointed procureur-général by Nubar to avoid having an Englishman, exposed many of these abuses in a scathing report, and the commissions were suppressed.

Cromer's explanation for the persistence of these evils for so many years under the British occupation was that after Nubar's refusal to accept the recommendations of Raymond West (the Anglo-Indian judge who was appointed to succeed Sir Benson Maxwell and who remained in office for an even shorter period) it was decided to 'see what the Egyptians could do in the way of judicial reform if left to themselves'. In 1890 he was able to pronounce the experiment a total failure and to insist on the appointment of Sir John Scott to a new post of judicial adviser with power to institute a thorough-going reform of Egypt's judicial system.

In his chapter on Reforms in *Modern Egypt*, Cromer identifies two types of reform which are possible for a country 'in a backward state of civilization'. First there are 'those which are manifestly possible if the reformer is provided with the money and the administrative agency necessary to their execution' and secondly 'those dealing with long-standing abuses or faulty habits of thought, which are ingrained to such an extent into the minds of the population as to require a social almost as much as an administrative revolution in order to ensure their eradication'.[2]

He cites as the three most prominent abuses reformed under his proconsulship the three Cs, the courbash (or *kurbaj*), the *corvée*, and corruption. We have already seen how the *corvée* virtually disappeared during the British occupation as much because of its inefficiency and impracticality as any conscious effort to abolish it. In the case of the *kurbaj*, a decree prohibiting its use was issued at the very start of the occupation on the initiative of Lord Dufferin. Ignoring the fact that an attempt had already been made under Ismail by Riaz Pasha to abolish both the *kurbaj* and the *bastinado*, Baring was initially much too optimistic about the effects of Dufferin's decree. In October 1884 he wrote on the basis of his consular agents' reports: 'An immense change has already been effected, the nature of which can perhaps only be fully appreciated by those who, like myself, are able to compare the Egypt of the present day with the Egypt of but a few years ago. . . . The old arbitrary system of governing Egypt is not moribund. It is actually defunct; and I venture to doubt the possibility of its revival'.[3]

Writing more philosophically twenty-five years later, Cromer admits that although 'Lord Dufferin dealt a staggering blow to the use of the courbash; nevertheless, that implement was plentifully used for some years after the issue of his epoch-making circular.'[4] He also clearly implies that this was just as well because the *kurbaj* was an essential element in the Egyptian system of justice. No Egyptian would have dreamed of giving evidence before a court (or commission of brigandage) unless he was forced.

The use of flogging to extract evidence could only be abolished through a fundamental change in the Egyptian attitude to the law. In Cromer's own words this required a 'social almost as much as an administrative revolution'.

When Sir Edward Malet was leaving Egypt he summed up the needs of the Egyptian people as 'Justice! Justice! Justice!' But the problem was much more easily stated than solved. The traditional patriarchal system whereby the *Omdehs* (i.e. village mayors) were endowed with autocratic powers had been open to grave abuses. The *Omdehs* had wide scope for the misuse of their authority. On the other hand, it was a system that was generally understood and accepted by the masses. Although the *Omdeh* was appointed by the Government, he was regarded by himself and the community as the champion of its interests and rights. He was amenable to any consensus of public opinion and in certain matters his powers were circumscribed by the judge or *qadi* who administers the Islamic Sharia law. In fact it was a blend of autocracy and democracy which is common to most conservative Islamic communities.

The erosion of the *Omdeh*'s authority by the advent of European individualist principles was bound to create a difficult period of transition until it was replaced by something that was both understood and accepted by the villagers.

The introduction of European principles of law into Egypt had started well before 1882 although the process was greatly speeded up under the occupation. Mohammed Aly and his successors took advantage of their initially *de facto* and subsequently *de jure* independence from Constantinople to diverge increasingly from the Ottoman system.

When the Ottoman penal code was finally adopted in Egypt in 1863 it was the new Ottoman Code of 1858, which was based for the first time in Ottoman history on French law, with numerous adaptations to Egypt's circumstances. The event of the most far-reaching significance was Nubar's introduction of the mixed courts in 1879 to exercise jurisdiction in all cases in which foreigners were involved. Although, contrary to Nubar's intentions, the mixed courts did not exercise jurisdiction in criminal as well as civil and commercial cases, owing to the opposition of the capitulatory powers, their creation was a vital step towards the establishment of the 'rule of law' and the independence of the judiciary. As a side effect also they created conditions for the development of a corps of Egyptian professional lawyers of high calibre who eventually formed the country's political elite. The mixed courts had a negligible influence on the lives of the mass of the people but they helped to shape the modern national movement.

A civil code, commercial code and a penal code (although this remained inoperative), all founded on French law, were promulgated in 1875 for the mixed courts. In 1880 a Law of the Sharia courts decreed by the Government of Sherif Pasha, effectively confined the prerogatives of the Sharia courts to questions of personal status (i.e. divorce, inheritance, etc.) and homicide.

It is clear that the secularist principles of the French Revolution had already been established in Egypt before the British occupation, but it was some time before their application was widened. In accordance with the liberal precepts of Lord Dufferin, the Khedive Tewfik's Organic Law of 1 May 1883 accorded the right of universal suffrage to male Egyptians over twenty years of age. The fact that the elected legislative and provincial councils remained largely moribund until they were abolished in 1915, does not mean that the Organic Law was of no significance. The declaration of such a revolutionary principle as universal suffrage was in itself important.

When the British arrived in Egypt it was clear that if the Egyptians were to have more justice it was the national courts, which now handled all cases not involving foreigners except the very limited matters dealt with by the Sharia courts, that needed to be reformed. Lord Dufferin wrote that they were 'so bad, so imbecile, and so corrupt' that almost any change would be an improvement. But a movement in this direction had already started in 1880. A civil code and codes of civil and criminal procedure had already been drafted and were promulgated in 1883. At the same time a decree for the reorganization of the national courts was issued. The new codes were very similar to those issued eight years earlier for the mixed courts. They were basically French with little derived from the Sharia.

The new system for the national courts was strongly criticized by Sir Benson Maxwell, the first procureur-général under the occupation, and his successor Raymond West. Both of them believed that the French code ('utterly unsuited to this country' in Maxwell's opinion) should be replaced by the Anglo-Indian law with which they were familiar. They could marshal some powerful arguments. The new courts were cumbersome and costly for the generally small matters they were called upon to deal with. The French practice of having more than one judge was unfamiliar to Egyptians, while the responsibility of the *juge d'instruction* for collecting evidence for the prosecution antagonized the police authorities.

On the other hand, French law was virtually the only non-Islamic law in use within the Ottoman Empire and it had provided the only basis of experience for Egyptian lawyers in the mixed courts. Nubar won the argument and the British made no further attempt to interfere with the ministry of justice for the next five years.

The original idea of the Egyptian reformers of the national court system was to have summary courts in the countryside as well as courts of first instance in the major towns and appeal courts in Cairo and Assiut. But there were too many difficulties in establishing the summary courts while the courts of first instance did not work well. The Belgian and Dutch judges brought in to administer them neither knew Arabic nor the special conditions of Egypt and within a few years most of them returned to Europe. The Egyptian lawyers and judges who remained were inexperienced and inadequately trained.

By 1890 Baring was ready to insist on an extension of British control over the judicial system. He now proposed the appointment of John Scott, an Anglo-Indian judge, as judicial adviser with the same right as the financial adviser to attend Cabinet meetings. He wanted Scott to head a corps of judicial inspectors similar to the inspectors of irrigation.

Predictably, the Egyptian reaction was strongly hostile. Hussein Fakhri, the minister of justice who had been one of the architects of the pre-1883 reforms, resigned and a few months later Riaz resigned also after vainly fighting Scott's appointment. However, Egyptian resistance to this attempt to take control of the entire judicial system was strong enough to prevent Baring and Scott from having all their own way. Judicial inspectors were not appointed but only a three-man committee of judicial control, headed by Scott. The judicial adviser secured the right to attend Cabinet meetings only when judicial affairs were being discussed.

Scott had an important advantage over Maxwell and West in

that before 1882 he had served on the mixed courts in Egypt. He was therefore familiar with French law as applied in Egypt as well as Indian law. He accepted that French law would continue to be the basis of the Egyptian judicial system but he aimed to modify it according to Anglo-Indian practice. He not only set up summary courts of justice in some of the smaller provincial towns but gave the *Omdehs* the power to settle minor civil and criminal cases subject to the right of appeal. Thus the *Omdehs* recovered some of their previous authority, although not their autocratic powers. His principal purpose was to make justice cheaper and more easily available to the Egyptians through decentralization, at the same time he tried to raise the standards of legal practice by weeding out the incompetent and reforming the Egyptian Law School. His committee of control visited each tribunal in turn to examine its files. A start was made on building new court houses while existing ones were for the first time provided with adequate law libraries.

In 1898 Sir John Scott, who was in poor health, retired to England where he was appointed judge advocate-general. He was succeeded by Malcolm McIlwraith, a brilliant young Scots lawyer with a French law degree but an unfortunate capacity for making enemies easily.* McIlwraith carried Scott's policy of decentralization one stage further by creating (after the Anglo-French agreement of 1904 had further freed Britain's hands in Egypt) *Markaz* (or district) tribunals in the sub-divisions of the provinces in which judges of the courts of first instance on circuit tried criminal cases. Prosecution in these courts was conducted entirely by the police, without the intervention of the Parquet, though subject to its supervision. The right of appeal in criminal cases was eliminated as the decisions of the circuit assize courts were made final except for references on points of law to the court of cassation.

McIlwraith acknowledged that the Egyptian codes of law had been 'more successful than one would have been entitled to expect', but some confusion had resulted from the British policy of applying piecemeal reforms to parts of the basically French system. He

---

* It is alleged that when McIlwraith offered to resign on condition that he received a pension of £1,200 a year the financial adviser was so eager to accept that he told his messenger 'Run! Run!' The messenger ran so hard that he broke his leg and then claimed compensation from the Government. (Marshall, *The Egyptian Enigma*, p. 81.)

set up a commission to revise the penal code and code of criminal procedure and new codes were promulgated in 1904 which followed the general lines of the 1883 legislation although they incorporated some sections of the new Sudanese penal code. In 1916 one further attempt was made to Indianize the Egyptian penal code by McIlwraith's formidable successor Sir William Brunyate, but the Egyptian nationalist movement had developed over the years and he was successfully opposed by the now substantial and experienced body of Egyptian legal opinion. His draft revised code was never adopted.[5]

The change from a judicial system based on traditional social and religious practice to one based on modern European principles was bound to be slow and difficult. The obstacles were numerous: despite all Scott and McIlwraith's efforts to bring justice closer to the people the Egyptians still found the law slow, expensive and frequently incomprehensible. Gradually the new tribunals began to gain public confidence. Revenue from fees rose until by 1906 the courts were virtually self-supporting. But it was a painfully slow process. One of the difficulties was the virtual impossibility of finding judges and magistrates who combined adequate legal training with an understanding of the society in which they were supposed to be administering justice. Only a small handful of the English judges had more than a rudimentary knowledge of Arabic and could avoid working through interpreters. In the early years they overawed their Egyptian colleagues but as the quality and standing of these improved, Anglo-Egyptian relations on the bench deteriorated with the rise of the national movement.

This does not mean that once the decision had been taken to Europeanize Egypt's judicial system – a decision that was supported by the great majority of the growing corps of Egyptian secular lawyers – the Scott and McIlwraith reforms were not both sensible and salutary.

While the British in Egypt were justifiably pleased with their efforts to give ordinary Egyptians easier access to justice through the courts, they were pained and mystified by the steady increase in crime during the occupation. In 1906, the last full year of Cromer's rule, 3,201 felonies were committed including 741 murders, 392 attempted murders, 497 robberies and no less than 521 cases of arson. Some of this could be attributed to improved reporting of crime but this could not be the whole explanation.

It is relatively easy to see now that this was the inevitable consequence of attempting to substitute a modern system for one that, however savage and unjust in some of its aspects, had achieved reasonably good results in controlling crime. The process was achieved partly by abolishing the old system and partly by reforming it. In some cases the reformers were obliged to retrace their steps. Thus the *Omdehs* had some of their powers restored to them with certain safeguards. When Kitchener became head of the police in 1890 after the death of General Valentine Baker, he attempted to reduce the number of the *Ghafirs* who had reached the ludicrous proportion of one to every six or seven villagers. Because they were unpaid and undisciplined they were not much use for preventing crime once the authority of the *Omdehs* and the provincial *Mudirs* had been relaxed. Towards the end of the occupation an attempt was made to give the *Omdehs* some legal training but as long as their general level of education was low it was hard for them to adminster a complicated new system.

The British reformers had hoped that the Egyptian people would become more law-abiding as well as more litigious. In his final report to the British government, Cromer admitted: 'I have no hesitation in stating that the increase of crime, to which I have frequently alluded in former reports, is the most unsatisfactory feature in the whole situation.' Two years earlier, in his report for 1905, he had put forward the superficially specious suggestion that this was due to the increased prosperity of the fellahin. 'Large numbers of persons, who but recently were very poor, have now become moderately rich. Having tasted the enjoyment of wealth, they wish to become richer, and in their desire to attain their object, they are far more frequently than heretofore brought into collision with others who are seeking precisely the same object as themselves.'

A year later, in his final report, Cromer seems to have changed his mind to a more familiar explanation. While repeating that there was no question of poverty being the explanation of the crime wave, he says: 'It is, I think, to be found in the fact that the law does not inspire sufficient terror to evildoers. Only 43·5 per cent of the crimes committed last year (1906) were punished. In the remaining 56·5 per cent, it was found impossible to discover the criminals, or if they were discovered, to prove their guilt.' He attributes this to the fact that under the new reformed system no one could be condemned without witnesses.

Cromer was older and wiser than when he wrote in 1884 that the old arbitrary system of governing Egypt was defunct. Belatedly he had concluded that an ancient system could not be changed by a stroke of the pen in the form of a decree abolishing the *kurbaj* but by a gradual process of education. The two different reasons he gave for the increase in crime – i.e. the 'lust for gain' and the 'law inspiring insufficient terror to evildoers' – were close to the truth. Over the years the fellahin had acquired some of the individualist profit motive; as a *laissez-faire* liberal in economic matters, Cromer had always hoped that they would. At the same time the introduction of laws of evidence meant that everyone went in less fear of the law. If fewer of the innocent were condemned than under the old system fewer of the guilty were condemned also.

Cromer regarded corruption as the third of the three Cs after the *corvée* and courbash that the British occupation could claim the most credit for having reformed. 'Corruption,' says Cromer, 'is the canker which eats away the heart of most Eastern governments.' He assumes that Egypt before the arrival of the British was in an especially parlous condition. Ismail had inherited a corrupt administrative system and 'by his own action, he made this system doubly corrupt'.[6] He implies that Ismail was merely showing a common oriental characteristic to an exceptional degree, although elsewhere he admits that Europe shared some of the blame when he says that under Ismail and his predecessors 'all that was least creditable to European civilization was attracted to Egypt, on whose carcase swarms of needy adventurers preyed at will'. Oriental corruption had taken on new dimensions through the agency of unrestricted western capitalism. 'It can be stated with confidence that at no previous period in Egyptian history has so little "bakhshish" been paid or received as a present;' he wrote after his retirement. As regards the taking of bribes by senior officials of the administration this was undoubtedly correct. The introduction of a proper system of accounting and auditing of state funds, which had started under the Dual Control, the practice of inviting tenders for government contracts and the regular payment of civil servants' salaries had all contributed to this improvement. In the countryside the removal of many of the *Omdeh*'s powers meant that there was less reason to bribe him, while the new judges and magistrates were largely incorruptible. Above all the injection into the higher ranks of the administration of a number of Englishmen who shared Cromer's late-Victorian sense of financial probity helped to reduce the public's cynical belief in the inevitable venality of government. 'The Egyptians pay an unconscious compliment to English integrity by very rarely offering bribes to British officials,' says Cromer.

On the other hand, his claim to have reduced the use of 'bakhshish', in the sense that it is most generally known as part of Egypt's social and economic system, is nonsense. 'Bakshish' means the tips or fringe benefits with which a large part of the urban population who, in the absence of industry, were engaged in trade or services, supplemented their meagre and irregular wages. The system can only be changed by the provision of mass regular employment in industry. It will be reinforced by a rapid increase in population which inevitably results in the over-staffing of the government services and by a growing disparity between rich and poor. Both of these trends occurred during Cromer's time in Egypt. Like the incidence of crime, bakhshish-giving tended to increase rather than decline with prosperity as there were more Egyptians asking for it and more who are ready to pay it in order to increase their own comfort.

12

SIRDARS AND SOLDIERS

After the Khedive Tewfik's laconic decree issued six days after the battle of Tel el-Kebir, 'L'armée Egyptienne est dissoute,' there was disagreement among the British occupiers as to whether the Egyptians should have an army at all. Some held the view that while it would be useless as a fighting force it would act as a breeding-ground for rebellion. They suggested the use of Turkish troops or European mercenaries instead. Lord Dufferin, however, 'decided to put aside all idea of enrolling Albanians, Circassians, or other waifs and strays of the Mediterranean',[1] and decreed that the new army which would be needed to keep internal order and protect the frontiers against marauding bedouin, would have to consist mainly of Egyptians. Its total strength would be about 6,000 and since 'Egypt had had enough of Mamelukes and their congeners', the officers and drill-sergeants would come from England.

Despite the widespread contempt for Arabi's soldiers among British and Indian Army officers, the Egyptian fellahin were not wholly unpromising military material. Although bullied and down-trodden by centuries of alien rule they had been fashioned by one of the Albanian waifs and strays – Mohammed Aly's son, Ibrahim Pasha – into the basis of a formidable army of a quarter of a million which won repeated victories over the Turks in the 1830s and, but for the intervention of the Powers, would most probably have occupied Constantinople. This was despite the fact that the fellahin showed no instinctive martial qualities and could only be recruited by savage and brutal means.

Admittedly, the Turkish forces they were fighting were at a low ebb following the massacre and dissolution of the Janissaries in 1826. All the officers and most of the non-commissioned officers in Ibrahim Pasha's army were Turks or Albanians who had developed a loyalty to Egypt and were quite prepared to fight their fellow-Turks on its behalf. But if properly led, the fellahin fought with discipline and courage. They lacked the panache of attack of the Sudanese (or 'black troops' as they were invariably called by the British) but they were particularly good at holding a defensive position. Unlike the Sudanese, their health stood up to campaigns in cold climates.

The Treaty of London of 1841 which followed the intervention of the Powers against Mohammed Aly and Ibrahim limited Egypt's army to 18,000 men. This effectively prevented them and their successors from campaigning outside the borders of Egypt and the Sudan. Said Pasha actually reduced the army further to 3,000 men but he took the politically significant step of allowing some fellahin NCOs to become officers. Under Ismail there were a number of colonels of fellah origin although, as we have seen, all the key posts in the armed forces were held by Turks or Circassians. These colonels became the spearhead of the national movement and one of their first demands was that the army should be increased in number to the 18,000 allowed by the sultan's firman. They aimed to form a national Egyptian army in which influence of the Turco-Circassian elements would be insignificant. Unfortunately their military capacities were not equal to their patriotism. As officers, although not as political leaders, they betrayed the trust of the rank and file.

The task of building up a new Egyptian army in 1883 was entrusted to Sir Evelyn Wood, who became sirdar or commander-in-chief, and twenty-six other officers. These included Grenfell and Kitchener (who both succeeded as sirdar) and a handful of other names that were to achieve high promotion. As Milner observed only ten years later: 'The Egyptian service, which was at first scoffed at as a career, had proved a road to advancement as good or better than any other in the whole wide field of British empire or influence. . . . British officers have done much for Egypt, but it is equally true that Egypt has done a good deal for them.'[2]

Conditions in the Egyptian army – especially for the ranks – had been so bad that it was not difficult to achieve a rapid and spectacular improvement. An army of only six thousand in a population of seven million meant that force no longer needed to be used for recruiting. Regular pay and medical services came as a pleasant surprise to the Egyptian soldiers. The fellahin have a fundamentally sturdy physique so reasonable care and training put them in good physical condition.

When the new army was recruited it was not contemplated using it outside Egypt's borders. The Sudan could be looked after by the existing garrisons and the remnants of Arabi's army (even if some of them had been sent to the Sudan in chains). All this was swiftly changed by the Hicks disaster, news of which reached Cairo in November 1883, and the Mahdi's sweeping successes. Although it was decided to abandon the Sudan for the time being, there were not enough British troops left in Egypt either to mount an expedition to rescue General Gordon when the need arose or even to defend the country's southern borders against a possible Mahdist invasion.

Egyptian soldiers were used in Wolseley's unsuccessful expedition principally to guard his long line of communications but afterwards they were employed in steadily increasing proportions to the British troops. When Evelyn Wood retired in the summer of 1885 his successor, General Grenfell, formed a Frontier Field Force of about equal numbers of Egyptians and British which successfully defended the new *de facto* frontier at Wadi Halfa for ten years until Kitchener began the re-occupation of the Sudan in 1895.

The size of the Egyptian army was steadily increased from the initial 6,000. Between 1884 and 1888 five Sudanese battalions – consisting mainly of Dinka and Shilluk tribesmen – were raised in addition to the eight 'fellahin' battalions, bringing the total strength (including cavalry and artillery) to about 12,000 in 1890. Expansion continued and at the Battle of Omdurman in 1898 Kitchener had 17,600 Egyptian and Sudanese regular troops under his command, in addition to 8,200 British.

After the reconquest of the Sudan the army was reduced again and by the end of Cromer's time in Egypt it amounted to 16,000 with 11,000 in reserve. Recruiting was by ballot and the period of service was five years with a further five years in the reserve or police or coastguard services. In theory, every Egyptian male of eighteen was liable to be balloted but the numerous rights of exemption (which included the payment of £40 which Edgar Vincent had initiated as a convenient means of increasing revenue) reduced the number of potential recruits each year from about 110,000 to about 70,000. In the years before the First World War the army cost between £500,000 and £700,000 a year but in addition Egypt had to pay about £100,000 annually for the cost of the British troops stationed in the country. The sprinkling of British officers in the Egyptian army was very small, although they held all the senior posts. In 1906 there were 63 British officers and 623 Egyptians and Sudanese. Four out of the five Egyptian battalions were commanded entirely by Egyptian officers.

The potential political danger of an Egyptian army with restored morale was never forgotten. The bulk of the Egyptian troops were kept in the Sudan; munitions were kept under British control and Cairo was garrisoned by British troops.

The British officers serving with the Egyptian army could not conceal their preference for the Sudanese troops. As long ago as 1874, Gordon had said: 'I cannot bear these Egyptian officers. They have no good quality. I like the blacks; now these black soldiers are the only troops in the Egyptian service worth having.'

Undoubtedly the majority of Egyptian officers at that period were of poor standard. The upper-class Turco-Circassians who filled the higher ranks had no concern for the welfare of their subordinates. Morale and discipline, for which they were responsible, were equally bad. But the British preference for the black soldiers persisted in the new army even when standards in everything had improved. Milner makes the reason fairly clear: 'A noticeable fact is the sort of natural "camaraderie" which seems rapidly to spring up between the blacks and Englishmen. The former very easily become attached to their British officers, and those officers, on their side, have a curious kind of fondness for the blacks, which they do not seem to feel in an equal degree for the native Egyptians. This feeling has been known to extend even to the private soldiers of our British regiments, who, on more than one occasion, have readily fraternized with the Sudanese. These grown-up children with their light-heartedness, simplicity, and unquestionable pluck, were regarded by Tommy Atkins with half-amused, half-admiring and inoffensively patronizing affection.'[3] Imperial Anglo-Saxons have always liked their subject races to be unsophisticated; hence the strong preference for Punjabis to Bengalis.

13

THE NEGLECT OF EDUCATION

No aspect of the British occupation of Egypt is more open to criticism than its effect on education. Its staunchest apologists in later years, such as Lord Lloyd and Sir Valentine Chirol,[1] could find little to say on this subject. Milner relegated education to a section of a chapter entitled 'Odds and Ends of Reform'.

In the first decade of the occupation the educational budget was actually lower than under Ismail in his financial straits. In all Cromer's years in Egypt the amount spent on education did not exceed one per cent of gross revenues. Although in the early years of the twentieth century the allocation was allowed to rise to £250,000 or about three per cent of the budget, this was totally inadequate for a population of ten millions. The consequence was that in 1910 the literacy rate was 8·5 per cent for males and 0·3 per cent for females. 'The mass of the Egyptian population,' said Cromer in a speech shortly after his retirement, 'is still sunk in the deepest ignorance, and this ignorance must necessarily continue until a new generation has grown up.'[2]

Cromer was unabashed by this performance although he could not ignore the criticism. His answer was to lump education with other fields of social reform in which his administration had a better record. In his farewell speech at the Cairo Opera House in 1907 he said: 'I hear it frequently stated that although the material prosperity of Egypt has increased marvellously of late years, nothing has been done towards the moral and intellectual advancement of the people. What! gentlemen, has there been no moral advancement? Is the country governed, as was formally the case, exclusively by the use of the whip. . . .?' He went on to enumerate the abolition of forced slavery, the decline in slavery and corruption and the reform of prisons and hospitals but said nothing more of 'intellectual advancement'.

In *Modern Egypt* he indignantly denies the view of 'critics of the baser sort', that the British occupation had aimed to keep the

Egyptians in a state of subservience. Fifty years before Tel el-Kebir, Macaulay had told the House of Commons that there was to be no question of keeping the people of India ignorant in order to keep them submissive and Cromer believed he had followed the same principle in Egypt. If progress had been slow, he would say it was because moral and intellectual advancement are always more difficult to achieve than material prosperity and in view of the conditions in which he found the Egyptians it was surprising how much, and not how little, had been done.

In one respect Cromer felt that Macaulay's policies had been misguided. The expansion of Western-style higher education in India had in his view manufactured a class of discontented and place-seeking demagogues who were divorced from the mass of their own people. His remedy for Egypt was to concentrate on the expansion of elementary and technical education while opposing the opening of a university. As he wrote to St Loe Strachey, the editor of the *Spectator* in 1906: 'Here I am trying to take to heart the lesson of India; that is without discouraging higher education, I am doing all I can to push forward both elementary and technical education. I want all the next generation of Egyptians to be able to read and write. Also I want to create as many carpenters, bricklayers, plasterers etc., as I possibly can. More than this I cannot do.'[3]

The trouble with this policy was that it was the equivalent to consigning Egyptians to manual and semi-skilled labour. It was all very well to say that he did not discourage higher education, failure to encourage it amounted to the same thing. While it was arguable that India was producing too many secondary school and university graduates, these were the men who would have to provide the country's administration if it was ever to govern itself. In asking himself the question whether Egyptians would become capable of self-government within the foreseeable future, Cromer replies: 'It is nothing less than this; that the new generation of Egyptians has to be persuaded or forced into imbibing the true spirit of Western civilization.'[4] Thus Cromer opens himself to the charge of trying to postpone indefinitely the date when self-government would become possible.

At the same time it must be admitted that even his policy of concentrating on elementary education was not very successful. When Cromer retired about 1·5 per cent of the population was receiving primary education as compared with 1·7 per cent in 1873. So far from all the next generation of Egyptians being able to read and write, illiteracy was still over 80 per cent in 1937 – thirty years after Cromer's retirement.

The truth is that Cromer did not regard education as of major importance. He knew much more clearly what he did not want – rebellious Egyptian intellectuals – than what he wanted. While he often stated his belief that Egypt could never have a genuinely civilized society under Islam – the position of women alone making this impossible – he opposed any attempt to remove religious control of education. He sympathized with Mohammed Abdu's efforts to reform the ancient and hidebound Islamic university of el-Azhar but considered them fruitless. 'Islam cannot be reformed,' he said shortly after his retirement, 'that is to say, reformed Islam is Islam no longer; it is something else; we cannot as yet tell what it will eventually be.' At the same time he did not hide his contempt for the 'Europeanized Egyptian' who though nominally a Muslim 'in reality he is generally an agnostic'. He described them as 'at the same time demoslemized Moslems and invertebrate Europeans'. In general he did not hold out much hope for the ambitious and intelligent young Egyptian Muslim.

As in all Muslim countries, Egyptian education was dominated by religion before the nineteenth century. The only opportunity of learning for the majority of Egyptian boys (for girls there was almost none) was at the local *kuttab* or Koranic school, where the pupils devoted most of their time to memorizing the Sacred Book. Secondary or higher education of a kind was provided by the thousands of *Madrasahs* attached to the Mosques with their apex at el-Azhar, where studies concentrated on Islamic theology, law and logic. Mathematics, astronomy and physics, in which the Arabs were once pre-eminent, were also taught but on medieval principles.

Mohammed Aly, though barely literate himself, had seen the importance of a modern system of education to achieving his ambitions for Egypt. As with his industrialization policy, everything was directed to strengthening the state, but his French advisers did succeed in creating a national system of education on European lines which, at least on paper, was highly impressive. He also arranged for several hundred students to continue their studies in Europe – mostly in engineering, industry and medicine.

Like most of Mohammed Aly's creations, his educational system did not long survive him. But the schools of medicine and law continued and his reign created an appetite for European culture. Ismail endeavoured to expand Mohammed Aly's system but his bankruptcy ultimately forced him to reduce it.

At the start of the British occupation, therefore, Egypt had a dual educational system: the Islamic, based on the *kuttabs* and including government primary and secondary schools, and the various higher institutes of learning and the numerous foreign mission (Greek, Italian, French and American) schools established in the country.

Cromer's first concern was to economize and his second was to limit both primary and secondary school graduates to a number that could be absorbed into the government administration. This double purpose was served by reversing Mohammed Aly's and Ismail's policy of providing free education in the government schools. Tuition fees were charged and raised when the number of applicants for entry into the primary schools was considered excessive. At the same time, Cromer instituted a system of examinations for primary and secondary school certificates which were required for entry into the appropriate levels of the civil service. The examinations were made difficult enough to ensure that a substantial number failed.

At the start of the British occupation, teaching in the government schools was principally in Arabic and, especially at the higher levels, in French. There were only a few classes in English. The first inclination of the British was to replace both Arabic and French with English as far as possible. Most British officials agreed with Cromer, who never learned more than a few words of Arabic in all his years in Egypt, that Egyptians could never be properly educated in their native tongue. As far as French was concerned, there was no need for the British to impose its replacement by English as the chief European language taught in the schools.* As English became the language used in most government depart-

---

* As Cromer somewhat disingenuously informed a young Englishman who in 1903 had just come to join the ministry of public instruction, there had been 'an extraordinary change over from French to English among Egyptian youth, without any influence direct or indirect emanating from the British agency'. (Humphrey Bowman, *Middle East Window*, p. 55).

ments the demand for English classes from ambitious young Egyptians and their parents increased.

On the other hand, there was no hesitation about imposing English methods of teaching and discipline on the Egyptian government schools. In 1890 Cromer recruited to the department of public instruction as a schools inspector, Douglas Dunlop, a dour Scots bachelor who had come out to Alexandria as a young man to teach at a missionary school. With Cromer's support, Dunlop rose rapidly to become adviser to the department and the dictator of Egyptian education. Although a few intimates claimed to have detected a warm heart in Dunlop, he appeared to most as cold, unimaginative and arrogant. He drilled his English and Egyptian staff like an army, imposing an absolute uniformity in curriculum and teaching methods throughout the country.

One difficulty was not of Dunlop's making. The department of public instruction (or PI as it was known) was badly paid and despised by the rest of the government service. In an effort to raise standards, Dunlop, who always regretted that he had not been to a public school himself, recruited a number of well-born young Oxford and Cambridge graduates ('Dunlop's Young Men') to the department.* Those who wished to remain in Egypt transferred as soon as possible to other more prestigious branches of the government service. This increased the resentment and depressed the morale of the handful of older and more experienced English teachers in the department who had no university degrees but usually knew Arabic well.

In the early years of the occupation the British did not interfere at all in the operation of the three higher institutes of learning which had survived from the reign of Ismail – the schools of medicine, engineering and law. The school of medicine, founded by Clot Bey,† the great French doctor, in the 1830s had been fully Egyptianized and instruction was mainly in Arabic. There were obvious defects in its training and administration but the Egyptians were proud of it and strongly resisted outside interference.

---

* Dunlop insisted that they should not know a word of Arabic because 'it only gave them romantic ideas about the natives, and they would waste their time explaining what they taught to the natives in Arabic instead of making them learn English'. (Blunt, *My Diaries*, 11, p. 40.)

† Chief surgeon to Mohammed Aly who made him head of Egypt's medical administration in 1836.

However, in the 1890s the British gradually gained control of the school which was finally completely reorganized, instruction changed to English and English teaching staff introduced. An examining committee, headed by an eminent British physician, came out regularly to report on the work of the school and Egyptian doctors were sent for further specialized training in England. The standard and reputation of the school improved considerably but, like Egypt's entire educational system, it was utterly inadequate for the country's needs. In some years there were no more than six graduates from the school. Consequently the Egyptian medical profession was dominated by Syrian, Lebanese and European doctors who concentrated in the wealthy cities of Cairo and Alexandria and often had dubious qualifications.

The law school was more difficult to Anglicize because it was under French control and, as we have seen, the reformed Egyptian legal system continued to be based on French law. It was not until 1899 that, against strong French opposition, an English section was introduced. A fierce rivalry ensued until in 1907 Dunlop succeeded in ousting the eminent French jurist, Edouard Lambert, from the directorship of the school and replacing him with a Canadian historian who had only just obtained his degree, at the second attempt, from the Ecole de Droit in Paris.

The British regarded (with good reason) the law school as a breeding ground for Egyptian nationalism and they accused the French teachers of encouraging subversion. Lambert signed the petition for the release of the Denshawai prisoners (see p. 168) and this was doubtless an additional incentive for Dunlop to be rid of him. By 1907 the Anglo-French agreement had virtually eliminated the power of the French Government to protect the position of its nationals in Egypt. But what is certain is that the law school continued to breed nationalists. Because of the lack of other outlets for the political energies of young Egyptians, the law school was the obvious ladder to a political career. Unlike the graduates of other schools, successful law students waived their right to enter the government service in order to be called to the Egyptian Bar. As the nationalist movement grew, the law school became the centre of anti-British propaganda and led the way with students' political strikes.

After Cromer's departure the drawbacks of teaching Egyptian students almost entirely in English became obvious even to

Dunlop. While such a system could be defended in the expensive private boarding schools, such as Victoria College, which were modelled on English public schools, it made nonsense in the ordinary government day-schools where the students all thought in Arabic and returned home in the afternoons to speak it with their families. The difficulties of the young English teachers, who as we have seen were not expected to know any Arabic, but had to teach history, geography and mathematics entirely in English, can easily be imagined. They were reduced to making their pupils memorize chunks of dictated notes – the very 'learning by rote' that Cromer had rightly stigmatized as the defect of traditional Egyptian education. Cromer persuaded himself that with the appointment of foreign teachers 'the time-honoured methods of loading the memory without exercising the mind had been abandoned'. But such was far from the case. Eventually Dunlop, although he never learned Arabic himself, came round to advising the English teachers to take Arabic lessons in their spare time.

Cromer acknowledged that in time Arabic would be restored as a teaching language 'as the number of highly trained Egyptian teachers increases'. But as with training Egyptians in the art of government, he did nothing to hasten the process. There was no training college for secondary school teachers in his time while the elementary school training college was of such a low standard that only students went there who were too poor or too unintelligent to go anywhere else. The few Egyptian teachers who went abroad for specialized training were at once taken by Dunlop for administrative work in the department on their return. It was not until some years after Cromer's departure from Egypt that a proper teacher's training college was opened as a branch of the Egyptian university.

However, before this happened and even before the end of Cromer's rule, Arabic began to be gradually restored in the primary and to a lesser extent in the secondary schools. This was both because teaching in English had proved to be difficult and ineffective and because of growing nationalist pressure supported by English Radical MPs, such as J. M. Robertson,* who harried the foreign minister with questions on the subject. Ultimately the trend was inevitable. In Egypt there was no question of English

* John M. Robertson (1856–1933) was a brilliant writer and literary critic of encyclopedic knowledge and humanist views.

acquiring the position that it held in India and many African states with no common national language of their own.

With few exceptions, the British in Egypt were unsympathetic towards proposals for establishing an Egyptian university. They feared that it would do even more to foster nationalism than the law school and their suspicions were confirmed when Mustafa Kamel's Nationalist Party began a campaign to raise subscriptions for one. Nothing was done until Cromer's departure from Egypt when, as part of the new policy of limited concessions to nationalism, his successor, Eldon Gorst, agreed to the establishment of the university at the end of 1908. At first it was financed entirely from private funds and although the Government later provided a small annual subsidy it remained for some time on a very limited scale. Most Egyptians who wanted a liberal university education had to seek it abroad and at their own expense since the practice of sending students to Europe with Government scholarships virtually ceased under the British occupation.

Sheikh Mohammed Abdu eloquently stated the Egyptian grievance when he wrote: 'The only schools which represent higher education in Egypt are the schools of law and medicine and the polytechnic. Of all the other sciences of which human knowledge is composed the Egyptian may sometimes obtain a superficial notion at the preparatory schools, but it is almost impossible for him to study them thoroughly, and often he is compelled to ignore them. The result is that we possess judges and lawyers, physicians and engineers more or less capable of exercising their professions; but amongst the educated classes one looks in vain for the investigator, the thinker, the philosopher, the scholar, the man in fact of open mind, fine spirit, generous sentiments, whose whole life is bound to the ideal.'

Cromer responded to these remarks, which were published in a book by a Frenchman, de Guerville, in his best headmasterly manner: 'not only with surprise but with a keen feeling of disappointment ... I had hoped for better things of him'. But he never really answered the point that Sheikh Abdu was making, which was not that the British had 'discouraged the acquisition of knowledge' by the mass of Egyptians but that they had tried to prevent the development of a liberally educated elite capable of governing a modernized Egyptian state. Unfortunately, Cromer never proceeded very far with his alternative policy – the provision of elementary education for the mass of the population. It is true that after 1900, when some additional funds became available for education, an attempt was made to improve the *kuttabs* which still provided the only education of any kind for most of the population. A few *kuttabs* were run directly by the Government, while others were given grants-in-aid and regularly inspected. By 1906 there were 165,000 pupils out of a population of 11,000,000. But since almost nothing had been done to raise the standard of their teachers the methods they employed remained the same. Educationally they were virtually useless; the most that could be said was that the additional funds meant that they were cleaner and better housed. When the agitation for an Egyptian university was at its height, the British gave some extra attention to the *kuttabs* as an alternative but this subsided after the Egyptian nationalists had had their way.

True to his policy of not interfering with the religious susceptibilities of the Egyptians, Cromer did nothing to promote female education, although he considered the lack of it to be the chief cause of Egypt's backwardness. In 1900 there were only 1,640 girls in *kuttabs* and although the number had risen to 17,000 by 1908 this was still barely one per cent of the girls of school age. Moreover, the extreme difficulty of finding trained female teachers meant that many of these were illiterate. Eventually Dunlop opened a teacher's training college for Egyptian women and sent a few girls for specialized training in England. But the effort remained on a tiny scale.

Cromer acknowledged that the demand for female education was growing as young Egyptian males began to look for wives with more knowledge of the world than they could have gained in the harem.* But he did not regard it as Britain's duty to help meet this demand and he remained pessimistic about the Egyptians' capacity for self-improvement. He believed that, contrary to the position in Christian Europe, Egyptian Muslim women were generally less religious than the males. This meant that they would be even more likely to become agnostic if they received a western education and 'a Europeanized Egyptian man usually becomes an agnostic, and often assimilates many of the least worthy portions

---

* 'Harem' refers to the part of Muslim houses reserved for the women; hence it was a collective term for all female members of the household and not only the wives.

of European civilization'. Despite this danger of wholesale production of debased Egyptian lady agnostics he still believed that 'the experiment of female education should certainly be continued with vigour'; although 'few people now living can hope to see its results'.[5] This last assertion was much too pessimistic. Cromer was writing in 1908; within thirty years it had been accepted by most of the population that girls should be educated and their position in society was being rapidly transformed.

At the basis of Cromer's attitude towards Egyptian education lay his *laissez-faire* principles. He positively disapproved of the state's expansion of secondary and higher education, partly because he thought it would produce a surplus of subversive demagogues divorced from the mass of their own people but also because, like most Victorian liberals, he did not believe that it was the state's duty to provide education. But the result of making the Egyptians pay for their children's higher education became the prerogative of the wealthy. Egypt's elite was not only divorced from the masses but had no common interest with them.

In the same way there was no concerted attempt to impose English culture on Egypt. Teaching in English was introduced into the government schools but, as we have seen, Arabic was restored long before the end of the British occupation. English rapidly replaced French as a second language in the schools,* but this was largely because of the material advantage of a knowledge of English in the government service to which most students aspired. To a remarkable degree French retained its predominance among Egypt's social and cultural elite.†

The French, who of course pursued a very different policy in their North African Arab possessions, never ceased to be astonished at Britain's apparent failure to impose its civilization on Egypt. They attributed it partly to the innate superiority of their own culture and its natural attraction to other Mediterranean peoples and partly to the anti-British sentiments of Egyptian

* Between 1889 and 1898 the number of pupils in the government schools who studied the English language increased from 1,063 to 3,859 while those who studied French dropped from 2,994 to 1,881.

† Ironically, the real change came with the 1952 revolution which created a new elite of Anglo-Saxon trained technocrats. Even so, several of the Free officers spoke French better than English while the traditional upper classes, who are far from extinct, usually speak both with the edge on French.

nationalists. But the real reason was that the British from Cromer downwards did not see their civilizing mission in these terms. In the field of education, British policy was symbolized by Dunlop – a man who was far too limited to impose his culture on anyone. What he did impose was a certain discipline and efficiency on the educational system. He established the valuable principle, for example, that students could not bribe or cheat their way to success in examinations. As in many other spheres, it was order and justice rather than enlightenment or understanding that the British brought to Egypt.

14

THE ROYAL REBEL

On 7 January 1892, the thirty-nine-year-old Khedive Tewfik died suddenly at the winter resort of Helwan, south of Cairo. His Greek doctor's report said that the cause of death was influenza, double pneumonia and an inflammation of the kidneys but the rumour that he had been poisoned by the Turks or even the British spread rapidly. Summoned to Helwan several hours before the Khedive expired, Cromer (he was made a peer in 1892) at once saw the necessity of proclaiming his successor. There was a small difficulty in that the heir, Prince Abbas Hilmi, who was at school in Vienna, was still six months short of 18, the age of majority fixed by the sultan's firmans of 1873. When someone pointed out that on the basis of the Muslim calendar year of 354 days the Crown Prince would have had his eighteenth birthday two weeks before, Cromer, in his words, 'jumped at the suggestion'.

Abbas Hilmi was more in the mould of his grandfather Ismail than his father, who had been content to act as the veil for the British 'protectorate'. He had been educated in Switzerland and, from the age of thirteen, at the Theresianum in Vienna; he arrived to ascend the throne of Egypt speaking Turkish and excellent German, French and English but no Arabic. From his French teacher and direct observation of separatist movements within the Austrian Empire he had learned the meaning of national independence. Already he was determined to assert himself against Cromer's authority.

Although Abbas could not have been aware of it in Vienna, Egypt was waiting for such a new departure. The national movement which had been crushed at Tel el-Kebir, was beginning to revive in a different form. Since his return from exile in 1888 Mohammed Abdu had abandoned political activity to concentrate on religious, social and educational reform but the anti-occupation movement had never died and, though denied any approach to real political power, was increasingly making itself heard. In Cairo the political salons of Riaz, Princess Nazli (the witty and still beautiful niece of Ismail who had been a bitter enemy of Tewfik) and Aly Pasha Mubarak, the distinguished engineer, writer and educator nurtured the political leaders of the future – such as Mustafa Kamel and Saad Zaghlul. In 1889 Sheikh Ali Yusuf founded the newspaper *al-Muayyad* which became the voice of moderate Egyptian nationalism alongside the pro-British *al-Muqattam* and the pro-French *al-Ahram* (which were both founded and owned by Syrian Christian immigrants). The Egyptian bar was beginning to produce a number of frustrated Egyptian lawyer-politicians.

Cromer regarded these first stirrings of nationalism as insignificant. He was convinced that the obvious advantages of the British occupation in national solvency, lighter taxation and a more just and orderly administration would outweigh the Egyptian people's regrets for an illusory lost independence. His only real concern was the recrudescence of reactionary pan-Islamic fanaticism. In a sense Cromer was right; anti-occupation sentiments – at least on the surface – were the monopoly of salon intellectuals with no roots in popular feeling.

But even Cromer could see that Abbas Hilmi's succession might endanger the system he had devised for governing Egypt. As he wrote later to Rosebery: 'Under Tewfik, I remained more or less hidden. I pulled the strings. ... It was an artificial and unsatisfactory system. Its only merit was that it worked fairly well and produced good results; moreover it was extremely difficult, if not impossible, to devise any other system.'

When Abbas arrived in Cairo on 17 January Cromer's immediate impression was favourable: 'He resembles a very gentlemanlike and healthily-minded boy fresh from Eton or Harrow – not at all devoid of intelligence, but a good deal bored with el-Azhar,' he wrote to Lord Salisbury. But he added the revealing caution: 'I really wish he was not quite so civilized.' Wilfrid Blunt, who was in Egypt for the winter, also realized at once that the situation had changed but welcomed it. 'I decided that the time was now come for me to make my peace formally with the Egyptian Government,' he wrote in his journal and persuaded Cromer to present him to the new Khedive. As they went in they were met by a young man in military undress whom Blunt took to be an aide-de-camp but who turned out to be Abbas himself;

'a quite unmilitary figure of proportions which made him look
like a woman dressed up in man's clothes'. But Blunt found that he
spoke well and had a pleasant smile. 'He reminded me much of his
grandfather, Ismail, and has just the same sort of French accent,
talking French well but not perfectly.' It was the touch of sarcasm
in his voice which particularly reminded him of Ismail.

Blunt noted that Cromer's manner was very abrupt, 'like that of
a schoolmaster to a schoolboy'. After the interview he remarked that
the Khedive would only be driven with a very light rein but was
told that it was necessary to treat orientals firmly. Blunt claims that
he warned Cromer he would have trouble.[1]

All went well at first. Sultan Abdulhamid tried to make use of
the young Khedive's inexperience to detach Sinai from Egypt in
the firman of investiture. Abbas needed Cromer and British
diplomatic support to retrieve the situation. 'I see that the young
Khedive is going to be very *Egyptian*,' wrote Cromer approvingly
to Salisbury. By 'Egyptian' he meant anti-Turkish but he was
nearer the truth than he realized.

At first Cromer was satisfied: 'The position here during the last
week or two has been rather delicate,' he wrote to Salisbury on
15 April. 'First, my poor little Khedive was bandied about like a
shuttlecock between rival interests; but he behaved very well.
Then we have a very honest and well-intentioned, but extremely
weak, prime minister (Mustafa Pasha Fehmi). Both he and the
Khedive cling to my skirts with a tenacity which is almost greater
than I could wish.'

Within a few months Abbas began to show his resentment
against Cromer's headmasterly manner towards him.

Abbas appointed his former tutor, Rouiller Bey, described by
Cromer as an 'Anglophobe Swiss', as his private secretary. On
political matters he listened to the advice of Tigrane Pasha,
Nubar's son-in-law, who, though an Armenian, at least professed
to be an ardent Egyptian patriot. He was described by Cromer as
one of those 'hybrid and nondescript Egyptians who had the ear
of the Khedive, and who, more than any other class, chafed under
British control'.[2]

Cromer was irritated by the young Khedive's behaviour but not
seriously alarmed. 'The Khedive has been very foolish about a
number of small things, but he is so young and inexperienced that
he ought not to be judged harshly,' he wrote to Rosebery on 12

November. The 'small things' Cromer referred to were the various ways in which Abbas was trying to prove that he was not a puppet. In his *Abbas II* he lists all the most trivial things (such as the Khedive's complaint that an English officer had come to one of his receptions wearing long boots instead of trousers) in order to portray him as petty and spiteful. But Abbas was also setting out to establish the more general principle that the members of the Cabinet were his ministers and not Cromer's. The principle had been established by Cromer that if the ministers visited the Khedive they should always be accompanied by the financial adviser, Elwin Palmer. When Abbas went on a tour of the Delta he ostentatiously failed to take Palmer with him.

The situation was not improved by the contemptuous teasing of Abbas on the part of Arthur Hardinge, the legation secretary, who acted as chargé d'affaires during Cromer's summer leaves. After a visit to England the Khedive complained to Hardinge that Queen Victoria had received him sitting under an umbrella in the garden instead of giving him a formal audience, adding, 'It is not in this manner that Her Majesty would have received the German Emperor or the Czar of Russia – not that I should put myself entirely on the same footing with these potentates'. Hardinge replied with a low bow, 'Your Highness is not the only one who would say so' and later recounted the anecdote to a delighted audience at the legation.

The Khedive was encouraged by the belief that if it came to a showdown with Cromer he would have the support of the sultan and of the other Powers – notably France. This was the impression he received from the pro-French press in Egypt, the French consul-general and reports of the activities of Anglophobe French political circles. He also believed that Gladstone's return to power in England in August 1892 would strengthen his position. Not for the first time, Gladstone had come out against the British occupation of Egypt in his speeches in opposition. Tigrane Pasha was an avid reader of the British press and reported all this faithfully to the Khedive. He did not, however, apparently understand the significance of Lord Rosebery's appointment to the foreign office in the new Government.

About the time of Gladstone's return to power Milner's *England in Egypt* was published. While it was well received in Britain as a masterly apologia for Cromer's policies, it had the opposite effect in

Egypt where it appeared simultaneously in an Arabic translation. It candidly revealed the workings of the Veiled Protectorate and gave the clear impression that, if Cromer had his way, the British would remain in Egypt indefinitely. Egyptian public opinion began to concentrate its hopes on Abbas to lead the resistance to this policy.

The Khedive had for some time been looking for an opportunity to get rid of Mustafa Pasha Fehmi, whom he regarded as weak and incapable of standing up to Cromer – a view that is confirmed by Cromer himself. His chance came at the end of 1893 when the prime minister fell dangerously ill with a congestion of the lungs. Cromer wanted to bring back Riaz as the least of alternative evils, but Abbas calmly informed him that he wished to appoint Tigrane. This started a prolonged and high-pressured correspondence between Cromer and Rosebery. The foreign secretary complained of Cromer's 'near-hysterical letters' and, at one point, of his 'tumultuous storm of sinister telegrams', but on essential matters he gave Cromer his support and rallied the wavering Liberal Government by threatening his resignation. He only asked Cromer to deal as far as possible directly with him. 'Pray remember very carefully the distinction between telegrams – it is only those marked *private* that I consider as personal to myself – all the others go into the hands of my sixteen colleagues. There are many "nuances" of the situation that, without any disloyalty to them, are better only seen by me.'

When Abbas insisted on appointing Tigrane, Cromer cabled to Rosebery asking for the British Government to express its disapproval. He gave as his reason that Tigrane, as a Christian, would be unacceptable to 'native opinion'. This was disingenuous; he had virtually imposed Nubar on Egypt before and was to do so again. His real reason was that Tigrane would be thoroughly unamenable. In his reply, Rosebery accepted that Tigrane was unsuitable but advised Cromer not to press his opposition too far if the Khedive insisted. This did not satisfy Cromer, who realized that if Abbas was to have his way the entire Veiled Protectorate system would collapse. When he still failed to extract an absolute veto on Tigrane from the British Government he even considered threatening the Khedive to have Tigrane exiled. This turned out to be unnecessary because after a talking-to from Cromer, doubtless at his most magisterial, Tigrane realized the risk he was running and advised the Khedive against appointing him. Meanwhile Mustafa Pasha Fehmi had recovered enough to be out of danger so there was no immediate necessity of finding a successor.

Cromer was by now seriously concerned with the conduct of his new senior prefect. He wrote to Rosebery: 'He is an extremely foolish youth. It is difficult to know how to deal with him ... I think he will have to receive a sharp lesson sooner or later – and the sooner the better.' The occasion arose soon enough. On 15 January – barely two weeks after the freezing of the Tigrane crisis – the Khedive's private secretary called on Cromer and advised him that Mustafa Pasha Fehmi had been dismissed and Fakhri Pasha appointed in his place. This was a deliberate provocation because Fakhri, whom Cromer described as Tigrane's 'alter ego', was thoroughly unreliable; he had resigned as minister of justice when Cromer overruled him on the question of Scott's judicial reforms. Cromer records that when the Khedive's secretary called on Fehmi to inform him of his dismissal, the latter 'gave his headstrong master some sensible advice, which he would have done well to have followed'. This advice was to consult Cromer before making any ministerial changes. This was, of course, precisely what Abbas was determined not to do and proof, if any was needed, that Fehmi was Cromer's puppet.

Cromer went to almost any lengths to alarm the British Government. The 'coup d'état' (for so it was described by the English officials in Egypt) he said had been planned by the sultan through his agent in Egypt, Ghazi Moukhtar Pasha. Abbas' grandfather, the ex-Khedive Ismail, was also involved as were France and Russia.

On 16 January Rosebery telegraphed: 'Her Majesty's government expect to be consulted in such important matters as a change of ministers. No change appears to be either necessary or desirable. We cannot therefore sanction the proposed nomination of Fakhri Pasha.' But this was not enough for Cromer who suggested that British troops should occupy the key ministries and the British adviser take over the departments. Again this proved unnecessary; after consulting Riaz and Nubar, Abbas surrendered. Fakhri resigned before his appointment was published in the official gazette and as a face-saving compromise agreed by Cromer and Abbas, Riaz once again became prime minister. As Cromer observed, he had thought 'it might perhaps be wise not to humiliate the young Khedive unduly. If he were treated generously, all excuse for future misbehaviour would be removed.'³ Also, Fehmi could always be brought back again later – as he was after eighteen months.

Cromer had won a victory and taught the Khedive a lesson. The trouble was that Egyptians did not see the incident in this light. Though reactionary, Riaz was far from being a British puppet and he now encouraged the Khedive to act independently. Public opinion rallied strongly behind them and British officials in Egypt who, with some justification, had just been congratulating themselves on the improved financial outlook, had to face a wave of hostile criticism.

Evacuation was out of the question for Cromer; annexation was unacceptable to the Gladstone Government as likely to provoke a European war. Accordingly Cromer did everything in his power to preserve the Veiled Protectorate, and because the Khedive was still being insubordinate – in spite of the lesson he had been taught – Cromer decided to wield the stick and asked Rosebery for the British garrison in Egypt to be strengthened. Deliberately resurrecting the spectre of Arabi Pasha, he informed the Government that the army supported the Khedive: 'It appears that all the young officers are in favour of Egypt for the Egyptians.' The request horrified most of the Cabinet and Gladstone remarked that they might as well ask him to put a torch to Westminster Abbey as to send more troops to Egypt. But Rosebery supported Cromer and since the Government's survival, together with Gladstone's hopes for Irish home rule, depended upon the foreign secretary remaining in the Cabinet, Rosebery had his way and the troops were sent.

The Khedive was still far from cowed into submission. With Riaz's encouragement he was beginning to lead what looked remarkably like a new Arabist movement with the Khedive at its head. But, like Arabi, he was learning how little he could expect in practical support from outside. For the time being, Cromer was reasonably satisfied. On 26 January he telegraphed to Lord Rosebery: 'The lesson which the Khedive has now received will, I am of opinion, cause his Highness to be very careful in his conduct for the present'. Later he wrote that the Khedive was to behave himself for just one year before his 'smothered hostility to England burst again into flame'.

In July 1893 Abbas paid a state visit to the sultan at

Constantinople, accompanied by Tigrane Pasha. His aim was to complain about Cromer's treatment of him and to elicit a firm guarantee of the sultan's support. The visit was not a success. The sultan received him amicably four or five times but characteristically promised nothing. Tigrane had a cool reception from the representatives of the Powers whom he canvassed. Russia, Germany, Austria and Italy had no desire to see an independent Egypt or British policy changed while France showed no inclination to back its hostile criticisms with action. A delegation of Egyptian Sheikhs and Notables who presented a petition against the British occupation only alarmed the sultan who, as Cromer remarked, 'disliked popular demonstrations of any kind'.

It was only at home in Egypt that Abbas's fledgeling national movement was making some headway. Although Cromer contemptuously insisted that it consisted of an alliance of self-seeking individuals who bore Britain a grudge and that the great majority of the Egyptians would have been horrified by a British evacuation, he admitted that it was having some practical success. 'English officials are being practically boycotted and so also are natives who sympathize with England.'

Cromer went home in early July 1893 for his annual leave and found on his return in October that the situation had deteriorated. Understandably discontented, British officials were demanding action. The legislative council, though consisting largely of docile government nominees, had summoned up enough patriotic courage to refuse approval of the army estimates in the budget.* Still Cromer held his hand knowing, as he said, that 'if I had the patience to wait, the folly of my opponents would afford me some suitable opportunity for striking a decisive blow'.

He did not have to wait for long. In December 1893 the Khedive announced that he intended to make a tour of inspection of Egyptian army units on the Nile between Aswan and Wadi Halfa. He took with him his recently appointed under-secretary for war, Maher Pasha, who was already suspected of Anglophobe tendencies. Kitchener, who was anxious to buttress the morale of the

* The Khedive told Wilfrid Blunt that he had the greatest difficulty in keeping up their courage. One member of the council had been terrorized by Kitchener when he had to ask the sirdar to get his son into the military school. Kitchener had pointed out to the father that he was one of those wanting to cut down the military estimates and shown him the door.

newly reconstructed army, laid on a series of parades and tattoos
in the Khedive's honour. But Abbas found fault with everything;
he criticized the standard of drill and smartness of the troops –
especially the Sudanese 'black' battalions which were mainly
under British officers. Finally, after a march-past of the Wadi
Halfa garrison, he remarked to Kitchener: 'To tell you the truth,
Kitchener Pasha, I consider that it is disgraceful for Egypt to be
served by such an army.' Kitchener, whose temperature had been
rising steadily during the previous days, at once offered his
resignation. The Khedive saw that he had gone too far and begged
him to withdraw. The next day he told Kitchener 'that on parade
the day before he had felt a rush of blood to the head, and that
when this occurred he hardly knew what he said or did'. But,
according to Kitchener's biographer Philip Magnus, the sirdar
rejected the olive branch because he did not wish to appear to
have resigned in a fit of pique, and Abbas never forgave him
because he felt he had humiliated himself for nothing. He had
already telegraphed a report of the incident to Cromer in which he
said that when the Khedive had assured him of his confidence
'I gave him to understand that I would not persist in my resignation, although I did not absolutely withdraw it'. This curious
circumlocution gave Cromer the opening he needed. Cromer
recorded later[4] that he was first struck by the gravity of the
incident in view of the dangers of trifling with the discipline of an
army in which the officers were Europeans and Christians while
the soldiers were African or Asiatic Muslims, and secondly that
'the opportunity for which I had been waiting had come'. Having
cabled for Rosebery's support, which was immediately forthcoming, he informed Riaz that he demanded Maher Pasha's immediate
resignation and the issue of a Khedivial statement praising the
armed forces. Riaz hastened to meet the Khedive who was returning
to Cairo and begged him to give way. Angry and resentful, Abbas
accepted Cromer's demands although he never forgave Riaz who
was obliged to resign three months later.

Writing after his retirement, Cromer said that there had been
two turning-points in Anglo-Egyptian relations since the occupation of 1882. The first had been in 1887 when the sultan's fortunate failure to ratify the Drummond Wolff convention had meant
that Britain had not been obliged to evacuate Egypt prematurely.
The second was in 1894 when the rebellious Khedive capitulated.

Abbas II was still to cause trouble 'but the battle for British supremacy was virtually fought and won during the eventful period when Lord Rosebery presided at the foreign office'.* He gave the credit to Rosebery 'for without his cordial support I should have been quite powerless'.

The royal rebel's frontal assault on Cromer's authority had been defeated. From then on he could cause Cromer irritation but never any serious alarm. He was obliged to pursue his campaign at second-hand through the press and the renascent nationalist movement which he helped to finance. But his spirit was broken and he devoted himself increasingly to his personal affairs and the enrichment of his private estates – often by devious means. In 1903, Wilfrid Blunt, who had placed such high hopes in him on his accession to the throne, 'found him grown older and less fat and gay, with a rather harassed look, like a man who had been worried and bullied, but whether by Cromer or by his new Hungarian mistress I do not know'.[5]

Abbas II was intelligent and at least at the outset ambitious but it would have required political genius, which he did not possess, to win with the cards stacked so heavily against him. Though determined not to follow his father's course of action as a constitutional façade for British rule he could not forget the fate of his grandfather Ismail, whom he admired. The threat of deposition was always in the background although Cromer and the other English officials took care never to mention it except in private correspondence. As long as Turkey and the Powers would give him no more than verbal support he had no real protection. Even British liberal and radical opinion, which might well have sympathized with the Khedive in his struggle with Cromer, was hostile. If he had a thoroughly bad press in Britain it was partly his own fault because he chose his ground badly – especially in the Wadi Halfa incident with Kitchener. Also Cromer, who was aware of the British tendency to sympathize with the underdog, carefully avoided humiliating him excessively.

Cromer and the other British officials in Egypt were not immediately aware that the victory for British supremacy had been won. Dawkins, who was assistant to Elwin Palmer the financial adviser, wrote to Milner in February 1895 to ask his advice on the

* Rosebery briefly became prime minister of the expiring Liberal Government in March 1894.

best means of deposing the Khedive. Although Milner had left Egypt in 1891 to take up the post of chairman of the board of inland revenue, he had maintained his interest in Egypt and kept up a rather surprising correspondence with Cromer's subordinates. He replied that English opinion was fed up with Abbas and that 'a bold act of usurpation' would be instantly condoned and applauded. 'The only thing needful is that there should be, or seem to be, a state of things sufficiently critical to justify it. Disturbances at Alexandria, even if they are not very bad disturbances, are quite good enough and they have the additional advantage of frightening the European "colonies", the most timorous aggregations of human beings in the world, and inducing them and their governments to look leniently on any action which may avert the danger, largely imaginary, of a repetition of the events of 1882.'[6] In expressing his hope for a small riot in Alexandria to justify the deposition of the Khedive and an intensification of British rule in Egypt, Milner was exhibiting a degree of moral blindness which was exceptional even among late nineteenth-century imperialists.

NATIONALIST RENAISSANCE

In 1895 Cromer had reason to be pleased with the shape of events. The Veiled Protectorate had been preserved and Egyptian officials taught that non-co-operation was useless. Of the former under-secretary of state for war who had encouraged Abbas in his fatal insubordination, he remarked: 'Like a good many other Egyptian officials, Maher Pasha soon learnt that his Anglophobia was a mistake. He eventually obtained civil employment and worked cordially with the British officials.' Even Riaz mellowed with time; in 1904 he caused a stir with a speech praising Egypt's progress under British auspices.

What Cromer failed to see was that the reviving national movement had not ebbed away but been diverted into other channels. He said that once Riaz had gone he realized that the day was past when Egypt could be governed by men of his type, but for the alternative – the 'Gallicized Egyptian' – he held nothing but contempt. This was true even of Nubar although he admired his intelligence. With the Khedive's sullen acceptance the now tired and elderly Armenian was brought back as prime minister in April 1894. Nubar despised those Egyptians who he said had encouraged the Khedive to rebel only to throw themselves at Cromer's feet at the moment of crisis. He endeavoured to retrieve what he could of the remnants of Egyptian independence but it was too late. He did succeed in restoring the police powers of the provincial *Mudirs* – the matter on which he had resigned ten years before – but since the police force was now controlled from the top by an English inspector-general working through his own inspectors in the provinces, it was a hollow victory. He even had to accept Eldon Gorst as under-secretary at the ministry of the interior; Nubar's semantic quibble that Gorst was merely attached to the ministry deceived no one. In April 1895 Nubar fractured his ankle and departed for England to convalesce; he returned in November broken in health and expressing a wish to retire. The way was open for the return of the loyally Anglophile Mustafa Pasha Fehmi, who in fact remained at the head of the Government for the remaining twelve years of Cromer's rule in Egypt.

These were years of a remarkable economic boom. The first decade of the British occupation, during which Egyptian Governments and their British financial advisers had devoted themselves to staving off bankruptcy, had been a period of austerity and skimp. The brief boom in foreign investment which had followed Ismail's abdication was abruptly halted by the Arabi revolt and the value of agricultural land declined sharply. Foreign investors began to recover their confidence in the early 1890s and capital flowed into Egyptian enterprises – new railways, irrigation and land reclamation. In 1897 £E11·9 million out of a total of £E13·9 million invested in Egyptian companies was foreign-owned. By 1902 this had risen to £E24·6 million out of £E26·3 million; in 1914 it was over £E100 million. Between 1900 and 1907 no less than 160 new companies were formed. French and British investors were predominant although Belgian investors had an important share. In Britain the lead in promoting Egyptian enterprises was taken by Sir Ernest Cassel, multi-millionaire financier and friend of Edward VII. We have already seen how he made the building of the Aswan Dam possible. In 1898, with two partners, he founded the National Bank of Egypt which became in fact the country's central bank and bank of issue. In 1902 the National Bank took over control of the Agricultural Bank which had been established by the Government to help small farmers. In 1908 he founded the Mortgage Company which aimed to encourage English financial interests to invest in Egyptian mortgages.

For the most part the Egyptians were only passive partners in this extraordinary boom. By 1914 some 92 per cent of the capital of joint-stock enterprises operating in Egypt was foreign-owned and interest liabilities to foreigners amounted to £E8·5 million a year. Egypt was no longer bankrupt but it had an enormous and growing overdraft.

According to Cromer's logic, prosperity must mean that the Egyptian people were fundamentally contented. They might grumble at their lost independence and the British occupiers could never expect gratitude for what they had done for Egypt, but he was convinced that the majority of Egyptians would have been horrified if the agitators had succeeded in forcing the English to evacuate.

There was some sound reason for his complacency. The bright young lawyers and journalists – the Gallicized Egyptians he so despised – and those who led the agitation against the British occupation in the 1890s had little comprehension of the feelings of the majority of the Egyptian people, the *fellahin*. But he was wrong to dismiss them entirely. If they lacked judgement and 'gravitas' this was at least partly because the Cromerist Veiled Protectorate denied them access to political or administrative power. The only outlet for their feelings was in the French and Arabic press which consequently was filled with polemical and ill-researched diatribes against the occupation. There was virtually complete liberty of the press because Cromer regarded it as unimportant.

This new wave of nationalism found a natural leader in a slender and passionate youth named Mustafa Kamel. Born of middle-class parents in 1874 he hurled himself into politics when still a schoolboy of 16. Kamel studied law first at the Cairo law school and then at Toulouse, where he graduated in 1894. He returned to Egypt to form a group with other young Egyptian lawyers and intellectuals which later took the official title of Hizb al-Watan or National Party. He had already made contact with the young Khedive soon after his accession. By 1895 Abbas had lost his own battle with Cromer but was prepared to continue the campaign indirectly by supplying the National Party with money and advice. It was decided that Kamel should go to Europe as the party's emissary to rally support for Egyptian independence.

Kamel's first action was to present to the president of the French chamber of deputies a propaganda picture representing France as liberator of the oppressed and Egypt brutally tied in chains by perfidious Albion. He also wrote a touching letter to the powerful elderly lady journalist, Mme Juliette Adam, editor of the *Nouvelle Revue des Deux Mondes*: '*Madame, je suis encore petit, mais j'ai des ambitions hautes. Je veux, dans la vieille Egypte, réveiller le jeune. . . .*' This began a friendship which lasted until Kamel's premature death at thirty-four. Through Madame Adam, Kamel met all the leading French political and literary figures who showed interest in Egyptian affairs including Pierre Loti, General Marchand (soon to confront Kitchener at Fashoda) and the well-known Anglophobe deputy Etienne Deloncle. He published articles in the *Nouvelle Revue* and other French papers; he addressed numerous private and public meetings. But though he achieved some eminence, was lionized and flattered, he came to realize that Egypt's liberty would not be achieved through the support of French political salons. Most of his new friends were only interested in his movement as a means of annoying the British. In this it succeeded although to the end Cromer dismissed the National Party as spurious and, astonishingly, fails to mention Mustafa Kamel in his two books on Egypt.

He did not confine himself to France but extended his activities to Austria and Germany. In 1896 he wrote to the aged Gladstone, then in opposition, to ask his advice on a solution of the Egyptian question and remind him of his advocacy of evacuation on various occasions since 1882. Gladstone replied courteously, but pointing out 'I am wholly devoid of power. My opinion has always been the same; that we ought to quit Egypt after having fulfilled the work for which we went there with honour and profit to that country. So far as I know that time arrived some years ago.'

Kamel had many of the qualities that Edwardian Englishmen were calculated to dislike. With his enormous liquid eyes and receding chin he was good-looking rather than handsome but undeniably attractive (or *séduisant*, as the French would say) to both sexes. With his lively mind and French education he was an excellent conversationalist but he was also a powerful orator. Between his frequent visits to Europe he made speeches in Egypt and wrote articles in the press. In 1900 he founded his own paper, *al-Liwa* (the Standard) which soon reached the remarkable circulation of 10,000. This was followed by a quarterly in 1902 and English and French editions of *al-Liwa* in 1907.

In the early years of his short political career, Kamel co-operated fully with the Khedive. On his advice he championed the pan-Islamic movement and cultivated relations with the sultan who made him a Pasha in 1904. Predictably, Cromer seized on the pan-Islamic element to accuse the National Party of 'fanaticism'. To counter this Kamel went out of his way to discountenance xenophobia among his followers and to encourage Egyptian Copts to join the national movement. But his simultaneous championing of Egyptian nationalism and the rights of the Ottoman sultan ultimately led him into a damaging false position. When in 1906 the sultan, who was building his Hejaz Railway to Medina, landed a force at the head of the Gulf of Aqaba and laid claim to the whole of the Sinai Peninsula, Kamel led the nationalists into a vigorous campaign in his support. Juridically the sultan had a fairly good case but it was left to Cromer to champion the cause of Egyptian territorial integrity. His principal concern, as of the British Government, was to keep the Turks away from the Suez Canal but many patriotic Egyptians saw no point in abandoning Sinai, which had widely come to be regarded as Egyptian territory, for the rather nebulous cause of Islamic solidarity.

Edward Grey, foreign minister in the new Liberal Government, assembled the British fleet at Piraeus and delivered a virtual ultimatum to the sultan who, since the expected moral support from the Kaiser had faded away, quickly backed down.

This incident was the signal for a group of moderate Egyptian nationalists, who were unenthusiastic about Kamel's pan-Islamic policies, to found their own newspaper and a year later their own political party, the Hizb al-Umma or People's Party. The leading intellect in the Umma Party was a radical young lawyer, Ahmed Lutfi al-Sayyid, but its members were far from revolutionary. They included Mustafa Pasha Fehmi and most of the ministers who were generally wealthy bulwarks of the establishment. They accepted co-operation with the British and only looked on Egypt's independence as a distant goal; for some it was so remote as to be out of sight. Cromer gave these men his cautious approval. One of his last acts was to have the rising young star of the party, Saad Zaghlul, who was Mustafa Pasha Fehmi's son-in-law, made head of the newly-created department of education. But this was too little and too late. The aspiring younger generation of Egyptian politicians, who were naturally more impatient than their elders, did not see the Umma Party as the likely instrument to achieve Egyptian self-government. Zaghlul himself, though warmly praised by Cromer in his Farewell address,* was to become the champion of Egypt's immediate independence and Britain's bitter enemy.

In the early years of the twentieth century it was the Nationalist Party which caught the imagination of Young Egypt. Kamel's oratory and personal magnetism transcended the illogicalities in his position.

The fact that he first made the Egyptian people aware of their

---

* 'He possesses all the qualities necessary to serve his country. He is honest; he is capable; he has the courage of his convictions; he has been abused by many of the less worthy of his own countrymen.'

patriotic feelings gave him the right to plead the cause of Turkey against Egypt's interests and to take most of them with him. It has been pointed out that Kamel was 'a typical nineteenth-century middle-class nationalist'.[1] His French education had imbued him with the principles of the French Revolution but he was un-influenced by Marx. He scarcely ever mentioned the need for social or economic reforms and when he did his views were con-servative. He was interested in education and helped to found a college in Cairo in 1898 but he looked on it essentially as a means to enable the Egyptians to wrest their independence from the British.

At the outset of his career he looked to France to help him achieve his goal. This belief was first shaken by France's retreat after the Fashoda incident which reduced the Khedive to a state of cynical hopelessness. Kamel's francophilia received its *coup de grâce* with the entente cordiale of 1904. As part of this important package deal which prepared the way for the Anglo-French alliance in the First World War, the rival imperial powers settled a number of outstanding differences over their colonial possessions in Africa and Asia. In particular the entente provided that Britain would renounce its rights and interest in Morocco while France would do the same in Egypt.

Cromer looked on the agreement as an unmitigated advantage. At one stroke the irksome financial restrictions on the Egyptian Government were removed together with the only potential threat to the British position in Egypt. But for Mustafa Kamel and the nationalists the entente cordiale was a disaster; the British occupation now appeared permanent and immovable. Kamel wrote bitterly to Juliette Adam: 'I would be an imbecile were I to believe for an instant that France could be the friend of Egypt or of Islam'. But this only served to emphasize something that Kamel had always been saying in his speeches to the Egyptian people: that if they really wanted their freedom they must struggle for it themselves.

Fortunately at this time there was in Japan an inspiring example of an oriental nation which had heaved itself up by its own efforts and was in the process of inflicting a humiliating defeat on Russia, one of the Powers. Kamel wrote a book on the subject entitled *The Rising Sun*, which appeared in 1904.

Nevertheless 1904–6 were difficult years for the nationalists. As we have seen, the Khedive had become totally discouraged and although he continued to provide funds for the National Party he was more interested in making money himself. There is some evidence that Kamel distrusted the Khedive although he continued to emphasize his importance as the symbol of Egypt's national independence. If this independence had been achieved and Britain had evacuated it is doubtful whether Kamel and the Khedive could have continued their co-operation.

There were many Egyptians who distrusted Kamel for his association with the Khedive and for what they regarded as his ill-considered political judgements. Some of these were mere collaborators who were doing well under the British occupation and saw no advantage in bringing it to an end. But others were what Cromer called 'the Girondists of the Egyptian national movement' and included Sheikh Mohammed Abdu, who died in 1905, and his spiritual disciples in the Umma Party. Kamel was the only Egyptian nationalist at that time who seemed to possess political charisma. His enemies charged him with demagogy and some of his oratory must bear this charge, although most of his speeches read surprisingly well today. He made good use of his ability to sway crowds but it would be difficult to think of a popular national leader who did not.

Nevertheless, in 1906 Kamel's movement was in danger of losing its impetus. Although his leadership survived the Aqaba crisis there must have been doubts among some of his followers. To some extent he was helped by Cromer's intransigent attitude towards the extension of self-governing institutions. He was ready to give the Girondists a pat of approval for their moderation but not any political power. Then in June 1906 something happened which rallied the patriotic instincts of every Egyptian and placed the collaborators in an unenviable position.

The Denshawai incident was a turning-point in the British occupation of Egypt comparable to the Amritsar massacre of 1919 in India. Every Egyptian schoolboy knows the story.*

Denshawai is a small village near Tanta in the Nile Delta, and like many Egyptian villages today the inhabitants raised pigeons which they kept in tower-shaped pigeon-houses of unbaked brick, a characteristic feature of the Egyptian countryside. In 1905 an

---

* And not only Egyptians. Shortly before the Suez crisis of 1956 Lebanese Druze student told the author that Denshawai explained the anti-British outpourings of Radio Cairo.

incident had occurred when a party of British officers had gone pigeon-shooting at Denshawai for sport. The villagers, led by one doughty old pigeon-farmer named Hassan Mahfouz, protested vigorously with little result, although orders were issued to the army that no one should shoot pigeons in the villages without the consent of the omdeh.

A year later, on 13 June 1906, a party of five British officers, an Egyptian policeman and a dragoman interpreter, which included one of the sportsmen from the previous year, appeared again at Denshawai at the invitation of a local landowner. The omdeh was absent but his deputy told them they would have to go away from the village to shoot; they retired for a few hundred yards and began shooting. At this moment a threshing floor in the village caught fire; the villagers, who were already angered by the pigeon-shooting, assumed that the sportsmen were responsible. Led by Hassan Mahfouz they attacked the British officers with their wooden staves in an attempt to take away their guns. The senior officer, Major Pine-Coffin (*sic*) told the others to give up their guns in the hope that it would calm the villagers, but in the scuffle a gun went off and wounded three men and a woman, who fell and was taken for dead. The villagers now attacked more strongly using stones as well as sticks. Another officer, Captain Bull, who had been severely beaten went to fetch help but died of concussion and heatstroke near the army camp. An Egyptian fellah who had tried to help him was found by a party of British soldiers who, assuming that he had murdered Captain Bull, beat him to death.

The tragedy had been caused by the British officers' insensitivity in the first place and by subsequent misunderstanding on both sides. But Cromer and the vast majority of the European communities saw it in a different light. To them it was one more symptom of the dangerous xenophobic fanaticism, fanned by the nationalists, that was sweeping the countryside. The cry for exemplary punishment was started by the European press and taken up by the London newspapers. 'Everything indicates that the outrage was much more serious than at first supposed and that it was prearranged,' wrote the *Daily Chronicle*.*

* In the preface to *John Bull's Other Island* Bernard Shaw wrote one of his best passages of acid polemic on the incident. 'Try to imagine the feelings of an English village if a party of Chinese officers suddenly appeared and began shooting the ducks, the geese, the hens, and the

A special tribunal was set up with three British officials and two Egyptians (Fathi Bey Zaghlul, brother of Saad Zaghlul, and Boutros Ghali, a Coptic Pasha who was President), but the Court's proceedings were virtually conducted by Sir Walter Bond, vice-president of the appeal court who, like his two British colleagues, knew little Arabic. According to Judge Marshall, 'The case was conducted with such a want of method that when minutes of the proceedings were called for by parliament in London, they had to be compiled from reports made by native journalists for their papers.'[2]

Of the fifty-two accused twenty-one were sentenced – four, including Hassan Mahfouz, were sentenced to death, two, including the husband of the injured woman, to penal servitude for life, six men to seven years in prison and the rest to fifty lashes. The sentences of hanging and flogging were carried out on the site of the incident and the villagers were compelled to watch.

When the incident occurred, Cromer was about to depart for England on his annual summer leave. He reported the matter to Edward Grey and then left, with the unfortunate Charles de Mansfeld Findlay (later British minister in Norway) in charge of the agency. He reported to London that: 'in native circles ... I understand, the conduct of the villagers is looked upon as casting discredit on the whole Egyptian people, as well as being indefensible in itself'. The Alexandria correspondent of *The Times* wrote (28 June): 'Opinion among Europeans and many respectable natives supports the verdict, the evidence having proved that the attack had been premeditated for months.' But neither Mansfeld Findlay nor any of his colleagues foresaw the Egyptian reaction to the savage punishment of the villagers. Editors, poets and politicians combined to denounce it. Many who hitherto had hardly been stirred by nationalist feelings were converted overnight, and Kamel gained a million new followers. The famous writer and disciple of Mohammed Abdu, Qasim Amin, who had hitherto supported the British occupation, wrote: 'Everyone I met had a broken heart and a lump in his throat. There was nervousness in

---

turkeys, and carried them off, asserting that they were wild birds, as everybody in China knew, and that the pretended indignation of the farmers was a cloak for hatred of the Chinese, and perhaps for a plot to overthrow the religion of Confucius and establish the Church of England in its place.'

every gesture – in their hand and their voices. Sadness was on every face, but it was a peculiar sort of sadness. It was confused, distracted and visibly subdued by superior force. . . .' Already the Denshawai pigeons were coming home to roost.

The uproar spread to Europe and in the House of Commons Sir Edward Grey, facing a barrage of hostile questions from Liberal MPs, defended the sentences as necessary to combat the growing fanaticism in Egypt. But Grey had serious misgivings. As soon as he had had Findlay's cable saying what the sentences were he had consulted Campbell-Bannerman and Asquith, and they had decided not to interfere only because 'Egypt was in a disturbed state. The effect of overriding the decision of the tribunal would have been incalculable. It would have spread an impression in Egypt that the officials on the spot were not to be supported from home.'[3]

Cromer was equally alarmed when he arrived in England and heard of the sentences and he hastened to tell Grey that if he had foreseen the outcome he would never have left Egypt before the trial was over. However, he confirmed Grey's opinion that it would have been a 'capital error' to override the tribunal when once the sentences had been pronounced.

CROMER BOWS OUT

In 1904 Cromer had ruled Egypt for twenty-one years and achieved most of what he had set out to do. The Egyptian Government was solvent, the Sudan had been reconquered and, finally, an agreement with France had been reached which though not exactly as Cromer would have wished, included the essential point that France undertook not to 'obstruct the action of Great Britain' in Egypt 'by asking that a limit of time be fixed for the British occupation or in any other manner'.* Although the Caisse de la Dette was not abolished, as Cromer had hoped, its powers were greatly reduced. It now became only a receiver of debt payments and any surplus after a reserve fund of £1,800,000 had accumulated in the hands of the Caisse was entirely at the disposal of the Egyptian Government.

He was now sixty-four years old but still contemplated staying in Egypt until he was seventy. He had been heavily stricken by the death in 1898 of his wife Ethel who, though suffering from the fatal Bright's disease, had insisted on returning to Cairo for Cromer to be there during the climax of the Sudanese campaign and she had died one month after the Battle of Omdurman. She had mastered her shyness to make herself a much-loved hostess at the residency where her gentle charm offset Cromer's occasional brusqueness. For three years after her death her place was taken by Cromer's niece, Nina Baring, afterwards Countess Granville, but in 1901 he married again. The second Lady Cromer was Lady Katherine Thynne, the thirty-six-year-old sister of the Marquess of Bath. Gifted and intelligent, and 'as noble in spirit as in appearance', she was well-suited and well-trained for the post of viceregal consort at the British agency.†

* Lord Zetland, the author of Cromer's somewhat uncritical authorized biography, appears to claim that Cromer was the chief architect not only of the entente cordiale but the Anglo-Russian agreement as well. (See Chapter XXIV, *Lord Cromer* by Zetland.)

† However, Ronald Storrs, who arrived in Egypt in 1904 as a young

Like most unconstitutional monarchs, Cromer did not contemplate abdication while still in sound body and mind. In 1905 he consulted numerous doctors who agreed that he was in good condition and could continue for some years. 'But', he wrote to the foreign secretary, Lord Lansdowne, 'they all say that I am, so to speak, living on my capital, and that I cannot stand for long the sort of work I have to take for nine months a year in this climate.' His annual leaves were further extended so that he would avoid all the hot weather; this was why he was absent for the Denshawai affair. But in 1906 his health deteriorated alarmingly; for some years he had suffered from bouts of nervous dyspepsia, to which his staff had loyally attributed his occasional extreme irritability. Now this reached a stage that he spent days in great pain when he could eat nothing but Benger's Food. His wife did her best to protect him; the daily luncheon parties were abandoned. But to his intimates he gave the impression that he was dying.

It is impossible to say how far Denshawai and its consequences were responsible for his decline but they must have had something to do with it. Cromer, though absent, had approved the decisions of the special tribunal. In later years he admitted that the sentences 'though not unjust, were . . . unduly severe'.[1] What Denshawai did was to give new life to nationalist agitation at a time when Cromer was no longer able to cope with it. He still wholly underestimated its importance but at the very end of his career it helped to convince him of the need to give some more encouragement to the moderate reformers as a counterweight. But it was too late, and Cromer was fundamentally too sceptical of the Egyptians' capacity to rule themselves to show any real enthusiasm for self-governing institutions. In 1904 he had written to Lord Lansdowne with heavy sarcasm, 'The Egyptian legislative assembly, which meets once in ten years, and has a right to *emettre des voeux* has just expressed its wishes. They are that the Koran should be more freely taught, that expenditure should be in every direction increased, that numerous taxes should be abolished, that the Capitulations should be swept away, and that a Parliament on a

---

recruit to the newly constituted Egyptian civil service, records that the second Lady Cromer 'cared little for diplomatic and social life, and was far more interested in Egypt, ancient, Saracenic and modern'. (*Orientations*, p. 53.)

European model should be created – altogether a fairly extensive programme. Possibly by the year 2004, some portion of it may have been adopted.' He did not see that the assembly was doomed to be irresponsible as long as it was denied responsibility.

A confidential pamphlet written in 1905 for the guidance of young recruits to the Anglo-Egyptian service is revealing.* In a brief 'Historical background' the pamphlet points out that the British occupation of Egypt 'is of a character wholly without precedent'. Whereas an occupation is usually the result of defeat in war, in this case Britain's sole object had been to restore order and re-establish the legitimate authority of the Khedive and his Government. 'The British occupation of Egypt may, therefore, be properly characterized as a friendly occupation, by mutual consent of the parties concerned, and not in any respect reducing the country to the position of a conquered state.' The pamphlet then goes on to describe the 'Tasks before the Young British Official'. 'When the work of reform first commenced, it was thought that the object in view would be best attained by limiting the number of British officials as far as possible. Their duty was to consist almost entirely in guiding and advising the native officials, in whose hands rested almost the whole of the executive business of administration. ... As time went on, and as the task which the British Government set themselves became more clearly defined, it was found that the maintenance of this system was incompatible with the true interests of the country, and that further English assistance was necessary if the objects in view were to be fully realized. A small number of high officials, with executive powers, were therefore appointed. ... Concurrently with these appointments, a moderate number of Englishmen had also been placed in subordinate posts of greater or less importance, but the principle had always been kept in view that Egypt should be ruled, as far as might be, by the Egyptians themselves. Unfortunately, and to the great regret of the authorities responsible for the gradual extension of British executive interference, this principle has not proved successful. Experience showed that the native official, considered

* The uncorrected draft, which had been prepared by Boyle for Cromer's signature, was found in Harry Boyle's papers after his death. It was never printed because they concluded that there was too much danger that a copy would find its way into the native press. (*Boyle of Cairo*, Clara Boyle, Chapter IV.)

as a class, however gladly he might welcome or intelligently receive the advice and instructions of his English superior, had not yet reached either the stage of intellectual development which would enable him to carry out those instructions with efficiency, or of moral courage enough to face the terrors of unsupported responsibility. . . . The one and only object which we should keep in view approaches almost pure altruism – it is, in few words, to confer upon a people whose past is one of the most deplorable ever recorded in history, those benefits and privileges which they have never enjoyed at the hands of the numerous alien races who have hitherto held sway over them; and to endeavour to the utmost of our power to train up, by precept and example, generations of Egyptians who in the future may take our place and carry on the tradition of our administration.'

It is not difficult to see why Boyle and Cromer were concerned that this paper should not fall into the hands of the nationalists, who would have made good use of selected passages. But what is interesting is not the overbearing self-confidence which is an essential ingredient of successful imperialism but the patent sincerity with which Boyle and Cromer declared that they were teaching the Egyptians to govern themselves as fast as was reasonably possible. There were few Englishmen who were prepared to point out that they were deceiving themselves. There was Wilfrid Blunt who was always ready to do battle in the British press and who published his *Secret History of the English Occupation of Egypt* immediately after Cromer's retirement.* But Blunt was so widely regarded as an egregious rebel that his criticisms merely confirmed the authority of Cromer's views. With Cromer's long tenure of office in Egypt even men like Rosebery, Salisbury and Lansdowne deferred to his judgement, whereas in Egypt no one on his staff was prepared to contradict him. Professor A. H. Sayce, the distinguished archaeologist who visited Egypt during most of the years of Cromer's regime, pointed out that 'the first-class men by whom Lord Cromer had been surrounded when he first went to Egypt had been succeeded by mediocrities. This was partly his own fault. Age and increasing authority made him increasingly autocratic; he became impatient of contradiction and preferred

---

* He sent copies to the prime minister, Grey, Churchill, the Kaiser and Roosevelt. But Cromer was able to answer several points in his *Modern Egypt* which was published the following year.

subordinates who accepted his views without question to men of independent thought.'²

In 1896 Alonzo Money, who was the British commissioner on the Caisse and therefore not under Cromer's authority, wrote an article for private circulation among his friends saying that Britain's claim to be prolonging the occupation to enable its reforms to work was bogus because in 'emasculating the governing classes' in Egypt it was ensuring that a British withdrawal was impossible. The article came into the hands of Cromer who was confident enough to send it to Salisbury as proof of Money's ignorance.

The weightiest criticism came from Edward Dicey. Unlike Blunt, he had always advocated that Britain should declare a protectorate over Egypt. As far back as 1878 he had crossed swords with Gladstone on the subject in the pages of the *Nineteenth Century*. Thirty years later he wrote a book called *The Future of Egypt* in which he paid a high tribute to Cromer's merits as an administrator but pointed out that his 'remarkable individuality' had unconsciously biased him in favour of a system of autocratic rule based on young British officials wholly subordinate to himself. Dicey said that these officials, who were not required to know Arabic, were positively discouraged from intimacy with their native colleagues or from discovering the views of the Egyptian people. Any experienced old hands, whether English or Egyptian, who did not share Cromer's views on the way Egypt should be administered, for many years had not been invited to the agency except on purely social occasions. Dicey added that he had no doubt that Cromer's self-isolation was not deliberate and that he honestly believed that what he was doing was in the interest of England in the first place and of Egypt in the second. But he was deceiving himself if he did not see that his policy was indefinitely prolonging the British occupation. Successive Conservative and Liberal Governments had been abetting him in also refusing to face the facts.

Cromer was sufficiently aware of this charge to answer it in his chapter on 'The British Officials' in *Modern Egypt*. After pointing out correctly that in the early years of the occupation a number of European engineers, lawyers and doctors had to be imported because there were not enough trained Egyptians to implement the urgently needed reforms, he says that lack of funds for education delayed the training of Egyptians to replace them. Now (1908) the situation had improved and he took a 'somewhat sanguine view' of the possibility of gradually substituting Egyptians for Europeans, although 'any attempt to hurry can only lead to disappointment'. The figures he quotes show that there had been no risk of haste. In 1896, there were 8,444 Egyptians and 690 Europeans in the civil service; in 1906 there were 12,027 Egyptians and 1,252 Europeans. Cromer points out that 303 of the total increase in Europeans was in the Railway Administration which had only recently come under the Egyptian Government's control, but the fact remains that in the last decade of his regime the number of Europeans involved in administering Egypt had increased by over 80 per cent. The great majority of course held the most senior and responsible posts. The situation in the education department was much the same; in 1896, Egyptians 631; Europeans 92 and in 1906, Egyptians 794; Europeans 160.

As we have seen, the policy at the end of Cromer's time was to recruit Oxbridge graduates fresh from the university as teachers. From the education department they were usually moved after a few years to other branches of the administration, especially finance and the interior.

The method of recruiting to the Egyptian civil service was not regularized until 1902 when the need to supply the recently reconquered Sudan with administrators caused Eldon Gorst, financial adviser in Egypt, and Sir Reginald Wingate, the governor-general of the Sudan, to devise a system of advertising the vacant posts in the major English universities and interviewing the applicants in London. There was no competitive examination as for the Indian civil service; it was more like entry into the diplomatic service. Although clearly an improvement on the former haphazard arrangement, the system does not appear to have worked so very well. Ronald Storrs, one of the better selections, spent six weeks doing nothing in the finance ministry after his arrival in 1904 until he confessed his idleness to Lady Cromer who passed on the message to 'the Lord'.

Clearly it had soon become an established notion that any young Englishman with a university degree could do a job better than any Egyptian, however experienced. In 1895 Wilfrid Blunt records coming across two Royal Engineers in their early twenties in charge of building a railroad in Upper Egypt. They had been given the rank of major in the Egyptian Army and were obviously enjoying themselves hugely. But the job was simple and could easily have been accomplished by Egyptian military engineers.[3] Hussein Heykal, the distinguished Egyptian writer and politician, records in his memoirs an occasion when the inspector of agriculture in his area of the Delta turned out to be his former geography teacher at school. Although he knew nothing about agricultural conditions in the area he had been sent because he happened to be staying in Egypt for the summer.[4] Ronald Storrs says in his memoirs that the theory of government put forward by Milner in the early days of the occupation (and not then considered slighting) had been 'British heads and Egyptian hands'. This had worked fairly well as long as there were only a handful of British advisers and inspectors. 'But by 1910 there were too many of the first and far too many of the second.'[5]

In the spring of 1907 there was no longer any doubt that 'the Lord' would have to go. One difficulty was that although his health was the principal reason the nationalists were certain to claim the credit for his departure. In an apocalyptic letter to Rennell Rodd on 27 April 1907, Harry Boyle described the political situation as 'simply damnable'. The nationalists, believing that they had the Khedive and a strong party in the British House of Commons on their side, had reached a new pitch of violence. They openly insulted anyone thought to be pro-British. 'In all our past troubles we have never been in such a position as now; our power is moribund and only the adoption of a very vigorous remedy – such as a repetition of the exodus in 1879 – can set things to rights.'

At the eleventh hour Cromer rallied to make his farewell address to a great gathering of Egyptian dignitaries and foreign diplomats at the Cairo Opera House on 4 May. The speech was masterly and delivered 'like an athlete of thirty', according to Boyle, although this enabled the nationalists to claim that he was retiring because his policies and not his health had failed. He commended Tewfik, Riaz, Nubar and Mustafa Pasha Fehmi, the still surviving premier, but ignored the Khedive except to advise him with pointed irony to help with the moral advancement of the people by putting a stop to financial scandals. Disarmingly he noted that whereas the French press in Egypt had once referred to him as 'le brutal Cromer' or even Moloch 'the most bloodthirsty of heathen gods', more recently he had been dubbed 'cet illustre vieillard' which clearly denoted a change of tone. He did not miss the chance of a parting thrust at 'this wholly spurious and manufactured movement in favour of a rapid development of parliamentary institutions' which 'should be treated for what it is worth'.

Two days later he left Cairo to take the boat from Port Said. His staff had feared a hostile demonstration by the nationalists but the crowd watched silently behind the British troops who lined the streets with fixed bayonets, and the occasion passed without incident. Cromer himself was never shaken by doubt. Except for his admission that the Denshawai sentences had been too severe, neither his two books on Egypt nor his numerous speeches and writings on the subject show anything but the fullest confidence in his achievement and contempt for his adversaries. As we shall see, he felt confirmed in his judgement by the apparent failure of the different policies of his successor. There is no doubt about his sincerity; Cromer was often pessimistic or harshly ironic but he was not cynical. He genuinely believed that British rule was the best that the Egyptian masses could hope for in the indefinite future. While he lacked any real sympathy with the people he ruled for a quarter of a century he would have been astonished to be told this by any of the few whose judgement he valued. Above all, he was a creature of his age – a late Victorian Liberal imperialist with all the assumptions of his breed concerning the natural world dominance of the Anglo-Saxon Protestant race buttressed by his own outstanding ability and strength of character.

GORST'S LIBERAL
EXPERIMENT

In Cromer's later years in Egypt, he would often say to Harry
Boyle that although in many respects Eldon Gorst was incompar-
ably the best choice as his successor, he had no intention of
proposing him as his defects outweighed his merits. Boyle and
other members of Cromer's staff agreed but when Cromer's health
collapsed there was no time to find an alternative. Cromer swal-
lowed his doubts and Gorst, who had powerful friends at court,
was immediately appointed by the Liberal Government.

Eldon Gorst was the son of Sir John Gorst, an able Tory radical
and member of Randolph Churchill's Fourth Party, who retired
from politics in 1908 an embittered failure. In 1886, after a brilliant
academic career at Eton and Trinity College Cambridge, the
twenty-five-year-old Eldon Gorst was appointed attaché at the
British agency in Cairo. Although small and unimposing in appearance, he was exceedingly ambitious, and worked hard to improve his position and salary. His natural talent was for finance
and in 1890 he became controller of taxes; in 1892 he succeeded
Milner as under-secretary of the finance department and in 1896,
on Elwin Palmer's sudden resignation, he was appointed to the
key post of financial adviser to the Egyptian Government. In this
capacity he conducted the negotiations in Paris which led to the
1904 Anglo-French agreement. In the same year he had left Egypt
to become assistant under-secretary of state at the foreign office;
his unpublished memoirs make clear that his principal reason for
returning to Whitehall was to ensure his chances of succeeding
Cromer.

In Egypt Gorst was not liked by his colleagues, who found something decidedly un-English about him. His undoubted, and on the
whole justified, sense of superiority was not effortless. He was
self-assertive, like many able and ambitious men of small stature,
and in his recreation as much as in his work he showed a Teutonic
earnestness of purpose which they found unappealing. In his

memoirs for 1890 he summarizes his own defects as 'a certain want of confidence in my own powers and a consequent tendency not to aim high enough, and secondly a humble appreciation of the position I had a right to occupy among my fellow-men'.

Kitchener, with whom he quarrelled in 1896, particularly disliked Gorst but Cromer could not dispense with his talents, and although he counted on Boyle for his intelligence reports he relied on Gorst to administer the Veiled Protectorate. After the resignation of Palmer (described by Gorst as of 'very inferior capacity' and given to 'dubious financial arrangements') Gorst claimed to have run Egypt under Cromer's influence.

At that time Gorst was still a bachelor. He discussed the matter with Cromer, who decided he should get married, but his first attempts were unsuccessful. His own conclusion was that his relations with the fair sex were too conciliatory and with his own sex not conciliatory enough. 'I made a further effort to get married,' he wrote in 1901. Finally, in 1903, on his forty-second birthday, his efforts succeeded with his marriage to Evelyn Rudd who was young, pretty and the daughter of a South African millionaire.

In 1902 Gorst had been made a KCB and he seized the opportunity of the investiture to make the acquaintance of Edward VII. With equal foresight he made friends with Mrs George Keppel in Cairo and in the following year he was satisfied that the King, Sir Ernest Cassel and Mrs Keppel would all help to ensure that he should succeed Cromer. Milner was still a threat but fortunately he declined to take a post abroad. Both Cromer and the foreign secretary, Edward Grey, were opposed to Kitchener at that stage, so when the time came Gorst had no serious rival in the eyes of the Liberal Government.

Gorst was thrilled to be stepping into Cromer's shoes. In his memoirs he wrote: 'Throughout the British Empire there is no place in which the occupant enjoys greater freedom of action than that of British agent and consul-general in Egypt.* The consul-general is the *de facto* ruler of the country, without being hampered by a parliament or by a network of councils like the viceroy of India and the interference of the home government has hitherto been limited to such matters as are likely to arouse interest or criticism in the British House of Commons.' Gorst was no more

* Gorst had forgotten that Egypt was not in the British Empire.

of a believer in representative institutions than Cromer but he did feel that radical changes were needed. On his return to Egypt he observed that under Cromer 'The whole machine of government absolutely depended on one man and that man had been going to pieces physically and morally'. In his opinion the financial adviser was incapable and disloyal.

Gorst decided on a discreet change of direction. 'While outwardly proclaiming that Lord Cromer's policy was unchanged [I decided] to apply the precepts laid down in his annual reports rather than to follow the actual practice of recent years – in a word to carry into execution the many excellent practical and statesmanlike maxims which abound in Lord Cromer's writings but which had remained in the state of "pious opinions". . . . [I wanted] to render our rule more sympathetic to the Egyptians in general and to the Muhammedans in particular by restoring good feeling between the Anglo-Egyptian officials and the natives of the country and preventing the British element riding roughshod over the Egyptians by putting a check on the annual British invasion of new recruits, by giving great encouragement to the Egyptian official class, and last, but not least, by giving a more national character to the educational system.' Above all, Gorst hoped that by satisfying nationalist feelings he could keep Egypt quiet for a time. He confided to Harry Boyle that the British Government was fed up with the Egyptian problem and that nothing would please them more than to hear nothing of Egypt for the next few years. If he could do this he might be promoted to Constantinople and then Paris, from where he could enter the Government as a cabinet minister.[1]

Gorst was alarmed by the state of the two key ministries with which he had been chiefly concerned during his Egyptian service – finance and the interior. He replaced both the British advisers and initiated reforms. In finance it was largely a question of economizing because Gorst's return to Egypt coincided with a break in the fifteen-year-old financial boom. This had culminated in 1906 with a wave of speculation in property and shares; a decline on Wall Street in the spring of 1907 had spread to Europe and Egypt. Gorst and his new financial adviser, Sir Paul Harvey, sharply pruned expenditure and succeeded in reducing the budget estimates from £E18,926,911 in 1907 to £E16,406,000 in 1911.

This was unpopular but it was relatively easy to achieve; the reform of the interior ministry was another matter. Gorst looked round for a new British adviser and chose Arthur Chitty, the highly successful director of customs at Alexandria. Though shy and retiring, Chitty was well liked by his staff, both European and Egyptian. But in Cairo he was suspected of excessive pro-Egyptian sympathies and in fact he enthusiastically endorsed Gorst's policy of promoting Egyptians to positions of responsibility wherever possible. Mustafa Kamel described him to Blunt as 'the only Englishman who could inspire us with any confidence'.

With Gorst's support, Chitty set about with a fair degree of ruthlessness, reducing the responsibilities of the British inspectors in the provinces and reviving the authority of the Mudirs. He persuaded the minister of the interior to replace many of the more traditional and reactionary Mudirs with better educated Egyptians who were mostly middle-class lawyers from Cairo. Gorst's next step was to breathe new life into the provincial councils which had been established as part of Lord Dufferin's recommendations by the Organic Law of 1883 but which had remained largely moribund for the past twenty-five years. They could impose no rates or grant any concessions. Their advice was not sought on any question of local government. Gorst now decided he would make them genuine advisory councils to the Mudirs. He gave them the power to raise revenue through increased land tax and apply the money to local government. In practice, the provincial councils devoted most of their funds to education and eventually took over control of all the state primary schools from the Government.

Gorst was aware that this moderate measure would not satisfy the demands of renascent Egyptian nationalism. He had come to the conclusion that Cromer's principal error had been his irreparable antagonization of the Khedive, who remained the constitutional head of the Egyptian state. He therefore abandoned the policy of promoting the moderates in the Umma Party, which Cromer had only tentatively adopted at the end of his career, and set out for a reconciliation with the Khedive. Abbas, whose self-esteem had been deeply wounded by Cromer, responded and the first part of Gorst's plan was successful. The removal of the British agency's hostility broke up the somewhat unnatural alliance between the Khedive and the nationalists. In February 1908 the thirty-four-year-old Mustafa Kamel died; he had been gravely ill for some time but kept up the struggle with the help of morphia and his own natural dynamism. Reuter reported that fifty thousand followed his funeral cortège in a great demonstration of national feeling. His successor as the head of the Nationalist Party, Mohammed Ferid, was a lesser personality than Kamel; 'Not first-rate, but sensible and honest,' was Wilfrid Blunt's conclusion. He improved the party's administration and established contact with radical and socialist groups in Europe. The break with the Khedive was final; in July 1908 the Young Turk Revolution which compelled Abdulhamid to restore the 1876 constitution, convinced Abbas of the dangers of encouraging young nationalists. From then on he was ready to co-operate with Gorst.

One of the first consequences of the rapprochement between Gorst and the Khedive was the resignation of Mustafa Fehmi, the prime minister for the last thirteen years whom Abbas had always disliked for his subservience to Cromer. The new ministry was headed by the Coptic aristocrat Boutros Ghali Pasha, and included the Khedive's favourite Mohammed Said as minister of the interior (although Saad Zaghlul, of whom the Khedive disapproved, remained as minister of education).

Gorst's misgivings in having a Coptic premier who had also been a member of the Denshawai tribunal, were overcome by the Khedive. In December the Denshawai prisoners were all released on the occasion of the Khedive's birthday and the new Government, which was both better educated and more representative of the Egyptian nation than any of its predecessors, enjoyed considerable popularity even among the nationalists.

Gorst's next step was to attempt to revive the legislative council which under Cromer's rule had been if possible even more impotent than the provincial councils. On Gorst's advice, Boutros Ghali and his ministers attended a meeting of the council and announced that in future they would be present whenever matters of importance were being discussed.

Gorst had achieved some striking initial success for his policies. He had 'restored' the Khedive and taken the wind out of the nationalist sails. But it was obvious that he could not carry through his reforms without the co-operation of the Anglo-Egyptian officials, and the attitude of most of these ranged from scepticism to outright hostility. One of his first aims had been to limit their numbers and promote Egyptians to positions of greater responsibility. In the spring of 1908 he called all the more senior officials together at the agency to explain his programme. Colonel Elgood, who was present, records his impression of Gorst's address as 'no more than a gentle reminder to the audience of Great Britain's earlier pledges on the subject of the occupation'.[2] But the majority of Gorst's audience was much less sympathetic; they foresaw a speedy handing over of power to the Egyptians and the demolition of the entire Cromerian system, and Harry Boyle, who was much closer to their mentality, records a quite different impression. For him, Gorst was announcing that Cromer's policy was to be reversed and Egypt would henceforth be governed through the Khedive. 'I have never seen a more curious scene in its way than the bearing of the audience as they left the ballroom. They went out in complete silence and as if stupefied.'[3] British officials who had acquired positions of unquestioned authority now found themselves demoted and forced to defer to the Egyptians who were their nominal superiors. Many of them showed their resentment while few of the Egyptian officials took pains to handle the matter tactfully.

The consequence was a wave of angry and often malicious criticism of Gorst from the British colony which soon found echoes in the London press. Gorst rather self-consciously attempted to modify Cromer's Olympian image of the British agent. He drove his own motor-car bare-headed through the streets of Cairo and made use of his Arabic to talk to passers-by; but he lacked the stature and inner self-confidence to shrug off the charge that he was undignified.

In contrast to his personal informality he revived, on an even more lavish scale, the viceregal style of entertaining of Cromer's earlier years. Harry Boyle had, on his own suggestion, taken over what he called the 'Lord Chamberlain's department' of the agency having realized that his political role was ended in the Gorst era. He records that Gorst employed 70 European and Egyptian servants, including the former chef of Baron Rothschild, who also played the violin brilliantly and was paid £500 a year. In the winter season daily lunches for twenty and weekly dinners for 36 were normal. But his generosity only provoked more criticism from the European colony because Gorst liked to invite as many Egyptians as possible.*

* The 'classic dialogue' recorded by Ronald Storrs sounds only too familiar. 'Were you at the agency last night?' 'No; but then you see I'm not a foreigner; I'm only British.' (Storrs, *Orientations*, p. 82.)

The consequence was that there was little mercy for Gorst when his policies began to go seriously wrong. Much of this was not the fault of the British agency. After Mustafa Kamel's death, for example, his policy of welding Copts and Muslims together in the national movement soon collapsed and relations between the two communities sharply deteriorated. Gorst was held responsible and even accused of deliberately encouraging religious divisions to weaken the nationalists. Had he not written of Boutros Ghali in his annual report that he was 'the first genuine Egyptian who has risen to the highest position in the country'? This was tactless and offensive, although it had more than an element of truth, but it does not prove Gorst's malign purpose and there is no doubt that he regarded the Coptic-Muslim troubles, which culminated in Boutros Ghali's assassination, with anguished dismay.

The truth is that Gorst lacked the gift of political imagination. He had correctly diagnosed the fault of the later Cromerian regime as the stifling of individual Egyptians' sense of independence and responsibility, but he failed to see that this was something that could not be hastily remedied. He pursued several simultaneous policies which appeared to be complementary but which were in fact mutually inconsistent. His reinforcement of the Khedive, who was by nature and inheritance an authoritarian ruler, conflicted with his aim of having more able and genuinely responsible ministers in the Government. At the same time, his strengthening of the Egyptian executive in the Central Government and the Mudirs in the provinces was incompatible, at least in the short term, with his encouragement of representative institutions in the provincial councils and the legislative council.

It was unlikely that the nationalists, who had been encouraged by Cromer's departure, would be satisfied with Gorst's liberalizing measures. Their agitation increased and the press heaped a crescendo of abuse on Egyptian ministers as well as the English occupiers. In some cases the real target was the Khedive but since he would have responded ruthlessly to any personal abuse the attacks were directed at his ministers instead. In the countryside there was an alarming new crime wave which was partly the consequence of the rebellious spirit of the nation. In 1909 Gorst re-established the press law of 1881 which gave the Government the power to suppress or suspend newspapers after due warning.

Cromer had never agreed to do this despite urgent requests from ministers or other notables who had been scurrilously attacked, both because he despised the native press and regarded it as a useful opening for Young Egypt to let off steam and because a free press was a useful symbol of English liberalism. The revived press law was robbed of much of its effect by the Capitulations which protected the foreign-owned press and allowed the Egyptian newspapers to evade suppression by transferring nominal ownership to a European front-man. In the same year (1909) Gorst had the so-called Relegation Law passed which gave the Government the power to deport the more troublesome brigands without trial to specially created penal colonies in the Kharga Oasis of the Western Desert. The law also provided for the creation of special committees of omdehs and notables who were required to tour the villages in their area and draft a list of all miscreants who were regarded as a danger to the peace. The defect in this law was that it provided unlimited opportunities for scoring off opponents in personal vendettas, and it was speedily abandoned under Kitchener. At the same time it was decided to give the 45,000 Ghafir force semi-military training and arm them with Remington rifles. The moving spirit behind this rash decision was André von Dumreicher, an Alexandria-born German who had joined the ministry of the interior after failing as a cotton merchant. It was not a success; the Ghafirs were delighted with their rifles but it was far from certain that they would use them on behalf of the law. The crime wave continued.

Neither the Relegation Law nor the revived press law were the actions of a weak man but they were confessions of failure. The most severe blow to Gorst's hopes was yet to come. The original concession of the Suez Canal Company was to run for 99 years from the date of opening, which meant that it would expire in 1968. In 1910 the company made a proposal for the extension of the concession for forty years in return for the payment by the company of a capital sum of £4 million and an annual share of the profits. Gorst and his financial adviser were both eager for this means of increasing revenue and urged acceptance. Boutros and his ministers agreed but there was an immediate public outcry led by the nationalists against any extension of the concession. True to his policy of encouraging Egyptian responsible government, Gorst agreed with the Khedive that the matter should be referred to the general assembly – the shadowy body created on Dufferin's advice which consisted of representatives from each province as well as the twenty-eight members of the legislative council which had a purely advisory function and met 'at least once every two years'. Only one member of the assembly had the courage to vote in favour of acceptance of the Canal Company's offer. Gorst had no alternative but to let the matter drop.

Cromer would not have made this error. He was aware of the Egyptian people's deep dislike of the Suez Canal Company, although he regarded it as merely one more example of their incorrigible lack of responsibility. Gorst himself was brought to see the fallacy in his own liberalizing reforms. He wrote: 'The policy of ruling Egypt in co-operation with native ministers is, at the present time, incompatible with that of encouraging the development of so-called representative institutions. The ministers are chosen from the most capable Egyptians, and are better educated with the real desires and opinions of their countrymen than the members of a council who in reality represent nothing but the class of wealthy Beys and Pashas.'[4] There was some truth in this, although if Gorst had wanted to make the council and the assembly more widely representative he might have pressed for the extension of the franchise. But it was incorrect to say that the assembly had rejected the Canal Company's offer without consideration. Their committee's report presents some sober and reasonable arguments against it. In refusing to commit future generations of Egyptians to the survival of a 'state within a state' (which is how the Canal Company was justly regarded) the wealthy Beys and Pashas were showing more foresight and imagination than either Gorst or the Khedive's Government.

Two days later on 10 February 1910 Boutros was assassinated as he was standing on the pavement outside his office. The murderer was a young Egyptian, Ibrahim al-Wardani, who declared that his victim had deserved death because as minister of foreign affairs he had signed away Egypt's sovereign rights over the Sudan in 1899; as minister of justice in 1906 he had presided over the Denshawai trial; as prime minister he had revived the press law and advocated acceptance of the Suez Canal Company's offer.

Wardani became a national hero, particularly with students who roamed the streets chanting:

Wardani! Wardani!
Illi 'atal al-Nusrāni.

(Wardani, who slew the Nazarene.)

But Gorst was now in a grimly determined mood and when Wardani was tried and sentenced to death by a court which included two Egyptian judges, he was promptly executed despite a widespread belief that he would be reprieved.

Gorst's policies were now in ruins and he was near despair. Criticism of his alleged weakness came from all sides. In the House of Commons, A. J. Balfour, the leader of the opposition, chose the occasion of a debate on the Egyptian situation to present his views on the philosophy of imperialism and the general inapplicability of the self-government principle to orientals who in any case hold the art of government in contempt. 'Every person, with an intimate knowledge of Egypt, to whom I have spoken . . . agreed with one voice that the position in Egypt is now eminently unsatisfactory. They also agreed that it is eminently unsatisfactory because the authority of what they frankly say is the dominant race – and I think ought to remain the dominant race – has been undermined.'[5] This view was echoed in more robust tones by the former US President Theodore Roosevelt, who stopped off in Cairo for two days on an African hunting tour to deliver his judgement that the British in Egypt should 'govern or get out'. He made a considerable impression when he repeated the advice in a speech at the Guildhall in London. With apparently unconscious irony, he argued that Boutros Ghali's assassination showed that the Egyptians were not ready for self-government. He had become president of the United States in 1901 as a result of the murder of President McKinley.

Harry Boyle was not an unprejudiced observer but he is probably correct when he says that in Egypt 'a sort of general slackness set in; the Anglo-Egyptian officials no longer felt the same keen interest in their work'. Gorst would have long interviews with the Khedive two or three times a week and pass on to his agency staff virtually nothing of what was said. Gorst himself ceased to be the dynamo of ambitious energy that he had always been known. He was constantly away from Cairo sailing at Alexandria, shooting ibex in the desert or fishing in the Red Sea. Such behaviour gave added opportunity for sarcastic criticism but those close to him were aware of the true reason; Gorst was in constant pain because he was dying of cancer of the spine. He fought death with as much determination to win as he had always been famous for playing games, but he lost. In April 1911, in acute agony, he dictated his last annual report to Sir Edward Grey, then left for leave in England where he died in July. The Khedive rushed over from Paris to see him on his deathbed.*

Gorst was harshly judged by most of his contemporaries. Ronald Storrs, who was one of his few admirers, expressed the wish that those historians who had devoted time and talent for the re-habilitation of Tiberius or Lucrezia Borgia 'could have devoted them to the vindication of an appreciated and calumniated servant of the British Crown'.[6] Storrs believed that Gorst's policies were showing signs of succeeding when they were fatally affected by the assassination of Boutros Ghali. Colonel Elgood, another sym-pathizer, thought that his ideas were fundamentally right but that he was continuously weakened by lack of support from British public opinion or the Anglo-Egyptian officials. Even Cromer conceded that the Gorst experiment had to be tried but only because its inevitable failure was needed to convince the Egyptian public and 'the extreme English sympathizers with Egyptian aspirations' that Egypt was incapable and quite unprepared for self-government.

In fact Gorst had set himself a task which, with his unimagina-tive self-confidence, he was unable to see was impossible. In 1907 a new policy was urgently needed. Cromerism was collapsing and no one – not even Kitchener – could have revived it. Gorst's answer was to take the superficially logical step of fulfilling the liberal proposals that Lord Dufferin had made in 1882. But times had changed; Abbas, who was more like his grandfather Ismail than his father Tewfik, was Khedive and Egyptian nationalism had revived in a different form. Gorst's principal success was to divide the opponents of the British occupation against each other but this was essentially negative and did nothing to help Egypt towards self-government. He has chiefly been blamed for having restored the authority and prestige of the Khedive. Abbas had many defects, as Cromer wrote his little book (*Abbas II*) to demonstrate, but this

* Cromer's comment was: 'It is the best act I have ever heard of his performing. Much may be forgiven him for the real feeling which he displayed on this occasion.' (*Abbas II*, xiii.)

is not why Gorst's plan was misconceived. A strong Khedive was incompatible with the British occupation, for an abler and more powerful character than Abbas – and he was far from insignificant – would have insisted on ruling Egypt alone, while a weaker character would have remained a British puppet. In either case, Gorst's hopes for a moderate Egyptian National Party moving steadily towards self-government under the Khedive's leadership and British guidance could not have been achieved.

RETURN OF THE SIRDAR

In 1911 both Edward Grey and Cromer, who still exerted a powerful influence on the Government's Egyptian policy, had overcome their doubts about sending Kitchener to Cairo. The respite from Egyptian troubles that the Asquith Government had hoped for when Gorst succeeded Cromer had not been forthcoming and it was clear to them that a firm hand was required. It was also a solution to the awkward problem of what to do with the hero of Khartoum. In 1911 Kitchener's prestige was at a peak. Six years earlier, as commander-in-chief in India, he had emerged victorious from a blazing row with the viceroy, Lord Curzon, on the question of the Indian Army's submission to viceregal control and Curzon had resigned. Kitchener had long had his eyes on the viceroyalty and he now hoped to succeed the ailing Lord Minto, who had replaced Curzon. Edward VII was enthusiastically in favour and Asquith was prepared to agree despite Liberal suspicions of Kitchener's strong Tory connections, but the decision rested with the secretary of state for India, John Morley. This spinsterish anti-militarist intellectual was resolutely opposed to the Field-Marshal's appointment as viceroy. He could point out with some logic that it would hardly look well to send a soldier to rule India so soon after the liberalizing India Councils Act of 1909. Morley was prepared to resign on the issue and Asquith, who was in the throes of the great constitutional crisis with the House of Lords, gave way.

An effort had been made in 1909 to persuade Kitchener to accept the post of commander-in-chief in the Mediterranean, which included the British forces in Egypt, and a seat on the committee of imperial defence. As an added bonus he was told he would be made a Field-Marshal. The Mediterranean Command had been somewhat over-hastily established in 1907 by Haldane, the secretary of war. The king's brother, the Duke of Connaught, had reluctantly accepted the post but within a year had resigned because he had concluded that it served no useful purpose. Kitchener was of the same opinion, and had only accepted on the strength of a personal appeal from the king, but when he discovered on his return to England that Edward VII regarded the Malta post as a 'damned rotten billet' and had only urged him to accept it on the advice of his ministers Kitchener felt that he had been tricked and withdrew his acceptance. In May 1910 Edward VII died, and with him Kitchener's last hopes of becoming viceroy of India.

So it was that when the nature of Gorst's fatal illness became known Kitchener saw the opportunity to achieve at least one of his principal ambitions (viceroy of India, ambassador at Constantinople or consul-general in Egypt) and the Liberal Government was glad to accede. Cromer added his support in a letter to Grey, saying that there was only one possible successor for Gorst and the new King George V expressed his warm approval.

In an interview with Kitchener, Grey told him that a strong hand was needed in Egypt but he did not want Gorst's liberalizing reforms to be reversed. He wanted him to direct Egyptian nationalism into constructive work. Above all he hoped that Kitchener would keep Egypt quiet as Gorst had failed to do.[1] On 16 July 1911 Grey informed the House of Commons that Kitchener had been appointed British agent, consul-general and minister plenipotentiary in Egypt; he assured the House that no change from civil and administrative reform to military reform was contemplated.

To emphasize this last point, on Grey's suggestion Kitchener arrived at Cairo station on 28 September wearing, to everyone's surprise, a top-hat and grey frock coat instead of his military uniform. In contrast to the icy silence in which Cromer had departed he was warmly received by the crowds. The nationalist press was hostile, referring to the 'Butcher of Khartoum', but Kitchener had glamour and style and only his positive achievements were remembered. There was also a sense of relief in some quarters that the years of chronic unrest would now be followed by a period of tranquillity.

Kitchener was as aware as Gorst had been of the British consul-general in Egypt's power of independent action, but much more capable of exploiting it. With his aura of prestige he established himself as an archetypal oriental potentate, accepting petitions

from the humble and proceeding from time to time on tours of the
countryside to observe how the peasantry was faring.* The
drawback of Kitchener's extreme authoritarianism was that since
he was disinclined to listen to other points of view he tended to
overestimate the abilities of those who agreed with him. As in his
earlier career, he had almost no intimates except for Major A.
McMurdo, who had been his ADC in Egypt in the 1880s, and the
faithful young Colonel Oswald Fitzgerald whom he brought with
him from India and who remained at his side until they were
drowned together on the *Hampshire* in 1916. Yet he extracted
devoted service from many of his subordinates.

Ronald Storrs, who had become very close to Gorst after he
succeeded Harry Boyle as oriental secretary in 1909, half expected
to be sacked by Kitchener who had detested Gorst. But Kitchener
soon came to rely heavily on Storrs who was widely popular and
enjoyed an entrée into many circles of Egyptian life. It is doubtful whether Storrs had any significant influence on Kitchener's
policies but he did on the way they were presented: 'I always
announce pleasant news myself, and unpleasant through Storrs,'
was Kitchener's comment. In return, Storrs described his time
with Kitchener in Egypt as 'three years of such happiness, interest
and responsibility as no gratitude could repay'.

Kitchener was neither a scholar like Cromer nor an intellectual
like Gorst. On a long trip up the Nile in 1910 his reading material
consisted of bound volumes of *Country Life* and the novels of
Stanley Weyman. Yet he was no mere polo-playing philistine. His
aloof and awe-inspiring manner concealed a feminine temperament
lit by flashes of intuition and sensitivity. He was a passionate
collector of antiques and works of art and one of his first actions
on taking up residence at the agency was to move his fine collection
of porcelain and Byzantine icons into the drawing-room. Unlike
Cromer, he was deeply interested in Egyptian antiquities and he
devoted himself to the improvement of Cairo's amenities. In his
earlier career in Egypt he had earned a reputation for thrift which

---

* He was usually received with sycophantic adulation – but not always.
At a garden party for Egyptian officers who had served under him in the
Sudan, he remarked to a group of them that they were all looking very old
and grey. One of them looked at Kitchener's head on which no sign of grey
could be detected and remarked solemnly, 'Hair-dye is very cheap, my
Lord'.

his enemies called meanness but he also had a taste for magnificence which he had been able to indulge to some extent in Simla and Calcutta and now more fully in Cairo. At the agency he ordered the construction of an enormous new ballroom and changed the servants' liveries from Gorst's chocolate and yellow to scarlet and gold.*

The first part of his instructions from the British Government – to restore order – agreed with his natural inclinations. With a new Press Censorship Act, Criminal Conspiracy Act and School Discipline Act he struck at the power of the nationalists. Their leaders were either imprisoned or went into exile. At the same time he effectively handled another potential source of trouble. On the day of his arrival in Cairo Italy declared war on Turkey and invaded the two Ottoman provinces of Tripolitania and Cyrenaica. Egyptian public opinion was overwhelmingly on the Ottoman side against the Italian invader but Kitchener agreed with the British Government that Egypt must remain strictly neutral. Although Egypt was nominally part of the Ottoman Empire, Turkish troops were not to be allowed to cross its territory to defend Libya. With the help of his prestige and such gestures as a personal gift of £100 to the Turkish Red Crescent, Kitchener kept Egypt quiet until the war ended a year later. The Egyptian Government even co-operated in helping to prevent the bedouin tribes who inherited Egypt's Western Desert from running guns into Tripoli for the Turks. The bedouin responded to Kitchener's threat to abolish their treasured exemption from military service.

Kitchener carefully avoided the impression that he was purely coercive. Having scattered the nationalists he made overtures to the moderate Umma Party and their associates who had been offended by Gorst's alliance with the Khedive and gone into opposition. The Khedive himself presented little threat to Kitchener's order. After the brief revival of his power through Gorst, he was furious and embittered at being landed with Kitchener, whom he detested since the Frontier Incident of 1894. Kitchener's view of him was similar to Cromer's – a contempt that varied between amusement

---

* When he was sirdar, Cromer had prevented him removing the tiles from the walls of a famous mosque in Damietta. Now he was in a stronger position and he virtually forced the unfortunate Swiss manager of the Gezira Palace Hotel to present him with the two marble lions which stand to this day at the doors of the British Embassy in Cairo.

and irritation. In his private letters to Lady Salisbury he referred
to him as the 'wicked little Khedive'.

Abbas attempted to strike back. When Kitchener began his
series of visits by special train into the countryside, where he
would receive petitions and hear classical poems chanted in his
honour, the Khedive followed in his footsteps on his own royal
tour. But Kitchener saw his chance to cut down the Khedive's
remaining source of power. First he did something which even
Cromer had not dared to do. In 1913 he established a Ministry of
Waqfs to administer the enormously wealthy Muslim religious
charities which had previously been controlled by the Khedive.
Abbas only consented when Kitchener threatened to expose all
his financial misdealings. At the same time Kitchener decreed that
the Khedive could in future only confer titles or decorations on the
recommendation of his ministers and with the approval of the
British agent. Even his right to preside at cabinet meetings was
removed. The Khedive had become a constitutional monarch in a
country without constitutional government.

In another respect he went a long way towards reversing Gorst's
policies. Whereas Gorst had shifted executive responsibilities on to
Egyptians wherever possible, under Kitchener the number of
British in the higher positions now rapidly increased again. But
Kitchener was not in favour of British social exclusiveness. In
India he had deplored it and blamed it on the club system, in
Cairo he pursued Gorst's habit of inviting as many Egyptians as
possible to the agency – with the difference that he does not appear
to have been criticized by the British and other European communities as a consequence. He did take fairly ruthless action to
force the Egyptian members to resign from the famous Gezira
Club, but this was not out of any belief in social 'apartheid' but
because of complaints that members of the Khedive's circle were
using the club to express anti-British opinions. With Kitchener's
approval another club was opened with mixed membership.

Kitchener was not unmindful of his undertaking to Sir Edward
Grey that he would not reverse the liberalization programme. But
the quiescent state of the country led him to believe there was no
need for haste. As he wrote to Grey six months after his arrival:
'I am glad to be able to report that . . . the consideration of practical reforms for the good of the country has apparently become
more interesting to the majority of the people than discussions of

abstruse political questions which are unlikely to lead to any useful result.' He shared Cromer's lack of faith in the application of Western parliamentary systems to oriental and Muslim peoples but, whether or not he was merely trying to persuade the Liberal in Edward Grey, he was more prepared than Cromer to see what was positive in existing Egyptian social institutions. 'Whatever the value of a party system may be in western political life, it is evident that its application to an intensely democratic community, the essential basis of whose social life is the brotherhood of man,* combined with respect for learning and the experience of age, is an unnatural proceeding fraught with inevitable division and weakness.'²

He consulted Cromer, who in reply repeated his view that Egypt was not a nation but 'a fortuitous agglomeration of a number of miscellaneous and hybrid elements'. He also urged Kitchener to wait and see. 'As regards any real representation of the Egyptian people which could ultimately, in some degree, take the place of personal government, probably the wisest thing for the moment is to leave the whole question alone. ... National representation in Egypt, in the sense in which that term is generally used, is a sheer absurdity.'³

By all appearances these delaying tactics were successful. Two years after Kitchener's arrival, Ahmed Lutfi al-Sayyid, intellectual leader of the moderate Umma Party and one of the most thoughtful men in Egypt, was writing: 'The nation's political consciousness has been numbed for the last two years. Some say that our political parties are no more, and that our interest in public affairs has waned.'⁴

While endeavouring to freeze Egyptian political life Kitchener devoted himself passionately to those 'practical reforms' which interested him. These were almost entirely concerned with the conditions of the fellahin. Like Cromer, he believed that they were the true Egypt – the only worthwhile section of Egyptian society – but his interest was much more direct and practical than Cromer's. Kitchener's attitude to financial and economic policy foreshadowed that of President de Gaulle; he believed that it should serve, rather than determine, the national interest. In this he was fortunate that

---

* Although Islamic society was restrictive and oppressive in some respects – especially for women – its relative lack of racial and class barriers was something western democracies could envy

economic recovery had begun after the recession which had coincided with Gorst's arrival in Egypt. One of his first actions was to enforce the resignation of Sir Paul Harvey, Gorst's able and influential financial adviser who had been responsible for the stringent economies of the past four years, and replace him with Lord Edward Cecil. A son of Lord Salisbury whom Kitchener warmly admired, Cecil had started his career as a soldier and had been Baden Powell's chief staff officer at Mafeking. He notoriously knew nothing of finance but he could be relied upon to carry out Kitchener's instructions.*

When Kitchener arrived in Egypt he had already made up his mind on two major agricultural reforms. One was to reduce the indebtedness of the fellahin, and the other was to solve the drainage problem by installing huge pumps at the tails of the main drains. He allowed no opposition and officials who valued their jobs always agreed with him. There was a verse circulating in Cairo:

> For ever with the Lord
> Amen so let it be!
> Promotion hangs upon the word
> Adds K to CMG!

His solution to the fellahin's debts (which Gorst had lately estimated at £16 million) was the Homestead Exemption Law, or Five Feddan Law as it was always known, which made it impossible to recover in the court of law any money lent to fellahin who owned less than five feddans – that is over 90 per cent of the total. The measure was highly controversial although it was based on the successful Punjab Land Alienation Act. William Willcocks, who had just returned to Egypt from Mesopotamia, thought the new law was disastrous because it dealt a fatal blow to the Agricultural Bank which had been founded in 1902 to lend money to the fellahin at 8 per cent or 9 per cent instead of the usurer's 20 per cent to 30 per cent. The Bank had had some initial difficulties through a lack of caution in its lending policy, especially during the economic recession after 1907, but was just over its teething troubles when the Five Feddan Law destroyed it. Willcocks also believed that many of the usurers were now the fellahin women

---

* Cecil was the author of the minor imperial classic, *The Leisure of an Egyptian Official*, which unconsciously explains much of the lack of harmony in Anglo-Egyptian relations.

who had acquired the money under Muslim law as a result of the men's improvident habit of divorcing their wives to marry a younger woman. Divorce was extremely easy for men but the property rights of divorced women were carefully defined.

Cromer's Victorian financial orthodoxy was outraged by Kitchener's action which, as he wrote in a letter, 'has given a very great shock to confidence among all the monied classes'.* This was precisely what Kitchener hoped he had done if by 'monied classes' Cromer was referring to the European financiers who had acquired a sizable financial stake in Egyptian agriculture through the commercial banks. In the long run the Five Feddan Law in itself could not solve the problem of peasant indebtedness, this could only be done through the co-operative system. But the law at least gave a temporary boost to the fellahin's morale and a feeling that the Government was on their side. Kitchener's initiative assisted agriculture in other respects: village savings banks were opened and for the first time proper methods of weighing and storing cotton were introduced, stagnant village ponds were drained and a scheme for training village midwives was started, new roads and light railways were built in the country-side. In 1911 Kitchener instituted an urgently needed campaign against cotton pests. But Kitchener was excessively impatient in his drive to increase the cultivated area. Without waiting for the elaborate surveys that were necessary before reclaiming un-cultivated land, he decided to concentrate his attention on Gharbiyeh Province in the Delta. The Mudir of Gharbiyeh, Muhib Pasha, was politically ambitious and favoured Kitchener's scheme, although he knew it was technically impracticable. Two model villages were built and Kitchener arrived in state for the inaugural ceremony which included the distribution of title deeds to landless fellahin. But despite their fear of their Mudir, the fellahin were reluctant to accept because they knew it would take three years for the land to be washed of salt and made fit for cultivation. Muhib Pasha was obliged to drag an unfortunate fellah selected from the crowd who was unaware of what was happening, to accept the deeds from Kitchener. It was also said that some of

---

* His critics even improbably referred to him as 'the Lloyd George of Egypt'. The difference, as someone shrewdly observed, was that whereas Lloyd George could feel *with* the masses, Kitchener felt only *for* the masses.

the Mudirs used to force the fellahin to borrow money at high rates of interest and deposit it in the new village savings banks on the eve of one of Kitchener's visits; the money would then be withdrawn the following day after Kitchener had been reassured that the banks were successful. Nevertheless, the general direction of Kitchener's policies was wholly correct and his tendency to break the rules was salutary in a society weighed down with tradition. The Gharbiyeh Province experiment was a failure but the experience helped towards the success of another at a later date.

In 1913 Kitchener's initiative established Egypt's first ministry of agriculture – an important step which should have been taken earlier. But Kitchener showed much less energy in tackling other reforms. Gorst's unpopular Relegation Law was allowed to lapse but nothing had been done to counter the rural crime wave or improve the inadequate police force, despite Kitchener's earlier connection with it, when his career in Egypt was cut short by the First World War. Kitchener was equally unconcerned with education.

In 1913 Kitchener decided that the time had come for some form of constitutional advance which would satisfy the Liberal Government and the moderate nationalists in Egypt. The result was the new Organic Law which replaced the moribund general assembly and legislative council, which had been half-heartedly resuscitated by Gorst, with a legislative assembly of seventeen nominated and sixty-six elected members. Kitchener claimed that this new body would have considerably increased powers. It could veto proposals for the increase of direct taxation; it could delay legislation for a limited period and compel ministers to justify their proposals at length, interrogate them and call for information. But the advance was minuscule and the assembly was still essentially an advisory body. Even so Kitchener was determined that it should be dominated by solidly conservative landed interests. The property qualification for the franchise was placed so high that there were only 2,000 electors who elected no less than 49 large landowners. Kitchener wrote to Grey: 'I hope that the lesson has been learned that noisy extremists and outside political influences must be eliminated if the assembly is really to represent the hard-working unheard masses of the people who desire reform and improvement in their condition of life, and look for this result from the representatives they send to assist the Government in working for their good.'⁵

Despite all his safeguards, Kitchener still believed that the assembly might indulge in 'unjustified hostility, unseemly bicker- ings, and futile attempts to extend its own personal importance', in which case 'it will convince all reasonable men that Egypt is not for the present fitted for those representative institutions which are now on their trial'. But Kitchener needed nothing to convince him that orientals were unready for representative institutions and his attitude to his own constitutional reform can only be described as cynical. As might have been expected, the majority of the assembly – since they had no real responsibility – devoted them- selves to making life difficult for the ministers. They had a leader in Saad Zaghlul who had resigned in 1912 after falling out with the Khedive and who was now elected first vice-president of the assembly where he began to reveal his remarkable gifts as a par- liamentarian. Zaghlul succeeded in discrediting Mohammed Said the prime minister, and the baiting of ministers reached such a pitch that they were delighted when the session ended. The First World War intervened before the next session and the constitutional experiment was over.

Throughout his three years in Egypt Kitchener was as much of an absolute ruler as Cromer but with more of the trappings of monarchy. He was courteous and friendly to the flood of Egyptian notables who called on him at the agency but there was never any doubt of who made the decisions of importance. When he first arrived in Egypt, Kitchener made an effort to free Britain's hands in Egypt entirely by getting rid of the Capitulations. He was encouraged by Edward Grey, who believed that since France was in the process of assuming full jurisdiction in Morocco, it would be ready to relinquish its remaining privileges in Egypt to Britain. Kitchener made some proposals involving the transfer of all criminal and civil jurisdiction other than questions of personal status from the consular courts to the mixed courts. He also proposed that the legislative and fiscal veto of the powers should be handed over to Britain subject only to certain undertakings which would be enforceable in the supreme court.

But Kitchener was not sufficiently interested in this complex problem to think it through. Already he was devoting his attention to plans for the fellahin. His proposals were unlikely to satisfy the powers while they would outrage the Egyptians, who would see them as forecasting a permanent British occupation. Grey asked Kitchener to revise them, which he finally did when the War intervened and it was too late. This did not stop Kitchener from entertaining a series of visionary plans for abolishing Turkey's nominal suzerainty over Egypt and Britain annexing Egypt to create a new viceroyalty of Egypt and the Sudan, with himself as the first viceroy. He shared Cecil Rhodes' vision of an all-red Africa from Cape to Cairo.

In the summer of 1913 he considered removing the first obstacle by deposing the Khedive. Cromer, who was much more capable of seeing the dangerous international repercussions of such an action, advised caution. (He had himself considered deposing the Khedive at one time but instead had succeeded in emasculating him politically.) Wisely Cromer warned Kitchener against excessive complacency. After Gorst's 'relaxation in the personal system which was a necessity in my day', he wrote to Kitchener, 30 July 1913, 'you were appointed, and we have now gone back to a system of personal government, probably in a more accentuated form than was the case in my day. For the time, everybody seems very well content, but do not imagine for one moment that this state of things will last . . .'

Kitchener remained as determined as ever and when he left Egypt for his 1914 summer leave he had decided to insist to the British Government on the Khedive's deposition. This proved unnecessary. Abbas left Egypt at the same time as Kitchener with the intention of ending his European tour in London. Kitchener saw to it that he was informed that if he came to England King George v would refuse to see him. Abbas was therefore in Constantinople when war broke out on 4 August. When Turkey joined the central powers on 5 November Britain decided to declare a protectorate over Egypt. Abbas issued a violently anti-British declaration and was told that he could not return to Egypt. Kitchener hastened to return to Cairo when war seemed imminent. He was on the cross-channel boat at Dover on 3 August, urging the captain to leave before the boat train arrived because he knew he might be recalled, when Asquith telephoned to bring him to London. Two days later he entered the Cabinet as secretary for war to loud public applause.

Whereas admirers of Gorst could argue that his career was cut short before his experiments had had any chance to succeed, Kitchener's reputation probably benefited from the briefness of his rule in Egypt. He had established his authority with the help of his own commanding personality and the popular reaction against the obvious failures in Gorst's system. To a remarkable degree he kept Egypt quiet for three years, as the British Government had requested. Revisiting Egypt at the end of 1913 Professor Sayce observed: 'Egypt was contented and prosperous; it had the government, or rather the governor, that suited it; and a native remarked to me "Grenfell and Scott were our fathers, but Kitchener is our master". But it was a master whom the fellahin trusted implicitly, and as long as the nine million of fellahin were content, upon whom the very existence of Egypt is dependent, it did not matter what the mongrel population of Alexandria and Cairo, or the schoolboys who are educated there, might say or do.'[6]

But it did matter. Kitchener succeeded in holding down the lid on the nationalist sentiments of the urban intelligentsia and the students; this was a relatively easy task since they had already been divided and weakened by Gorst and their enthusiasm dampened by the death of the charismatic Mustafa Kamel. But though these emotions were buried they were not dead; after the interregnum of the war they led to the explosion of 1919. We can only speculate what would have happened if Kitchener had remained in Egypt a few more years but it is unlikely that his luck would have lasted.

THE GREAT WAR

The guns of August 1914 were only faintly heard in Egypt but the anomalies of the Veiled Protectorate were immediately exposed. Although occupied by a belligerent power, Egypt was officially neutral as Kitchener had insisted during the Turco-Italian war of 1911. But as long as Turkey kept out of the war, the difficulty could be surmounted by a typically British compromise. The British Government declared that it 'did not propose to alter the status of Egypt', while in return the amenable Egyptian prime minister, Hussein Rushdi Pasha, issued a declaration stating that since war had unfortunately been declared between England and Germany the presence of His Majesty's Army of Occupation rendered Egypt liable to attack by His Majesty's enemies. Accordingly no resident or visitor might conclude an agreement with any country at war with Britain or contribute to a loan issued by such a country or enter into any kind of business with enemy subjects. No vessel flying the Egyptian flag might enter an enemy port while British Naval and Military Forces were authorized to exercise all the rights of war in Egyptian ports and territories. Egypt was *de facto*, if not *de jure*, a belligerent.

Hussein Rushdi, the prime minister, although quick-witted and able, was no heroic national leader, and he bowed to the inevitable.* Britain's chief concern was the Suez Canal which was of little interest to Egypt in 1914. At that stage of the war there seemed no reason why Egypt should suffer any internal disruption. Prompt action to declare the pre-war note issue inconvertible followed by a five-day banking moratorium, successfully prevented any commercial panic. The most serious potential problem was the food supply. Cereal production had declined steadily over the years because cotton, despite the alarming fall in yields, was

* Small and birdlike in appearance, he was descended from an Albanian officer who accompanied Mohammed Aly to Egypt, but he was not cast in the same mould.

more profitable. In 1913 Egypt had imported 260,000 tons or one third of its requirements of wheat and now some of the obvious sources of supply, such as Russia, would be cut off by the war. The issue of ration cards to a population which was 90 per cent illiterate was ruled out, so it was decided to decree a limit to the cultivation of cotton to one quarter of the cultivable land.

In the first weeks of the war the British Government wisely decided to replace the general officer commanding the troops, General Byng, with General Sir John Maxwell. Byng was pre-eminently a fighting soldier while Maxwell had long experience both of Egypt and administration; nicknamed 'Conkey' he was bluff but tactful and humane. One of his first tasks was to decide on the deportation and internment of enemy aliens, many of whom were Levantines who had only adopted German or Austrian nationality for convenience. Maxwell helped them out of their difficulty, to the furious resentment of some of the British community who had succumbed to the wave of Germanophobia which swept England in 1914. Egyptian citizens who were regarded as potential security risks fared less well. It was difficult to draw the line between those Egyptians who merely disliked the British occupation and those who were likely to give active assistance to the enemy.

The Egyptian Government could hardly be expected to make this distinction so the matter was left to the British authorities; in Cairo it was Philippides, the Levantine director of the political CID, who investigated and recommended who should be deported. He turned out to be a dubious character who made use of the opportunity to pay off some old scores. Later in the war he was found guilty of corruption and sent to prison for a long term. Philippides had the full confidence of Harvey Pasha, the blimpish commandant of the Cairo police. His exposure was carried out by Thomas Russell who was later to become an almost legendary figure as inspector general of the Egyptian police. Russell risked his career in challenging powerful vested interests to bring Philippides and his formidable wife to trial by proving they had extorted bribes from police officers with promises of promotion. Russell's action earned him the lasting gratitude of a wide circle of Philippides' victims.

The relatively satisfactory situation in Egypt from the British viewpoint would be upset if Turkey entered the war on the side of the central powers. It was not so much that Turkey was Egypt's nominal suzerain; that difficulty had been ignored or surmounted on previous occasions. While the Veiled Protectorate had satisfied the British dislike of logic it would not be too difficult to devise a new formula. But what of the familiar spectacle of Mohammedan fanaticism? No one knew how the Egyptians would react to the inevitable call to *Jehad* or Holy War against the infidel. Moreover, there were numerous influential Turks in Egypt especially, as Ronald Storrs noted, in the harems of the aristocracy.

In 1914 Turkey was effectively ruled by a triumvirate of Young Turks, Enver, Talaat and Jemal, who had long since discarded the democratic ideals of their Revolution of 1908. They were alarmed at Turkey's isolation in the face of Russia's threat to Constantinople but it was far from a foregone conclusion that they would turn to Germany as an ally despite Kaiser Wilhelm's energetic courting of Turkish and Muslim sympathies. Since December 1913 there had been a German military mission in Constantinople headed by General Liman von Sanders but it was not outstandingly popular and the Turks had good reason to fear the imperial ambitions of Germany and her partners in the Triple Alliance – Austro-Hungary and Italy. Talaat and Jemal were in favour of a Turkish neutrality benevolently inclined towards England and France in the expected forthcoming European War. But circumstances were unfavourable. France was relying heavily on its alliance with Russia while in England the Liberal Government had inherited Gladstone's Turcophobia and even the Tory Opposition had abandoned its traditional view that the survival of the Ottoman Empire was the best protection of Britain's imperial interests. Yet all was not lost. Anglo-Turkish negotiations to delimit their respective zones of influence in Arabia and the Persian Gulf were reaching a success-ful conclusion in the summer of 1914. A British naval mission headed by Admiral Limpus was liked and trusted while the British Ambassador, Sir Louis Mallet, had excellent relations with the Turkish Government.

Ultimately the matter was decided because Enver Pasha was inclined towards Germany and he was the dominant figure in the Turkish Government. On 2 August 1914 the Germans succeeded in concluding a secret alliance with Turkey in Constantinople. Any doubts whether this would involve Turkey in the war against the Allies were removed on the same day when the British

Government commandeered two Turkish battleships which were on the point of completion in British shipyards. This high-handed action caused a wave of anti-British feeling throughout Turkey. Although strictly legal in wartime it was two days before Britain declared war on Germany and the immense cost of the battleships (£7·5 million) had mostly been raised by public subscription in Turkey.

Eluding the British fleet in the Mediterranean, two German warships, the *Goeben* and *Breslau*, were rushed to Constantinople where the German Ambassador placed them at Turkey's disposal. Although apprehensive at the prospect of being hastened into war before Turkey had time to mobilize, Enver and his colleagues were trapped. The Germans poured naval personnel into Constantinople while the British fleet blockaded the Dardanelles and demanded that Turkey justify its neutrality by expelling the German military mission. On 28 October the German admiral took the Turkish fleet into the Black Sea to bombard Russian ports and on 3 November the British fleet shelled the Turkish ports at the entrance to the Dardanelles. Turkey declared war on the Allies on 5 November.

Since the Allies were ignorant of the Turco-German alliance, the British in Egypt did not regard war with Turkey as a certainty in August 1914 but it seemed highly probable and discussion began at once on Egypt's future status. There was a powerful body of opinion in England in favour of the elimination of the Mohammed Aly dynasty followed by the outright annexation of Egypt and its incorporation into the British Empire as a Crown colony. This was vigorously opposed by Milne Cheetham, Acting British Agent in Kitchener's absence, and Sir John Maxwell who argued in favour of Britain replacing Turkey as Egypt's suzerain. In this way the *status quo* would be continued; only the flimsy veil over the British protectorate would be removed. Abbas Hilmi would have to be deposed but a suitable replacement existed in his elderly uncle, Prince Hussein Kamel, the senior member of the Khedivial family.

Cheetham and Maxwell understandably shrank from the task of ruling Egypt directly without the intermediary of Egyptian ministers, which would have been the consequence of annexation. It would also have meant that England was finally using the excuse of the war to renege on all the repeated solemn undertakings of the past thirty years at a time when Germany was being accused of infamous conduct in treating the Belgian treaty as a scrap of paper. It might have been thought that the effect on England's reputation would have seriously concerned Sir Edward Grey and his colleagues but it was they who decided a week after the outbreak of war with Turkey to overrule Cheetham's arguments by annexing Egypt. Only Cheetham's urgent eleventh-hour protests persuaded Grey to change his mind and agree to a protectorate.

When war with Turkey had become a certainty Sir John Maxwell proclaimed martial law (2 November 1914) in terms calculated to cause the least alarm and resentment among the civilian population. He declared that martial law was intended to supplement, not to supersede, the civilian administration; compensation would be paid for requisitioned property – and no civilian would be interfered with provided he conformed to all orders given by the competent military authorities. Three days later, when war was declared, he announced that Britain was fighting to protect the rights and liberties of Egypt won upon the battlefield by Mohammed Aly, and to secure the continuance of the peaceful prosperity which Egypt had enjoyed from the British occupation. For good measure he added that Great Britain accepted the sole burden of the war without calling upon the Egyptian people for aid.

Once Grey had agreed to the protectorate the next task was to persuade Hussein Kamel to accept the throne without conditions. The old gentleman was both honest and honourable but he had inherited a stubborn streak from his father Ismail. He wanted to be King of Egypt but since this would have given him the same title as his new suzerain, King George v of England, a compromise was reached, at Ronald Storrs' suggestion, on sultan (which happened also to be the title of his ex-suzerain) with the style *Son Hautesse* to distinguish him from the numerous *Altesses* at his court. Sultan Hussein Kamel still only agreed under strong persuasion to accept his proclamation without any mention of the hereditary rights of the Mohammed Aly dynasty or his right to choose his own flag. Finally, on 18 December, the declaration of the protectorate was issued in the form of a letter to Prince Hussein Kamel Pasha from Milne Cheetham. After condemning Turkey and Abbas Hilmi for throwing in his lot with His Majesty's enemies, the declaration roundly stated: 'it results that the rights over Egypt, whether of the Sultan, or of the late Khedive, are forfeit to His Majesty'. It added that 'by reason of your age and experience, you have been chosen as Prince of the Family of Mehemet Aly most worthy to occupy the khedivial position, with the title and style of Sultan of Egypt'. The declaration repeated Maxwell's acceptance of Britain's 'exclusive responsibility' for the defence of Egypt.

The British in Egypt had some reason to be pleased with their handling of this delicate situation. The Egyptian people took their transfer from Muslim to Christian suzerainty with remarkable calm. Pro-Turkish opinion remained largely theoretical for the Egyptians had no desire to be ruled by Turks in practice. Storrs observed: 'Pious Muslims shake their heads and say, "We wish the Turks all success – from afar," the last portion of the benison receiving the emphasis.'[1] The declaration of the protectorate had tactfully stated that the British Government was 'animated by no hostility towards the khaliphate. The past history of Egypt shows, indeed, that the loyalty of Egyptian Mohammedans towards the khaliphate is independent of any political bonds between Egypt and Constantinople.'

Pan-Islamic feeling scarcely affected the Egyptian armed forces as had been feared. It was only some Muslim troops in two Indian battalions of the Suez Canal defence force who deserted to the Turks. Those who were caught were shot and the trouble was prevented from spreading. A succession of Indian Muslim ruling princes visited the Canal Zone to help stiffen the morale of the troops.

Sultan Hussein Kamel undertook his new duties with enthusiasm. He swiftly transformed the Byzantine atmosphere of corruption and intrigue which had characterized the court in the later years of Abbas Hilmi's reign. In return he was humoured in some of his whims which his British advisers regarded as harmless megalomania. His right to bestow Turkish orders on his subjects, which Kitchener had taken from Abbas Hilmi, was restored. His civil list was raised from £100,000 to £150,000 and he exchanged the sombre travesty of the European frock-coat which the Turks had imposed on the Egyptian court, to a magnificent musical comedy uniform of gold lace. He was hospitable, dignified and generally popular – especially in the countryside where he was known as a model landowner.

Subsequent events were to show that for the sake of the immediate advantage of keeping Egypt peaceful a number of awkward questions had been postponed to a time when they would be much more difficult to answer. Was Egypt an ally of England in the war with Turkey and the central powers? General Maxwell had clearly implied that it was not but within days of his proclamation artillery units of the Egyptian army were on their way to the Suez Canal to defend it against a Turkish attack. In 1916 the Army Reserve was called to the colours and by 1917 there were 21,000 Egyptians serving in camel transport in the Auxiliary Egyptian Corps. Of these 220 were killed, fourteen thousand were wounded and no less than four thousand died in hospital.[2] The Labour Corps casualties were lower since it normally operated away from the front line but it was scarcely less unpopular with the fellahin. While conscription for these two Corps was never introduced because the Egyptian Government refused, despite British persuasion, the result was much the same. When volunteers were not forthcoming the Government instructed the Mudirs to reimpose a form of the *corvée* which obliged them to produce a quota of recruits from each village. Similar methods were used to procure the thousands of camels and donkeys that were needed in Palestine but which were almost as precious to the fellahin as their own sons.

Another question that had not been answered related to the status of Egyptians under the British protectorate. Were they British subjects or not? In fact there was no general agreement as to whether Egypt was now part of the British Empire. Lord Cromer, in England, assumed that it was but the British in Egypt thought differently. Lord Lloyd, writing some twenty years later, records with regret that the opportunity of incorporating Egypt into the Empire was missed in 1914.[3] The declaration of the protectorate itself avoided the issue by begging the question when it stated with the establishment of the protectorate, 'all Egyptian subjects, wherever they may be, will be entitled to receive the protection of His Majesty's government'.

The only respect in which Egypt's system of government was altered by the declaration was the abolition of the foreign minister. Relations between the Egyptian Government and the representatives of foreign powers, 'should henceforth be conducted through His Majesty's representative in Cairo'. But this was a purely nominal change. Egypt had had no foreign policy of its own since 1882 and the foreign minister was a cypher. The real trouble lay elsewhere. The effect of the protectorate declaration was to freeze Egypt's political development for the duration of the war. However inadequate and superficial Kitchener's experiments in the creation of representative institutions may have been, they at least created an illusion of progress. In December 1914 Kitchener was replaced as high commissioner, as his title became automatically with the declaration of the protectorate, by Sir Henry MacMahon who came to Egypt from the very different post of political secretary at Simla. Though able and sympathetic he had no opportunity or official encouragement to attempt any constitutional experiments. His time in Egypt is chiefly remembered for his negotiations with the Sherif Hussein of Mecca to initiate the Arab Revolt against the Turks. In Egyptian affairs he generally submitted to the guidance of Lord Edward Cecil, the financial adviser, and Sir William Brunyate, the judicial adviser.

The legislative assembly was supposed to begin a new session in November 1918. It was postponed several times and then *sine die* – to the infinite relief of Rushdi Pasha and his ministers who had no wish to face a barrage of questions from Saad Zaghlul and his followers on the effects of legislation decreed under martial law. In October 1914 a hurriedly drafted law declaring the assembly of five or more persons, unless previously authorized, to be a penal offence virtually paralysed Egypt's political life. Under army orders the Government muzzled the press so severely that *The Times* was moved to remark that the Egyptian censorship was 'the most incompetent, the most inept, and the most savagely ruthless in any country under British control, not excepting Mesopotamia'. The British were determined to keep Egypt quiet for the duration of the war.

At the time it seemed wholly preferable to the British in Egypt that repression should be exerted on Britain's behalf through the intermediary of Egyptian ministers. But it is at least arguable that annexation followed by direct rule would have avoided some of the later confusion and bitterness. In one respect annexation would have been wholly advantageous; the Capitulations would have been abolished with little difficulty. The protectorate declaration admitted that they were no longer in harmony with the development of the country but concluded that their revision must be postponed until the end of the war. General Maxwell was able to make some use of martial law to eliminate abuses by the foreign

communities of their extraordinary privileges under the Capitulations. In 1915 European residents were for the first time made to
contribute to local security forces through payment of the Ghafir
tax. Severe restrictions were imposed on the manufacture of
unadulterated liquor and suspected premises were entered for the
first time without consular authority. In 1914 there were over 100
distilleries in Cairo alone – mostly, though not exclusively, owned
by foreign subjects. The alcohol, which was distilled from molasses,
was injurious to health, to say the least, and one cynical visitor
was moved to remark that the only unadulterated drink you could
buy in Egypt was poison. General Maxwell's chief concern was
with the effect on the British troops in Egypt but it was not only
they who drank it. Despite the prohibition of Islam, the Greek
shopkeepers sold quantities of this vicious spirit to the Egyptians
while successive Egyptian Governments tried unsuccessfully to
control the trade.

Egypt's silence under repression did not mean acquiescence.
The students, though leaderless and confused, were still fervently
nationalist and their cafés and clubs seethed with bitter opposition
to the Government and occupation. Secretly they applauded two
unsuccessful assassination attempts on the life of the Sultan in
1915. For the time being the countryside was relatively content but
when the fellahin also became disaffected as a consequence of the
requisitioning of their animals and the reintroduction of the corvée,
an unusual synthesis of urban and rural discontent resulted in the
rebellion of 1919.

But all this was hardly suspected by the British in Egypt in 1914;
their immediate concern was the possibility of a Turkish attack
on the Suez Canal. Jemal Pasha, who had been appointed commander-in-chief of the army in Syria, was reported to have told
his friends as he stepped on the train 'I shall not return until I have
entered Cairo'. Jemal was an able general and his chief of staff
was Kress von Kressenstein, the brilliant Rommel of the First
World War. The British Army of Occupation had been withdrawn
in August 1914 to reinforce the Expeditionary Force in France and
it was replaced by a territorial division of the 42nd Lancashire*
regiment and some yeomanry squadrons. This new force was not

* 'Lancashire spins cotton,' said Kitchener when he decided to send
them. 'Not a bad thing, then, if Lancashire men see how the raw material
is grown.'

ready to take the field when it arrived. They were reinforced by an equally untrained contingent of the Australian and New Zealand Imperial Forces, two Indian infantry divisions and the Egyptian artillery.

Jemal Pasha assembled an army of twenty thousand rifles in southern Palestine and in January 1915 marched across Sinai to attack the canal near Ismailia in the central sector. Some units succeeded in crossing the canal but were repulsed with the help of the fire from two French cruisers and a sandstorm. Jemal had hoped that the Egyptian troops would mutiny and the civilian population rise against the British occupiers. When this failed to happen he had to give up all hope of taking Cairo. However, with the help of the unruly bedouin tribesmen in Sinai von Kressenstein kept a substantial British force tied down on the canal for the first two years of the war. In the Libyan Desert the Germans also succeeded in persuading the Senussi, the warlike bedouin tribesmen of Cyrenaica, to rise against Britain. The Cairo intelligence service had failed to appreciate the threat and the Germans supplied the Senussi with money and arms. In November 1915 they occupied the Egyptian frontier town of Sollum and although they offered no serious military threat and were easily dislodged they too pinned down large forces in patrolling Egypt's western frontier.

Meanwhile Egypt had become deeply, if indirectly, involved in the Gallipoli campaign – the imaginative attempt by the British and French to open a second front to encircle the central powers and relieve the hard-pressed Russians. Egypt became the base for the Expeditionary Force and it is at least arguable that this was the chief reason for its failure. The time taken to assemble such a large force in Egypt removed the essential element of surprise and enabled the Turks to strengthen their almost non-existent defences of the Dardanelles.

Egypt's role was to be first a vast Allied war camp and shortly afterwards a military hospital as well. The English civilian community in Egypt had begun by taking the war very calmly. Senior officials in the government service insisted that none of their Anglo-Egyptian staff could be spared for military service and visitors from home were critical of the manner in which the whisky-drinking, polo-playing, Gezira Club life continued unruffled while appalling casualties were already being suffered on the Western Front. Attitudes changed to some extent during 1915.

The English ladies of Cairo volunteered enthusiastically for war work and ultimately provided invaluable assistance to the over-stretched hospital staff, treating the wounded from Gallipoli.* Some of the men decided to form their own volunteer reserve and doggedly drilled themselves under the Egyptian sun. But they had to do it without rifles for Maxwell had none to spare and they were the object of ribald comment from those who stood aloof and dubbed them 'Pharaoh's Foot'. The survivors of the Mediterranean Expeditionary Force were established in Egypt as part of the newly constituted Egyptian Expeditionary Force (EEF) under its commander, Sir Archibald Murray, who moved his headquarters from Ismailia to Cairo. In March 1916 he took over from Sir John Maxwell who was dispatched to Ireland where the nationalists were proving rather more rebellious than the Egyptians.

Once again a soldier rather than administrator was in command in Egypt. Unlike Maxwell, Murray was not interested in the tactful application of martial law but only in the prosecution of the war; he was respected but not liked. The Egyptians were shortly made aware that their country was not occupied by a small British garrison but an immense foreign army engaged in war. The towns were invaded by tens of thousands of servicemen and while their spending brought great wealth to some it only meant a crippling rise in prices for most of the inhabitants. On the other hand, the uninhibited behaviour of the soldiers – especially the Australians and New Zealanders – caused less offence than might have been expected to the urban Egyptians who are rarely sullen and respond easily to cheerful friendliness. Ronald Storrs records that the Australians were 'terrifying but popular'. Colonel Elgood remarked that their magnificent physique made them 'supermen from another world' but added, rather primly, 'Unfortunately the self-control of some of these giants was in inverse ratio to their bodily proportions. ... There seemed sometimes no form of temptation, however repulsive, which one type of Australian could resist.' However, 'the fault was not wholly his: for Egypt pandered gladly to his grosser appetites'.[4] Whereas Wellington's armies had been decimated by dysentery, improved sanitation

---

* At first their enthusiasm outran their ability. Maxwell's reply to one pertinacious lady was: 'Everyone expects me to find him or her suitable military work and no one seems to have any qualifications. I want dispatch riders. Can you ride a motor bicycle?' She could not.

ensured that this was not a threat to the Egyptian Expeditionary Force; its place was taken by venereal disease. As we have seen, the sale of alcohol could be restricted and controlled under martial law but the Capitulations and contemporary prejudice combined to prevent the same being done for prostitution. In 1916 the average annual incidence of venereal disease was twelve per cent for the Expeditionary Force and as high as 25 per cent in some units.

The failure to deal sensibly with the problem was vividly illustrated by the authorities' action in Cairo. The principal red-light district in the capital was the officially tolerated Wasa'a quarter, near the Opera and Ezbekiyah Gardens, with its extension, the Wigh el-Birka. According to Thomas Russell, the assistant commandant of police in Cairo, the Wasa'a was where 'the Egyptian Nubian and Sudanese women plied their one shilling trade in conditions of abject squalor, though under government medical control'. While the Wigh el-Birka was staffed by European women 'of all breeds and races other than British, who were not allowed by their consular authority to practise this licensed trade in Egypt',[5] the Wasa'a quarter was ruled by a huge transvestite Nubian, known as el-Gharbi whom Russell describes as a 'repulsive pervert' but seems to have been an efficient and relatively humane employer.

Because of the capitulations little could be done to clean up the Wigh el-Birka even under martial law, but in 1916 Harvey Pasha, the unimaginative martinet who was Russell's superior, decided on drastic action 'to clear up the scores of free-lance girls and catamite boys who had sprung up outside the licensed quarters'. A special internment camp was set up at Hilmiya into which the police threw as many of 'these long-haired degenerates' as they could find. Russell was annoyed to discover not only that el-Gharbi had not been arrested but that Harvey Pasha had never heard of him. When Russell informed him he sent for el-Gharbi and 'demanding what the hell everyone meant by bringing that disgusting patchouli-scented sodomite into his presence' had him handcuffed and thrown into the Hilmiya camp. He was released after one year but later sentenced to five years in prison where he died. Russell admits that el-Gharbi's removal 'was not altogether a blessing for the brothel organization of the country' as he was good and just to his women who only had to find themselves new and less scrupulous protectors.

In 1916 the Canal Zone was made a restricted area; no Egyptian or European was allowed to enter without a permit. Under General Murray's direction an elaborate system of pipelines, railways and roads was built to connect Egypt with the canal and beyond into Sinai. An auxiliary labour corps of some three thousand Egyptians had been sent to the Dardanelles in 1915 with outstanding success. An Egyptian fellah was much better at digging than an English tommy. Many more were now needed but volunteers were not forthcoming as the fellahin, who were always reluctant to leave their villages, had an additional incentive to stay at home in the high agricultural prices. In the summer of 1916 von Kressenstein received reinforcements from Enver Pasha in Constantinople; a squadron of German aircraft also arrived and proceeded to make regular air raids on Port Said which intimidated the civilian population. One German plane even reached Cairo and dropped a few bombs. In August von Kressenstein launched a final offensive against the canal with twenty thousand troops. But General Murray's defensive system proved highly effective; the Turks were driven off with heavy casualties and four thousand prisoners were taken.

General Murray now decided to clear Sinai of the Turks. Slowly and deliberately he advanced across the Peninsula to occupy the coastal town of el-Arish in December 1916. The Turkish forces withdrew to Gaza. In April 1917 Murray attacked but was heavily repulsed and for three months the Expeditionary Force remained in front of Gaza. Morale was low; Murray kept GHQ in Cairo where staff officers who had never been near the front received high awards for gallantry. Then at the end of June Murray was replaced by Allenby who at once removed GHQ to Palestine and in a short time immeasurably improved the morale of the EEF. At the end of October he launched his offensive and swept on to enter Jerusalem on 11 December 1917.

With the withdrawal of the immediate Turkish threat to their country, the Egyptians found their involvement in the war increasingly burdensome. Allenby's victories in Palestine inspired little enthusiasm. At the same time the British who were entering their fourth year of war were little inclined to care about Egyptians' susceptibilities. The army's demands for camel transport and the auxiliary labour corps grew increasingly peremptory while the British Government was not prepared to see any reassertion of the authority of the Egyptian Government *vis-à-vis* the military occupation. Sir Reginald Wingate, who succeeded Sir Henry MacMahon in December 1916, had the vital advantage of experience of Egypt having been governor-general of the Sudan since 1899. But his position was unenviable for while the foreign office ignored his advice on Egyptian politics he suffered constant criticism from the army for the inadequacy of Egypt's war effort.

In May 1917 deep resentment was caused by the decree of a new law requiring all Egyptians to surrender their arms. A similar law in 1904, which had been aimed at rural lawlessness, had been largely ineffective as the fellahin merely buried their weapons. The new law was issued on the authority of the army and was not connected with domestic crime but military security; it included severe penalties for contravention. The fellahin were angered because they felt they had done nothing to provoke this action; there had been no hint of armed rebellion in Egypt since the outbreak of war.

Control of the cotton market was established early in the war to try to prevent the sale of Egyptian cotton to the enemy through Switzerland. This proved only moderately effective and in 1917 it was decided that the entire crop should be purchased at slightly above the current rate. But since this rate was rising so rapidly (from $42 per cantar in 1918 to $90 in 1919) Egyptian farmers felt they had been cheated. The fact that the Cotton Control's windfall profit was later handed back to pay for war pensions failed to alleviate their sense of grievance.

During the summer of 1917 the sharp decline in Sultan Hussein Kamel's health reopened the question of Egypt's status. Once again the annexationists put forward their arguments but this time they were supported by the British high commissioner Sir Reginald Wingate in a letter to A. J. Balfour* the foreign secretary (27 July 1917): 'I am of opinion that, provided the act was made tactfully and at a favourable juncture, annexation would be accepted passively, if without enthusiasm, by the bulk of the population, and would tend to facilitate and strengthen our control and influence on the administration of the country, and ultimately to improve and solidify our relations with the natives.' Brigadier Gilbert Clayton, the brilliant director of the Arab intelligence bureau in Cairo, was

---

* Balfour had replaced Grey at the foreign office when Lloyd George became prime minister in 1916.

still more specific in a Note on the Future Political Status of Egypt.[6] After summarizing and dismissing all the arguments against annexation he concluded, in familiar Cromerian terms, 'I venture to think that somewhat undue weight is given to the aspirations of the small and interested ruling class in Egypt to the detriment of the great mass of Egyptians – a submissive and amenable community – to whom the high official is inaccessible; and whom many years of subjection have entitled to just and efficient rule.' But all this was of no avail. Egyptian affairs were handled by the foreign office not the colonial office and it was concerned less with Egypt's internal administration, or even its position in the Islamic world, than with Britain's relations with other Mediterranean powers. The foreign office was resolutely opposed to any renunciation of the protectorate declaration of 1914 and the question of annexation was finally dropped.

The succession posed a serious problem. The Sultan Hussein's son, Prince Kemal el-Din, was a shy recluse who had voluntarily renounced his claims to the succession. The next possibility was the Sultan's younger brother, the 49-year-old Prince Ahmed Fuad.* He was far from satisfactory because although he was no Anglophobe like his nephew Abbas Hilmi, he had been brought up in Italy where he had gone into exile with his father Ismail, spoke little Arabic and made no attempt to hide his lack of sympathy for Egypt or its problems.† Unlike Hussein Kamel (or Abbas Hilmi for that matter) he was incapable of representing any section of Egyptian opinion to England and this proved disastrous in the aftermath of the war. But there was no obvious alternative and he was duly installed as Sultan Fuad I after Hussein Kamel's death in October 1917.

While the British Government did not wish to consider any change in Egypt's status while the war continued, it had not forgotten the promise included in the declaration of the protectorate to revise the Capitulations treaties as soon as it was over. The

---

* In 1921 a Sheikh of al-Azhar remarked of the last three rulers of Egypt: 'Abbas Hilmi was a Turkish Pasha, Hussein Kamel an Egyptian farmer, Ahmed Fuad is an Italian Count.'

† Sultan Fuad's ludicrous blunders in Arabic were common currency in Cairo gossip. His voice was also an unfortunate dog-like bark as a result of a shooting incident with his jealous brother-in-law who was in love with his own sister, Fuad's first wife.

recommendations made by the committee set up by Kitchener in 1913 were now outdated and permanently pigeon-holed. A new Capitulations Commission was therefore established in March 1917 to make proposals which the British Government hoped would lead to an Anglo-French convention finally regularizing the two countries' respective positions in Egypt and Morocco. Some of the more spirited Egyptian ministers were also looking forward to the end of the war. Two of them – Adly Pasha Yeghen and Sarwat Pasha, who were both destined to play an important part in the political life of independent Egypt – proposed that the whole question of legislative reform apart from the Capitulations should be revived. Wingate agreed and another special commission for this purpose was set up at the end of 1917. Wingate, however, opposed the new Sultan's request, made at the suggestion of the prime minister Rushdi Pasha, that Zaghlul should be brought in to strengthen the Government. Possibly much trouble would have been avoided if this had been done.

Unfortunately, the principal influence on the work of the two Commissions was the judicial adviser, Sir William Brunyate, a ponderous and politically insensitive lawyer who had been brought out to Egypt in the 1890s by Sir Malcolm McIlwraith to vet the English business contracts of the Egyptian Government; his natural dictatorial inclinations had been enhanced by Sir Henry MacMahon's enforced reliance on his judgement. A year later Brunyate produced a note which, though lucidly argued, was quite out of touch with the political realities of Egypt in 1918. Starting from the assumption that the overriding need was for efficiency in administration to match Egypt's undisputed economic progress, he concluded that the Egyptians' share in government should be reduced to a minimum. He therefore proposed the creation of a legislature of two chambers of which the Upper House would be the more important. This would include Egyptian ministers, British advisers and representatives of the foreign communities elected by special electorates. Brunyate's view was that since Egypt's financial interests were largely in foreign hands the Egyptians had no right to a dominant voice in legislation affecting them.[7]

Brunyate's proposals were a more detailed expression of the views expressed by Cromer on the future government of Egypt shortly before his retirement. Cromer had said that since a 'true

Egyptian' was indefinable, any 'Egypt for the Egyptians' policy was nonsense. 'The only real Egyptian autonomy . . . is one which will enable the dwellers in cosmopolitan Egypt, be they Muslim or Christian, European, Asiatic, or African, to be fused into one self-governing body.'[8] Accordingly Cromer had said that all the foreign communities should have special representation in any future legislative body. Brunyate went further to propose that they should form the overwhelming majority. Egypt would in effect be governed by a five per cent minority of non-Egyptians.

Brunyate's proposals were useless because they ignored the state of Egyptian public opinion. The fact that they were not intended for public discussion but for the consideration of the British foreign minister was irrelevant; it only meant that Balfour (who succeeded Grey in 1916) was being misled as to the real alternatives for British policy in Egypt. In any case the matter did not remain private for long; details of Brunyate's note leaked out in November 1918 and added to the newly rising tide of nationalist feeling. A revealing, even if apocryphal, anecdote of the day related that when Rushdi Pasha objected to Brunyate that his proposals would set the country in a blaze, he replied '*Je l'éteindrai avec un crachat*'.

20

UPRISING

Despite the genuine causes for grievance, it could be argued that Egypt was one of the most fortunate countries to be involved in the First World War. While it had suffered no devastation and no more than a few thousand casualties, its national wealth had immensely increased. Cotton prices and exports rocketed and because imports were limited by shortages of shipping and overseas supplies, a substantial favourable trade balance was built up by the end of the war. At home, increasing personal prosperity was reflected in the growth of deposit banking and the repayment of mortgage debts.

Yet because the Government was devoid of any social policy the new wealth created more bitterness than satisfaction in the nation as a whole. The cotton boom primarily enriched the big and medium landowners who formed less than ten per cent of the cultivators but owned nearly 75 per cent of the cultivated area. In the towns an even smaller class profited or profiteered from the presence of Allied troops. Wholesale and retail businesses made fortunes while the foundations of Egyptian industry were laid behind the protection of wartime import restrictions. Not all the new rich in the country or the towns were from the pasha class; a few were illiterate fellahin. Egypt took on a few of the superficial aspects of western capitalist society, but no substantial new property-owning middle class was created during the war. The reality for most of the people was that prices more than doubled between 1914 and 1918 and went on rising when the war was over. As cotton prices rose, landowners ignored government restrictions to plant cotton and wheat and food became scarce and expensive. A devastating comment on the nation's ill-health, despite its increased income, was the sharp rise in the death rate which actually exceeded the birth rate in the last year of the war.

The classical circumstances for a social upheaval had therefore been created in Egypt by the war. The sudden wealth and success of a minority had raised the expectations of the rest and sharpened their discontent.

Politically, the same situation applied. Egypt, like every nation under foreign rule, had taken note of President Wilson's advocacy in 1918 of the universal principle of self-determination which even his allies had apparently adopted. In November 1918 an Anglo-French declaration promised self-determination to the peoples freed from Turkish rule. Already the Arabs of Arabia, whom the Egyptians regarded with some justice as more backward than themselves, were looking forward to independence and preparing to send a delegate to the peace conference. Two days after the Armistice Zaghlul Pasha presented himself at the residency at the head of a delegation and informed Sir Reginald Wingate that the Egyptian people wanted their complete independence.

Zaghlul, of whom Cromer had once spoken so highly, was now to succeed Mustafa Kamel as the arch-enemy of the British occupation. Ultimately his leadership was detrimental to Egypt because his undoubted gifts which enabled him to gain such a hold on the nation's imagination only served to conceal his inadequacies as a statesman. Tall and craggy in appearance, he was a splendid orator who interspersed his rhetoric with the kind of jokes and colloquial proverbs that Egyptians love. At times he could be noble and commanding but at others he was nervous and indecisive. Above all he exemplified Egypt's misfortune in the domination of its political life by lawyers and judges who confused forensic skill with statesmanship. It was scarcely their fault; it had been Cromer's policy of denying political responsibility to independent-minded young Egyptians which had forced them to seek an outlet for their ambitions at the Bar. Zaghlul was one of the very rare exceptions who had enjoyed responsibility as minister of education and then of justice but he had fallen foul of the Khedive, Abbas, and resigned in 1912. As vice-president of the legislative assembly he had discovered his real talent for rousing the national feelings of the Egyptians against the ministers who were co-operating with Britain. Although outwardly restrained and moderate in his behaviour during the war years, he had used his time to build up his following while the Government was taken up with interpreting the orders of the military authorities and softening their impact on the Egyptians.

When Zaghlul presented himself to Wingate his claim to represent the Egyptians was justified if not formally correct. Wingate was taken by surprise and instead of objecting, as he might have done, that he could only deal with Rushdi Pasha as prime minister, replied that he had not yet been informed by His Majesty's government of their intentions concerning Egypt. Two days later Zaghlul returned to the charge with a request to proceed to London with his delegation (Wafd)* to present Egypt's case. This request was sharply refused by Balfour. Rushdi now saw his opportunity and proposed that he and his colleague Adly Pasha Yeghen were the ones who should go to London. Wingate forwarded this request with a strong recommendation that it be accepted but Balfour's reply was that 'no useful purpose would be served' by the visit. He had the valid reason that the forthcoming peace conference was occupying all his attention but the reply could at least have been couched in more diplomatic terms. The Egyptians were being curtly informed that, unlike the Arabians, Cypriots and Armenians, they would have no say in any discussions on their own future. Balfour made this clear in a despatch to Wingate on 27 November. 'His Majesty's government desire to act on the principle which they have always followed of giving the Egyptians an ever-increasing share in the government of the country. . . . As you are well aware, the stage has not yet been reached at which self-government is possible. His Majesty's government have no intention of abandoning their responsibilities for order and good government in Egypt and for protecting the rights and interests both of the native and the foreign populations of the country.' The Egyptian reaction was predictable and Zaghlul at once seized his opportunity. Pointing out that the British Government had spurned the Egyptian prime minister, he launched a nation-wide campaign by setting up local committees and collecting signatures to back his claim to be the true representative of Egypt.

Under strong urging from Sir Reginald Wingate, Balfour eventually relented to invite Rushdi and Adly to London in February 1919. But it was now too late; Rushdi realized that he had been outflanked by Zaghlul who would at once denounce any agreement he might reach as a betrayal. He therefore proposed that Zaghlul should accompany him to London. Although Wingate advised acceptance, Balfour again rejected this proposal, adding that he could not allow extremist and unrepresentative Egyptian

* His political party later came to be known as the Wafd.

politicians to bring their demands to London or anywhere else. Rushdi and his whole cabinet then resigned on 1 March 1919 with the full approval of Sultan Fuad.

Wingate had been recalled to London for consultations and Milne Cheetham was once again in charge of the high commission. Despite, or perhaps because of, the great increase in the number of British officials in Egypt during the war, the high commission was sadly misinformed of the true state of Egyptian opinion. The social gulf between English and Egyptians was wider than ever as even the contacts with the pashas and upper class Levantines maintained by Cromer and Harry Boyle and later by Ronald Storrs (who had left Egypt at the end of 1917 to become military governor of Jerusalem) had come to an end. Intelligence reports Cheetham received must have been wildly misleading for him to write to Balfour on 24 February in reference to the nationalist leaders, that 'the agitation which they have organized is dying out, or is at any rate quiescent in the country at large. A noteworthy feature is that this agitation has from the beginning been entirely pacific in character. . . . We still, no doubt, have to reckon with discontent among the upper classes, the landed proprietors and professional elements. Most of these people vaguely desire some form of autonomy, which would make them individually more important, but the situation does not seem to me to differ materially from that of 1914 when Prince Hussein and the leading ministers refused for a long time to accept a protectorate without concessions which we were not able to make. . . . The present movement, however, cannot be compared in importance with that of Mustafa Kamel, and there seems no reason why it should affect the decisions of HM's government on constitutional questions and the proper form to be given to the protectorate.'[1]

This was not the first occasion – and unfortunately it was not the last – that a senior British representative in a Near Eastern state failed to gauge a revolutionary situation. As Zaghlul increased his agitation following Rushdi's resignation, Cheetham decided that all that was needed was to remove him from the scene. He recommended that he should be deported to Malta and Balfour agreed. Because martial law was still in force this was simply done and Zaghlul and three of his colleagues* were bundled on to a train

* Two of these, Ismail Sidky Pasha and Mohammed Mahmoud Pasha, were future prime ministers, as well as Zaghlul.

at Cairo to be taken by a British destroyer from Port Said to Malta. No special security precautions were taken and there was no liaison between the ministry of the interior and the armed forces.

As soon as the news spread in Cairo, university and secondary school students poured into the streets to demonstrate. They overturned trams, smashed windows and street lamps and paraded through Cairo chanting Zaghlul's name. The riots worsened as the students were joined by others more interested in looting than politics, and on 11 March the student strikes spread to government offices, doctors and lawyers; business in the capital came to a standstill in what amounted to a general strike. Shops in central Cairo and the offices of Faris Nimr's Anglophile *al-Muqattam* newspaper were sacked. British troops were called out; several rioters were shot and many more arrested. To the astonishment of the vast majority of Anglo-Egyptians who had assumed that the fellahin were impervious to student agitation, the trouble now spread to the countryside. There was rioting at Tanta, Damanhour, Zagazig, Mansura and many other Delta towns. Crowds gathered to tear up railway tracks and burn down stations. Telegraph wires were cut and communications throughout the country came to a standstill. At Tanta fourteen rioters were shot when they tried to rush the railway station. Planes dropped leaflets all over the country warning the population that anyone attempting acts of sabotage was liable to be shot under martial law, but these had no effect because the whole country had been roused by the shootings of demonstrators which had already taken place. In the towns their funeral processions were followed by great crowds of men and lamenting women who halted at intervals to hear impassioned speeches. Throughout the country the crowds concentrated their attacks on the symbols of authority, such as law courts and government offices. At Zagazig and Minieh they created their own provisional 'republican governments' and even some villages set up 'soviets'.

On the fourth day (14 March) the first Briton was murdered in a Delta town and on the following day the uprising spread for the first time to Upper Egypt. At Wasta a British railway official was murdered and the situation took a new turn for the worse as the bedouin flocked in from the desert to join the fighting. But with the help of the few regular troops available, including a small Indian detachment which was rushed in from Fayoum, British residents in Upper Egypt were able to hold out against ill-disciplined mob attacks until relief came. The worst incident for the British side was the murder of seven unarmed soldiers and one civilian returning by train from Luxor to Cairo. At each station that the train pulled into, carrying their mutilated bodies, a frenzied crowd shouted with joy when they heard the English had been killed until the bodies were taken off the train and buried at Minieh.*

On 17 March General Bulfin, who had taken over command of the Egyptian Expeditionary Force in Palestine when Allenby left to go to Paris for the peace conference, arrived by car in Cairo to take charge of the situation. An energetic and powerful personality, he at once issued the sternest warning to notables and government officials and, hastily collecting all the troops available, including an Australian division awaiting demobilization, despatched mobile columns into every province where there was trouble. Planes bombed every suspicious gathering and armoured cars and planes fired on any suspect groups near roads and railways. From then on the security situation improved and within two days trains were running again in the Delta. The pacification of Upper Egypt, where the trouble had been worse, took longer and General Shea's punitive column did not reach Aswan until 18 April. But in most of the country the rebellion was over by the end of March, even if sporadic incidents continued.

As in 1882, the Egyptian Government accepted responsibility for damage to property and in October 1919 the finance ministry paid £1 million to a commission appointed to investigate individual claims. A military proclamation prevented the mixed and native tribunals from contesting its decisions. General Bulfin also set up special military tribunals, with British judges as advisers, to try the principal offenders in the rioting; he correctly assumed that the Egyptian judiciary would sympathize with the defendants. Within three months 2,304 cases had been heard and 1,613 convicted. Sentences of death were passed on 102 of which 55 were commuted by the high commissioner.[2]

---

* Only a prostitute (or 'public woman' as Lord Wavell charmingly describes her) showed pity in trying to protect the bodies. Later the British community in Egypt considered offering her a piece of land in recognition of her action but she preferred jewellery and was presented with an inscribed gold bracelet and signet ring.

After an initial hesitation due to surprise the uprising had been swiftly stamped upon. But who was really to blame? Anglo-Egyptian officials were inclined to hold Zaghlul morally responsible; but no one could seriously contend that he had actually organized the rebellion. He was already out of the country when it started and his replacement as president of the committee of independence, Ali Pasha Sharawi, had been all too clearly out of control of the situation from the beginning. The manner in which the uprising had spread haphazardly from one province to another argued against the existence of any kind of revolutionary master-plan. It is true that Milne Cheetham on the first day of the outbreak was hinting at a 'Bolshevik tendency' and 'extraneous influence' because of the destruction of property while the official memorandum on the Unrest in Egypt of 9 April 1919 went further to suggest that the 'hand of the Young Turk, and even German agent, is clearly discernible' on the ground that the 'premeditated and organized plan of campaign corresponds to the programme drawn up by the Germans and Young Turks for an attack in the autumn of 1914, which was revealed to the Egyptian authorities by the German spy, Mors, captured at Alexandria'.[3] How either the Bolsheviks or the prostrate Germans and Turks could have been in a position to promote rebellion in Egypt in 1919 was not explained and not a shred of evidence was ever offered in support. As Lord Lloyd tartly remarks: 'It was perhaps inevitable that the authorities should seek in this way to console themselves for their ignorance of conditions precedent.'[4]

News of the alarming events in Egypt was as unwelcome as it was unexpected to the Lloyd George Government which was heavily involved in the affairs of the Paris Peace Conference. Allenby, the conqueror of Syria from the Turks, arrived in Paris on 19 March to give his views on the Syrian question to the Allies. With one of his intuitive flashes, Lloyd George decided that Allenby was the right man to restore order in Egypt. The unfortunate Wingate, who was still kicking his heels in London, was summarily superseded despite the fact that his advice, which had been consistently ignored, had been proved resoundingly correct. Within thirty-six hours of his arrival in Paris Allenby was on his way to Cairo.

General Sir Edmund Allenby had ended the war with an outstanding reputation among all the Allied generals. His earlier career in France and Flanders was controversial – especially during the first battle of Arras in April 1917 where his efforts to achieve surprise by improving on the then accepted tactical methods of position warfare were unfavourably regarded by GHQ. He had his admirers but he also aroused widespread hostility through his occasional fits of brusqueness and bad temper and his extreme self-confidence which verged on arrogance. But all was forgiven when he took over command of the Egyptian Expeditionary Force in June. He infused a new spirit in this weary and demoralized force and went on to win a brilliant campaign in Palestine. He was fortunate in being a victorious commander in virtually the only theatre of war in 1914–18 to which any glamour could be attached in contrast to the unrelieved hell of the Flanders trenches, but much of the public's adulation was fully deserved. He was that rare combination of a daring and imaginative tactical commander with a genius for administration. His universal nickname of 'the Bull' may have originally been acquired by his choleric manner and appearance but later it referred as much to the impressive force of his strength and courage.

Lloyd George and his Cabinet considered that Allenby's strong personality and prestige would pacify Egypt but they clearly did not expect him to do much more than this. His instructions were 'to exercise supreme authority in all matters military and civil, to take all measures necessary and expedient to restore law and order, and to administrate in all matters as required by the necessity of maintaining the King's protectorate over Egypt on a secure and equitable basis'. Lloyd George held a low opinion of the political acumen of generals, with some justification, but he should have been forewarned that Allenby was different when he argued during his brief stay in Paris that if French rule was established over Syria against the clearly expressed wishes of its inhabitants, there would be serious trouble. Allenby at least half believed in the principle of self-determination which was fifty per cent more than the British and French politicians who had publicly adopted it. On one point there can be no doubt: Allenby had a better knowledge and instinctive understanding of the complex political problems of the Middle East than any member of the British Cabinet.

Within twenty-four hours of his arrival in Cairo, Allenby had revealed his liberal inclinations. He called together an assembly of

Egyptian notables at the residency and informed them that his intentions were:

First, to bring the present disturbances to an end;
Secondly, to make careful inquiry into all matters which have caused discontent in the country;
Thirdly, to redress such grievances as appear justifiable.

A week later he cabled to London recommending that Zaghlul and his three colleagues should be released from Malta and allowed to proceed to Paris. The British Government and the Anglo-Egyptian community were equally taken aback. Curzon, who was in charge of the foreign office during Balfour's absence at the peace conference, had just made a characteristically patronizing speech in which he had referred to the uprising in Egypt as 'predatory rather than political' and added that a redeeming feature had been the loyalty of most Egyptian officials, the army and police. Government officials promptly went on strike to disprove his assertion. Now Allenby, who had been sent to Egypt as a stern disciplinarian, in recommending Zaghlul's release was apparently justifying the political aims of the uprising. Curzon consulted Wingate who, although he had argued in Zaghlul's favour in the past, recommended against his release on the ground that this would appear as a surrender to the forces of disorder. This view was later echoed by Lord Lloyd (Allenby's subsequent successor as high commissioner) who held that however unwise and unjust the original decision to deport Zaghlul and withdraw his passport, to reverse the decision would prove 'that violence had succeeded where constitutional methods had failed'.

Allenby was not the sort of man to waver under criticism. When he arrived in Cairo on 25 March the first part of his mission was already accomplished as General Bulfin was already on his way to mastering the security situation. Allenby's diagnosis was that behind the uprising lay a legitimate grievance which should be remedied and Bulfin supported his view that political concessions were necessary. Although the British Cabinet were extremely reluctant to permit Zaghlul's release they could hardly refuse the first request of the man they had just sent to Egypt with special emergency powers.

On 7 April a proclamation announced that Zaghlul and his three colleagues would be released; Egypt went wild with joy, and

Rushdi agreed to return to office as prime minister. But Allenby's hopes that the nationalists would now be ready to co-operate with the new Government under the protectorate were soon disappointed. Zaghlul had gone straight to Paris from where he sent back wildly over-optimistic reports that the peace conference was insisting on an immediate British withdrawal from Egypt. His followers in Egypt renewed their demands for the abolition of the protectorate. Mass rioting was impossible in the face of General Bulfin's security measures but the nationalists had learned the technique of political strikes. Students, civil servants, lawyers, post office, tram and railway workers all came out in turn. A newly organized unofficial force of national police helped to enforce the strikes in the name of restoring order. There were sporadic assassinations of individual British soldiers and officials and of Greeks, Armenians and other foreign minorities.

The timid Rushdi was quite unable to cope with the situation and resigned on 21 April with all his cabinet. Allenby was forced to act and on the following day issued a proclamation reaffirming the protectorate and stating that if civil servants were not back at work the following day they would be considered to have resigned. He also threatened to close all the schools permanently unless the students ended their strike. Simultaneously the Egyptian nationalists suffered a severe setback as the US Government announced its formal recognition of the British protectorate.

Something like normality was restored as the nation returned sullenly to work. It was a month before a new prime minister could be found in Mohammed Said, a thick-skinned Turkish Pasha of the old school; but in the meantime the budget and other bills could be passed by decree under martial law. But Allenby knew that he had only a temporary respite; he also understood, as the Government at home did not, that the protectorate would have to go. The Government had already decided to send out to Egypt a high-level commissioner of enquiry under Lord Milner, who was then in the Cabinet as colonial secretary. When Curzon had first proposed the commission as an alternative to Zaghlul's release Allenby had stubbornly refused. But he still regarded the commission as essential and at once began urging that it should come out immediately. Curzon replied that Milner would not be ready before September.

In his first few weeks in Egypt, Allenby had earned the

confidence of 'moderate' Egyptians such as Rushdi and Adly. He had
not reconciled the extreme nationalists; his greatest failure in
Egypt, which was probably inevitable, was that he never achieved a
working relationship with Zaghlul. But he was shrewd enough to
know that it was Zaghlul and not Rushdi who represented the
spirit of Egypt at that time and this assumption remained the
basis of his policy. His action in releasing Zaghlul earned him
the lasting hostility of much of the Anglo-Egyptian community.
Some of the criticisms of Gorst were revived and echoed by visiting
tourists. The Allenbys were said to be inviting more Egyptians than
Europeans to the residency. At a time when the common British
view was that the spirit of Cromer needed to be revived the high
commissioner was allowing himself to be influenced by native
opinion. Allenby, who regarded the accusation of being pro-
Egyptian as a compliment, ignored these criticisms. Moreover the
attitude of England in general was very different. He could take
comfort in the very different attitude of the home country. In
July, Allenby's viscountcy* was announced together with a grant
of £50,000. He was also promoted to Field-Marshal and during
his brief summer leave at home was greeted with greater public
enthusiasm than any other British military commander.

* He took the title of Megiddo, the site of his greatest victory over the
Turks, and Felixstowe to please his mother who lived there.

21

MILNER'S MISSION

Lord Milner's mission finally arrived in Egypt on 7 December 1919. Its other members included Sir Rennell Rodd, who had served with Cromer in his early years and who had been ambassador to Italy since 1908; Cecil Hurst, principal legal adviser of the foreign office; J. A. Spender, former editor of the *Westminster Gazette* and a prominent Liberal; Sir John Maxwell, officer commanding the troops in Egypt in the first two years of the war, and General Sir Owen Thomas, a Labour MP. The high level of the mission and the weight of experience it embodied might have been regarded as a compliment to Egyptian nationalism in an earlier age. But this was nullified in Egyptian eyes by its terms of reference which were: 'To enquire into the causes of the late disorders in Egypt and to report on the existing situation in the country and the form of the constitution which, *under the Protectorate*, will be best calculated to promote its peace and prosperity, the progressive development of self-governing institutions and the protection of foreign interests.' In other words the mission was to be based on the assumption that the protectorate was to be maintained. This had been emphasized in strong words by Balfour in the House of Commons on 17 November: 'Let me, therefore, say that ... the question of Egypt, the question of the Sudan, and the question of the Canal, form an organic and indissoluble whole, and that neither in Egypt nor in the Sudan, nor in connection with Egypt, is England going to give up any of her responsibilities. British supremacy exists, British supremacy is going to be maintained.' Balfour added that if certain 'unrealizable expectations' were fulfilled, they would 'damage Great Britain, would damage the world, and would damage most of all the Egyptian population itself'. In referring to Britain's 'responsibilities' in Egypt Balfour was blandly begging the question for it was Britain that had taken the responsibilities upon itself.

The truth was that the course of the Great War had appeared to justify the British occupation of Egypt and the change in focus of British Near Eastern policy from Constantinople to Cairo which had occurred almost accidentally in the nineteenth century.

The existence of a British military base in Egypt in 1914 had prevented a Turkish seizure of the Suez Canal. Later it had immensely facilitated Allenby's Syrian campaign and made possible Britain's sponsorship of the Sherif Hussein of Mecca's Arab Revolt. At the end of the war Britain therefore enjoyed an important advantage over France in the division of the corpse of the Ottoman Empire. Furthermore, Egypt not only lay across the route to India but was the key to Africa in which Britain had recently enlarged its colonial possessions through the break-up of Germany's East African Empire. It was hardly surprising, therefore, that no British statesman at that time was prepared to contemplate abandoning control of Egypt. For the Egyptians, on the other hand, the distinction between being incorporated into the British Empire as a Crown Colony and the continuation of the protectorate was largely academic.

As soon as the British Government's attitude was known, in November, Zaghlul in Paris saw his opportunity and sent word that the mission was to be boycotted entirely.

Mohammed Said Pasha and his Cabinet resigned on the apparently logical ground that the mission should be postponed until after the conclusion of a peace treaty with Turkey. With some difficulty a replacement was found in Yusuf Wahba, a harmless Copt. The most that his Government could achieve was to remain in office; the nationalists dominated the country. Elaborate precautions had to be taken to protect the mission for everywhere they went they were greeted by strikes and hostile demonstrations. The boycott was almost total; the only prominent Egyptians who would agree to speak to them were the Sultan Fuad, members of Yusuf Wahba's colourless cabinet and a handful of ex-ministers such as Rushdi and Mohammed Said Pasha. Even these refused to express any opinion on the future relationship between Egypt and England but confined themselves to describing the current condition of the country. The heads of el-Azhar University and six of the Royal Princes published manifestoes demanding complete independence and a British withdrawal.

It was a disheartening experience for the mission. J. A. Spender's visit to the Delta town of Tanta was followed by several days of rioting. When Cecil Hurst went to a law court the Egyptian law-yers left in a body. During their stay the mission received 1,131 hostile telegrams and only 29 of welcome from personal acquain-tances. The sixty-five-year-old Milner, aged beyond his years and exhausted by his work in the War Cabinet, was looking forward to retirement. Despite his reputation from South Africa as an arch-imperialist he soon reached the conclusion that the protectorate should be abolished and that no solution imposed upon the Egyptians would work. Some of the demands for complete inde-pendence from prominent Egyptians were at least partially insincere in that they were made through fear or a desire to curry popularity, and the mission was able to comfort itself with the thought that 'they (the extremists) certainly failed in their main object, for it was impossible not to come to the conclusion that, if the Egyptians were really so unanimous as we're intended to think, we should have been left to find that out for ourselves by going about the country without let or hindrance'. But this negative assumption was not something on which a policy could be based. The only possible conclusion was that Egyptian opinion was in extremist (i.e. nationalist) hands.

Within three weeks of their arrival in Egypt the mission made a conciliatory gesture of great significance in a public declaration which said: 'The British mission has been struck by the existence of a widespread belief that the object of its coming is to deprive Egypt of rights which it has hitherto possessed. There is no foundation whatever in this belief. The mission has been sent out by the British Government, with the approval of parliament, to reconcile the aspirations of the Egyptian people with the special interest which Great Britain has in Egypt and with the mainten-ance of the legitimate rights of all foreign residents in the country.'

The purpose of this statement was to encourage timid moderates to overcome their fears and express their views to the mission but in its failure to include any mention of the British protectorate it was conceding the principal demand of the nationalists.

The mission left Egypt at the end of March; despite its almost total failure to break through the boycott it had reached certain definite conclusions about what should be done. But first of all in its report it attempted to clear up the ambiguity which had characterized Anglo-Egyptian relations since 1882. 'We have never honestly faced the Egyptian problem, and our neglect to do so is in a measure responsible for the present situation.' And it went on to grasp the nettle, 'It appears to be frequently assumed in current talk and writing in this country that Egypt is a part of the British Empire. This is not and never has been the case.' In fact, as we have seen, this question had been dodged when the protectorate was declared. Cromer had assumed that Egypt had become part of the Empire in 1914 and the mission was showing some courage in contradicting his memory (he died in 1917) but the mission was certainly correct. All the same, Egypt had been part of the British imperial system since 1882, and even more so after the Anglo-French agreement of 1904 gave England a free hand in Egypt. As Lord Lloyd points out: 'From 1904 onwards there had been, as a matter of hard fact, apart from the khedivial position, only one difference between the state of affairs in Egypt and in similar parts of the British Empire. That difference had been the existence of the capitulations. . . . The British Government had in practice controlled the internal and external affairs of Egypt.'[1]

Nevertheless the fact that Egypt had never been made *de jure* part of the Empire, and was never coloured red on the map, was not without significance; even more important was the undeniable truth that the Egyptian people had never regarded themselves as British subjects or looked upon the king-emperor as their sovereign. Unlike most other parts of the colonial Empire, Egypt had not become a nation under British rule; it had already been a nation for several thousand years. Although its people were accustomed to living under foreign domination it had not lost its identity.

This was the reality that the mission was acknowledging when it recommended that the protectorate should be replaced with a bilateral treaty between England and Egypt. But with whom should the treaty be negotiated? The mission did not make the mistake of thinking that any purpose would be served in negotiating with an Egyptian Government formed under British pressure, which would be quite unrepresentative of Egyptian opinion. Almost everyone they did speak to told them that Zaghlul was their leader, but Zaghlul had refused to come out to Egypt to meet them during their stay.

An unexpected development then occurred to break the deadlock. Adly Pasha was the only Egyptian politician of note who was on good terms with Zaghlul but retained his independence. He now went to Paris and persuaded Zaghlul to meet the mission; Zaghlul and his delegation proceeded to London where negotiations opened in June 1920. These progressed laboriously for several weeks because although the Wafd had gained their principal demand in the abolition of the protectorate they sought further concessions, which the mission was reluctant to give, such as the right for Egypt to have its own diplomatic representatives abroad. However by August agreement had been reached on the points which should provide the basis of the Anglo-Egyptian Treaty to replace the protectorate.

Egypt was to be recognized as an independent constitutional monarchy with representative institutions and the right to diplomatic representatives abroad. At the same time Egypt's independence would be qualified in a number of respects by its special relationship with Britain. An alliance would be formed by which England would defend the integrity of Egypt's territory and Egypt, in case of war, would render England all assistance even if its integrity was not affected. England would have the right to maintain a military force on Egyptian soil for the protection of her 'imperial communications' (i.e. those between the mother country and her Asian and East African Empire) but 'the presence of this force shall not constitute in any manner a military occupation of the country or prejudice the rights of the Government of Egypt'.

England would have the right to maintain a financial adviser and a permanent official in the ministry of justice to safeguard the interests of foreign governments after the abolition of the Capitulations and the Caisse de la Dette. The British representative would be accorded an exceptional position in Egypt, and entitled to precedence over all other representatives.

From the British view, immense concessions had been made to Egyptian nationalism. The proposals shocked imperialist opinion and aroused strong parliamentary opposition led by Winston Churchill. Zaghlul therefore had reason to feel that his intransigent struggle had won a great victory. Yet with hindsight it is possible to see that this arrangement could not last, for once the principle of independence had been accepted no nation would accept permanent limitations to its sovereignty. The Veiled Protectorate had given place to the official, but unilaterally declared, protectorate of 1914. Now Egypt was to become a semi-protectorate and Britain's dominant position would no longer even be limited by the established rights of other foreign governments. Nevertheless, Egyptian nationalism had achieved at least half its objectives and it was at this point that Zaghlul showed his fatal lack of vision and the true qualities of leadership. His agreement in London still had to be incorporated in a Treaty and his prestige with the Egyptians was such that he could have persuaded them to accept the mission's terms. Under any system of representative institutions he would inevitably have been prime minister and in a strong position to extract further concessions from Britain. But he now hedged and hesitated. On the superficially logical plea that any acceptance of the scheme must be endorsed by the Egyptian people, he sent four of his delegation to Egypt to sound out their views. But although he was their spokesman and leader he offered no guidance. The emissaries returned with inconclusive results and further desultory discussions had to take place. Seeing that no progress was being made, Milner submitted his report at the end of 1920 and it was published and presented to parliament the following February.

The British Cabinet was notably unenthusiastic about Milner's proposals and took the line that it was not bound by the mission's recommendations despite the fact that Milner, who was a senior member of the Cabinet, had always been represented to Egypt as a plenipotentiary. Partly for this reason and partly because he wished to retire, Milner resigned. In laying his report before parliament the Government did concede that the protectorate was no longer a satisfactory relationship between Britain and Egypt, but it decided to attempt what both Milner and Allenby had wished to avoid – that is to by-pass Zaghlul and negotiate an agreement with the 'moderate' Egyptian elements.

Allenby was told to consult Sultan Fuad and the Egyptian government on the formation of an official delegation to come to England to negotiate a treaty. This proved extremely difficult because Zaghlul was still easily the most popular figure in Egypt. The only man who could offer any challenge to his leadership was Adly Pasha, and on 16 March he formed a new government. Zaghlul at once decided to return to Egypt to press his claims to lead the delegation.

It was now two years since the 1919 rebellion; martial law was still in force and no political progress had been made. Strikes, demonstrations and intermittent bomb outrages and assassination attempts on the lives of European and Egyptian officials continued.

Allenby stood by his policy of using British troops to the minimum and encouraging the Egyptians to take responsibility for keeping order. He had tactfully spent the first six weeks of 1920 touring the Sudan to leave the field free for the Milner mission. Later he had unsuccessfully urged that the mission's recommendations should be kept secret until the Cabinet had made its decision to avoid their becoming 'a cockshy for criticism by everyone'. Now he had the unenviable task of getting together a delegation for negotiations which he knew in advance would be fruitless.

On 5 April Zaghlul arrived back in Egypt to a hero's reception. Vast cheering crowds lined the railway all the way from Alexandria to Cairo. ('Saad Zaghlul arrived in Cairo yesterday,' wrote Allenby to his mother, 'I kept all officers and soldiers out of the streets and left the whole management to the Egyptians. There was a gigantic and enthusiastic but quite orderly crowd, and not a single mishap occurred.') Adly Pasha welcomed Zaghlul and attempted to secure his co-operation. But it was not long before Zaghlul was denouncing him as a traitor and his Government as a British creation. His followers responded and public agitation culminated in a serious riot in Alexandria on 23 May, (known as 'Red Monday') in which thirty Egyptians and fourteen Europeans were killed and scores more injured.

An eye-witness of these events was the now elderly Harry Boyle who was brought out of retirement by the foreign office and sent out on a private mission to Egypt to assess the situation and 'to reassure native opinion as to the genuine desire of His Majesty's government to achieve a solution of the present situation satisfactory both to Great Britain and Egypt'. Unfortunately, Boyle was in no position to do this. He was showered with invitations from his old acquaintances of the Cromer era and spent much of his time with the two Syrian editors of the Anglophile *al-Muqattam* newspaper. But he felt no kind of sympathy for the new nationalist movement. Zaghlul, whom he described in a letter to his wife as 'the idol of the moment', received him courteously but showed no interest in compromise. 'He is quite, quite impossible' was Boyle's comment on the meeting.[2]

Boyle was convinced that the majority of Egyptians looked back on the Cromerian era as a Golden Age. Unlike most of the Anglo-Egyptian community he strongly approved of Allenby, whom he described in his diary as 'the one only good point I can find in the whole horizon'. This was surprising in view of the high commissioner's 'Egypt for the Egyptians' policies which Boyle had so strongly criticized Gorst for pursuing. But Boyle concluded that 'a great part of his (Allenby's) success with the native element was due to his extraordinary resemblance to Lord Cromer, both in physique and manner'.

Whatever nostalgia Boyle believed the Egyptians harboured for past British rule he had no illusions about their current feelings. The memorandum he wrote for the foreign office on his return began: 'It would be useless to attempt to palliate the fact that, as matters now stand, we do not possess a sincere friend in the country, that is to say, one who would desire to see the continuance of British predominance in its present form. Strong and just government, bringing with it light taxation, public order, and security to life and property, is what the Egyptian people crave, and this, they consider – with the exception of the first requisite – has not been afforded to them under British auspices for many years past.'³

At length an official delegation headed by Adly Pasha was formed and left for England on 1 July 1921. Zaghlul was not included because he insisted that he should lead the delegation and Adly held that this would be inconsistent with his dignity as prime minister. The political situation in Egypt had now resolved itself into a struggle between Zaghlul and Adly; but the struggle was unequal. 'Long live Saad', 'Down with Adly', chanted the demonstrators in the streets of Cairo and Alexandria. Exactly as Allenby and Milner had foreseen, Adly was hamstrung in the negotiations because he did not dare to make concessions which would at once be denounced as treachery by Zaghlul. The negotiations stuck on several points of which the most important was the question of where the British force should be stationed in Egypt. The Egyptians demanded that they should be restricted to the Canal Zone; understandably, they considered that any alternative would constitute a continuation of the occupation.

Curzon was conducting the negotiations on the British side. He was inclined to sympathize with most of the Egyptian demands and he realized that coercion was no solution. The foreign secretary had mellowed since the days when Lord Salisbury used to complain that his under secretary wanted him to conduct Britain's foreign policy as if he had half a million men under arms. But the Lloyd George Coalition Cabinet as a whole was more rigid. It had been influenced by a meeting of the imperial conference where the supreme importance of the security of the Suez Canal was stressed. On 21 October Curzon wrote to his wife: 'The Cabinet are all much stiffer than I am in the matter, and I am sure we shall have an absolute rupture with another Ireland in Egypt.' Unfortunately Curzon had neither the character nor determination to impress his views on his colleagues and when the negotiations failed he temporarily lost his nerve.

Fruitless discussions continued for several weeks and broke down finally in November. In an angry mood Curzon sent a headmasterly rebuke to Egypt in the form of a note which Allenby was instructed to deliver to the Sultan. The tone of the note was revealed in the sentence, 'The progress of Egypt towards her ideals will not only be retarded, but completely jeopardized, if her people are tempted to indulge their national aspirations, however sound and legitimate in themselves, without sufficient regard to the facts which govern international life.' It pointedly added that England 'could exercise the right of re-entry into Egypt, if, left to her own unaided counsels, she should revert to the waste and disorder of the last century'.

While the negotiations had continued Egypt had been relatively quiet under the acting premiership of the minister of the interior, Sarwat Pasha. The visit in October of four Labour MPs who showed warm sympathy with Egyptian nationalism was an occasion for Zaghlulist demonstrations but not for the first or the last time some of the British in Egypt believed that Zaghlul was losing ground to moderate opinion.

Allenby was under no such illusion. The Curzon note had already aroused nationalist opinion when Adly ventured to announce the failure of the negotiations and resign. Not surprisingly, no one could be found to take his place; but Allenby was now determined that a settlement of some kind must be reached. Anglo-Egyptian officials were demoralized because most of them realized that independence was now inevitable and had no idea what their own future would be. Allenby reached the conclusion that nothing could be done while Zaghlul was still in Egypt. He banned a mass meeting Zaghlul had called for 22 December and when Zaghlul challenged the decision he had him arrested and deported to Aden, from where he was later removed to the Seychelles.*

With a heavy show of force Allenby ensured that Zaghlul's second deportation was not followed by the same violent outbreak as the first. The strikes ceased and the under-secretaries of state, who were all British except for one Egyptian, carried on the administration in the absence of a Government. But Allenby knew that this was only a very temporary arrangement. Realizing that no Egyptian Government could be found which would be prepared to accept formally the limitation of independence on which the British Government was insisting, he now urged Curzon that the right thing to do was for Britain to make a unilateral declaration of the abolition of the protectorate and Egypt's independence while reserving the right to freedom of action on certain 'reserved subjects' (such as the Capitulations, the location of British troops in Egypt and the status of the Sudan)† until such time as an Anglo-Egyptian agreement covering these matters could be reached.

Allenby forwarded this proposal to Curzon on 12 January. The foreign secretary was inclined to agree with it, although he thought that at least some specific undertakings should be extracted from Egyptian ministers before independence. But the Cabinet was adamant that the protectorate could only be abolished within the framework of a comprehensive bilateral treaty guaranteeing British interests in Egypt, and Curzon had insufficient conviction or strength of character to persuade them. He temporized by suggesting that Allenby send home two of his advisers to explain his proposals further; Allenby curtly replied that his advisers fully agreed with his proposals and they needed no further explanation. When Curzon still demurred Allenby sent him a personal cable which amounted to an ultimatum. After pointing out that 'The long delay has caused a rapid deterioration in the political situation.

---

* He was entertained on Christmas Day at Suez by British officers and is said to have won all their money at poker.

† Under Cromer's arrangement of 1898, the Sudan was theoretically governed jointly by England and Egypt through a condominium. In fact it was under British rule as Egyptians were excluded from the higher administrative posts and the determination of policy. Egyptian nationalists were pressing strongly for an adjustment of this position with independence.

What was possible last week may be impossible next week. I have dealt with Zaghlul and enemies of order, and now is the time to show confidence in and uphold those who are ready to work with us in the interests of Egypt.' Allenby added that if his advice was not accepted he would have to resign.

The reaction of the majority of the British Cabinet was that the resignation of Allenby and his advisers should be accepted, and a cable was sent summoning him home for consultations. But Curzon and the foreign office made a serious mistake in accusing Allenby in the same telegram of having suddenly reversed the British Government's policy which had been formulated with his advice. Allenby had little difficulty in showing that this was not true.

The British Government had placed itself in an awkward position. Allenby had secured the trust of the Egyptian moderates and their reaction to his summons to England and expected dismissal showed that it would be virtually impossible to replace him with someone who could obtain their co-operation. He had also obtained a valuable and unexpected ally in Lord Northcliffe, the proprietor of *The Times*, who after stopping in Egypt on his way home from a world tour, had been convinced that Allenby and his advisers were right.

'The Bull' arrived in London on 10 February in his most stubborn mood and armed with a skilfully drafted but angry memorandum refuting the Cabinet's allegations which he clearly intended to make public after his resignation. Curzon was in despair when his efforts to persuade Allenby to withdraw the memorandum failed, and he is said to have ended one meeting in tears. The Cabinet was divided fairly equally with the new colonial secretary, Winston Churchill, leading the anti-Allenby faction. But the decision ultimately rested with the prime minister and Lloyd George was the first man to see the danger to his shaky Coalition Government of a full-blooded attack from Allenby in the House of Lords.

Lloyd George and Curzon met Allenby with his two principal advisers, Gilbert Clayton and Maurice Amos, on 15 February. The prime minister began by raising the sternest objections to Allenby's proposals, saying that he was asking him 'to abandon our entire position in Egypt without guarantee'. Allenby's blunt response was that it was no good disputing any further; he had given his advice which could be accepted or rejected. 'I have waited five weeks for a decision and I can't wait any longer.' 'You have waited five weeks, Lord Allenby,' said the prime minister, 'Wait five more minutes.' He then capitulated by accepting all Allenby's proposals except for a few unimportant drafting amendments. A last minute attempt by Curzon, who was by now personally antagonistic to Allenby, failed to reverse the decision and it was accepted by the Cabinet.

Allenby returned to Egypt for an enthusiastic public reception and the declaration of independence was published the following day 28 February 1922.

'Whereas His Majesty's government, in accordance with their declared intentions, desire forthwith to recognize Egypt as an independent sovereign State; and

'Whereas the relations between His Majesty's government and Egypt are of vital interest to the British Empire;

'The following principles are hereby declared:

1. The British protectorate over Egypt is terminated, and Egypt is declared to be an independent sovereign State.

2. So soon as the government of His Highness shall pass an Act of Indemnity with application to all inhabitants of Egypt, martial law, as proclaimed 2 November 1914, shall be withdrawn.

3. The following matters are absolutely reserved to the discretion of His Majesty's government until such time as it may be possible by free discussion and friendly accommodation on both sides to conclude agreements in regard thereto between His Majesty's government and the government of Egypt:

(a) The security of the communications of the British Empire in Egypt.

(b) The defence of Egypt against all foreign aggression or interference, direct or indirect.

(c) The protection of foreign interests in Egypt and the protection of minorities.

(d) The Sudan.'[4]

On the next day (1 March) Sarwat formed a government and two weeks later Sultan Fuad assumed the title of King Fuad 1 of Egypt. Because of Britain's privileged position in Egypt, Allenby retained the title of high commissioner instead of becoming ambassador. On 4 March the House of Commons had approved the Government's Egyptian policy by 202 votes to 77 after Austen Chamberlain, the foreign office spokesman in the Commons, had given the impression that it was Allenby who had yielded to the government's views. He was not a member of the Cabinet and probably did not know that precisely the reverse had happened.

The arrangement that had been made was unsatisfactory because it left a number of vital questions unsettled with no guarantee that they would be any easier to settle in the future. Allenby was perhaps over-sanguine about this and he was bitterly criticized for his leniency towards Egyptian nationalism by Anglo-Egyptian officials outside his immediate circle of advisers (often referred to contemptuously as his kindergarten) and as forcefully, if in more measured terms, by his imperial-minded successor Lord Lloyd. Admittedly Lloyd had the task of representing Britain in a relationship with Egypt which was unique and ultimately unworkable. But there is no reason to believe that either he or Allenby's other critics could have produced a more workable solution to the almost impossibly difficult problem presented by Anglo-Egyptian relations in the aftermath of World War I.

Criticism of Allenby was on two levels which both stemmed from his original action in allowing Zaghlul to return from his exile in 1919. In the first place he was accused of 'encouraging extremism' and then of excessive leniency and a reluctance to use force to combat violence. Allenby's views were quite clear on this point. As he wrote to his mother after some disturbances in May 1921: 'I bide my time, as I want the Egyptians to settle their politics for themselves and I don't want to interfere with my troops unless the life, limb or interests of Europeans are in danger.' In the handling of political strikes and mass demonstrations this policy was broadly successful. But he did fail to prevent the continuation of attacks on individual Anglo-Egyptians. A British Union was formed of members of the community which held angry protest meetings at Shepheard's Hotel, at which the high commissioner was the target of criticism even if his name was not mentioned. But this form of violence is notoriously difficult to counteract. Severe repression of the Egyptians as a whole would hardly have been effective even if the British troops had been available to make it practicable.

The second charge against Allenby was that he was too eager to sell out the interests of the British Empire to Egyptian nationalism. But Allenby could reply that Lord Milner, whose enthusiasm for the British Empire none could doubt, had independently reached the same conclusions as himself. This could also be said of

Gilbert Clayton and Harry Boyle. His assumption that no purpose would be served in trying to reach an agreement with the moderate Egyptians which Zaghlul would inevitably repudiate, was certainly correct. As it happened, it soon became clear that agreement with the moderates was equally unattainable for they had no wish to go down in their country's history as traitors. When this became obvious, Allenby insisted that Britain should give just as much as it was prepared to give; he was convinced that the British forces in Egypt and even more British naval power in the Mediterranean would be enough to preserve vital imperial interests. What can hardly be disputed is that further delay would not have made a comprehensive Anglo-Egyptian agreement any easier to achieve.

22

SEMI-INDEPENDENCE

If Egyptian sovereignty was still severely limited, British dominance in Egypt was also sharply reduced. In effect Allenby's voluntary practice of leaving the management of the country's affairs as far as possible to the Egyptians had now been formalized. Henceforth, instead of the British residency being the only real centre of power in the country it was to be one of four alongside the Palace, Zaghlul's Wafd and the 'moderates' such as Adly and Sarwat who now formed themselves into a Liberal Constitutional Party. As long as British troops remained in occupation British power could always be exerted but it was at increasing cost and diminishing effectiveness.

King Fuad, the youngest son of the Khedive Ismail, had the temperament but not the aptitude of a royal autocrat. He was ambitious but lacked the nerve to impose his authority openly, and he was handicapped by his ignorance of the nation's character. His talent was for backstairs intrigue and manoeuvre. It cannot be said that he was deeply concerned with the welfare of his people.

Inevitably the revival of Egyptian autonomy meant the recovery of some of the power of the house of Mohammed Aly. The extent of the restoration depended upon the constitution that was to be adopted and this was Egypt's first concern after the declaration of independence. A constitutional commission of prominent politicians, jurists, religious leaders and government officials was set up under the chairmanship of Rushdi Pasha, the wartime premier. After six months the commission produced a draft constitution based on the Belgian model and a draft electoral law providing for universal suffrage. The draft constitution declared Egypt to be a sovereign independent state with Islam its religion and Arabic its official language. The legislature would consist of a Senate partly appointed by the King and partly elected and a wholly elected Chamber of Deputies.

Article 23 declared 'All authority derives from the nation,' but despite the clear intention of a majority of the commission to establish a constitutional monarchy the final draft was a compromise to meet the ambitions of the king, who had to ratify the constitution before it became law. Apart from his right to appoint senators the monarch had the power to dissolve parliament and to appoint and dismiss ministers. Nevertheless, King Fuad was dissatisfied and used his influence to have the draft amended to increase his powers. Allenby felt obliged to intervene to restrain his attempts to establish a royal autocracy by law.* An even more controversial issue was the attempt by the monarchist and nationalist members of the commission to declare Fuad King of Egypt and the Sudan. Allenby went as far as to threaten the king with deposition to coerce him into accepting that Sudan should be dropped from his title 'until authorized delegations fixed the final status of the Sudan'.

The 1923 Constitution, as it became known, was finally promulgated on 19 April. The controversies over the constitution had forged an unnatural and temporary alliance between the king and the Wafd, who for fundamentally different reasons were opposed to the Liberal Constitutionalists who were co-operating with Allenby. The king succeeded in getting rid of Sarwat in November 1922 but he could only replace him with political nonentities. Accordingly he turned to the Wafd for support although it must have been with some apprehension about the consequences.

Egypt had acquired a fairly liberal constitution on western parliamentary lines. For this Allenby bore a large share of responsibility; the declaration of independence had said nothing about representative institutions but this had been the recommendation of the Milner mission and Allenby felt it his duty to see that it was carried out. Critics ranging from Lord Lloyd to Gamal Abdul Nasser have pointed out that such a system was quite unsuited to Egypt's needs. In a sense Egypt was the forerunner of scores of European colonies and protectorates which discovered

---

* 'If you want this Bolshevik constitution then I claim all the powers and privileges of a Lenin,' the king remarked to a leading member of the commission. To the reply that it was not a Bolshevik but a democratic constitution he retorted: 'Then I claim all the powers and privileges of the president of the United States.' Ultimately his position was comparable to that of a US President with the important difference that he did not have to stand for election every four years. But he never forgave Allenby for imposing constitutional government on him.

that the parliamentary constitutions they acquired at independence were unworkable. Yet in 1922 the only alternative to representative government was a return to the royal autocracy of the Khedives and there is no reason to believe that this would have worked any better in the absence of a ruler of exceptional capacity. Moreover constitutional parliamentary government was what the great majority of politically active Egyptians wanted at that time.

During 1923 other practical obstacles to the transfer of power were overcome. Before martial law could be abolished an Act of Indemnity was needed to prevent legal proceedings being taken against measures enforced under martial law, which is unrecognized by civil law. This act was passed on 5 July 1923 and martial law, which had been in force for nearly nine years, was at once abolished. The effect was to remove most of Allenby's residual powers.

A more difficult problem was the settlement of terms of compensation for British and other European officials who would now be replaced by Egyptians. The constitution stated that all public and military employment was to be restricted to Egyptians except where provided by law. Eventually foreign officials were given the choice of retiring on 31 October 1923 or of remaining in service provisionally until 1 April 1927. The amount of compensation, which finally cost the Egyptian treasury about £7 million, was less than the British Government had intended to insist upon although the Egyptians regarded it as more than generous. The British side accepted it because it assumed quite correctly that a popularly elected Egyptian Government would offer much less.

Now that martial law had been abolished Zaghlul could no longer be legally kept in exile. The climate of the Seychelles having proved bad for his chronic bronchitis, he had been moved to Gibraltar where he was released in March. In September he returned to Egypt and another wildly enthusiastic popular reception.

Although now an ailing septuagenarian, Zaghlul had lost none of his force. The effectiveness of the Wafd had been weakened during the two years' absence of its leader but it now recovered its position as the strongest political factor in the country. In the general elections of January 1924 the Wafdist victory was overwhelming; out of 214 members of the Chamber of Deputies 190 were declared supporters of Zaghlul. The king's prime minister, Yehya

Ibrahim, lost his seat and resigned and Zaghlul became Egypt's first premier under the new constitution. Allenby had diplomatically absented himself in the Sudan during the elections. On his return he called on Zaghlul – a portent of change in itself because previously the first act of any Egyptian prime minister had been to call at the residency. Zaghlul was touched but his liking for Allenby was never reciprocated.

King Fuad temporarily accepted the dominance of the Wafd and bided his time. For the remaining twenty-eight years of the Egyptian monarchy the same pattern was constantly repeated. Whenever there was a free election under the 1923 Constitution the Wafd invariably won a sweeping victory. King Fuad – and later his son Farouk – would then seek ways of ousting the Wafd from power and ruling without them. He would succeed for some time and the Wafd was usually restrained from pursuing a full-blooded anti-monarchist policy by the fear of a repetition of the British intervention of 1882, but the Wafd would always return in time because the king would fall out with the non-Wafdist politicians or because the British Government, for its own reasons, which will appear later, wanted the Wafd in power.

Zaghlul became prime minister of Egypt at the same time as Ramsay MacDonald took office as head of Britain's first minority Labour Government. The outlook seemed favourable for a settlement of the four 'reserved points' in the declaration of independence. MacDonald had met Zaghlul and established a relationship with him; the Labour Party had declared its support for complete Egyptian independence. One of MacDonald's first acts was to agree to Zaghlul's request for an amnesty for those imprisoned by British military courts.

For the first time, but certainly not the last, the Labour Party was to prove itself less radical on a colonial issue in office than it had been in opposition. MacDonald wanted Allenby to make a preliminary agreement with Zaghlul in Cairo but Allenby insisted that direct negotiations would have to take place in London. As soon as it became clear that the MacDonald Government was not going to evacuate Egypt, Zaghlul began to take what limited counter-measures he could. In June the Egyptian parliament cancelled a £150,000 credit for maintenance of the British garrison and discontinued the service of the Ottoman Loans, secured on the Egyptian tribute. Zaghlul informed Allenby that he intended to modify the law passed the previous year to cover the indemnities to be paid to retiring European officials. In his speeches Zaghlul declared his refusal to compromise on any of Egypt's sovereign rights, including those over the Sudan.

. When Zaghlul finally arrived in London in September with demands for what amounted to full Egyptian independence, including the withdrawal of British troops from Egyptian soil and the dropping of Britain's claim to protect foreign minorities and the Suez Canal, he was surprised to find that MacDonald considered that Britain had already given Egypt as much independence as it deserved or needed. After the inevitable failure of the talks Zaghlul returned to Egypt in a defiant mood. He appointed two ministers who had been imprisoned for their alleged connection with terrorism and released under the amnesty. He endeavoured to intimidate the king by threatening resignation.

Within three years of the declaration of independence a direct clash between Britain and Egypt seemed inevitable. As it happened, when the clash came it concerned the Sudan. For the first twenty years of the anomalous arrangement of the Anglo-Egyptian condominium it had run fairly smoothly because both Egypt and the Sudan were effectively under British control. Egypt's claim to the Sudan was only symbolically maintained by the illogical and inconvenient arrangement whereby the governor-general of the Sudan was also the sirdar of the Egyptian Army. With the revival of Egyptian nationalism after the First World War the situation changed. Inevitably the Wafd reasserted Egypt's claims while the king and the 'moderates' were unable to do less. The Sudanese were far from immune to the influence of the Egyptian national movement. This did not mean that they were anxious for a resumption of Egyptian rule in the Sudan but that the nationalist fever in Egypt affected them.

British administrators had preferred to govern through the conservative notables with whom they had established relations of mutual respect but they had little contact with the new educated urban middle class and it was this – especially in northern Sudan – which was affected by the radical ideas emanating from Egypt. There was rioting and demonstrations in several towns during the summer and in August an armed demonstration by the Sudanese cadets of the military school coincided with a mutiny of the Egyptian Railway Battalion at Atbara.

Anglo-Sudanese officials reported that the troubles were entirely due to Egyptian instigation and bribery, but unquestionably an element of Sudanese nationalism was involved. It had a leader in Ali Abdul Latif, a former Sudanese army officer who had been imprisoned for political activities and who was now ready to co-operate with the Egyptians against the British.

In the fevered atmosphere in Egypt of the summer of 1924 there had been a renewal of the political violence against individuals which had quietened down for a time after Zaghlul's return to Cairo. In July there was even an attempt on Zaghlul himself which was believed to be an extremist warning against any compromise with Britain. On 19 November the sirdar, Sir Lee Stack, was shot at and mortally wounded by a group of Egyptian terrorists, as he was driving through Cairo.

As sirdar of the Egyptian Army and governor-general of the Sudan, Sir Lee Stack symbolized the continuation of British power in the Nile Valley. Allenby was personally outraged at the murder but he also realized that it gave him the opportunity to bring down Zaghlul and settle the Sudanese problem. The Egyptian prime minister had doubtless reached the same conclusion for as soon as he heard the news he hastened to the residency to express his profound regret. He was confronted by the high commissioner who pointed to Stack's wounded A D C chauffeur, saying 'This is your doing'.

Allenby decided to act at once. Immediately after the funeral and without waiting for the deciphering of a long foreign office cable on the subject because he was afraid that Zaghlul might forestall him by resigning, Allenby drove with a cavalry escort to parliament where the deputies were assembled to deliver a harsh ultimatum. After a preamble which declared that the murder 'holds up Egypt as at present governed to the contempt of civilized peoples', it went on to demand an ample apology, condign punishment of the criminals, the banning of all popular political demonstrations, payment of a £500,000 fine, the withdrawal from the Sudan within twenty-four hours of all Egyptian officers and the purely Egyptian units in the Sudan Army, acceptance of an increase in the irrigated area of the Sudan from 300,000 feddans to an unlimited figure and the withdrawal of all opposition to the British Government's wishes concerning the protection of foreign interests in Egypt. A separate document explained that the Sudanese units in the

Egyptian Army were to be made into a Sudan Defence Force owing allegiance only to the Sudan Governments, that the conditions of retirement of European officials were to be revised according to British wishes and the British financial and judicial advisers were to be retained.

When Allenby returned to read the foreign office telegram he found that it proposed the exclusion of any demand for an indemnity and the inclusion of an assurance that the extension of the Gezira cotton irrigation scheme would not be detrimental to Egypt. The British Government (Baldwin and the Conservatives had returned to power in October) had rightly foreseen that Allenby's ultimatum would lay Britain open to the charge of seeking vindictive revenge and of cynically using the opportunity of Stack's murder to secure its interests in the Sudan. The whole incident only served to emphasize that the declaration of independence had been unilateral. It was still Britain that decided just how independent Egypt should be.

The Zaghlul Government's reply accepted the indemnity but rejected the rest of the ultimatum; thereupon Allenby ordered the military occupation of the Alexandria customs until the two Sudanese demands had been met. As he had hoped, Zaghlul resigned and was replaced by Ziwar Pasha, a non-Wafdist, who accepted all Allenby's demands. The king seized the opportunity to dissolve the Wafdist parliament on 24 December. When fresh elections were held in March the Wafd, which was demoralized and put no effort into the campaign, won barely half the seats. Nevertheless, when parliament met Zaghlul was elected president of the chamber by a 3 to 2 majority; he was still the nation's political leader. The king at once dissolved parliament again with the intention of having the electoral law revised before further elections were held.

For a time the country was relatively quiet. Largely through some skilful detective work by British police officers, Sir Lee Stack's murderers were caught and brought to trial. Six were sentenced to death and five were executed. Allenby could claim that his harsh ultimatum had served its purpose, but he could not fail to be aware that Egypt's stability was merely superficial. He had broken irretrievably with Zaghlul while the 'moderates' he had hoped would govern independent Egypt had shown their incapacity; the result was a shaky royal autocracy.

Austen Chamberlain, whom Allenby had not forgiven for his misrepresentation of the genesis of the 1922 declaration of independence, was now foreign secretary. Chamberlain, who was strongly influenced by Churchill, had doubts about Allenby's capacity and resolved to get rid of him. In November he announced that he was sending Nevile Henderson (later Britain's disastrous ambassador in Berlin) to the residency as minister plenipotentiary with a rank immediately below the high commissioner. As soon as Allenby realized that Henderson's appointment was a deliberate declaration of lack of confidence in himself and his staff (Henderson had no previous experience of Egypt) he offered his resignation, which was finally accepted in May 1925. He departed to genuine expressions of regret from the Egyptian public including the Zaghlulists. The British press, which had often been savagely critical of his Egyptian career in the past, now praised his achievements. His errors of judgement, which were undeniably many and serious, were outweighed by his unusually sympathetic understanding for Egyptian nationalism.

Allenby's successor, Lord Lloyd, offered a strong contrast in style and approach. A friend of Winston Churchill's whose outlook he shared, Lloyd was a British imperialist who refused to accept that the Empire was in decline. Compton Mackenzie who was with him at the Dardenelles GHQ remarked, 'I began for the first time to appreciate that Imperialism could touch a man's soul as deeply as religion.'[1] At the same time Lloyd possessed an incisive intelligence and un-British logicality which often enabled him to see to the heart of a problem while his more liberal-minded colleagues were fumbling with its exterior. Energetic and ambitious, he was respected rather than popular except, with a few close friends. He was small, slim and elegant and his high-pitched voice, in the words of one obituarist, 'was almost a parody of the governing class accent'. He was nicknamed the Black Panther.

Lloyd had travelled widely in the Middle East and served with distinction in the intelligence branch of Allenby's staff during the war. Recognizing his abilities, Edwin Montagu, the secretary of state for India, had offered him, at the age of 39, the governorship of Bombay. His five years in India covered a period of dramatic change as the Montagu-Chelmsford reforms laid the foundations of Indian self-government. Lloyd was not opposed to the principle of these reforms because he was clear-sighted enough to see that Indian 'loyalists' must be given something to combat what he regarded as the insidious appeal of extremist agitators such as Mahatma Gandhi and his non-co-operation movement. But he had no doubt that the agitators must be firmly suppressed and he quarrelled seriously with Lord Reading, Chelmsford's successor as viceroy, because he hesitated to sanction Gandhi's arrest and prosecution.

Lloyd had no doubt that one of his duties was to impress the inhabitants of West India with the dignity of the king-emperor's representative. The Prince of Wales is reported to have remarked that he had not known what regal splendour was until he visited him in 1922.*

When Lloyd arrived in Cairo enough of his reputation had preceded him to allow the Anglo-Egyptian community to hope for a Cromerian restoration. The new high commissioner realized at once that the declaration of independence made this impossible. However mistaken this declaration and the Milner mission's conclusions which led up to it may have been in Lloyd's eyes, he characteristically decided that it must be rigorously upheld. The advice of Ramsay MacDonald, leader of the opposition, before his departure from England stuck in his memory: 'Be as liberal as you may be but be firm, eternally firm.' His lucid mind rapidly concluded that no Egyptian politician of any standing would dare to negotiate a settlement of the four reserved points in the declaration which would be acceptable to the British Government. He therefore decided to employ his restless energy in maintaining the *status quo*.

The first threat to the letter and spirit of the 1922 declaration came not from the Wafd but the palace. King Fuad was blatantly attempting to establish the royal autocracy which had been withheld by the 1923 constitution and was contrary to the declaration of independence which Lloyd was determined to uphold. Nashat

* When the Lloyds arrived in Cairo, Lady Lloyd was appalled at the low standards of accommodation the Allenbys had evidently accepted. 'The inside of the house – furniture, decoration, and general equipment – is about as bad as can well be, and the whole impression bleak and desolate to a very marked degree ... the hall is carpeted with vivid mustard-coloured squares and hung with faded nondescript velveteen curtains edged with little woolly balls.' (C. Forbes Adam, *Life of Lord Lloyd*, p. 204.)

Pasha, his chef de cabinet was interfering in all branches of the Government* and the prime minister was planning to introduce a new electoral law which would have ensured the defeat of the Wafd in the forthcoming elections. Lloyd decided the king's wings must be clipped. He used his influence to have Nashat Pasha sent to the Egyptian legation in Madrid and the Electoral Law of 1914 restored. Since this provided for adult male suffrage, the elections held in May 1926 resulted in another sweeping victory for the Wafd.

Lloyd was now confronted with a new problem. As leader of the majority party in parliament, Zaghlul should constitutionally be prime minister. Apart from the clear threat this would present to British interests in Egypt, Allenby had promised the Anglo-Egyptian community in January 1925 that 'the wicked old man' (as he called him) would never again head the Egyptian Government. At first Zaghlul showed signs of understanding Lloyd's dilemma and agreeing that his old rival Adly Pasha should become prime minister, but as he realized that his popularity in the country was undiminished he decided that there was no reason why he should give up his right to the premiership.

With Austen Chamberlain's approval Lloyd presented Zaghlul with an ultimatum. The announcement of the results of the elections had coincided with the acquittal of four leading Wafdist politicians accused of complicity in the murder of Sir Lee Stack. This heartened the Wafd as much as the election results but shortly afterwards Judge Kershaw, the single British member of the court, declared his disagreement with his Egyptian colleagues and resigned. Lloyd considered that this action strengthened his hand in showing the depth of British feeling against the Wafd. For good measure he asked for a British battleship to be sent to Alexandria with the result that the Wafdist deputies, fearing a suspension of the 1923 constitution, this time with British backing, persuaded Zaghlul to stand down on the ground of his age and failing health. Adly Pasha formed a Coalition Government of three Liberal Constitutionalists and seven Wafdists.

Lloyd had won the round but he was under no illusion that he

* Before Lloyd's arrival Nashat Pasha had suggested to Nevile Henderson that the new high commissioner would naturally be bringing letters of credence to present to His Majesty – something that none of Lloyd's predecessors had done. Lloyd ignored the suggestion.

had permanently defeated the Wafd. ('Adly Pasha in Office – Saad Zaghlul in Power' is his title to Chapter XI of *Egypt Since Cromer* dealing with these events.) No one in parliament dared to stand up to Zaghlul who had only to shout '*Uskut*' (Shut up!) at an orating deputy for him meekly to sit down. In the first weeks of the new parliamentary session Zaghlul was inclined to avoid doing battle with Adly or Lloyd but the king, who disliked any degree of co-operation between the Wafd and the high commission because it weakened his own position, began taunting Zaghlul with his moderation through the palace-subsidized newspapers. A renewed clash between Lloyd and the Wafd could not be long delayed.

Lord Lloyd was convinced that in order to uphold the reserved points in the 1922 declaration it was absolutely essential that a minimum of British officials should be retained in key ministries such as finance, war and justice. Since 1922 Egyptian pressure had reduced the number of Anglo-Egyptian officials by about 50 per cent while the authority of those that remained had been progressively diminished and their contracts were due to expire in April 1927. The Milner mission had been optimistically unperceptive in this matter. 'The idea of any Egyptian Government, however free to do so, attempting to make a clean sweep of its foreign officials is a chimera. . . . No sensible Egyptian seriously wishes to dispense with foreign aid.' Lord Lloyd determined to fight on this issue and was alarmed to find that the foreign office urged extreme caution on the ground that Egyptian hostility to the employment of Englishmen was understandable. But at this point the Wafd played into his hands by attempting to eliminate British control of the Egyptian Army, which was something on which it was relatively easy for Lloyd to persuade Austen Chamberlain it was necessary to take a firm stand. In 1925 Allenby had allowed an Egyptian Army Council to be formed which promptly arranged for officers to be appointed and promoted by an officers' committee instead of by the British sirdar. The British inspector-general of the Egyptian Army was increasingly by-passed and ignored by the minister of war. Early in 1927 the Wafdist parliament proposed measures to increase the size of the army, create a military air force and abolish restrictions on the carriage of arms.

Foreseeing an incipient Arabist movement, Lloyd decided that another ultimatum was necessary. Among other points this demanded that the inspector-general should retain all his functions, that a British second-in-command should be appointed and that all the remaining British officers in the Egyptian Army should remain in their posts. Adly had resigned as soon as he realized that the Wafd was heading for a struggle with Britain, and had been replaced by a more pliant Sarwat. His evasive reply to Lloyd's ultimatum, which neither accepted nor rejected it, was clearly unsatisfactory but even now it was necessary for Lloyd to exert all the pressure at his command on a cautious British Government (Chamberlain was in Geneva and Baldwin was conducting foreign policy) before they would back him to the full. Once more a British warship was dispatched to Alexandria at Lloyd's request; Sarwat, with Zaghul's reluctant approval, accepted Lloyd's demands.

Despite this success Lloyd was unhappy and frustrated by his role in Egypt. As he wrote to a friend at about this time: 'I repeat what I have said before to you – that our present position is impossible. . . . We cannot carry on much longer as we are. We have magnitude without position; power without authority; responsibility without control. I must insure that no foreign power intervenes in education, aviation, wireless communications, railways or army (where all seek to do so), and I must achieve this without upsetting the parliamentary regime which we forced upon the country in the face of the king's wishes; without weakening the power or alienating the loyalty of the monarchy which we set up, and without displaying that military power which is in fact our sole remaining effective argument. I must maintain and respect Egyptian independence and yet justify our army of occupation. . . . I must secure mobility for our troops, but must not interfere with the railways. I must insure the efficient lighting of the Red Sea, but have no effective say in the administration that organizes these services. . . .'[2]

The anomalies of the British position in Egypt were not his only cause for concern. Despite Baldwin's warmly congratulatory telegram on his handling of the Army crisis, he was becoming aware of a lack of confidence in his judgement in the foreign office where his pro-consular approach was regarded as unnecessarily undiplomatic.

In the summer of 1927 King Fuad paid a state visit to England accompanied by Sarwat Pasha. While they were there, Austen Chamberlain took the opportunity of discussing with Sarwat the possibility of negotiating an Anglo-Egyptian Treaty. At this point the Egyptian department of the foreign office, without informing Lloyd who was on leave in England, took over the negotiations with Sarwat. These resulted in a draft Treaty of Alliance which was approved by the Cabinet. It was only then that Lloyd was informed what had happened; he at once predicted that Sarwat would never be able to obtain Egypt's acceptance of the treaty. The aged Zaghlul had died suddenly in August and he was the one man who could have secured the approval of the Egyptian parliament in the unlikely event of his being willing to try. Nahas Pasha, his 50-year-old successor at the head of the Wafd, had none of his hypnotic control over the deputies. He was now principally concerned to show that he was as fervent a champion of unfettered Egyptian independence as his predecessor. After weeks of aimless political manoeuvres the Egyptian Government rejected the proposed treaty on 4 March 1928 and Sarwat resigned. The British Government received the result with pained surprise and Lord Lloyd with understandable *schadenfreude*.

While attention was concentrated on the abortive treaty negotiations Nahas Pasha and the Wafd were pushing ahead with legislation to strengthen their hold on the country. One bill aimed to have the Omdehs appointed by direct election while another, known as the Assemblies Bill, would have removed from the Government all power to suppress or control public meetings and demonstrations.

After Sarwat's resignation the king had no alternative to asking Nahas to form the new Cabinet, which he did on 15 March. As soon as he made clear that he would proceed with the Assemblies Bill the British Government instructed Lloyd to issue one more ultimatum (although no gunboat was considered necessary on this occasion). Nahas's reply was in conciliatory terms saying that he would postpone the proposed legislation until the next session of parliament. This satisfied the British Government but not the high commissioner who was considering what measures would be necessary to bring Nahas to heel when providence intervened on his behalf in the form of a financial scandal which was of the kind which would eventually destroy the Wafd. The press published the text of an agreement between Nahas and two other lawyers whereby they undertook to use their influence in parliament to remove the estates of Prince Seif el-Din (the king's brother-in-law who had been declared insane after attempting to assassinate him in 1897) from the king's control to that of the prince's mother in return for the handsome sum of £130,000. In the ensuing uproar Nahas had to resign.

As after the murder of Lee Stack, King Fuad seized his opportunity. He appointed as premier Mohammed Mahmoud, an able and ambitious Oxford-educated Liberal Constitutionalist,* and the new Government promptly petitioned the king to dissolve parliament and postpone elections for three years, which His Majesty was pleased to do with alacrity. On this occasion neither Austen Chamberlain nor Lord Lloyd saw any reason to intervene to restore parliamentary democracy.

The Wafd had been defeated without Lloyd having to raise a finger, but the high commissioner was the first to realize the victory was ephemeral. The new Government's ill-judged decision to refer Nahas Pasha and his two colleagues to a Council of Discipline aroused public sympathy on their behalf and when it resulted in an acquittal restored the Wafd's morale. There was one positive achievement of the Mahmoud Government which the absence of parliament doubtless made possible: the Nile Waters Agreement of 1929. The harsh terms of the Allenby ultimatum of 1924 had been dropped by the Baldwin Government and an Anglo-Egyptian commission formed to propose a basis for the allocation of the Nile Waters between Egypt and the Sudan. The 1929 Agreement abandoned the principle of a fixed irrigation area for the Gezira and made Egypt's share of the Nile Waters twenty times that of the Sudan. The Sudanese were not party to the agreement and Sudanese nationalists later regarded the Sudanese share as far too small.

In June 1929 the British general elections brought Labour back to power with greater strength than in 1924 but still dependent on Liberal support. It was inevitable that the new Government would want to replace Lloyd, who represented a romantic right-wing form of Toryism.† In the spring of 1929 Lloyd had been involved in a dispute with Austen Chamberlain and the foreign office over an Egyptian request for British 'sympathy in principle' for the appli-

---

* A contemporary remarked that he resembled an Englishman in every respect except that he did not wear a bowler hat, disliked marmalade and did not sing in his bath.

† In no way incompatible with the excellent personal relations he had established with Ramsay MacDonald.

cation of four new taxes to foreign residents in Egypt. This would have amounted to an important revision of the Capitulations and an expression of Egypt's sovereignty and independence, Chamberlain had been inclined to support the Egyptian request but Lloyd had strongly opposed any blanket approval on the ground that one of the taxes – a stamp tax – was unnecessary since the Egyptian Government's existing revenues were adequate while the existing form of another – the municipal tax – was chaotic and required clarification. Once again Lloyd found himself in dispute with the British Government over its interpretation of Anglo-Egyptian relations. As Lloyd wrote to Chamberlain in his last dispatch to the outgoing foreign secretary: 'If I may venture to offer a criticism of the main conclusion at which you arrive, viz., that intervention in the internal affairs of Egypt is to be confined to those cases where vital imperial interests are directly involved, it will, I think, be this: The Declaration of 1922 was, and still is, a unilateral act. It has never been accepted by Egypt, and even the friendliest Egyptian Government would not voluntarily consider accepting it today. . . . It has always seemed to me . . . a most dangerous course to make further substantial concessions to Egypt, however reasonable in themselves, except as part of a general settlement involving Egypt's acceptance of our minimum requirements.'

Arthur Henderson became the new foreign secretary and one of his first acts was to write Lloyd a letter in terms which amounted to a request for his resignation. When he came to give an account of his action to the House of Commons he based his decision primarily on the disagreement between Lloyd and his predecessor, Austen Chamberlain, revealed in their correspondence. Henderson was saying: If Lloyd was too pro-consular for a Tory foreign secretary how could he work with a Labour Government? Chamberlain said nothing to deny Henderson's charges and Lloyd's defence in the House of Commons was left to Winston Churchill.*

Lloyd left Egypt to the regret of the Anglo-Egyptian community. Without doubt he had been shabbily treated because however incompatible his High Tory style might be with the liberal image that the Baldwin and MacDonald Governments wished to display, the assumption that no British Government would offer what the

---

* Churchill was able to make amends when Lloyd became secretary of state for the colonies and leader of the House of Lords in his May 1940 Coalition Government shortly before his premature death at 61.

Egyptians really wanted was perfectly correct. His self-confident rightness did not add to his popularity in Whitehall.

Lloyd could have felt justified by the events that followed his resignation. The Labour Government optimistically engaged in negotiations with the Mohammed Mahmoud Government. A sixteen-point draft agreement was made but the Wafd was strong enough to insist that elections for a new parliament should be held before it could be ratified. The inevitable sweeping Wafdist victory followed and Nahas became prime minister on 21 December 1930 with a mandate to complete the negotiations. Agreement was reached on thirteen of the sixteen points, including the withdrawal of British forces to the Suez Canal Zone, but not for the last time negotiations broke down on the Sudan when Nahas demanded the right to raise the question of revision of the 1899 condominium within a year. (The Sudan was a question which could rouse the whole country; even the illiterate fellahin were aware of its importance to the Nile flood on which their lives depended.)

Nahas and the Wafd were reduced to concentrating on the defence of parliamentary government against the king's continued attempts to establish a royal autocracy. When the king refused to sign two bills they presented to parliament Nahas resigned in the belief that Fuad would be unable to withstand the Wafd's popular strength. But there was one man in Egypt who was capable of leading an anti-democratic counter-revolution, which the king had neither the character nor ability to command on his own. This was Sidky Pasha, a former associate of Zaghlul who had held office with ability in various governments since 1908 but who had always followed his own path with ill-concealed contempt for his fellow Egyptians. His cool ironic manner offset his energy and ambition. He was not a king's man and had more than once opposed the palace in the past but he was now prepared to establish a quasi-dictatorship under royal auspices. His strong nerves enabled him to prick the Wafdist bubble. With the help of British troops he suppressed popular demonstrations and went on to amend the 1923 constitution and the electoral law to increase the king's powers and ensure the defeat of the Wafd in the 1931 elections.

Britain was not going to intervene to help Nahas and Sir Percy Loraine, the new high commissioner, remained benevolently neutral towards Sidky. At the same time, Sidky's position was immeasurably strengthened by the fact that he was clearly no puppet of Britain, the palace or anyone else. He muzzled the press and hamstrung the Wafd by preventing it from using its most powerful weapon – control of the streets. He made use of the political moratorium to exhibit his talent for finance. A millionaire businessman, Sidky had been one of the original promoters during the First World War of Egyptian-controlled capitalist enterprise. His ability was suited to dealing with the consequences of the world depression and shielding Egypt from them as far as was possible. His regime marks the beginning of the move away from free trade liberalism installed under Cromer towards today's total Egyptianization of the economy.

Inevitably resistance grew to Sidky's reactionary authoritarianism; Wafdists and Liberals united against him and student protest grew louder. More ominously, Nahas Pasha began to think of a rapprochement with the British residency. As the demoralization of public life continued, the situation was clearly satisfactory to no one, including Britain. In August 1933 Sir Percy Loraine was removed from Egypt to become ambassador to Turkey and to be replaced after an interim by the overpowering figure of Sir Miles Lampson (later Lord Killearn) who was to preside over most of what was left of the British occupation of Egypt.

In September 1933 Sidky Pasha suffered a stroke and departed to England for medical treatment. He was replaced by two political nonentities – first Abdul Fattah Yehya, an Alexandrian merchant, and then Tewfik Nessim, widely and justifiably regarded as a British puppet. But the British Government was far from certain what it wanted in Egypt. The Labour Party had been swept from power in the electoral holocaust of 1931 and replaced by the superficially self-confident MacDonald-Baldwin National Government, with Sir Samuel Hoare as foreign minister. With the rise of fascism in Europe and of anti-colonial movements in Asia and Africa, the devaluation of sterling and mass unemployment at home, these were alarming years for the British Empire. In Africa Mussolini's ambitions were the principal concern. Obviously a government was needed in Egypt with some popular support but the British Government was reluctant to see the 1923 constitution restored since this would inevitably mean the return to power of the Wafd. King Fuad, on the other hand, was prepared to envisage this possibility since it would gain him some popularity. In November

1934 Sidky Pasha's 1930 constitution was abrogated and Egypt was governed for a year without a constitution.

In November 1935 Sir Samuel Hoare made the British Government's policy as clear as he could in a speech: 'There is no truth in what has been claimed, that we are opposed to Egypt's returning to a constitutional order suited to her special needs. It would be contrary to our traditions to do any such thing. But when our advice was asked it was opposed to a return to the constitution of 1923 or the constitution of 1930 because the former had proved unworkable while the latter is against the will of the people.'

Egyptian public opinion was outraged at what it regarded as a blatant attempt to prevent the restoration of the 1923 constitution. The press protested and the students demonstrated; in a mêlée with the police the tall, rather solemn leader of the Cairo secondary school students, named Gamal Abdul Nasser, was grazed on the forehead by a bullet.

A month later the king was pleased to restore the constitution he had always detested. (A few days after this, Sir Samuel Hoare, driven from office by the scandal of his Abyssinian Pact with Pierre Laval, was replaced by the young Anthony Eden.) A powerful factor behind this royal *volte face* was the king's chef de cabinet, Ali Maher, who possessed considerable political talent but ultimately helped the Egyptian monarchy to its downfall. The return of the Wafd after elections was inevitable but in the interregnum Ali Maher became prime minister.

On 28 April 1936, King Fuad died. Political intriguer to the last, his final gesture of restoring parliamentary government had not sufficed to make him popular. Since 1922 he had been a substantial force in Egyptian political life but never as much of one as he wished. When he died his sixteen-year-old son Farouk was in England where he had just failed the entrance exam to the Royal Military Academy at Woolwich.* He returned to an enthusiastic popular welcome in Egypt; the sentimental Egyptian crowd was ready to take to their hearts this attractive, smiling boyish figure who, unlike his father, had been brought up in Cairo. At first all went well; the Egyptian press and even foreign journalists smothered him with sycophantic praise. The Government trans-

---

* He expected the answers to be given him while he was doing the exam – as had always happened in Cairo. (Barrie St Clair McBride, *Farouk of Egypt*, p. 51.)

ferred his power to a regency council headed by his elderly Anglophile uncle Prince Mohammed Aly until Farouk should attain his majority at eighteen (according to the Muslim calendar) in July 1937.

23

A TREATY AT LAST

The first important event of the young king's reign was the conclusion on 26 August 1936 of the Anglo-Egyptian Treaty, at
which no less than six unsuccessful attempts had been made in
the past fourteen years. There were two main reasons why this
effort had succeeded where the others failed. First, the Wafd was
now an ageing party with declining revolutionary ardour but
undiminished appetite for power. Nahas Pasha, a lesser man than
Zaghlul although of the same populist mould, had established good
relations with Sir Miles Lampson. He and his party had begun
to learn the lesson that they could never hold power for long
against British opposition. At the same time, Egyptians of all
parties had become aware of Egypt's vulnerability in the face of
Italian imperial ambitions in Africa and its dependence on
Britain for defence.

Despite the immense and intoxicating prestige that the Wafd
still enjoyed with the Egyptian masses and that its adversaries had
never succeeded in eroding, the party had acquired a measure of
political wisdom during its long spells in opposition. While the
Wafd never moderated its hostility towards the palace, preferring
to accept the resignation of some of its prominent members
rather than yield to the king's demands, it had adopted an increasingly moderate attitude towards Britain. From 1928 onwards
the Wafd began to lobby Westminster and other branches of
the British Establishment. On his frequent visits to London,
Makram Ebeid Pasha, the suavely polished secretary-general of
the party, pointed out that the Wafd was 'neither anglophobe nor
xenophobe'. All that the Wafd wanted was the 'restoration of constitutional government' and in order to obtain this it was prepared
to compromise on Zaghlul's original objective of total and immediate British evacuation. This was already apparent in the Wafd's
attitude towards the 1930 Anglo-Egyptian negotiations which
broke down over the Sudan and not over the question of Britain's

right to maintain a military base in Egypt. However, the Wafd was still not moderate enough for Britain's purposes and as long as Sidky Pasha's iron rule was maintained, this seemed a satisfactory alternative. But Sidky's health failed and he was succeeded by lesser men. The British Government then considered the possibility of a new constitution which would be neither that of 1923 nor the guided democracy of 1930, on which a new basis for Anglo-Egyptian relations would be established. The popular outcry showed that this was not feasible but the most important factor behind the British Government's acceptance of the restoration of the 1923 constitution, which inevitably meant the return to power of the Wafd, was the changed attitude of the party as a result of the further chastening experience of five years in opposition. This, combined with the Italian threat, created the conditions for a settlement between Britain and the popular party for the first time since 1918.

All the preliminary negotiations took place in Cairo between an all-party Egyptian delegation and a British civilian and military team headed by Lampson. This in itself was an Egyptian concession; Zaghlul would have insisted on negotiating directly in London. In May elections were held in Egypt under the 1923 electoral law; after the usual Wafdist victory Nahas, as prime minister, headed the delegation to London to sign the treaty.

If the 1922 declaration gave Egypt semi-independence, the 1936 treaty went half the rest of the way. The treaty was for twenty years; both parties were committed to a further alliance in 1956 but Egypt would then have the right to submit to third-party judgement the question of whether British troops were any longer necessary in Egypt. The British occupation of Egypt was formally ended but this did not mean that British troops would leave the country. As Egypt's self-defence capability improved they would be withdrawn gradually to the Canal Zone and Sinai where their number would be limited to 10,000 land forces and 400 air pilots. The Royal Air Force could still fly over Egypt for training purposes. More significant, as it turned out, Britain reserved the right of re-occupation with the unrestricted use of Egyptian ports, airports and roads in the event of war. On the other hand the treaty did mean that Egypt was to gain control over its own security forces for the first time since 1882. The British inspector-general of the Egyptian Army was replaced by an

Egyptian, military intelligence was Egyptianized, military attachés sent to Egyptian embassies abroad and Europeans in the Egyptian police scaled down at the rate of twenty per cent a year.

However, Russell Pasha remained at the head of the Cairo police until his retirement in 1946 when the first Egyptian commandant was appointed. Although one of his principal duties was the control of political (i.e. anti-British) demonstrations, at which he was a familiar sight mounted on his white horse, he was never a target for Egyptian nationalist resentment and after the 1952 Revolution no question was ever raised about the payment of his pension. One reason was that all responsible Egyptians acknowledged the work of the Central Narcotics Intelligence Bureau (CNIB) which he had established in 1928 under Mohammed Mahmoud's Government. The Bureau's achievements were considerable in combating the smuggling and sale of 'hashish' and more particularly the traffic of opium and heroin which were introduced during the First World War and were sold mainly by non-Egyptian chemists under the protection of the Capitulations. In 1929 Russell estimated that about half a million Egyptians or one quarter of the male population between the ages of 20 and 30 were addicts. Of these about half were taking heroin intravenously. Russell had some success in rousing international opinion through the League of Nations even before Egypt became a member in 1937. He also developed the CNIB into an effective organization which incidentally raised the reputation of the Egyptian police force as a whole through its co-operation with anti-narcotics services in European and American police forces. As an Edwardian who began his career under Cromer, Russell had a naturally paternalistic attitude towards Egypt but his love for the country was genuine and he was totally opposed to the faction among the British community who favoured a return to direct rule during the Second World War.

One side-effect of the treaty ultimately paved the way for the 1952 Revolution and the end of British influence in Egypt. The Egyptian Army was not theoretically an ally of the British so Britain was anxious to improve it; the Wafd also needed popularity. For the first time the Military Academy was opened to young men who came from classes other than the land-owning aristocracy. Apart from Gamal Abdul Nasser, a dozen of the future Free Officers entered the army in this way.

Some of the changes brought by the treaty were symbolic but not insignificant. Sir Miles Lampson was henceforth ambassador instead of high commissioner and at least nominally ceased to be *primus inter pares* among foreign diplomatic representatives. Britain undertook to sponsor Egypt's entrance into the League of Nations, which it made the following year. Most important of all for Egypt's sovereignty, Britain undertook to bring the Capitulations to a speedy end. At the Montreux conference with all the capitulatory powers in the spring of 1937, Egypt obtained full rights of jurisdiction and taxation over all residents. The mixed courts took over all the jurisdiction of the consular courts for twelve years when they too would be abolished. The vestigial Caisse de la Dette was to be wound up, which it finally was in 1940.

The Sudanese situation was not radically altered by the 1936 Treaty, the question of sovereignty was shelved and the 1899 Condominium Agreement left intact. However, the terms of the 1924 Allenby ultimatum were reversed. Egyptian immigration into the Sudan was no longer restricted 'except for reasons of public order or health'; Egyptian as well as Sudanese and British troops were to be placed at the disposal of the governor-general. Egyptian officials were to be employed where no Sudanese was available. However, this did not mean even that the pre-1924 *status quo* was restored because the modern Sudanese national movement had developed and more Sudanese had qualified as government servants. The reality of an Anglo-Egyptian Condominium over the Sudan was almost as remote as ever.

Of the four reserved points in the 1922 declaration – defence, imperial communications, the Sudan and the Capitulations – the 1936 Treaty fully respected Egyptian sovereignty only in the last. Nevertheless, Nahas and the Wafd could regard it as an achievement. The British military occupation was being reduced as far as was compatible with Egypt's security in the face of the Italian threat. Nahas was cheered wildly in the streets; even Sir Miles Lampson was applauded. But many Egyptian students were absent from the crowds, they regarded the treaty as a betrayal and the Wafd could no longer automatically command their loyalty. Some of them looked to a new leader – a small and eloquent ex-school teacher named Hassan al-Banna whose Muslim Brotherhood movement, founded eight years earlier, was spreading throughout the country. Banna issued a denunciation of the Wafdist treaty.

Nahas remained in power for nearly two years until the end of 1937. The Wafd was in a slow but inexorable decline; it could still be called the political expression of Egypt but it no longer had the unrivalled control over the masses of Zaghlul's day. Two prominent Wafdists – Nokrashy Pasha and Ahmed Maher (Ali Maher's brother but politically dissimilar to Ali Maher) – were expelled and formed their own party which they called the Saad Wafd or Saadists to support their claim to have inherited Zaghlul's true tradition. A more serious challenge came from the palace. The young king, who came of age and officially ascended the throne in July 1937, showed his independence by appointing Ali Maher as his political adviser and chef de cabinet. He soon revealed his father's taste for political intrigue but with the difference that he could command his own secret police. Also, a fascist-type royalist youth movement had been formed to rival the Wafdist Blue Shirts. These frequently came to blows in universities and schools and in the streets although, as we have seen, with the passage of time these attacks became increasingly a form of exhibitionism as the Wafd moved towards a compromise with Britain. In 1937 Nahas was shot but survived.

The king's hand was strengthened by his continued popularity and the Wafd's striking failure to maintain public order. In December 1937 he seized the opportunity to dismiss Nahas 'for having violated the spirit of the constitution' and replaced his Government with a non-Wafdist Cabinet. The Wafd had no spirit to react and was heavily defeated in the subsequent elections which, though partially rigged, were held under the 1923 constitution that had previously always ensured a Wafdist victory. For eighteen months the elderly Mohammed Mahmoud held on to power against mounting vociferous opposition until in August 1939, barely two weeks before the outbreak of the Second World War the king felt able to replace him with Ali Maher.

The first seventeen years of autonomous government in Egypt had not been encouraging. The triangular balance of forces between the palace, the British residency and the Wafd had been maintained only in the sense that a repetition of the 1919 Revolution had been avoided and at the cost of failure to achieve the structural changes Egypt needed. The Wafd had some reformist drive but the system kept it out of power for all but five of the seventeen years and, whether in office or in opposition, it found attacking Britain easier than promoting social reform. It could claim some achievements such as the foundation in 1930 of the Agricultural and Co-operative Credit Bank to help small farmers and the industrial accident law of 1936. But there was no question of radical, still less of revolutionary, change. That the Egyptian masses expected little to ameliorate their lot from the parliamentary system is evident from the touching optimism in their hopes for a new dawn with the accession of the young King Farouk.

In one field – education – independent Egypt had shown some determination to repair the neglect of the Cromer era. One of the first acts of the Zaghlul Government in 1923 was to declare education free and compulsory. The ministry of education budget rose steadily from 4 per cent of the national budget in 1920 to 13 per cent in 1951. The number of pupils in school rose from 457,000 boys and 89,000 girls in 1915 to 678,000 boys and 204,000 girls in 1934. The increase was most striking in secondary education. In 1913 there were 2,500 boys and no girls enrolled in government secondary schools, by 1933 there were 15,000 (of whom 1,500 were girls). In 1920 there were 2,250 university students and in 1935 6,712. But this achievement had two serious defects. In the first place very few new schools were built so classes increased in size and standards declined. Secondly, the expansion in secondary education was still not accompanied by any structural change in the social and economic system, while no attempt was made to adapt the output of the schools to Egypt's needs. There was consequently a growing body of graduates from the state secondary schools and universities unable to find employment.

The problem was compounded by the existence of an entirely separate network of foreign secular and religious schools alongside the Egyptian state system. These had higher prestige, which was usually justified, but nothing did more to accentuate class divisions and to prevent the emergence of a responsible and socially conscious upper class. The Egyptian upper bourgeoisie grew up speaking French (or, less commonly, English) as their first language and despising the mass of their fellow-countrymen.

Foreign companies in Egypt favoured the products of the non-Egyptian schools and if the country's educational system was far from Egyptianized this was even more true of the economy. Despite the growth of native Egyptian industry after the First World War European companies still accounted for 86 per cent of local investment in 1933 (as compared with 96 per cent in 1897). The Egyptian share was rising slowly but at the outbreak of the Second World War it was still less than 25 per cent. Cromer's and Brunyate's plans for the non-Egyptian communities to be given formally entrenched political power in the constitution to match their economic position had been finally discarded by the 1922 declaration, and no independent Egyptian Government was likely to resurrect them. But Egypt at the outbreak of the Second World War retained many of the characteristics of a colonial society. In 1939, out of a total population of 16·5 million, foreigners numbered about 250,000, of whom nearly half were Greeks. There were about 60,000 British, who included about 50,000 Maltese, Cypriots, Indians, etc., with British passports. This 1·5 per cent foreign minority was a privileged caste which could be compared with the *colons* of French North Africa. The abolition of the Capitulations would eventually remove most of their legal privileges but they remained dominant in the higher levels of finance, trade and industry.

24

RE-OCCUPATION

The Anglo-Egyptian 1936 Treaty might have provided a satisfactory basis for relations between the two countries for some years although the inequality implicit in the treaty could hardly have been tolerated by Egypt indefinitely. The question remains academic because within three years of the treaty's ratification the outbreak of war with Germany caused Britain to invoke Article VIII which, in placing all Egypt's facilities at its disposal, implied the virtual re-occupation of the country. The prime minister declared a state of siege which amounted to the imposition of martial law with himself as military governor. Egypt did not declare war on Germany. A few leading politicians were in favour but the majority were opposed either because they felt that it was not Egypt's war or they were far from certain that the Allies would win. On the other hand, Egypt more than fulfilled its obligations under the terms of the treaty. German nationals in Egypt were interned and German property placed under sequestration.

As long as the war was kept out of the Middle East and North Africa a fair degree of Anglo-Egyptian harmony could be maintained. Italy's entry into the war in June 1940 at once transformed the situation. British forces in Egypt were engaged against the Italians in Libya and those in the Sudan with the Italian garrisons in Eritrea. Wavell, who had taken over command in Cairo in August 1939, had a total of 55,000 troops in Egypt and the Sudan. Clearly Egypt was in danger of a full-scale Italian invasion. Italian aircraft dropped bombs on Egyptian soil within a few days of the declaration of war.

Egyptian neutrality suited Britain because of the advantage of continued Axis acceptance of Cairo as an open city, but an immediate difficulty arose in the King and Ali Maher's reluctance to take action against Italian nationals and firms in Egypt. King Farouk had no special affection for Germany but many of his closest circle were Italian (including the notorious Antonio Pulli who rose from the post of palace electrician to become the king's most intimate companion). Lampson at once began to exert pressure on Farouk to dismiss his Italian court officials and when the prime minister still failed to act against Italian nationals in Egypt he told the king to replace him.*

The relationship between Lampson and Farouk closely paralleled that between Cromer and Abbas Hilmi. Behind a façade of formal politeness he treated the young king with overbearing condescension, although, unlike Cromer, Lampson was only an ambassador and Farouk, unlike Abbas Hilmi, was head of state of a sovereign country.

Lampson had first intervened in Farouk's career when he successfully persuaded the elderly and ailing Fuad to send his son to school in England rather than Italy against the strong protestations of Queen Nazli. The fourteen-year-old Farouk had taken an instant dislike to Lampson when he arrived in Egypt in 1934 and the antipathy grew with the years. Farouk would probably have resented anyone who so manifestly represented the limitations to his power and reminded him of his irksome duties as a constitutional monarch. The fact that most Egyptian politicians, including Nahas Pasha, were overawed by Lampson's personality, only deepened his resentment. But Lampson scarcely bothered to conceal his contempt for the Egyptian monarchy and its young representative to whom he was in the habit of referring as 'that boy'. Some of the British in Egypt were later to ascribe Farouk's rapid deterioration to Lampson's high-handed treatment of the young and sensitive monarch. A few were old enough to recall how Farouk's cousin, Abbas Hilmi, had given up the unequal struggle with Cromer to devote himself to his mistresses and the acquisition of wealth. Such critics were silenced by the events of the war when Farouk's pro-Italian sympathies, although they were personal rather than political, made him appear as a danger to security. When Farouk returned to Egypt on his father's death and was waiting to attain his majority, Lampson persuaded the headmaster

* The fact that Lampson's wife was the daughter of an Italian professor was the subject of Farouk's sarcastic comment. Instead of refusing Lampson's demand that he dismiss the Italian members of his household, Farouk characteristically attempted to circumvent it by conferring Egyptian nationality on them and having them circumcised for good measure. Those who refused were drugged before the operation.

of Eton, who had rejected Farouk as a pupil before he was sent to Woolwich, to send one of his masters to act as the young king's private tutor. The head recommended Edward Ford (later private secretary to King George VI) who duly arrived in Egypt in August 1936. But Farouk was not interested in applying himself to serious study; he preferred duck shooting or driving fast in his new sports car. Ford accompanied the king on a tour of upper Egypt and to Europe for the coronation of King George VI in May 1937, but his tutorials were reduced to a minimum.

When Farouk attained his majority on 29 July 1937, he understandably felt even more that he should do as he pleased. This was not Lampson's intention but, unlike Cromer, who had appealed in alarm to Lord Rosebery for support in dealing with the rebellious young Abbas Hilmi, he reassured the foreign office that he was perfectly capable of handling Farouk. This could be seen as a measure of the extent to which the British occupation had become entrenched since Cromer's day in spite of Egypt's nominal independence.

Farouk lacked the courage and strength of character to choose a position on which to stand his ground against Lampson. Instead he found ways of provoking and irritating the British ambassador on minor matters such as by keeping him waiting for appointments. Lampson took to making satirical remarks on social occasions about the king which were invariably relayed to the palace. Their relations naturally deteriorated further. When the war came new friction arose over the question of the king's pro-Italian sympathies but here again he gave in on the major matter of Ali Maher's premiership.

He dismissed Ali Maher and replaced him with Hassan Sabry and, after his death in November 1940, by Sirry Pasha. In September 1940 the Italians under Graziani invaded Egypt from Libya and reached Sidi Barrani on the coast; intermittent Axis air attacks continued. Ahmed Maher, the Saadist president of the chamber of deputies, now strongly criticized the Government for failing to declare war on Italy and following his lead the four Saadist ministers in the Cabinet resigned. However, both Hassan Sabry and Sirry did their utmost for the Allied cause short of declaring war.

In 1940 the British Government purchased the entire Egyptian cotton crop which had been cut off from its European markets. In

1941 and 1942 it only purchased half the crop as it was felt that the burden on the British taxpayer was excessive. Although Egypt was not suffering severely from the war the country was restive. Food shortages increased and the omnipresent Allied forces were blamed, although the real cause was that no attempt had been made to grow cereals instead of cotton.

In the Egyptian parliament the redoubtable Sidky Pasha, now restored to health, led the criticism of the Government. After Wavell's spectacular victories over Graziani at the end of 1940, which drove the Italians out of Egypt, the Germans reinforced the Italians and the Axis forces re-entered Egypt in April 1941. Enemy air-raids on the Alexandria area increased and 650 civilians were killed during the summer. (Cairo suffered no serious raids – almost certainly because of Churchill's warning in April 1941 that if either Cairo or Athens were attacked Britain would 'begin the systematic bombing of Rome'.)

Sirry Pasha did not waver, and in August 1941 Egyptian troops took over guard duties in the Suez Canal area. But there were many in Egypt, including the king and Ali Maher, who were so doubtful about the outcome of the war that they felt Egypt should have a more neutral government as insurance against an Axis victory. Others went further in believing that Egypt should actively assist such a victory and they included General Aziz al-Masri the Egyptian Chief of Staff and a young Captain, Anwar al-Sadat (now President of the United Arab Republic), one of the Free officers who led the 1952 Revolution and afterwards right-hand man to Abdul Nasser.*

The British prime minister had never had much patience with Egyptian nationalist feelings and he had none in time of war. When Eden was on one of his many visits to Cairo in March 1941, Churchill instructed him to inform the Egyptians of British security requirements. 'It is intolerable that the Roumanian legation should become a nest of Hun spies or that the Canal Zone should be infested by enemy agents. I am relying on you to put a stop to all this ill-usage we are receiving at the hands of those we have saved.'[1] He did not regard Egypt in any sense as an independent state. In December 1940 one of his speeches included the phrase, 'While the Italians invaded Egypt, which is under British protection' and a ruffled Egyptian prime minister had to be

* Gamal Abdul Nasser himself was stationed in the Sudan until 1941.

reassured by Sir Miles Lampson that this only meant that the British were there to keep Egypt out of danger.[2] As soon as Churchill became aware of the doubtful loyalty of the Egyptian Army to the Allied cause he insisted that Egyptian troops be sent back from the Western Desert to the Delta and General Aziz al-Masri should be dismissed. Any thought of allowing King Farouk to bring back Ali Maher was ruled out.

The crisis between the Egyptian king and Britain came to a head early in 1942. On 6 January the Sirry Pasha Government decided under Allied pressure to break relations with Vichy France. Not only was Vichy helping to supply the Axis armies through Tunisia but the Free French had established themselves in Egypt and Britain felt they should be encouraged. However, Farouk was furious at the decision, which was taken in his absence from Cairo and insisted on the foreign minister's resignation. Three weeks later Sirry Pasha, harassed by the opposition and without support from the palace, resigned also.

This gave Britain its opportunity. Sir Miles Lampson had for some time wanted to see a Wafdist Government installed; the Sirry Government had lost its impetus and was failing to deal with the pro-Axis sympathizers who were still at large. Rommel was advancing in Cyrenaica and the cry of 'Long Live Rommel' was being heard in the streets of Cairo; there was a rumour that a suite had already been booked in his name at Shepheard's Hotel.

The Wafd still enjoyed widespread national popularity and Lampson knew that a Nahas Government would provide the most effective support for the Allies. When Sirry resigned on 2 February Lampson pressed Farouk to send for Nahas.

But Farouk was determined to appoint a new palace government. Ideally it would be led by Ali Maher but if this was too provocative he would form a coalition of court politicians in which Ali Maher would be the real power. Lampson decided to act at once. Six months before, Oliver Lyttelton (later Lord Chandos) had been taken out of the board of trade to become minister of state for the Middle East with a seat in the British war cabinet.* When the

* The suggestion for the creation of this new post to relieve the commander-in-chief of some of his political responsibilities had originated with Randolph Churchill. When Winston Churchill told Lyttelton of the appointment at a private champagne dinner he chaffed him about his prospects as satrap of the Middle East 'holding the gorgeous East in fee'.

crisis in Cairo broke he was in Tehran attempting to settle a financial problem with the Persians and Lampson's telegrams hastily summoned him back to Cairo. He called together the defence committee which he had created when he arrived in the Middle East and which included the three service chiefs, Claud Auchinleck, Arthur Tedder and Andrew Cunningham. Clearly the security of the British military position in Egypt would be in danger if a pro-Axis government was formed in Cairo, but it was the civilian Lampson who proposed the use of force to prevent it.* As Lyttelton recalled in his memoirs: 'The ambassador favoured strong action. It was clear that words would be futile and that a show of force would be necessary if we were to get our way. The C-in-C and the military demurred, but I asked that at least the necessary measures should be concerted so that if an ultimatum from us became necessary, we would enforce its terms. The abdication and removal of the king might be involved. They reluctantly consented to make a plan but at the same time pointed out that we should probably have tumult in Cairo and a sit-down strike of all civilian labour upon which we relied. I reported that the disturbances which would follow the flouting of the popular party were likely to be much more severe because backed, and rightly, by the mass of the people. The army rapidly began to formulate and plan in great detail, and as it developed, their objections and queasiness seemed to fade away.³' The plan involved kidnapping Farouk and holding him on a British cruiser in the Red Sea.

With the support of the defence committee, Lampson went to see Farouk to tell him he must appoint Nahas. Farouk neither accepted nor refused the demand. He was appalled by the thought of recalling Nahas and the Wafd but he had already sensed the kind of action the British were planning against him. He attempted to compromise by asking Nahas to join a coalition government with non-Wafdists but Nahas had already accepted Lampson's instructions to reject anything except a purely Wafdist government. Lampson therefore sent the king an ultimatum telling him that unless he had sent for Nahas by 6.0 pm the following evening (2 February) he would have to face the consequences.

To Lampson and the king this meant the same thing—abdication. By a convenient chance, Walter Monckton had recently become

* Lyttelton observed that Lampson was 'quite unlike the urbane, cynical and detached ambassadors of the films'.

attached to the British embassy as director of propaganda services for the Middle East. Since he had drafted the instrument of abdication for Edward VIII he was obviously the man to do the same for Farouk. Lampson and the service chiefs by now were fully prepared to whisk the king away from Cairo by night as soon as he had signed.

But Farouk was still unprepared to face the choice of martyrdom or surrender to Lampson's terms. His next move was to call together a handful of ex-premiers, including Sidky Pasha, and presidents of the national assembly and to draft with them a letter to the British embassy protesting against the ultimatum as a gross infringement of Egypt's sovereignty. This reached the embassy at about the time when the ultimatum expired.

The British plan was then set in motion. Lampson and General R. G. W. H. Stone, Commander of British Troops in Egypt, were to present the abdication instrument in person after the Abdin Palace had been surrounded by a strong force of tanks and infantry. But first Lampson and Lyttelton had a long discussion of what they should do if Farouk capitulated at the thirteenth hour and agreed to call Nahas. Would they still insist on his abdication because the ultimatum had already expired? Reluctantly, Lampson agreed that if the king accepted their terms they should rest content.

At 9.0 pm Lampson and Stone, brushing aside the palace guards and flanked by their own armed ADCs, marched up the stairs of the Abdin Palace and into the king's private study, where Farouk was waiting. Lampson then read out in his stentorian voice a prepared statement which declared that in violating the terms of the Anglo-Egyptian Treaty, by accepting the advice of Britain's enemies and refusing to accept a government with popular support, the king had shown himself unfit to rule. He then presented Walter Monckton's draft instrument of abdication. Farouk appeared nonplussed and undecided; his first comment was that it was written on a dirty piece of paper.* Finally he took up his pen to sign but at the last moment pathetically asked Lampson if he would give him another chance. Reluctantly, Lampson had to

---

* Commenting in his diary on the singular coincidence that he should have twice in his life written an instrument of abdication, Monckton said that Farouk's remark on the inadequacy of the paper ('for that I was not responsible') reminded him of Edward VIII's observation that there was no ink in the pot. (Lord Birkenhead, *Walter Monckton*, pp. 198–9).

stand by his agreement with Lyttelton that if Farouk would appoint a purely Wafdist Government headed by Nahas, he could keep his throne.

The Duff Coopers, who were staying at the British embassy on their way back from Singapore, had been dining with the American minister that evening. On their return they found most of the principal actors in the crisis 'discussing the evening as people discuss the first night of a play when nobody is sure whether it has been a success or failure'.[4] There can be no doubt that in Lampson's eyes it had been a very limited success because the villain had survived the final curtain. He would have much preferred to be rid of Farouk and replace him with his reliably Anglophile uncle, Prince Mohammed Aly.

This incident was a seminal event in the history of modern Egypt. Its immediate effect was to upset the twenty-year-old triangular balance of forces in Egyptian political life; ultimately it destroyed the monarchy, the Wafd, and, in helping to provoke the 1952 Revolution, the British position in Egypt. The angry but helpless Farouk conceived a hatred for Lampson which he never forgot; non-Wafdist politicians were resentful but resigned to the result. Most Egyptian Army officers felt that the country had been humiliated in the person of Farouk. General Mohammed Neguib (who ten years later was to head the Council of the Revolution) sent the king a note: 'Since the army was given no opportunity to defend Your Majesty I am ashamed to wear my uniform. I hereby request permission to resign from the Egyptian Army.' Lieutenant Abdul Nasser, who had returned from Sudan to Egypt to be posted at Alamein, wrote to a friend who had described the incident to him in a letter: 'When your letter first arrived I almost exploded with rage. But what can we do about the *fait accompli* to which we have surrendered without a struggle? ... As for the army, it has been thoroughly shaken. Until now the officers only talked of how to enjoy themselves; now they are speaking of sacrificing their lives for their honour.'[5] If Farouk had been made of different material, there is every chance that by abdicating under pressure he could have returned later to his throne as a national hero like Sultan Mohammed v of Morocco who was deposed and exiled by the French.

The fateful consequences were not apparent to the British Government which had won its immediate objective of securing the

Egyptian domestic front in the face of Rommel's threat. Nahas
Pasha faithfully upheld his side of the bargain. New elections
which were held in March 1942 were boycotted by the non-Wafdists and 231 Wafdists were returned in a Chamber of 264. With
this power behind him, Nahas interned all suspected Axis sympathizers, including Ali Maher the ex-premier, and closed the Royal
Automobile Club which had become their meeting-place. He did
not lose his nerve during the high tide of Axis fortunes with
Japanese victories in South East Asia and Rommel's advance to
within fifty miles of Alexandria.

In August 1942 Churchill came to Cairo and it was agreed that
Montgomery should take over the Eighth Army. On 23 October
the Battle of Alamein marked the beginning of the Axis decline;
within seven months the remaining German and Italian forces
had evacuated North Africa.

As the war receded rapidly from Egypt, Nahas faced new
difficulties of which he was only partially aware. By 1943 there were
a vast number of Allied servicemen either stationed in Egypt, in
transit or on leave. The Anglo-American Middle East Supply
Centre made Egypt the focus of the allied war effort in the Middle
East and North Africa. Inevitably there was friction between this
vast occupying army and the Egyptians as only a small minority
of Allied servicemen had either the inclination or opportunity to
develop their knowledge or understanding of the country. For the
average British soldier a typical Egyptian was a Cairo prostitute
or a Port Said pimp selling Spanish fly and tickets to a blue film.
After a few beers he would be ready to belt out the British army
version of the Egyptian national anthem:

> King Farouk, King Farouk,
> Hang your bollocks on a hook
>
> or
>
> Queen Farida,
> Queen of all the Wogs.

Most Egyptians knew enough English to understand, and if they
did not the sentiment was clear. They were not especially proud
of their monarch but he remained Egypt's head of state.

Apart from the alien occupation, war conditions caused violent
social change as in 1914–18. In Charles Issawi's words: '. . . the
imposition of twentieth-century inflation on a social structure in

many ways reminiscent of the eighteenth century. The gap between rich and poor, already great, was further enlarged; the unskilled rural and urban labourers suffered severe privations; and the salaried middle and lower-middle classes, whose money incomes rose very little, were relentlessly pressed down.'[6] The relatively high wages offered by the services attracted many more fellahin to the towns than could find employment but by the end of the war the Allies were employing 200,000 Egyptians as clerks or skilled and unskilled labourers.

Secure in the knowledge that the Wafd was still the popular party, Nahas was unaware of the strength of the new forces arising in Egypt. One was the Muslim Brotherhood to which not only students but intellectuals, teachers and government servants were turning in despair and disgust with the failure of leadership of the politicians. The other was the movement among young army officers which was now led by Gamal Abdul Nasser, who had been promoted to captain and appointed instructor at the military academy.* Patiently he began to build up the cells of Free Officers (as they were later called) within the army with the long-term aim of overthrowing the monarchy and parliamentary regime.

But the Brotherhood was the significant revolutionary movement in Egypt at that time. It had been founded in Ismailia in 1928 by a 22-year-old elementary school teacher named Hassan al-Banna, a gifted leader of remarkable eloquence. At first the Brotherhood had been a purely religious revival movement concerned with protecting Islam against the forces of immorality and secularism encouraged by western influence. Al-Banna called for a return to the laws of the Koran and the Tradition. But during the 1930s he expanded his programme to positive demands that the entire political, legal and administrative system should be based on the Koran maintaining that Islam could provide everything needed for the social order without recourse to alien western systems such as communism or fascism. At first he had appealed mostly to the poor and uneducated but in 1934 he moved his headquarters to Cairo and began to attract supporters from all classes including students, teachers, civil servants and army officers.

In his speeches, Banna frequently called for the freedom and

---

* Anwar al-Sadat had been caught by British intelligence and interned. In 1944 he escaped but had to go into hiding.

independence of the whole Islamic world. In Egypt it was inevitable that the movement's xenophobia and anti-westernism should turn against Britain, the occupying power, and in 1936 Banna denounced the Wafdist Government's treaty with Britain as a betrayal. The Brotherhood had established a network of branches which undertook the indoctrination and education of its new members. It also started para-military training for its youth groups and in the 1940s the Brotherhood turned increasingly to terrorism and assassination to achieve its ends. The growth of the movement was the most striking consequence of the failure of Egypt's parliamentary system either to take root or to secure the country's genuine independence.

The Wafd had not been long in office before it showed signs of its chronic tendency towards internal disruption. In May 1942, Makram Ebeid the able Coptic finance minister resigned to form a new group. Ebeid then produced his famous black book which was a catalogue of the corruption of Nahas, his wife and wife's family. In 1944 Nahas used his powers as military governor to have Makram interned. Nahas continued to run his Party in an autocratic manner based on the assumption that it was an expression of the popular will, but he could not fail to be sensitive to the charge that the Wafd had been forced into power by the British. So while remaining steadfast in his support for the Allies in the war he continued to champion the cause of Egyptianization of the state. Perhaps the most significant measure in this direction was a law making the Arabic language compulsory for all official correspondence and commercial accountancy. The British chamber of commerce, in common with all the foreign communities, protested vigorously. As Tom Little remarks, 'notwithstanding the 1936 Treaty, the British and other foreigners in Egypt, and to a large extent the British press, continued to behave towards Egypt as though it were a subject country and to hark back to days when Britain could wield power inside it'.[7]

In return for Nahas' support for the Allies Lord Killearn (as Sir Miles Lampson had now become)* prevented King Farouk from dismissing him on more than one occasion. But the scandalous corruption of the Wafd, the distress caused by inflation and a

* Noel Coward is alleged to have remarked to the new peer at dinner: 'I hear, Sir, you are much more popular than your predecessor Lampson.' (Barrie St Clair McBride, *Farouk of Egypt*, p. 131.)

malignant malaria epidemic in Upper Egypt, which the authorities failed to combat and which killed over 50,000, combined to make Nahas' Government increasingly unpopular in the country. Finally, in October 1944, the king seized his chance when Killearn was out of the country, dismissed Nahas and replaced him with Ahmed Maher Pasha, the genial brother of Ali Maher, who formed a new government without the Wafd and including Makram, whom he released from internment.

Despite his undiminished dislike for Killearn, the king no longer felt it necessary to hedge his bets with the Axis after Alamein. At Christmas 1942 he made a personal donation of £2,000 for the Anglo-American troops in Egypt. Since 1940 Ahmed Maher had fought to have Egypt declare war on the Axis in order to ensure its place at the peace conference and now the Yalta Conference had decided that only those states which had declared war by 1 March 1945 would become members of the projected United Nations Organization. On 24 February 1945 Ahmed Maher announced Egypt's declaration of war to parliament; as he left the National Assembly he was assassinated.

Although the young assassin was said to be a member of the neo-fascist Misr al-Fatat (Young Egypt) organization it seems more likely that the murder was planned by the new terrorist wing of the Muslim Brotherhood. Without doubt it was the first of a series of political murders which were primarily the work of the Brotherhood and continued until the Revolution of 1952. Egyptian political life became violent as it had after World War I but with the difference that this time the victims were mainly prominent Egyptians.

Despite the prime minister's assassination, Egypt declared war, Ahmed Maher was succeeded by his foreign minister Nokrashy Pasha and the Cabinet remained unchanged. The Wafd had boycotted the elections held in January 1945 which had therefore resulted in a large anti-Wafd majority. In opposition the Wafd, which was still seeking to justify its nationalist credentials, conducted an anti-British campaign which grew increasingly virulent after the lifting of censorship with the final defeat of the Axis in August 1945.

In 1943 Lord Killearn had assured the Egyptian Government in a letter that 'His Majesty's government will exert its good offices with a view to ensuring that Egypt is represented on a footing of equality in any peace negotiations whatever which may directly affect her interests. Furthermore, His Majesty's government will not, in the course of any such negotiations, discuss any question directly affecting the interests of Egypt without consulting the Egyptian government.'

But Egyptian politicians of all parties went much further than this in believing that as a reward for Egypt's contribution to the Allied war effort, Britain should evacuate Egypt entirely and accept the unity of Egypt and the Sudan.

Tentative British proposals for continuing after the war the regional economic planning which had been initiated by the Middle East Supply Centre in Cairo, but with Middle East Governments in future taking part on an equal footing with the interested great powers, were rejected by the Egyptians. The Egyptian delegate to the United Nations Conference on International Organization at San Francisco in April 1945 said Egypt wished to limit membership of 'regional arrangements' provided under the draft UN Charter to nations having 'immediate geographical vicinity'. The Egyptians were determined to prevent the UN from being used as a means for perpetuating its satellite status.[8]

Heading a weak Government, Nokrashy Pasha had to follow the lead taken by the Wafd. Makram Ebeid, who was still finance minister, announced on 9 July that there would be no budgetary provision for building barracks in the Canal Zone to receive the British troops who were due to be withdrawn there from Cairo and Alexandria under the terms of the 1936 Treaty.

Once again Egyptian politicians were encouraged by the advent to power of a Labour Government in Britain. When Clement Attlee took office on 26 July, the right-wing Sidky Pasha greeted the event as a sign of the 'new spirit prevailing throughout the world'. On 30 July the Wafdist opposition presented Lampson with a memorandum containing Egypt's full demands and Nokrashy Pasha had no alternative but to endorse them.

Sir Edward Grigg (later Lord Altrincham) who was British minister resident in the Middle East until 12 August advised the Attlee Government to defuse the situation with a firm announcement that British troops were to be withdrawn from Cairo and Alexandria and to carry out the withdrawal as soon as possible. But the Labour Government was chiefly concerned with maintaining Britain's dominant military position in the Middle East and was not prepared for any hasty revision of the 1936 Treaty which, in its view, had stood the test of time. The consequence was that British soldiers remained in the citadel, the Kasr el-Nil barracks and the Ezbekiyeh Gardens to remind the Egyptians of the foreign occupation. Their evacuation would not have solved the Anglo-Egyptian problem but it would have done much to create good feeling between the two nations.

At the end of September 1945, Crown Prince Mohammed Aly returned from a visit to Britain and said that the great powers were so preoccupied with major post-war problems that those of Egypt and the Middle East would have to wait for the present. But pressure on Nokrashy from the Wafdist opposition and members of his own cabinet was mounting and on 20 December he formally asked for negotiations for the revision of the 1936 Treaty to begin as soon as possible. His note said that Egypt had concluded the treaty 'in the middle of an international crisis when the spectre of war was already appearing' and had accepted the restrictions on her independence only 'because she knew that they were of a transitory character and destined to disappear'. It added that Egypt's wartime collaboration with Britain had surely dispelled the British mistrust 'which had not yet entirely disappeared in 1936'.[9]

The British Government was heavily occupied with the crisis caused by the Soviet intervention in Iran which was the preliminary to the cold war. However, in its reply on 27 January, it said it had authorized the British ambassador to open preliminary negotiations with the Egyptian Government but took leave to observe that one of the lessons of the Second World War had been the essential soundness of the underlying principles of the 1936 Treaty.

This was highly unsatisfactory to Egyptian nationalist opinion. Anti-British agitation increased and in February 1946, there were massive demonstrations of students and workers with many casualties. Significantly, this first serious rioting since before the war was organized and led as much by Muslim Brothers and communists as by the Wafdists. Nokrashy Pasha resigned to be succeeded by the now tired and elderly, but still formidable, Sidky Pasha. Sidky Pasha acted against the extremist organizations but disorders and violent attacks on British soldiers and civilians continued. A general strike on 21 February was accompanied by widespread burning and looting of British property in Cairo and during demonstrations in Alexandria on 4 March a mob set fire to a

British military police outpost and stoned two of its five occupants to death. Sidky Pasha blamed Britain for the loss of British and Egyptian lives and ominously the Soviet press expressed sympathy for Egyptians killed demanding their national liberation.

In this heated atmosphere Sidky formed a delegation for negotiations with Britain. He included most leading Egyptians and representatives of all political parties except the Wafd which was insisting that it should have a majority on the delegation and that Nahas should be its chairman. It was not until 30 March that it was announced that Sir Ronald campbell, the British ambassador (who had succeeded Killearn a month before) would head the British delegation of senior military experts and embassy officials. Sidky, who was handling an explosive domestic situation, was highly displeased with this announcement. His delegation was at the highest level whereas the British delegation was to be led by an ambassador who was fresh to Egypt with the assistance of the same officials who had helped to plan and carry out his predecessor's unpopular policies.

Britain's Labour Government, which was now adopting a more sympathetic attitude towards Egyptian aspirations, responded to Sidky's protests and Ernest Bevin, the foreign secretary, announced that he would head the British delegation himself; preliminary negotiations would be led by Lord Stansgate, secretary of state for air, with the head of the foreign office Middle East department, Sir Kinahan Cornwallis, and the three commanders-in-chief in the Middle East. Sidky was especially pleased with the appointment of Stansgate who as Wedgwood Benn, MP, had been known as an outspoken supporter of Egyptian nationalism.

History relentlessly repeated itself. Stansgate arrived in Egypt to find that no responsible Egyptian politician was prepared to risk proposing anything less than complete British evacuation. In vain his military advisers urged on the Egyptians the dangers of the incipient Soviet cold war threat to the Middle East and Egypt's essential position as the base for a regional defence system. This type of argument had been heard in Egypt too often before. To the Egyptians it simply meant that they were never to be their own masters.

The British Government decided to break the deadlock by accepting the principle of total evacuation. On 7 May 1946 Attlee announced in the House of Commons that the Government intended to withdraw British forces from Egypt according to a timetable to be jointly agreed upon and to negotiate a new treaty of mutual assistance. As leader of the opposition, Winston Churchill strongly attacked the decision, describing the Government's policy of evacuating Egypt and defending the Suez Canal as 'a complete and total contradiction in terms'. As shadow foreign secretary, Eden criticized the Government for not withdrawing British troops from the Delta to the Canal Zone. Somewhat defensively, Ernest Bevin replied that while he believed in the new basis of approach that the British Government had offered, he would never agree to the creation of a vacuum. There must be a regional defence or other organization after Britain's departure.

The idea of an Anglo-Egyptian alliance which would give Britain the right to re-activate the Suez Canal base under certain circumstances even after evacuation, was still repugnant to many Egyptians but the real prospect of a total withdrawal of British troops from Egyptian soil gave Sidky room to manoeuvre. At least he now had the possibility of negotiating an agreement which would be ratified in spite of the certain opposition of the Wafdists. In the negotiations which continued throughout the summer, attention was now concentrated on the period to elapse before the final British withdrawal. The British negotiators wanted five years and the Egyptians one year. Eventually a compromise was struck at three years. Disagreement also arose over the circumstances under which Britain would be able to re-activate the Suez base after it had withdrawn. The Egyptians wanted these to be limited to an attack on Egypt or one of its immediate neighbours while the British, who were concerned with the Soviet threat to Iran, Turkey and Greece in those early days of the cold war, wanted them extended to include those countries on the periphery of the Middle East.

A compromise was reached on this point also whereby Britain agreed that in the case of an aggression against those more distant countries, Egypt's obligation would be limited to 'consultation on the action to be taken'.

Field-Marshal Montgomery arrived in Egypt in June on a tour of inspection of British troops overseas before taking up his new post of CIGS. He had been asked by Bevin to 'ginger up' the evacuation of the Delta cities – a task for which he was well suited.

But he was convinced that Britain must maintain a military base in Egypt in peace-time in case the Third World War were to break out and tried to impress this on King Farouk and the prime minister. He had no response from Farouk who merely repeated that Egypt was suffering from forty years of British misrule but Sidky Pasha 'displayed much more understanding'. He could afford to do this because Montgomery had already come to the conclusion that the base in Egypt could be maintained in peace-time by the Egyptians although he estimated that it would take at least five years to evacuate the Canal Base.

Attlee remarked later that the difficulties of reducing the number of troops in the Canal Zone was the 'plague of my life', because of the inexhaustible military capacity for delay. He was constantly told that it was necessary to guard the huge mass of valuable stores in the base but no one knew whether they were useful or obsolete. In fact, they did not even know what some of them were because 'some bright boy during the war had failed to put any marks on our cases'. Attlee was convinced that the military tended to cling to Egypt because it was a pleasant place to live in compared with 'Aden or some other God-forsaken place' and, in general, he thought that the supreme importance attached to the Middle East as a base was an imperial hangover from the days when the Middle East was an essential link between Britain and India. 'But India had ceased to be a British Imperial place of arms and the Suez Canal had never been a particularly good waterway in war-time and the idea of the Mediterranean as a kind of covered passage for Britain had also been exploded.'[10]

Montgomery had only concluded that Britain could afford to evacuate its troops from the Suez base provided it could maintain troops in Libya, Trans-Jordan and Palestine as well as the bases in Malta and Cyprus. He also believed that 'it was vital to remain strong in the Sudan, in case of difficulties with the Egyptians. The weaker our position in Egypt the greater our need for strength in the Sudan – so as to be able to control the Nile, the life-blood of Egypt'.[11]

Here was the cause of the collapse of the most promising opportunity for an Anglo-Egyptian settlement for decades. The British Government and the military were equally agreed that the Sudan must be kept separate from any settlement with Egypt. Since the details had been agreed in Egypt, when Sidky went to London in

October 1946, he fairly rapidly reached agreement with the British foreign minister on a draft treaty which became known as the Sidky-Bevin agreement. This provided for all British forces to be withdrawn from the Cairo and Alexandria areas by 31 March 1947 and from the whole country by September 1949. A joint board of defence would be established to ensure military co-operation if Egypt was attacked or if Britain was involved in a war as a result of an attack on any country adjacent to Egypt.

This treaty gave Egyptian nationalists virtually everything they wanted for Egypt. Had it been ratified the modern history of the Middle East would have been different; conceivably the monarchy and parliamentary system would have survived. But the draft treaty glossed over the problem of the Sudan in saying that the 1899 Condominium Agreement would remain until common agreement after consultation with the Sudanese could be reached on the Sudan's future status 'within the framework of the unity between the Sudan and Egypt under the common Crown of Egypt'.

On his return to Egypt Sidky understandably interpreted this diplomatically-worded text to mean that Britain had accepted Farouk as king of Egypt and the Sudan. But the British Government had no such intention. The governor-general of the Sudan had already given an assurance to the advisory council of the northern Sudan which had been set up during the war (without consultation with Egypt) that the British Government firmly intended to consult the people of the Sudan regarding the future of their country. There were now two main political groups in the Sudan: the Umma Party, with its Ansari supporters, who looked to the original Mahdi's posthumous son, Abdul Rahman al-Mahdi, for leadership, and the Ashiqqa or Brothers led by Ismail al-Azhari allied to the Khatmiyeh sect of the Mirghani family. The Umma wanted to achieve independence for the Sudan through co-operation with Britain, while the Ashiqqa sought the closest co-operation with Egypt as protection against the recrudescence of Mahdism. Understandably, if ironically, the British supported the Umma and Egypt the Ashiqqa. Since 1899 the British had developed a corps of able and devoted administrators for the Sudan who treated the country no differently from the African colonies; only perfunctory lip service was paid to the notion of the Anglo-Egyptian Condominium. The Sudanese political service would have put up the strongest resistance, with certain support from the British parliament, to any proposal to return the Sudan to Egyptian rule.

As soon as it became clear that the British Government was far from committed to Egyptian-Sudanese unity Sidky resigned and was succeeded once again by Nokrashy Pasha. The Sidky-Bevin agreement was shelved and the new Government was incapable of starting fresh negotiations. With the Wafd in opposition baying for blood it would have been impossible for Nokrashy to make any concession on the principle of *Wihdat al-Nil* (Nile Unity). Although it had been exploited for their own purposes by the palace and some politicians, the whole country was now genuinely roused on this issue. As the British governor-general of the Sudan instituted new moves towards Sudanese self-government Nokrashy referred the whole matter to the UN Security Council in August 1947. The Arab League states had endorsed Egypt's claim to the Sudan but this was virtually its only support. The Soviet Union was opposed and Egypt achieved nothing at the UN.

Anglo-Egyptian relations were as bad as they had ever been but Britain did unilaterally fulfil part of the terms of the Sidky-Bevin agreement as all troops were withdrawn from the Delta to the Canal Zone. However there were over seven times as many as the 10,000 stipulated by the 1936 Treaty.

25

EGYPT GOES TO WAR

At this point Egypt's attention was temporarily diverted from its quarrel with Britain. Since 1840, when Mohammed Ali's wings were clipped by the powers, Egypt's only important concern outside its borders had been the Sudan and this, since 1882, to the extent that Britain permitted. The Khedive Abbas had dreamed of a revived Arab caliphate under Egyptian temporal protection but it had remained a dream. If kings Fuad and Farouk had held similar ambitions their purpose was essentially to gain prestige and strengthen their position in Egyptian political life; they had support from some ambitious religious leaders such as Mohammed al-Maraghi, who was rector of el-Azhar from 1935 to 1945, but the politicians were almost invariably hostile. Egyptian popular leaders from Arabi to Nahas were essentially Egyptian nationalists absorbed by Egypt's problems. Pan-Arabism meant little to them and if Mustafa Kamel was an advocate of Islamic unity this was essentially a means to secure Ottoman support against the English occupiers.

But if Egypt abstained from pursuing a dynamic Middle Eastern policy after it had regained some control over its foreign affairs in 1922, national pride demanded that as the largest, richest and most advanced Middle Eastern Arab state it should refuse to be excluded from developments in the area. Educated Egyptian opinion began to take an interest in the Arab-Jewish struggle for Palestine in the 1930s and the Syrian and Lebanese efforts to establish their independence in the 1940s. Arab delegates to the Palestine Round Table Conference in London in 1939 assembled first in Cairo.

In May 1941 Anthony Eden had said in a speech that the British Government would give full support to any scheme that commanded general approval among the Arabs for the strengthening of the political, economic and cultural ties between the Arab States. In December 1942 the pro-British prime minister of Iraq,

Nuri al-Said, put forward his own scheme for the unification of Syria, Lebanon, Palestine and Trans-Jordan with 'semi-autonomy' for the Jews in Palestine as a first step towards Arab unity. But neither King Farouk nor Nahas Pasha had any intention that Egypt should be left out of the Arab unity movement. One of Nahas' last political acts before resigning was to preside over a conference of Arab leaders in Alexandria in September 1944. When the conference broke up on 7 October it had laid the foundations of the Arab League, which was legally established in March 1945 when the six Arab states which had become independent since 1919 (Egypt, Syria, Iraq, Trans-Jordan, Saudi Arabia and Yemen) signed a covenant in Cairo forming a loose confederation.

The scheme had been born under the aegis of the British Government but from the outset there was no doubt that Egypt was to be the dominant member. The permanent secretariat was established in Cairo and the first secretary-general, Abdul Rahman Azzam Pasha, was an Egyptian with an unqualified belief in Egypt's right to Arab leadership.

Nevertheless, when the prospect arose of Arab League intervention to prevent the creation of Israel and the partition of Palestine against the wishes of its Arab inhabitants, Egypt's participation with the other League members was far from a foregone conclusion. Egypt's pan-Arabism was still superficial; Nokrashy Pasha was prime minister instead of the more flamboyant and ambitious Nahas, and Nokrashy had no illusions about the inadequacy of the Egyptian armed forces with their total strength of about 10,000 men.

But Egyptian public opinion had been roused. The Muslim Brotherhood wanted to fight for Palestine and the Mufti of Jerusalem, Hajj Amin al-Husseini, who was in Egypt, exerted a powerful influence; of greater importance was King Farouk's determination that the Egyptian Army should enter the war. With deep misgivings Nokrashy's Government decided to intervene on 12 May 1948. Three days later the British mandate in Palestine was terminated, the state of Israel was declared and units of the Egyptian Army crossed into Palestine.

At first all went well. The Egyptians occupied Gaza and Beersheba and linked up with the Arab Legion near Bethlehem. But the Israelis, better armed and fighting desperately for survival, launched a violent counter-offensive. After a short truce arranged by the United Nations, fighting resumed and lasted until the armistice in January 1949 by which time the Israelis had captured most of Palestine except for two slices of territory to the north and south of Jerusalem. The Egyptian Army was shut up in the Gaza strip near the sea and in two pockets to the north-east.

The main effect of the war on the Egyptian Army was to convince the younger officers of the criminal incompetence of the men ruling Egypt. Food and medical supplies were inadequate and irregular while arms were obsolete and in some cases worthless. Senior officers gave contradictory and meaningless orders while some showed downright cowardice. (An outstanding exception was Major-General Mohammed Neguib who was desperately wounded.) Abdul Nasser, recently promoted to Major, was wounded and distinguished himself in a defensive engagement at the Irak el-Manshia pocket. But his most vivid memory of the war was the words of Colonel Ahmed Abdul Aziz shortly before he was killed: 'Remember the real battle is in Egypt.'

Even while the war was still in progress Egypt's sham democracy began to disintegrate as the extra-parliamentary forces gathered strength. The most obvious beneficiary was the Muslim Brotherhood which had gained new prestige as many of its members fought and distinguished themselves as para-military volunteers in Palestine. In November 1948 Nokrashy Pasha had made use of wartime martial law to declare the Brotherhood dissolved and its branches closed. On 28 December Nokrashy was assassinated in the presence of his own police. Ibrahim al-Hadi, the head of the Royal cabinet, who succeeded him, pursued his actions against the Brotherhood. Two months later the Supreme Guide of the Muslim Brothers, Sheikh Hassan al-Banna, was himself shot down – almost certainly by a wing of the state counter-terrorist police although not necessarily with the knowledge of the king or prime minister.

The Brotherhood was temporarily weakened by this shattering blow and remained quiescent until it was able to regroup after the election of a new Supreme Guide in 1951. The prime minister took repressive action against the communists and other groups; the country was superficially quieter than it had been for some time. But there was one group that Ibrahim al-Hadi failed to combat – the clandestine movement in the army which had also gained new recruits as a result of the Palestine war. He came near to penetrating the movement through the close connections of some of its members with the Brotherhood but the organization of the Free Officers, as they now called themselves, remained unscathed.

The Egyptian premiership was no sinecure at this time and Ibrahim al-Hadi had some of the necessary courage and ability. But since he had no political backing he could not remain in office without support from the Palace. Farouk disliked him and he made no secret of his disapproval of the king's behaviour. The way was now open for an improbable eleventh-hour reconciliation between Farouk and the Wafd. The king dismissed Ibrahim al-Hadi and in the subsequent elections in January 1950 the Wafd won its usual sweeping victory.

That Farouk should have been prepared to seek a rapprochement with his old enemy Nahas showed that he had become cynical but that he had not lost his taste for power, for a palace-Wafd coalition could always hope to govern the country as long as it could be sustained. The truth was that Farouk was now no longer even capable of the effort and application required for his father's style of political intrigue. In fourteen years the handsome and wildly popular boy-king had been transformed into a cartoon satire of middle-aged debauchery. Inherited glandular trouble allied to a Gargantuan appetite caused his extraordinary obesity. His character defects were doubtless innate but they had been accentuated by several factors such as his unsuitable education, unwise parental guidance and subsequent mistreatment at the hands of a domineering British ambassador. Although intelligent and quick-witted, he lacked *gravitas;* his character was as light as his body was heavy.

The decline in his popularity, at first imperceptible, had now gathered momentum. At the height of the Palestine war he had divorced his well-loved Egyptian wife Farida but his voracious and undiscriminating taste in women was already notorious.* The frivolous luxury of his life in Mediterranean resorts during the Egyptian troubles seemed a callous insult to his impoverished subjects.

---

* Despite, or more probably because of, his increasing sexual impotence caused by an endocrine disorder known as 'adipose gynandrism'. There is an interesting discussion of this in Hugh McLeave, *The Last Pharaoh*, pp. 158–62.

Nevertheless in 1950 some people imagined that a Wafd Government supported by the king could bring stability to Egypt. 'This was not the British Government's idea, for Mr Bevin was not the man to play around with the internal affairs of a country like Egypt,' says Tom Little, 'but people of some importance in the British embassy and the British community gave the impression that it would be an arrangement highly satisfactory to Britain.'[1] They were soon disillusioned. Superficially there were some improvements in Britain's relations with Egypt, and especially the Palace. In January Ernest Bevin came to Cairo for talks; in March the Duke and Duchess of Gloucester paid a visit and the Duke made Farouk an honorary Major-General in the British Army. Several other British generals and admirals, including Sir William Slim and Earl Mountbatten, passed through Egypt and Farouk even paid a state visit to Mountbatten's flagship in Alexandria. Since the replacement of Lord Killearn by Sir Ronald Campbell the king had been on better terms with the British embassy. But none of this was of any significance in the absence of a final Anglo-Egyptian political settlement. The king himself was the despair of any Egyptian who wished to see the monarchy preserved, in October 1950 a group of leading non-Wafdist politicians dared for the first time to present a petition criticizing Farouk's entourage.

Although the left wing of the Wafd showed some awareness of the need for social reform and the foundations of Egypt's first social security scheme were actually laid in 1950, the main plank in the Wafd platform was uncompromising nationalism which, in this case, meant the demand for immediate Egyptian-Sudanese unity under the Egyptian crown. This the British Government refused but during 1951 it made some attempt to prevent the situation from deteriorating by showing good will. In March an agreement was concluded, against sharp Conservative Opposition criticism in the House of Commons, for the progressive release of Egypt's blocked sterling balances.* For the first and last time British and Egyptian troops and naval forces held joint manoeuvres. The Labour Government had worked out plans for a combined Middle Eastern command with the US, Turkey and

---

* These had accumulated to about £400 million by the end of the war and they helped to cover Egypt's trade deficits in the immediate post-war years. But Britain's share in Egypt's foreign trade was steadily declining. Egypt left the sterling area in July 1947.

France, which it was hoped that Egypt would join. This was essentially a cold war move aimed to keep the Soviet Union out of the eastern Mediterranean, but already it was doomed to failure. Neutralist feeling was already nascent in the Middle East where the old imperial powers were regarded as a more serious threat than Soviet communism. The Iranian leader Mossadek's struggle with Britain for control of the Iranian oil industry in the Abadan crisis gave added impetus to the movement. The plan was eventually presented officially to Egypt a few days after the Nahas Government had decided to abrogate the 1936 Treaty in October 1951. Not surprisingly, it was flatly rejected.

Opposition to the Wafd was gathering strength and Nahas found it necessary to step up his anti-British campaign to divert attention from his domestic difficulties. Wafdist corruption became still more scandalous and the progressive-minded minister of social affairs resigned while the finance minister was dismissed. An initially successful attempt to secure the party's popularity in the countryside by maintaining cotton prices at their level, inflated by the Korean war, turned out to be economically disastrous. Opposition leaders issued a manifesto accusing the government of attempting to set up a virtual dictatorship.

If anyone had dictatorial ambitions in the Wafd it was the secretary general, Fuad Serag ed-Din, who was minister of finance and the interior and whose bulky figure overshadowed that of Nahas. But the king disliked him and was rumoured to be considering dismissing the Wafd Government. It was at this point that Nahas and Serag ed-Din decided on the desperate course of unilaterally abrogating the Anglo-Egyptian Treaty of 1936 and declaring Farouk King of Egypt and the Sudan. This move was wildly popular in Egypt but it was dangerous because in its struggle with Britain the Government had to enlist the support of all the anti-constitutionalist forces in the country. Nahas declared a state of emergency and took steps to cut off fresh food supplies from the British troops in the Canal Zone and withdraw most of the Egyptian labour on which they heavily depended. But this was not enough; Nahas and Serag ed-Din went further to encourage the formation of volunteer 'Liberation' squads to carry out sabotage and guerrilla attacks on the Canal Zone, and for these the obvious recruits were Muslim Brothers, communists, neo-fascist socialists or any other group with valuable terrorist experience. Some of the Free Officers helped them with training these groups behind the scenes and the Government allowed the auxiliary police to co-operate with them.

One of the Labour Government's last acts was to reinforce the garrison in the Suez Canal.* The Conservatives won the October 1951 election and Anthony Eden returned as foreign secretary. Immediately after taking office he sent the Egyptian Government a curt note rejecting the unilateral abrogation of the 1936 Treaty and reaffirming the 1899 Condominium agreements on the Sudan. He did not underestimate the seriousness of the situation. As he wrote in his memoirs: 'The position I had to face in Egypt was more forbidding than anything which was happening in Persia. I was convinced that there the situation had been made worse by some unimaginative mishandling, which I believed could be remedied. In Egypt the outlook was much darker; almost everything seemed rotten in the state.'²

Eden emphasizes the deterioration inside Egypt which was undeniable; it was equally true that Britain's position in Egypt was becoming untenable. The Egyptian Government's actions had rendered the Canal Base militarily useless. The immediate problem of the loss of Egyptian labour had been overcome by importing East African soldiers but the 80,000 British troops in the base were now fully occupied in protecting themselves and their installations against guerrilla and sabotage attacks. The only alternative would have been the re-occupation of Cairo which was something the aged Winston Churchill was unwilling to contemplate.

When the 'Liberation' squads stepped up their attacks in January the British extended their counter-measures by occupying areas where the attacks had occurred and arresting guerrilla suspects who included the auxiliary police. Then on 25 January a strong British force surrounded the police headquarters at Ismailia at seven in the morning and issued a one-hour ultimatum for its occupants to surrender. Serag ed-Din ordered the Egyptian police to resist, which they did with great courage, until some fifty were dead and many more injured.

* Herbert Morrison, who was the Labour foreign secretary, was almost as unsympathetic towards Egyptian nationalism as Winston Churchill. He favoured a stiff line and later blamed Egypt's nationalization of the Suez Canal Company on the Conservatives' decision to abandon the Suez base. (See Herbert Morrison, *Autobiography*, p. 282.)

The next day came to be known as Black Saturday. In a reaction to the Ismailia massacre a frenzied Cairo mob burned the centre of the city destroying some 400 buildings. Particular attention was paid to British property, such as the Turf Club, and to establishments with foreign associations such as the famous Shepheard's Hotel. Shops and restaurants owned by Italians, Greeks and Jews went up in flames. It was evident that the anger of the mob was directed as much against the foreign commercial classes as the British. The responsibility for the disaster has never been clearly established; almost certainly it should be shared by many. The initial acts of arson were organized by Muslim Brothers, Misr al-Fatat and other militant groups; subsequent damage and looting was carried out by the mob that followed in their wake. Fuad Serag ed-Din very probably connived with the first attacks but did not foresee how they would spread; King Farouk was entertaining senior Egyptian police officers to lunch and made no attempt to intervene. It was not until the evening that regular troops were called in and brought the city under control. Subsequently the king and Serag ed-Din blamed each other for the delay.

The belated move to call in the army was prompted by the very real fear that the British troops might intervene from the Canal Zone. They could have been in the capital in two or three hours. No Egyptian in authority had forgotten that the Alexandria riots had been the chief justification for the British invasion seventy years before. Eden records that a plan had already been worked out with General Erskine, the Commander-in-Chief of British troops in Egypt, for his forces to intervene in Cairo and Alexandria to protect the lives and property of British subjects (who included many Maltese and Cypriots). During Black Saturday General Erskine cabled to the British Government to say that in view of the fierce resistance of the Ismailia police post he doubted whether he could risk detaching enough forces from the Canal Zone to carry out the plan. After consulting with the Lord Chancellor, Lord Simonds, the only cabinet minister available that weekend, Eden instructed Erskine to intervene if necessary whatever the risks. By evening the Cairo rioting was over (Alexandria was quiet throughout) and the threat of a new British military occupation had been averted.

The attacks of the rioters had been directed against property rather than people or the loss of life would have been much greater. As it was, the loss of British property alone in Cairo was estimated at between three and four million pounds – an indication of its extensiveness.

Egypt's regime gave off the smell of death. The Wafd had been totally discredited; Serag ed-Din's callous order to the Ismailia police to resist aroused as much public anger as the British action which caused their death. The king seized the chance to dismiss Nahas and his Cabinet and bring back his old wartime ally, Ali Maher, but the monarchy's stock had fallen even lower than the Wafd and Farouk made no effort to mend his ways. Ali Maher struggled on for a month to be replaced by a prominent and respected lawyer, Neguib al-Hilali, who made an even more determined effort to save the regime despite itself. He suspended the Wafdist-controlled parliament and promised an energetic purge of corruption.

The king had known for some time from his secret police of the existence of the clandestine movement in the army. Since the end of the Palestine war the Free Officers had been distributing their famous mimeographed tracts denouncing the regime. In 1950 Gamal Abdul Nasser had been formally elected president of the Free Officers' Executive Committee and at that time the organization planned to move into action in 1954 or 1955. Nasser was aware that when the time came to overthrow the monarchy they would need a senior officer with a well-known name who would act as their figurehead and give their movement weight and respectability at home and abroad. The average age of the Free Officers was little more than thirty. They found the man they wanted in Brigadier-General Mohammed Neguib, who was known to be sympathetic. They contacted him and he joined the Free Officers as their president in January 1952. In the same month the king was enraged by Neguib's election as president of the Army Officer's Club committee and the defeat of his own nominee. But owing to Colonel Nasser's careful security the Free Officers' organization network remained undiscovered.

After Black Saturday the Free Officers knew that they would have to act much earlier than they had planned. They fixed a date for March although this later had to be postponed.

The British and American embassies, especially the latter, knew of the Free Officers but at that time they were still working on the assumption that the regime would survive. Anthony Eden recognized that al-Hilali was the most honest and well-intentioned prime minister Egypt had had for some time and he was prepared to try to ease his way. In April Britain made a further release of Egypt's blocked sterling balances and withdrew the outposts of British troops back to the Canal Zone. But the old dilemma remained; without any political base al-Hilali could not possibly accept less from Britain than the Wafd had demanded, which in this case was the union of Egypt and the Sudan. On taking office Eden had been more than a little irritated to discover that the US Government was pressing Britain to relax its position over the Sudan to the extent of recognizing Farouk as king of Egypt and the Sudan pending a decision about the Sudan's future status.* The US Government considered that Eden's abrupt dismissal of the Egyptian Government's proposal for a plebiscite in the Sudan as pure propaganda had created a bad impression.

All that Eden was prepared to do was to encourage direct negotiations between the Egyptians and the Sudanese. These came to nothing because Abdul Rahman al-Mahdi was adamant in refusing to acknowledge Farouk as king of the Sudan. Despite continued American pressure, no progress was made towards a settlement between Britain and the Egyptian Government. In June the Hilali Government resigned; it was Farouk's last chance of survival but various elements who feared Hilali's efforts to combat corruption brought pressure on the King's inner circle to get rid of him. Farouk had now reached the ultimate stage of folly. He called on Hussein Sirry Pasha, a political nonentity, to form the next cabinet which included Karim Thabet, a Lebanese palace official who was widely regarded as the worst of the many evil influences surrounding the king. Sirry lasted a few days until Hilali returned, but with Farouk insisting on having his own brother-in-law Colonel Sherin as minister of war.

If the king was now totally cynical about his country's political life, he still believed that he could preserve his throne by maintaining control of the armed forces and suppressing the rebellious officers' movement. No doubt he recalled the fate of his uncle the Khedive Tewfik. In July 1952 his military intelligence had come

---

* A special target for Eden's dislike was the US ambassador in Cairo, Jefferson Caffery, who was a warm sympathizer with Egyptian nationalism.

close to uncovering the Free Officers' entire organization and it was on 20 July that Colonel Nasser and his friends received word that Colonel Sherin was to become minister and proceed immediately with their arrest. They decided to strike at once. That Farouk was in his summer palace at Alexandria made their task much easier.

On the night of 22–23 July Egyptian Army units loyal to the Free Officers occupied Army Headquarters in Cairo, the radio station, the Almaza Airport and all key communication centres. There was only token resistance and only two private soldiers lost their lives in the whole operation. By 7 a.m. Anwar al-Sadat was broadcasting a message to the people of Egypt announcing the revolution from Cairo Radio and crowds filled the streets dancing and cheering.

The capital had fallen but the king was still on his throne and because the Free Officers were convinced that Britain would intervene to keep him there they had to act swiftly. Early on the morning of 26 July tanks surrounded the Ras al-Tin Palace in Alexandria. Some of the royal guards resisted and seven were wounded in the skirmish. By this time the king was afraid for his life and he signed the act of abdication in favour of his infant son with a trembling hand. On the evening of the same day he left for Naples and exile with his young wife Narriman and his son Ahmed Fuad. Theoretically Egypt was to remain a monarchy for another eleven months but in fact the century and a half of the Mohammed Aly dynasty had come to an ignominious end.

During the day of 26 July the Free Officers' Executive Committee had urgently discussed whether Farouk should be exiled or put on trial and executed. They were divided and it was largely the influence of Abdul Nasser that swung them in favour of exile on the ground that the task of purging the country of corruption was their first priority. He wrote in a memorandum, 'We cannot execute Farouk without a trial. Neither can we afford to keep him in jail and preoccupy ourselves with the rights and wrongs of his case at the risk of neglecting the other purposes of the revolution. Let us spare Farouk and send him into exile. History will sentence him to death.'

Almost certainly an additional factor in Nasser's mind was that a trial would give time for the counter-revolutionary forces to rally. In the minds of the Free Officers these included Britain.

Farouk was of the same opinion. From the morning of 23 July he had begun urgently telephoning the American ambassador to point out that only foreign intervention could save him and his dynasty. 'Foreign intervention' at that time could only mean British. General Neguib asserts in his book *Egypt's Destiny* (p. 127) that Farouk was not satisfied with Caffery's assurances that the lives of the king and his family would be protected and that the Free Officers intercepted direct radio appeals for intervention from Farouk to the British commander in the Canal Zone. He adds that the request was referred to Eden who consulted the US secretary of state, Dean Acheson, and that it was only on being told that the US Government was totally opposed to foreign intervention under any circumstances that Britain decided not to intervene. This must remain a matter of supposition. Eden himself says that he instructed the British embassy in Cairo to inform Neguib that while we had no wish to intervene in internal affairs in Egypt, we should not hesitate to do so if we thought it necessary to protect British lives. 'For this reason we had issued instructions to our forces which would bring them to a state of readiness.'

Neguib at once gave the necessary assurance. Since the country was entirely calm and there was no sign of danger to British lives or property the question of intervention hardly arose. Farouk was so discredited that an 1882-type of operation to restore him would have daunted a more imperial-minded statesman than Eden. But if there had been a split in the Egyptian Army and fighting had lasted several days the situation would have been entirely different and the urge to intervene could have been irresistible. In 1956 Eden was to show by his actions that he regretted the lack of justification for occupying Egypt four years before.

26

REVOLUTIONARY EGYPT

In a letter to Lord Lloyd after the publication of the second volume of his *Egypt Since Cromer*, T. E. Lawrence had said: 'Of course Zaghlul was *echt*-Egyptian: it just shows how the natural leader will be of Nile blood, and not a Turk, or Albanian Pasha. First Arabi, then Zaghlul.'[1]

In July 1952 Gamal Abdul Nasser, the successor to Arabi and Zaghlul, emerged from the shadows. Few Egyptians or foreigners gave him any special notice at first. The tall, impressive but rather sombre young colonel was just one of the dozen Free Officers surrounding the smiling, avuncular · Neguib who now formed themselves into a Revolutionary Command Council with Neguib as its president. As the Free Officers had planned, the outside world looked upon the benign reassuring figure of Neguib at this stage as the true leader of the 1952 Revolution, unaware that he had had almost nothing to do with its planning or execution.

Gamal Abdul Nasser was unmistakably '*echt*-Egyptian'. Like Colonel Arabi, who was the son of a village Sheikh, he had roots in the Egyptian countryside. His father, who had been of a poor fellah family in the village of Beni Morr in Upper Egypt, had earned the primary school certificate which enabled him to enter the Egyptian white-collar class as a post office official. Nasser had been born in Alexandria and passed through secondary school to enter the military academy in 1937 after this had been opened to the sons of other than Pashas and Beys as a result of the Anglo-Egyptian 1936 Treaty.

As a student he had already shown his qualities of leadership and his passionate devotion to Egypt. He had read voraciously outside the normal school syllabus – especially history and biography (Napoleon, Alexander the Great, Julius Caesar, Gandhi, Rousseau and Voltaire) and the western classics. He also devoured the works of Egyptian and other Arab and Islamic writers and was familiar with the writings of the nineteenth-century nationalists and reformers. His reading had helped him to understand why Egypt's earlier national leaders – Arabi, Mustafa Kamel and Zaghlul – had failed in the supreme objective of ridding the country of foreign domination. In some respects his analysis of his country's ills remained naïve and over-simplified. In 1952 he had read almost nothing of economics or political theory but he had an unshakeable belief in the power of a united Egyptian people to achieve its goal with honest and determined leadership. He had the utmost faith in the innate qualities of the true Egyptians; it was the corruption of the monarchy and the political parties which had kept Egypt in servitude to foreign interests. Two goals were therefore to be pursued simultaneously – a British evacuation and the purging of Egypt's social and political life.

Immediately after taking power the Revolutionary Command Council made a momentous decision. In August 1952 it announced its willingness to separate the question of the Sudan from that of the Suez Canal Zone in negotiations with Britain, and at one stroke removed the chief obstacle to an Anglo-Egyptian agreement. The decision was sensible and statesmanlike but it was not unduly difficult. The claim to sovereignty over the Sudan had long had little more than symbolic importance and once Farouk was out of the way there was little point in maintaining it. As a member of the United Nations Egypt had already conceded the Sudanese people's right to self-determination. At the same time the Free Officers genuinely believed that when British control had been removed the majority of the Sudanese would opt for union with Egypt. In other words they thought that in accepting Sudanese independence they were calling Britain's bluff.

To some extent this belief was justified. The decision opened the way to an agreement with all Sudanese political groups including the supposedly anti-Egyptian and pro-British Umma Party. The British Government had been proceeding with plans for Sudanese self-government under a British governor-general responsible for external affairs which would have been introduced by the end of 1952 if necessary without the approval of the Egyptian Government. Under the monarchy this would undoubtedly not have been forthcoming. The pro-Egyptian Ismail al-Azhari and the Ashiqqa were in eclipse and there was every likelihood that Sudanese political life would be dominated by the Umma. Now the situation had radically changed. The Egyptians skilfully proposed a number of amendments to the British-inspired draft constitution which the Sudanese leaders could hardly refuse since they provided for more rapid Sudanization. On 10 January 1953 the four main Sudanese political parties signed an agreement with the Egyptian proposals.

Eden saw at once that Britain would have to make the best of this situation and an Anglo-Egyptian agreement on the Sudan was reached on 12 February 1953. Under this agreement the governor-general's powers were to be limited by the appointment of a three-man commission to assist him in the exercise of his powers with a Pakistani chairman and two Sudanese proposed respectively by the British and Egyptian Governments. There was to be a transition period of three years self-government at the end of which a specially elected Sudanese constituent assembly would exercise the right of self-determination in deciding whether to opt for independence or 'to link the Sudan with Egypt in any form'.

Eden was faced with some sharp criticism of the Anglo-Egyptian Agreement on the Sudan from back-bench Tory MPs and members of the cabinet, including the prime minister. ('I think that Sir Winston was influenced on this occasion by his own memories of the Sudan many years before.')[2] He succeeded in bringing them round although he appears to have had to threaten resignation.

The new Egyptian regime had reason to feel that it had scored a striking success in a field in which the experienced politicians had consistently failed; its optimism was confirmed when al-Azhari's National Unionist Party, which had campaigned for unity with Egypt, won an absolute majority in the constituent assembly in the December 1953 elections. The results came as a shock to British administrators in the Sudan who had expected the Umma Party to win. But the Egyptians also suffered from self-deception for as soon as the prospect of the ending of British rule became a reality Sudanese nationalists of all parties showed that they had no intention of replacing it with Egyptian control. Moreover the Egyptians aroused the suspicions of the Sudanese through their blatant attempts to influence the elections in their favour. Neguib, who was half Sudanese and had partly been educated in the Sudan, was the only member of the RCC who had any popular following in the Sudan and by November 1954 he had been ousted from power by Nasser.

Al-Azhari was determined to speed up the process of independence. In August 1955 the Sudanese parliament passed a resolution demanding the evacuation of both Egyptian and British forces as a preliminary to self-determination, and on 19 December it declared the independence of the Sudan. On 1 January 1956 the fifty-seven-year life of Cromer's curious brainchild, the Anglo-Egyptian Condominium of the Sudan, came to an end. For Britain it had been a fairly satisfactory arrangement; its rule had been one of the more successful examples of enlightened colonial administration although marred by the failure to pursue a consistent policy of uniting the country, including the non-Arab southern provinces, in preparation for self-government. The Sudan itself had both benefited and suffered for the same reasons. But for Egypt the Condominium had been consistently harmful. Originally conceived as a means of salving Egypt's pride, in its own semi-colonial status under British occupation, it had created an illusion of power without reality. It had not only obstructed an agreement with Britain and therefore postponed the ending of the occupation, it had also fostered the belief in Egyptian minds that only Britain was preventing the Sudanese from accepting a renewal of Egyptian hegemony.

The British Government's initial reaction to the new revolutionary regime in Egypt had been patronizing, sceptical but faintly optimistic. The British embassy in Cairo had been instructed to advise General Neguib to maintain the institution of monarchy as a stabilizing factor. The advice had not been taken but the Free Officers had shown that they could maintain public order to a degree that had not been known in Egypt for decades. The Wafdist politicians and the ex-king's cronies aroused little sympathy when they were put on trial. The land reform which the new regime introduced immediately was not only overdue but a long way from Bolshevism. Articles appeared in the British press describing Neguib as Egypt's Cromwell.

However, the foreign secretary was not especially interested in Egypt's internal development except as it affected its foreign policy and for Eden this meant its willingness to co-operate with the Western Alliance. Early in 1953 Eden set down a summary of his proposals for his colleagues:

1 A phased withdrawal of British troops from Egypt.

2 Maintenance of a military base in the Canal Zone under

conditions which would enable us and our allies to have immediate use of it in war.

3 An Anglo-Egyptian organization for the air defence of Egypt.

4 Egypt's participation in a Middle East defence organization.

5 A programme of military and economic assistance to Egypt by the United Kingdom and the United States.

Eden said that he considered all these points to be interdependent. Unmistakably he still regarded Egypt as a western protectorate in the sense that it would continue to depend upon western protection even after a British withdrawal. With the Suez Canal running through its territory Egypt could never be wholly sovereign and independent. On the other hand, Britain could afford to be more flexible in its attitude towards Egypt since it was no longer the linch-pin of its Middle Eastern strategy. The situation had been transformed by Turkey's joining NATO in the autumn of 1952. ('I admired the peasant toughness of the Turk and knew him for a loyal friend.')[3] In December 1952 the British Government decided in principle to transfer the joint armed forces HQ to Cyprus.

United States support was clearly essential for the British Government's policy towards Egypt. Eisenhower, who had just taken office as president, agreed with Eden that it was essential to maintain the base in Egypt. He was 'clear and firm on this point', but this was 'in contrast to Dulles', the secretary of state. Here was the first sign of the mutual dislike and incomprehension between Eden and Dulles which was to reach a climax in the Suez crisis three years later. The Republican administration showed itself as irritatingly sensitive to Egyptian nationalist feelings as its Democrat predecessors. Thus, although Eisenhower agreed in principle with Eden's request to send a US military representative to take part in the Anglo-Egyptian negotiations, he would only do so if the Egyptians agreed. He insisted on this point even when Eden pointed out 'that the Egyptian army would have to be equipped largely from American resources and that the Egyptians had already asked to be supplied with arms'. The Egyptian RCC refused to allow the Americans to participate on the grounds that Middle East defence as a whole could only be discussed after agreement had been reached on evacuating British troops from Egypt. With Britain refusing to concede in advance the principle of total evacuation, preliminary negotiations with the British ambassador and the commander-in-chief in the Middle East were broken off almost as soon as they had begun in May 1953.

At this point Eden was upset by the news that the US was about to make an arms delivery to Egypt. He informed Washington that he had always understood that the Americans would not contemplate the delivery of any lethal weapons 'while the political situation in Egypt and relations with us remained disturbed'. In 1953 the United States was prepared to give the new Egyptian regime the benefit of British doubt. The Free Officers had shown no sign of being pro-Soviet; if anything they were strongly anti-communist. Apart from land reform, which could have been drafted by a liberal American economist, their economic policies were orthodox and they had even repealed some of the 'Egyptian-izing' protectionist legislation of the latter years of the monarchy. There was a powerful body of opinion in the State Department (and the CIA) which accepted Jefferson Caffery's contention that, given the right encouragement, Egypt's patriotic young revolution-aries would form the most effective barrier to communism in the Middle East.

Although formal Anglo-Egyptian negotiations had been broken off in May 1953, informal contacts continued during the rest of the year. Eden was ill and away from the foreign office from May until October while Abdul Nasser, who was in charge of the negoti-ations with Britain, was concerned with consolidating his hold on the country. Yet he never forgot for one moment his overriding aim of bringing the occupation to an end and for this he was prepared to make some concessions. The British government wanted the Egyptians to concede two main points: the right to keep up to seven thousand British servicemen in the Suez base to run the existing depots and installations, and the right to re-activate the base in the event of an attack on any Middle East country. Initially Nasser conceded the second point for an attack on any Arab country but not on Turkey or Iran; eventually he compromised by agreeing to include Turkey. But on the first point – the right to keep British servicemen in Suez – Nasser was adamant. He was prepared to have British 'technicians' in civilian clothes but not soldiers in uniform who would have represented the maintenance of the occupation. The overwhelming symbolic importance of this to the Egyptians seems to have escaped the British.

As negotiations dragged on fitfully into 1954 Nasser decided to step up pressure on Britain by launching saboteurs and guerrillas again at the Canal Zone. But this time they were under the control of the army. British public opinion – especially in the Conservative Party – was becoming increasingly hostile towards the new Egyptian regime and Nasser had begun to be singled out as Britain's special *bête noire*. Anglo-Egyptian rivalry in the Sudanese elections followed by the victory of the pro-Egyptian parties had not helped matters. A strong body of Tory opinion (the Suez Group in embryo) was in favour of breaking off the negotiations and holding on to the base by force. But the armed services chiefs had already come to realize that the base would be militarily useless without Egyptian acceptance and co-operation and their advice carried the day with Eden and Churchill. Negotiations were not broken off.

Eden still considered that the Americans were 'withholding the whole-hearted support which their partner in NATO had the right to expect'.[4] In his report for 1953 the British ambassador in Cairo commented that US policy seemed to be conditioned by the belief that Egypt was still the victim of British 'colonialism', and as such deserving of American sympathy. However, Jefferson Caffery was continually urging the RCC to reach a settlement with Britain with the inducement of a promise of American aid after agreement had been reached.

On the British side both Lord Alexander, the minister of defence, and Anthony Head, the secretary of state for war, were in favour of reaching a settlement even if it meant dropping any insistence on keeping British troops in the Canal Zone. As it stood the base was fairly useless and would become more so each year. On 12 July 1954 the British Government outlined its new proposals which included an undertaking to evacuate all British troops and maintain the base on a seven-year lease with a cadre of British civilians on contract to British firms. A few days later Head led a delegation to Cairo which initialled a Heads of Agreement on 27 July. These were elaborated in a final agreement signed in Cairo on 18 October by Anthony Nutting, minister of state at the foreign office, and Colonel Nasser.

The agreement provided for the complete withdrawal of all British forces from Egypt within twenty months of its signature.

The Canal Base would be maintained by civilians but could be reactivated in the event of an attack on any Middle Eastern Arab country or Turkey. The RAF would have over-flying and landing facilities. Both parties agreed to uphold the 1888 Convention guaranteeing freedom of navigation in the Suez Canal.

At the signing of the Heads of Agreement, Nasser remarked: 'A new era of friendly relations based on mutual trust, confidence and co-operation exists between Egypt and Britain and the Western countries. . . . We want to get rid of the hatred in our hearts and start building up our relations with Britain on a solid basis of mutual trust and confidence which has been lacking for the past seventy years.'

In the House of Commons Winston Churchill was taunted by Attlee, the leader of the opposition, for supporting a withdrawal of British troops from the Canal Zone which he had so vigorously attacked when the Labour Government proposed it in 1946. Obviously nettled, Churchill could only reply that the military situation had changed. Captain Charles Waterhouse MP, leader of the 40-strong 'Suez Group' of Tory back-benchers, had no doubts about the iniquity of the agreement which he said was 'not a sell-out but a give-away'. In the Lords, the Marquess of Salisbury uneasily defended the Government's action against the strictures of Lord Hankey and the indefatigable Lord Killearn.

A thirty-six-year-old Egyptian colonel had finally succeeded, where so many others had failed, in ending the foreign occupation of Egypt. Circumstances had assisted his efforts; the worldwide movement towards decolonization combined with the depletion in Britain's military and economic strength favoured a withdrawal. But Nasser himself showed strategic and tactical skill in diplomatic bargaining remarkable in one so inexperienced. Having singled out the essential (which meant separating the Sudanese issue from that of the British occupation) he went on to assess the true balance of strength between the two parties. Provided he could gain the essence he was prepared to compromise on other seemingly important matters. Also he was not obliged to explain his actions to parliament or the palace.

There was bitter opposition to the Anglo-Egyptian Agreement of 1954 within Egypt – notably from the Muslim Brotherhood and some disgruntled politicians. They argued that, in according Britain the right of reoccupation in the event of war, the new agreement was merely an extension of the 1936 Treaty which would have expired in any case in 1956. Moreover the Wafdist Government had denounced the Treaty in 1951. Nasser replied to his critics that the 1936 Treaty made no provision for unilateral abrogation and it committed both parties to a further alliance after 1956. Since Britain was the stronger party it was clearly necessary to terminate the Treaty by mutual agreement.

On 24 October 1954 a member of the Muslim Brotherhood attempted to assassinate Nasser at a public meeting in Alexandria. He was then able to suppress the Brotherhood and confiscate the arms of its terrorist wing. The subsequent trial of the leading brothers revealed a connection between them and President Neguib. This gave Nasser the opportunity to bring his prolonged power struggle with Neguib to a head. No real evidence was produced of Neguib's complicity in the assassination plot but it was enough that he had been in contact with the Brothers and come under their influence. (One of the Brotherhood's secret pamphlets had consisted of a statement by Neguib denouncing the Anglo-Egyptian Agreement.) On 14 November Neguib was removed from the residency and placed under restriction in his house in the suburbs of Cairo.

Nasser was now undisputed master of Egypt and in a position to silence opposition to the agreement with Britain. As the British troops began visibly to withdraw it became increasingly difficult to oppose on patriotic grounds an agreement which had achieved this result. On 31 March 1956, at least three months earlier than was provided in the agreement, the 2nd Battalion of the Grenadier Guards and D Squadron of the Life Guards embarked at Port Said and there were no more British soldiers on Egyptian soil. *The Times* correspondent wrote on 2 April 1956: 'Their departure was almost as silent and devoid of ceremony as presumably was the nocturnal disembarkation of General Wolseley's forces which captured Port Said 74 years ago.'

27

TWO NATIONS

Since this is intended to be an account of three-quarters of a century of British hegemony in Egypt, the brief and abortive Anglo-French invasion of 1956 hardly comes within its scope. British troops remained barely six weeks in Port Said before they were ignominiously withdrawn under world pressure. The only influence their presence had on the internal situation in Egypt was immensely to increase the strength and prestige of the regime. The consequences were the loss of Britain's rights under the 1954 agreement and the equipment and stores in the Canal Zone, the expulsion of all British subjects (some of whom had lived in Egypt for decades) and the Egyptianization of most of the still considerable British economic assets in Egypt. Doubtless all these would have happened within a few years even if there had been no Suez invasion but they would have been less abrupt and painful in their effect.

Nevertheless this dishonourable episode in modern British history is relevant in the light it throws on British attitudes towards Egypt. How was it that Eden, with his justified reputation for cool-headed international diplomacy, could have been driven to a pitch of anti-Egyptian hysteria which bordered on insanity? ("'But I don't want an alternative," [to destroying Nasser] Eden shouted at me. "And I don't give a damn if there's anarchy and chaos in Egypt.")[1]

A vain and sensitive man, Eden had suffered from criticisms of his alleged lack of firmness. As Churchill's successor to the premiership his position was difficult because the public compared him with Winston as he was in the war years rather than in the last months before his overdue retirement. Eden had an urgent need to show that he too could take command in a storm; it was almost as if he needed a dictator to defy.

But this provides only part of the explanation. He might contend that Nasser was to Russia what Mussolini had been to Hitler, and that 'Russia was the real danger in the Middle East',[2] but this was only a rationalization of his unbridled hatred of the young Egyptian leader. The true nature of his feeling is revealed in his angry outburst to Anthony Nutting: 'But what's all this nonsense about isolating Nasser of "neutralizing" him, as you call it? I want him destroyed, can't you understand?'[3]

Apart from its assumption that a British prime minister may order the elimination of an Egyptian president, the significance of this remark is that it was made several months before the nationalization of the Suez Canal. Relations between Britain and Egypt had already deteriorated sharply since the false dawn of the 1954 agreement. The Eden government had numerous grievances against Nasser's Egypt: first the challenge in the Sudan, then its wider support for anti-colonial movements throughout Africa and finally the outspoken opposition to Britain's plans for an anti-Soviet Middle East Defence Organization – the Baghdad Pact. Because it was militarily weak, Egypt used other weapons in its anti-British campaign – notably the newly-established Voice of the Arabs radio station which poured out a colourful stream of anti-imperialist invective. Much of it was highly unscrupulous in detail but it struck a responsive chord in the deep-seated resentment against the old colonial powers among the Arab masses. Eden had come to believe that every sign of hostility towards Britain, whether it was the dismissal of Glubb Pasha, the Commander of the Arab Legion (the immediate cause of the outburst quoted above) or an anti-British demonstration in Bahrain, had been instigated by Nasser. Even when he was presented with evidence that this was not so he refused to believe it.

Eden had never been a member of the Suez Group in the House of Commons; in 1954 he had skilfully neutralized their opposition to the Anglo-Egyptian agreements on the Sudan and the Suez Base. He would have regarded Lord Hinchingbrooke MP's contention that 'The Suez Canal and the area surrounding it are in some essential sense part of the United Kingdom' as an exaggeration. In his view, if the Egyptians churlishly refused to have anything to do with a pro-Western Middle East defence alliance that was their misfortune; they would merely be isolated. But what Eden could not tolerate under any circumstances was that Egypt should presume to pursue its opposition to British interests outside its own borders and within a sphere of traditional British influence.

A remark of Abdul Nasser's provides a partial explanation of Eden's attitude. He said of the only occasion that they met that Eden gave the impression 'he was talking to a junior official who could not be expected to understand international politics'.

The truth is that of all Cromer's 'subject races' the Egyptians were the most despised. Cromer held the view which was shared by nearly all his colleagues that in Egypt only the Turco-Egyptian Pasha retained the traces of governing capacity. ('The glamour of a dominant race still hovers as an aureole, albeit a very dimmed aureole, round his head.')⁴ This class had been gradually eliminated from power and the idea that the 'pure Egyptian' who now controlled Egypt should remain content with a permanently subordinate position in the world underlay all British thinking. This helps to explain the degree of British hostility towards Nasser which bears no comparison with that towards other nationalist leaders, from Nehru to Nkrumah, who have challenged British authority. The clash was the more inevitable because Nasser himself, as a deeply patriotic Egyptian, held the view that the Egyptian people have inherited the qualities of the men who built the Great Pyramids.

As we have seen, Cromer and Kitchener, were both much concerned with the welfare of the fellahin and their attitude was shared by most of the Anglo-Egyptian officials. It was the city-bred *effendi* or Gallicized Egyptian they could not tolerate. This attitude is reflected in countless memoirs of the heyday of British rule in Egypt. The most memorable of these, because the best written, is Lord Edward Cecil's *The Leisure of an Egyptian Official*. Most of it consists of humorous sketches that he wrote for his family about his life and work as financial adviser to the Egyptian government in the years before the First World War which is why it is much more revealing of the British attitude than any considered study of Anglo-Egyptian relations.

In the 1890s Lord Edward Cecil had the reputation of being the wittiest Englishman in Dublin. *The Leisure of an Egyptian Official* is often hilarious and brilliantly satirical, it is also nasty, snobbish and racialistic. In his active social life Cecil seems to have mixed exclusively with other British (and an occasional Frenchmen) but his work obliged him to associate with Egyptians. These are variously described as dirty, obsequious and dishonest. The only one for whom he shows any liking is the 'minister of arts and crafts': 'personally, I have a sneaking affection for him, as he has the rough, rather jolly way of the peasant, which contrasts very favourably with the oily snake-like manner of the town-bred Egyptians, and he has a sense of humour of an elementary kind'. This supercilious comment is the most favourable that Cecil could muster for the people among whom he worked for most of his active life.

It may be said the Cecil has as much fun at the expense of other races (especially the Americans) but it is not the same; at least he includes them in his own species, which he hardly does for Egyptians. Significantly, in describing his fellow-countrymen, he reserves his heaviest contempt for visiting radicals who sympathize with Egyptian nationalism or a few earnest young Anglo-Egyptian officials who are attempting to understand the Egyptian way of life. An even less favourable view of the Egyptians was taken by Ethel Smyth, eccentric, composer and militant suffragette who spent the winter of 1913–14 in the Tewfik Palace Hotel at Helwan near Cairo. In the short intervals between writing her comic opera *The Boatswain's Mate*, playing golf and writing passionate letters to Emmeline Pankhurst she found time to reach some conclusions about the Egyptian character which she recorded years later in an autobiographical fragment 'Egypt Before England's Exodus'. 'I think I said that when first I arrived in Egypt my ideas as to what the Anglo-Saxon angle towards "subject races" ought to be were rather in a state of flux – result, I suppose, of Suffrage associations. . . . In a word, it is ridiculous to apply western democratic notions to a people so brutish, so insensitive, so mentally deficient as the Egyptians.' She could not understand why her friend Ronald Storrs did not accept what she regarded as self-evident: that the Egyptians only interpreted kindness as weakness. She attributed it to his own 'kindly, even tender, nature'.[5]

Ethel Smyth's dislike was partly motivated by the inferior status of Egyptian women which revolted the champion of female equality who greatly preferred her own sex.*

---

* Her humour improved on a brief trip to the Sudan, where she found the Sudanese 'thoroughbred, and though (or should one say "because"?) untouched by civilization, have great dignity and beautiful manners'. She was introduced to a young hermaphrodite camel-breeder who had been married briefly to a tribal sheikh but was now known as Mohammed. She was allowed to photograph Mohammed in the nude in her cabin on

Indeed the seclusion of Muslim women was one of the important reasons for the social *apartheid* between the races and explains why when the barriers were crossed it was mainly by Egyptian Copts, Jews and Levantines. But even they did not find it easy. Dr Faris Nimr, a Syrian-born Christian Arab who was one of the most enthusiastic supporters of Cromer and the English occupation, attributed the unrest at the end of Cromer's rule in Egypt to English social exclusiveness. 'The English are the ruling nation, and the best Egyptian natives, highly educated by school and travel, naturally associate with them. They find the French and other residents fairly sociable, they drive out with them, they meet them in cafés and in social life. But the English mix mostly with one another.'[6] Dr Nimr's family ultimately surmounted the barrier when one of the daughters married Sir Walter Smart, Oriental Counsellor at the British Embassy. But this was years later when racial attitudes were slowly softening. Before the First World War, Anglo-Saxon arrogance was at its height. A. B. de Guerville, a French travel writer who spent the winter season of 1905–6 in Egypt and Sudan, records that English residents in Egypt (although not officials) referred to Egyptians, Greeks, Turks and Armenians equally as niggers. 'I am not joking, and extraordinary as it may seem, Englishmen, intelligent, educated and charming, will speak of a Greek as "that black man" or "that nigger". And there is no way of changing them.'

The extreme social exclusiveness of the English in Egypt had long been a subject of observation.

As early as 1842 the French poet Gerard de Nerval, who spent several months in Mohammed Aly's Cairo where he plunged himself into the main stream of Egyptian life complained of 'those gentlemen, always hatted and gloved, who dare not mix with the people to observe some curious detail such as a danse or ceremony, who would be afraid to be seen in a café or a tavern, to follow a woman or even to fraternize with a friendly Arab who cordially offers you the mouth of his long pipe or a cup of coffee when he sees you have stopped out of curiosity or fatigue. Above all it is the English who are perfect and they never fail to cause me

the boat and 'moved by the compassion I always feel for women who have been up against the prejudices of their world . . . what did I do but embrace Mohammed'. To her bitter disappointment the photographs were a total failure.

the greatest amusement. Imagine a gentleman seated on a donkey with his long legs almost reaching the ground. His round hat is covered with a thick piece of white cotton; an invention which is supposed to protect him against the sun by absorbing its rays. On his eyes he has something like two nutshells with blue steel shades to counteract the glare from the sun and walls; on top of all this he wears a green woman's veil against the dust. His rubber overcoat has yet another covering of waxed cloth as protection against the plague and contact with passers-by. His gloved hands carry a long stick to fend off any suspicious-looking Arab and normally he never goes out without his groom and dragoman on either side'.[7]

There were exceptions of course. The admirable Lucie Duff Gordon, who in the 1860s spent the last seven years of her life in Egypt in a vain attempt to recover from tuberculosis, did all she could to know and understand the Egyptians as human beings. But she could not help observing the different attitude of most of her fellow-countrymen.

When her cousin Harriet Martineau published a book on Egypt it was crammed with statistics but barely mentioned the Egyptians. Lady Duff Gordon commented: 'The people are not real people, only part of the scenery to her, as to most Europeans. She evidently had the feeling of most people here that the difference of manners are a sort of impassable gulf, the truth being that their feelings and passions are just like our own.'

Under the British occupation when the Englishmen in Egypt were not only tourists but administrators, the situation barely changed. Cromer, Gorst and Kitchener invited prominent Egyptians to official receptions at the agency but there were scores of English families who devoted the best years of their lives to the Egyptian service and saw nothing surprising in the fact that their servants were the only Egyptians to have entered their villas in Zamalek or Maadi. Wilfrid Blunt, who was an exception, was regarded as an eccentric *poseur*.

W. Basil Worsfold, an observant literary barrister who visited Egypt in the winter of 1898–9 remarked that: 'The English residents have no more to do with the picturesque ruins and mud-heaps of Medieval Cairo than the average West End Londoner has to do with the Mile End Road and Tower Hamlets.'[8] Except when they wanted to show a visitor the tombs of the Khalifs or the

Pyramids they only left their villas in the European quarter to drive
to their offices or the Gezira Club. The hot weather was regarded
as intolerable for Englishwomen and children and they were
dispatched home from May to November. Their husbands normally had a summer leave every second year; those that stayed
behind became even more dependent on their clubs.

The long periods of separation from their wives raises the question of the celibacy of the Anglo-Egyptian officials. Did they form
liaisons with 'native girls' as their pre-Victorian grandfathers or
their contemporary equivalents in French colonies would have
done? Gerard de Nerval went so far as to buy himself a Javanese
girl in the Cairo slave-market although he came to regret his action
because she expected him to employ servants to look after her.
The reticence of English published memoirs of the veiled protectorate makes assertion difficult but it is reasonably certain that
any open relationship between an Anglo-Egyptian official and an
Egyptian would have been frowned upon by the agency and a sure
barrier to his promotion. The same did not of course apply to the
tourist visitors.

We know that already by the turn of the century Cairo and
Alexandria had a reputation for offering pleasures that were
more varied and exotic but also cheaper and more easily available
than at home. Sydney A. Moseley who edited two newspapers in
Cairo during Kitchener's regime wrote an astringent little book
on his experiences entitled *With Kitchener in Cairo*.* Remarking
that the Wigh el-Birka brothel quarter was 'not three minutes
from two of Cairo's largest hotels' he says that a certain type of
tourist seemed to go to Cairo simply to enjoy these disreputable
scenes. According to Russell Pasha, a stroll through the narrow
and crowded lanes of this quarter 'reminded one of a zoo, with its
painted harlots sitting like beasts of prey behind the iron grilles
of their ground-floor brothels, while a noisy crowd of low-class
natives, interspersed with soldiers in uniform and sight-seeing
tourists, made their way along the narrow lanes.'[9] Nearby were
the famous Cairo music-halls of which Moseley also complains.
'There was nowhere in Cairo where one might take a lady without
affronting her modesty. The kind of veiled – and often unveiled –
indecency is no stranger in music halls in England, but it must be

* Kitchener was not amused and set up a revising committee which
tried unsuccessfully to make substantial changes in the manuscript.

admitted that Cairo went a shade or two farther. This low kind of cosmopolitan continentalism ought to be got rid of now we are in full control in Egypt. Englishmen in the audience, as I have said, did not set much of an example.'[10] It was not only the tourists who took advantage of Cairo's facilities. Moseley who seems to have visited such places regularly (presumably alone) points out that some of the worst exhibitions of misbehaviour were by men 'whose public position should have been a guarantee of their good behaviour'. There was not even the excuse, as there was in India, that a class of Europeans of a 'lower social grade' than the men who formerly came out to mercantile houses and other business establishments had been imported. These were not of this grade and if they had been they would have been dealt with by the authorities.

In one sense it was the wealthy tourists wintering in Egypt who made the most direct contact with the native population. A. B. de Guerville,[11] remarked that there was something in the air of Egypt which seemed to excite almost everyone and 'which almost maddens certain natures, especially of the weaker sex'. Young foreign girls had a pronounced weakness for the Egyptian. which sometimes led to a striking disregard for convention. One young Egyptian 'glib of tongue and an excellent dancer' confided to de Guerville that he and his friends found that foreign girls threw themselves at their heads. 'Several of us, for sport, formed a society which we called the "terrassiers" because we "did" the terraces of the various hotels: but it was no use, we had to give it up; no constitution could stand the success which crowned our efforts.'

De Guerville asserts that the adventures of these well-born young Egyptians were nothing compared with those of the dragomans (the tourist guides and interpreters) 'these splendid men, built like Hercules, strong as houses, and so picturesque in their native costume'. His testimony is born out by Captain Nelken y Waldberg who spent three years in Egypt at this period as editor of *La Bourse* and *Le Petit Journal Egyptian*. He remarks that the most successful were the guides at the Giza Pyramids. One very wealthy young English lady rented a house near the Pyramids for seven months one winter so that she could have one guide all to herself. A fair number of male foreigners had similar interests and in Egypt they found a congenial and tolerant atmosphere. When the homosexual scandals involving the Kaiser's adviser Prince Eulenbourg broke in 1906 the reaction in the fashionable Cairo Automobile Club was one of astonishment that the Germans should make such a fuss over something so natural – especially when it concerned a prince. It was generally agreed that article 175 of the German penal code, under which the Prince was charged, would have little success in Egypt and some European members of the Automobile Club even suggested that contravention of Article 175 should be a condition of entry. One young Frenchman remarked to Captain Nelken 'In Paris we have the Palmyra and Moritz Bars but you are much better off in Egypt, you have dahabiehs (houseboats) picturesquely anchored on the Nile.'[12]

This type of contact between the tourists and the native population hardly added much to their understanding and knowledge of Egypt (even, if we are to believe Captain Nelken, it resulted in a certain degree of mixing of the races). The English did not form the majority of tourists, they were outnumbered by Americans, Germans, French and other Europeans. Thomas Cook might have a monopoly on excursions to Upper Egypt and his steamers transported Kitchener's Army up the Nile to subdue the Sudan but the principal Cairo hotels – Shepheard's, the Gezira Palace and the Savoy – were managed by Swiss and Central Europeans and their atmosphere was cosmopolitan. Tourists were heavily occupied with their social activities or 'kodaking' (Edwardian slang) the fabulous ruins of Ancient Egypt.

One problem was a simple failure of communication. Cromer himself knew no more than a dozen words of Arabic after twenty-five years in Egypt. He had some Turkish because that was the language of Egypt's traditional governing class; Arabic was the language of servants.* Thus the concept of the romantic and aristocratic Arab Sheikh beloved of English Arabists did not apply to Egypt. T. E. Lawrence was one more Englishman who never

---

* W. Basil Worsfold observed in 1899 that the lack of knowledge of Arabic among English residents was one of the reasons for their belief that the Egyptians made very bad servants. The English gave orders that the native servants were too polite or timid to admit they did not understand. However, Worsfold expressed optimism that the increasing amount of education provided for Egyptian girls in the mosque schools would eventually provide 'a new and more reliable class of servants'. (*The Redemption of Egypt*, p. 195.)

concealed his dislike or contempt for Egyptians. 'Those Egyptians are such worms (though they can dig)' he wrote summarizing his attitude after employing some fellahin on an archaeological excavation in 1912.[13] His views did not mellow with time. When Robert Graves was offered the post of Professor of English Literature at Cairo University in 1925, he wrote to his friend T. E. Lawrence for advice and an estimate of the fellahin. Lawrence replied, 'Egypt, being so near Europe, is not a savage country. The Egyptians are very bestial, very savage: but you need not dwell among them. Indeed it will be a miracle if an Englishman can get to know them.'[14]

Anglo-Egyptian officials, on the other hand, had no time for the bedouin who lived in the Egyptian deserts and on the fringes of the Nile valley and who until recent times were usually referred to as Arabs in contrast to the Egyptians who were not regarded as Arabs at all. The bedouin were considered to be the real source of lawlessness in the countryside which so plagued the British authorities in Egypt. Judge Marshall expressed a typical view in a memorandum to Kitchener in 1912: 'The tent-dwelling Arab in Egypt is a loafer of the very worst class. Treacherous and vindictive, with a dislike to honest work amounting to aversion, he should be summarily dealt with, and treated in the same way that America has treated her Red Indians – put on a reservation out of which he could not emerge without being shot on sight. These Bedouin are responsible agents of all the smugglers who import hasheesh, arms and gunpowder into the country.'[15]

In contrast, the mass of the Egyptian people were regarded as simple, downtrodden and gullible and therefore in need of constant protection against unscrupulous political agitators. Because the fellahin had been oppressed and exploited for much longer than any living memory they welcomed the relatively honest and enlightened administration of the British in the early years of the occupation even if there was a lack of any real comprehension between the two races.

The British from Cromer downwards were so certain of their knowledge of the characteristics of the 'subject race' they assumed that the acquisition of a 'governing capacity' was well beyond the desires and abilities of the Egyptians. As the assumption of superiority of the members of the master race no longer needed proof, but was taken for granted, it inevitably influenced their character and behaviour. The moral climate of the occupation deteriorated. In a remarkable chapter of his *With Kitchener in Cairo* (published in 1917) Sydney A. Moseley considers 'Why the Englishman is Disliked?'[16] He suggested that the fault lay on both sides. On the one hand the British had been unwise in their choice of civil servants in Egypt. 'We appear,' he says, 'to have been at pains to send our snobs to Egypt.' Too many of the British officials were tactless, narrow-minded, bumptious and stand-offish towards the Egyptians. On the other hand, the 'educated complaining Egyptian official' should admit that his people were still too deferential in their attitude. 'The Egyptian is passing through a state of transition which has not altogether thrown off the unattractive and unhealthy characteristics of the past. No liberated subject race can at once possess that frank, open manly attitude born of freedom and fearlessness.'

Moseley illustrates his thesis with a striking anecdote. 'A friend of mine, a type of our officials in Cairo, in other respects quite a decent, polished, Englishman, took me along with him in the side-car of his 4-hp motor-cycle to the Pyramids. He was out to break records, and incidentally any obstacle that interfered with this object. The policemen on the road were, as they usually are to Europeans and especially Englishmen, quite humble, and fearful of this Englishman on his tearing motor-cycle. (If it had been one of his own race!) Coming back from this record-breaking journey, I noticed a little half-naked boy on an obstinate donkey, riding near the middle of the road. We passed him by merely swerving to the right a little. Then my friend slowed down.

"Why?" I asked.

In answer he called a policeman whom he had espied.

"Take that boy to the *caracol*,"* he commanded.

The lad, scenting danger, had veered the donkey round and tried to make off.

"My good fellow leave him!" I protested.

But my friend took the policeman's number, and that frightened individual set off on a trot after the unfortunate lad.

"You see," explained my friend triumphantly, "the policeman knows I have his number, and if he doesn't arrest the boy he'll catch it himself, I've had four this week."

* Police station.

"And what will they do to the wretched lad? Execute him?" I asked despairingly.

"Oh, they'll impound his donkey for three or four days."

"His sole means of livelihood—"

"Serves him right for getting in the road." '

Moseley concluded that 'the cringing and abjectness of the native have transformed many responsible Britons in Egypt from masters tolerant towards their inferiors into the kind of tyrant who recalls Egypt's darkest history'.

The testimony of Sydney Moseley, like that of Dr Faris Nimr, is the more valuable because he was no opponent of the British occupation. On the contrary he believed that both Cromer and Kitchener, despite the grudge he bore the latter for trying to have his book censored, had brought immense benefits to Egypt. It was not British policy that was wrong but 'the crass stupidity and overwhelming conceit – which always go together – of individual officials'.

As Britain relaxed its hold on Egypt's administration and British officials no longer manifestly formed the governing class, the opportunities for mutual comprehension between the races increased. If few of these opportunities were taken it was partly due to 'the increasing political friction between a resurgent Egyptian nationalism and what Britain still regarded as its imperial interests and partly to the ancient barriers of religion, culture and social mores. A small English-educated Egyptian elite existed but they were almost totally alienated from their own people. The soul of Egypt remained a mystery for the British.

Relations between the ordinary British soldier stationed in Egypt and the Cairo underworld with which was his chief point of contact with the country were friendly as far as they went. We have already mentioned the Wigh el-Birka quarter which Russell Pasha attempted to clean up, with only limited success, during the First World War. Walter Tyndale, a distinguished Edwardian water-colourist who was a frequent and observant visitor to Egypt, remarked that 'Tommy Atkins' not only spent his money more freely than the Levantine but he was a jolly fellow and 'a bit of rough fun appeals to the lower orders in Cairo'. He was more doubtful whether Cairo was conducive to the soldiers' morals. In the late evening a common sight in the drinking shops of the Ezbekiyeh quarter was a Tommy filled with several glasses of

1 spirit brewed by the Levantine landlord singing to an admiring Egyptian crowd some mawkishly sentimental song from the London music-halls such as 'The soldier dropt a tear'.[17]

Mutual tolerance and good humour of this kind were valuable but their long-term influence on Anglo-Egyptian relations was as negligible as the wealthy Edwardian lady's liaison with her dragoman. All the evidence from the past is supported by the testimony of one of the most prominent contemporary Egyptians. Writing in the *Sunday Times* (10 September 1967) Abdul Nasser's close friend and confidant, Mohammed Hassanein Heykal, pointed out that throughout the British occupation of Egypt the two nations never mixed. 'There were Englishmen who devoted their lives to Egypt but their interest was in things rather than people (such men were Professor Creswell, the great scholar of Muslim architecture, or H. E. Hurst who wrote the classic work on the River Nile). Only some of the schools and universities really knew and understood the Egyptians, while some of our boys who went as students to England came back with a true idea of what it was like.

'In the Second World War about two or three million troops spent some time in Egypt but this still did not bring our two nations any closer. The ordinary soldiers mixed with the lowest elements: shoe-shiners, pimps, pickpockets, belly dancers and bartenders who formed their idea of the *Gyppo*. On the other hand, officers met only the Circassian Turkish upper class, the circles connected with the royal family and centred on the Gezira Club – a cosmopolitan society isolated from the real Egypt. No British soldier ever entered an Egyptian home and our two nations never met.'

Yet it is possible to see now that the self-imposed limits to Britain's penetration of Egypt have one tremendous advantage. No attempt at cultural colonization, which would have certainly been disastrous, was ever attempted.

Under the British occupation Egypt's personality may have been crushed but it was not destroyed. Cromer's view, which was shared by most other Englishmen in Egypt, was that Britain's role was restricted to keeping the Egyptian inn on the British imperial highroad to India clean and orderly. It should make a profit, the servants must be well treated and the senior staff should be British; but there was no question of transforming it into an all-British hotel. Equally, they believed that the day when it could be transferred to purely Egyptian management was so remote as hardly to be worth considering.

Cromer, of course, took it for granted that the imperial race would be ruling for several more centuries. In 1970 it is possible to forget that as recently as the Second World War men like Winston Churchill and Lord Lloyd assumed the British Empire (and above all British possession of India) to be permanent and therefore rejected all possibility of Egypt acquiring full sovereignty over its territory. Yet because the British in Egypt kept aloof and made no serious attempt to transform the structure of Egyptian society,* the Egyptians were more able to respect the qualities for which they could be admired: their integrity, honesty and sense of justice – even their love of taking exercise – which were in sharp contrast to their previous alien rulers. The British may not have been very human but they were generally humane. That the Denshawai affair was regarded with such horror was in a sense a tribute to the physical mildness of the occupation. All this helps to explain Tom Little's wise observation, that 'the Egyptians are by temperament pro-British and by political conviction deeply against Britain'. The occupation did produce a small fringe of pipe-smoking blazered pseudo-Englishmen comparable to the Etonian Indian princes, but the vast majority of Egyptians never lost their identity. Consequently they did not have to rediscover it after independence as so many black and brown Frenchmen have been obliged to do.

Britain's troubled relations with Egypt over the past century have sometimes been compared with the Anglo-Irish problem, and there are many points of similarity in their emotional impact and the sorry tale of lost opportunities for reconciliation. There were several occasions between 1880 and 1922 when the British Cabinet was discussing the two questions simultaneously and appears to have had them confused. Yet, fortunately for anyone who loves both England and Egypt, the two problems were essentially different. In contrast to Ireland, religious differences were not seriously involved. Because Cromer and Brunyate's proposals for giving the non-Egyptian communities an established political dominance were not implemented, Britain never found itself in

* A task for which most of them were unequipped. As we have seen, Cromer knew no more than a dozen words of Arabic after twenty-five years in Egypt.

the disastrous position of supporting a racial and religious minority against the indigenous majority, while the Egyptians did not have to fight against the control of a foreign settler community. The Anglo-Egyptian problem is dead whereas the Anglo-Irish problem is still thriving.

There are grounds for hoping that as the incidents of the political struggle between the two nations recede into time, the positive aspects of the British occupation will be recalled. Egyptians may acknowledge that it was the best of the Anglo-Egyptian administrators, engineers, teachers and doctors who challenged Egypt to prove that it could provide its own. For Britain's part there are already encouraging signs that recognition of some of independent Egypt's achievements is dissolving that racial contempt which is as morally corrupting for those who show it as it is galling for those who are its object.

REFERENCES

Foreword

1 Tom Little, *Egypt*, London 1958, p. 56.

Chapter 1 The Roadside Inn

1 Remusat, Comtesse de, *Mémoires*, Paris 1893, **I**, p. 274.
2 A. W. Kinglake, *Eothen*, London 1896, p. 286.
3 *Les Lettres de Gustave Flaubert*, Paris 1965, p. 175.
4 J. H. Rose, *Life of Napoleon*, London 1902, **I**, p. 181.
5 A. E. M. Ashley, *Life and Correspondence of Palmerston*, London 1879, p. 338.

Chapter 2 The Arabi Revolt

1 *Khedives and Pashas, by one who knows them well* (C. F. M. Bell), London 1884, p. 166.
2 Cromer, *Modern Egypt*, London 1908, **I**, p. 179.
3 Cromer, *Modern Egypt*, **I**, p. 183.
4 Cromer, *Modern Egypt*, **I**, p. 186.
5 W. S. Blunt, *Secret History of the English Occupation of Egypt*, London 1907, p. 153.
6 Robinson, Gallagher and Denny, *Africa and the Victorians*, London 1961, p. 95.
7 Cromer, *Modern Egypt*, **I**, p. 203.
8 Cromer, *Modern Egypt*, **I**, p. 218.
9 Blunt, *Secret History*, p. 127.
10 Blunt, *Secret History*, p. 129.
11 Robinson, Gallagher and Denny, *Africa and the Victorians*, p. 97.
12 Blunt, *Secret History*, p. 144.
13 Cromer, *Modern Egypt*, **I**, p. 237.
14 Blunt, *Secret History*, p. 180.
15 Afaf Lutfi al-Sayyid, *Egypt and Cromer*, London 1968, p. 16.
16 Cromer, *Modern Egypt*, **I**, p. 226.
17 Gwynn and Tuckwell, *The Life of the Rt. Hon. Sir Charles E. Dilke*, London 1917, **I**, p. 459.

Chapter 3 Ultimatum and Invasion

1 Theodore Rothstein, *Egypt's Ruin*, London 1910, p. 215.
2 Lutfi al-Sayyid, *Egypt and Cromer*, p. 25.
3 De Freycinet, *La Question d'Egypte*, Paris 1904, p. 281.
4 A. M. Broadley, *How We Defended Arabi*, London 1884, p. 124.
5 Blunt, *Secret History*, p. 282.
6 Blunt, *Secret History*, p. 296.
7 C. Royle, *The Egyptian Campaigns 1882–5*, London 1900, p. 321.

Chapter 4 Lord Dufferin's Mission

1 Broadley, *How We Defended Arabi*, p. 322.
2 Blunt, *Gordon at Khartoum*, London 1911, p. 9.
3 D. M. Wallace, *Egypt and the Egyptian Question*, London 1883, p. 379.
4 Broadley, *How We Defended Arabi*, p. 488.
5 Cromer, *Modern Egypt*, I, p. 356.

Chapter 5 Baring in Command

1 Zetland, *Lord Cromer*, London 1932, p. 21.
2 H. D. Traill, *Lord Cromer*, London 1897, p. 343.
3 Traill, *Cromer*, p. 345.
4 William Willcocks, *Sixty Years in the East*, London 1935, p. 116.
5 Rennell Rodd, *Social and Diplomatic Memories 1894–1901*, London 1922–5, p. 6.
6 Rodd, *Memories*, p. 19.
7 Lytton Strachey, *Eminent Victorians*, London 1920, p. 278.
8 Rodd, *Memories*, p. 16.
9 Clara Boyle, *Boyle of Cairo*, Kendal 1965, p. 23.

Chapter 6 Sudanese Disaster

1 P. M. Holt, *A Modern History of the Sudan*, London 1963, p. 77.
2 Cromer, *Modern Egypt*, I, p. 423.
3 Cromer, *Modern Egypt*, I, p. 428.
4 Anthony Nutting, *Gordon: Martyr and Misfit*, London 1966, p. 253.
5 Philip Magnus, *Kitchener*, London 1958, p. 128.
6 Holt, *Modern History of Sudan*, p. 114.

Chapter 7 1883–1892

1 Cromer, *Modern Egypt*, **II**, p. 417.
2 Cromer *Modern Egypt*, **II**, p. 351.
3 Mary Hollings, *Life of Sir Colin A. Scott-Moncrieff*, London 1917 pp. 176–7.
4 Cromer, *Modern Egypt*, **II**, p. 340.
5 Blunt, *My Diaries*, London 1919, **I**, p. 54.
6 Blunt, *Gordon at Khartoum*, p. 56.
7 Zetland, *Lord Cromer*, p. 164.
8 D'Abernon, *Portraits and Appreciations*, London 1931, p. 22.
9 Cromer, *Modern Egypt*, **II**, p. 131.

Chapter 8 Restoring Egypt's Credit

1 *St Antony's Papers* No. 17, Middle East Affairs No. 4.
2 Auckland Colvin, *Making of Modern Egypt*, London 1906, pp. 136–7.
3 Willcocks, *Sixty Years in the East*, p. 89.
4 Cromer, *Modern Egypt*, **II**, p. 448.
5 Cromer, *Modern Egypt*, **II**, p. 447.

Chapter 9 Economic Strategy

1 Charles Issawi, *Egypt at Mid-Century*, London 1954, p. 31.
2 Anouar Abdel-Malek, *Egypte: Société Militaire*, Paris 1962, p. 21.
3 Cromer, *Modern Egypt*, **II**, p. 451.
4 Issawi, *Egypt at Mid-Century*, p. 34.

Chapter 10 The Water Engineers

1 Milner, *England in Egypt*, London 1892, p. 289.
2 Hollings, *Scott-Moncrieff*, p. 201.
3 Hollings, *Scott-Moncrieff*, p. 177.
4 Willcocks, *Sixty Years in the East*, p. 115.

Chapter 11 Law and Order

1 Colvin, *Making of Modern Egypt*, p. 193.
2 Cromer, *Modern Egypt*, **II**, p. 397.
3 Rothstein, *Egypt's Ruin*, p. 284.
4 Cromer, *Modern Egypt*, **II**, p. 404.
5 See J. N. D. Anderson, 'Law Reform in Egypt 1850–1950' in Holt, *Political and Social Change in Modern Egypt*, London 1968.
6 Cromer, *Modern Egypt*, **II**, p. 420.

Chapter 12 Sirdars and Soldiers

1 Cromer, *Modern Egypt*, **II**, p. 473.
2 Milner, *England in Egypt*, p. 172.
3 Milner, *England in Egypt*, p. 182.

Chapter 13 The Neglect of Education

1 See G. A. L. Lloyd, *Egypt After Cromer*, London 1933–4 and Valentine Chirol, *The Egyptian Problem*, London 1921.
2 Cromer, *Speeches 1882–1911*, **I**, p. 377.
3 Cromer, *Speeches*, **I**, p. 128.
4 Cromer, *Modern Egypt*, **II**, p. 538.
5 Cromer, *Modern Egypt*, **II**, p. 542.

Chapter 14 The Royal Rebel

1 Blunt, *My Diaries*, **I**, p. 79.
2 Cromer, *Abbas II*, London 1915, p. 9.
3 Cromer, *Abbas II*, p. 26.
4 Cromer, *Abbas II*, pp. 152–3.
5 Blunt, *My Diaries*, **II**, p. 37.
6 See Lutfi al-Sayyid, *Egypt and Cromer*, p. 125. Milner Papers, Milner to Dawkins 18 February 1895.

Chapter 15 Nationalist Renaissance

1 Issawi, *Egypt at Mid-Century*, p. 43.
2 J. E. Marshall, *The Egyptian Enigma*, London 1928, p. 83.
3 Grey of Fallodon, *Twenty-five Years*, London 1925, **I**, p. 224.

Chapter 16 Cromer Bows Out

1 Cromer, *Abbas II*, p. x.
2 A. H. Sayce, *Reminiscences*, London 1923, p. 286.
3 Blunt, *My Diaries*, **I**, p. 245.
4 Quoted by Afaf Lutfi al-Sayyid in her *Egypt and Cromer*, p. 141.
5 Ronald Storrs, *Orientations*, London 1937, p. 79.

Chapter 17 Gorst's Liberal Experiment

1 Boyle, *Boyle of Cairo*, p. 157.
2 P. G. Elgood, *Transit of Egypt*, London 1928, p. 185.

3 Boyle, *Boyle of Cairo*, p. 157.
4 Egypt No. 1, 1911.
5 Hansard, 13 June 1910.
6 Storrs, *Orientations*, p. 90.

Chapter 18 *Return of the Sirdar*

1 Magnus, *Kitchener*, p. 259.
2 Magnus, *Kitchener*, p. 263.
3 Magnus, *Kitchener*, p. 268.
4 Quoted by Jamal Mohammed Ahmed in *The Intellectual Origins of Egyptian Nationalism*, London 1960, p. 85.
5 Annual Report, 28 March 1914.
6 Sayce, *Reminiscences*, p. 407.

Chapter 19 *The Great War*

1 Storrs, *Orientations*, p. 154.
2 P. G. Elgood, *Egypt and the Army*, London 1924, p. 244.
3 Lloyd, *Egypt Since Cromer*, I, p. 210.
4 Elgood, *Egypt and the Army*, p. 116.
5 Thomas Russell, *Egyptian Service 1902–1946*, p. 179.
6 Lloyd, *Egypt Since Cromer*, I, p. 290.
7 Cromer, *Modern Egypt*, II, p. 568.
8 Lloyd, *Egypt Since Cromer*, I, p. 276–8.

Chapter 20 *Uprising*

1 Lloyd, *Egypt Since Cromer*, I, p. 290.
2 Elgood, *Transit of Egypt*, p. 244.
3 Lloyd, *Egypt Since Cromer*, I, p. 300.
4 Lloyd, *Egypt Since Cromer*, I, p. 301.

Chapter 21 *Milner's Mission*

1 Lloyd, *Egypt Since Cromer*, II, p. 18.
2 Boyle, *Boyle of Cairo*, p. 209.
3 Boyle, *Boyle of Cairo*, p. 223.
4 Lloyd, *Egypt Since Cromer*, II, p. 64.

Chapter 22 *Semi-Independence*

1 Colin Forbes Adam, *Life of Lord Lloyd*, London 1948, p. 94.
2 Forbes Adam, *Life of Lloyd*, pp. 198–9.
3 Lloyd, *Egypt Since Cromer*, II, 322.

Chapter 24 Re-Occupation

1 Churchill, *The Second World War*, London 1950, **III**, p. 95.
2 Jean Lugol, *L'Egypte et la Deuxième Guerre Mondiale*, Cairo 1945, p. 162.
3 Chandos, *The Memoirs of Lord Chandos*, London 1962, p. 276.
4 Duff Cooper, *Old Men Forget*, London 1953, p. 308.
5 *Nasser* al-Musawwar Biographical Edition, Cairo 1958, p. 86.
6 Issawi, *Egypt at Mid-Century*, p. 262.
7 Little, *Egypt*, p. 161.
8 Royal Institute of International Affairs, *Great Britain and Egypt 1914–51*, p. 82.
9 *Britain and Egypt, 1914–51*, p. 84.
10 Francis Williams, *A Prime Minister Remembers*, London 1961, p. 178.
11 Montgomery of Alamein, *Memoirs*, London 1958, p. 422.

Chapter 25 Egypt Goes To War

1 Little, *Egypt*, p. 179.
2 Anthony Eden, *Full Circle*, London 1960, p. 226.

Chapter 26 Revolutionary Egypt

1 *The Letters of T. E. Lawrence*, London 1938, p. 822.
2 Eden, *Full Circle*, p. 247.
3 Eden, *Full Circle*, p. 244.
4 Eden, *Full Circle*, p. 257.

Chapter 27 Two Nations

1 Anthony Nutting, *No End of a Lesson*, London 1967, p. 35.
2 Nutting, *No End of a Lesson*, p. 69.
3 Nutting, *No End of a Lesson*, p. 35.
4 Cromer, *Modern Egypt*, **II**, p. 172.
5 Ethel Smyth, *Beecham and Pharaoh*, London 1935.
6 J. Alexander, *The Truth About Egypt*, London 1911, p. 63.
7 Gerard de Nerval, *Voyages en Orient*, Paris 1950, **I**, pp. 336–7.
8 W. Basil Worsfold, *The Redemption of Egypt*, London 1899, p. 189.
9 Russell, *Egyptian Service 1902–1946*, p. 179.
10 Sydney A. Moseley, *With Kitchener in Cairo*, London 1917, p. 207.
11 A. B. de Guerville, *New Egypt*, London 1905, p. 33.
12 Capitaine Jorge Nelken y Waldberg, *Mes Mémoires en Egypte*, London, pp. 351–4.

13 *The Letters of T. E. Lawrence*, p. 135.
14 T. E. Lawrence, *To His Biographers*, London 1963, p. 35.
15 Marshall, *The Egyptian Enigma*, p. 133.
16 Moseley, *With Kitchener in Cairo*, pp. 177–80.
17 Walter Tyndale, *An Artist in Egypt*, London 1912, p. 133.

Suggested Further Reading

Cromer by John Marlowe (New York).
Egypt's Ruin by Theodore Rothstein (London).
Egypt by Tom Little (London).
Egypt and Cromer by Lufti al-Sayyid (London).
Intellectual Origins of Egyptian Nationalism, by Jamal Muhammed Ahmed (London).
The Modern History of Egypt by P. J. Vatikiotis (London).

INDEX